FUNCTIONAL LIVING SKILLS FOR MODERATELY AND SEVERELY HANDICAPPED INDIVIDUALS

✓ 1999 revised ———

Curriculum :
Elementary / Middle School . . . .

$38.—

7/6 - sending a review copy -

FUNCTIONAL LIVING SKILLS FOR MODERATELY AND SEVERELY HANDICAPPED INDIVIDUALS

Paul Wehman
Virginia Commonwealth University

Adelle Renzaglia
University of Illinois

Paul Bates
Southern Illinois University

5341 Industrial Oaks Blvd.
Austin, TX 78735

Printed in the United States of America

Library of Congress Cataloging in Publication Data

Wehman, Paul.
  Functional living skills for moderately and severely handicapped individuals.

  Includes bibliographical references and index.
  1. Handicapped—United States—Life skills guides. 2. Handicapped—Education—United States. 3. Rehabilitation—United States. I. Renzaglia, Adelle. II. Bates, Paul. III. Title.
  HV1553.W44 1984   362.4'0483'0973   84-5057
  ISBN 0-936104-49-X

pro-ed

5341 Industrial Oaks Blvd.
Austin, Texas 78735

10 9 8 7 6 5 4 3 2 1   89 88 87 86 85

To Brody, Cara, Dylan, Laurel, Lauren, Lindsay, and Megan

CONTENTS

2   COMMUNITY-BASED LIVING FACILITIES 23
Ernie Pancsofar, Ph.D.

3   DOMESTIC/HOME LIVING SKILLS 45

9   FUNCTIONAL ACADEMICS   221

10   ADVOCACY AND COMMUNITY INTEGRATION   249

PREFACE

As special education and rehabilitation increasingly focus on educational and community integration of handicapped people, greater attention is being given to the importance of teaching *functional* living skills. Functional living skills include those behaviors and activities that are basic to independence at home, at work, and in the community. They involve crossing streets, preparing meals, holding a job, using leisure time constructively, and so forth. In this book we address what these skills are, why they are important, and how they can best be taught. The information presented draws from the most recent research literature as well as our direct instructional experiences.

We are emphasizing programs for moderately and severely handicapped individuals in this book. There are two major reasons for this emphasis. First, this population has traditionally been ignored and considered unable to benefit from educational and rehabilitative services. This text addresses their needs specifically. The second reason is that while mildly handicapped persons can integrate much more easily into society without direct instruction, moderately and severely handicapped individuals need the highly focused curriculum and instructional approaches that we present in this book.

The major theme of our work is that training must be practical and take place in natural settings. To train an individual in a school classroom or adult center to cross a street or bus a table without providing training in real streets or real food service establishments will likely lead to failure. What this book proposes is community-based instruction in the practical life skills that are critical to helping moderately and severely handicapped persons become independent. We describe how home living, recreation, social, vocational, academic, and travel skills play a role in the educational planning and program development of the severely handicapped population. Throughout the chapters a recurring emphasis is on the collection of program data or verification that skills have actually been acquired.

This text is aimed at teachers in training as well as those direct service providers already in the field who interact daily with moderately and severely handicapped people. We believe it is these service providers who influence the direction of the field. Regardless of the numbers of books published, curricula developed, and conferences presented, without initiation and follow through by service providers in the field, widespread change will not occur. Hence the narrative, tables, figures, and references included in this book are designed for direct service personnel who plan programs for moderately and severely handicapped people regularly.

ACKNOWLEDGMENTS

A number of people have positively influenced our work and, specifically, the development of this book. We would like to acknowledge these individuals and thank them for their assistance and support.

First, we are indebted to Ernie Pancsofar for contributing an excellent chapter on community residential living. Ernie is an extremely hard worker and highly competent professional, and we are grateful to him for his work.

We would also like to thank Sherril Moon, Meg Hutchins, Grant Revell, Wendy Pietruski, Katty Inge, Janet Hill, Mark Hill, Sue Morrow, Patricia Goodall, John Kregel, Vicki Brooke, Keith Storey, Harold Hanson, Dee Hayden, Mary Beth Bruder, Marti Snell, and Fred Orelove for the influence their thought and actions have had on our philosophies and writing as we shaped the chapters in this text.

Joyce Bollinger and Simone Worden played an important part in typing the manuscript, and we greatly appreciate their patience and quality of work.

Special thanks goes to Dean Charles Rich and Dr. William Bost for their unflagging support of the senior author.

The service providers in the schools and other adult service agencies have greatly shaped our views on high priority material to present in this text. We are grateful to these individuals.

We would also like to thank the U.S. Department of Education for their partial support of our work over the past five years. Specifically, the Division of Innovation and Development in Special Education Programs, the Special Projects section of the Rehabilitation Services Administration, and the National Institute of Handicapped Research have played a major role in helping us develop and implement our thoughts. We are grateful for this assistance.

Finally, we are indebted to Barb Bates, Claiborne Winborne, and Jim Dubnicek who have been patient and supportive of us through the development of this text. Their help and assistance has helped make this work possible.

INTRODUCTION

LEARNING GOALS

1. *Specify the primary learning and behavioral characteristics of moderately and severely handicapped persons.*
2. *Describe a rationale for community-based instruction for moderately and severely handicapped persons.*
3. *Discuss what the community-based instructional model is and why it is important.*
4. *Identify and describe 10 guidelines essential in appropriate program development and implementation.*
5. *Describe strategies for implementing the community-based model of instruction.*
6. *Define the following: age-appropriate, interaction with nonhandicapped individuals, skill generalization, least restrictive environment, functional curriculum, reinforcer sampling, ecological analysis and integrated therapy.*

The development of special education programs for moderately and severely handicapped students has begun to receive increasing attention in recent years. There seems to be a greater sensitivity by special educators to the fact that handicapped children must learn skills that will prepare them for greater independence in home and community living and vocational areas. The challenge that is in front of special and vocational educators alike is how to select and teach skills that are functional, i.e., have high utility for handicapped students.

The importance of targeting career education and vocational education skills that are high in utility for handicapped students has been noted frequently (e.g., Wilcox & Bellamy, 1982). The selection of much of the traditionally academic-oriented curriculum for handicapped pupils has, regrettably, impaired the facility with which many secondary level students have developed competence in skills essential for independent living and employment. Use of classroom confined instructional experiences coupled with academic-oriented curriculum is especially restrictive to moderately and severely handicapped students. The problem of nonfunctional curriculum is exacerbated when students become older and move into middle and secondary schools then adulthood. What follows are several reasons why there is an emphasis on functional curricula for middle and secondary level students.

First, since P.L. 94-142 was officially signed into law in 1975, many handicapped children have grown into early, middle, and late adolescence. These students and their parents have high expectations for quality individualized programs that will help prepare them for independent or semi-independent living and vocational competence. Educational programs must prepare these students for the crucial transition to adulthood.

A second reason for this emphasis is because many community service adult day programs in many states have insufficient funds and staff to perform the necessary training. As noted in Chapter 2, there are far too few group homes, supervised apartments, and other community living facilities available, as well as trained staff necessary for domestic and community skill training. Similarly, job training and placement opportunities are severely limited to the moderately and severely handicapped population. Hence, much of the training must be started intensively even before the secondary school age level.

The approach we advocate in this text of functional curriculum and community-based instruction is also highly consistent with the third reason for emphasis in the secondary area. At this age level, many students who have physically grown in stature begin to exhibit increased behavior problems, grow more bored with traditional classroom activities, and continue to exhibit poor transfer of training abilities. The opportunity to receive some instruction outside the classroom and in high utility activities will stimulate the student and teaching staff in a positive way. The latter part of this chapter specifically addresses guidelines for this approach.

Finally, it is important to note that this age period is the *last chance* for school personnel to affect positive change in students. If many of the programs provided earlier in the student's time at school were nonfunctional and bore no relation to life skill competence, then the burden falls on the secondary teacher. Even though this is an unseemly burden due to the limited time left for the student before graduation, it is this teacher who can select the most functional skills and help effectively plan for the transition to adulthood.

In the section below we begin to take a closer look at these individuals who we call "moderately and severely handicapped." We use the terms *student* and *client* interchangeably because many schools and residential facilities use both.

CHARACTERISTICS OF MODERATELY AND SEVERELY HANDICAPPED INDIVIDUALS

The moderately and severely handicapped population includes a broad range of students who have been labeled "trainable," "severely/profoundly retarded," "deaf-blind," "autistic," or "multihandicapped." The common characteristic that each category has is a substantial *combination* of physical, learning, and/or behavior problems that significantly impair learning. (See Justen, 1976, for a more elaborate treatment of definitions of severely handicapped individuals.) The moderately and severely handicapped population may be verbal or nonverbal, may engage in self-abusive behaviors, be physically involved and nonambulatory, and usually requires intensive and systematic instructional procedures to learn (Snell, 1983). It is this challenging and diverse population to whom the content of this book is directed.

Social Behavior

A frequent characteristic of moderately and severely handicapped individuals is unacceptable social behavior. This may take the form of a behavioral excess such as stereotypical (nonfunctional) body rocking behavior, strange shrieking, or hugging strangers on the street. A social behavior deficit, on the other hand, may involve socially withdrawn behavior, being unresponsive to greetings, or not exhibiting awareness of other people in the environment. Inappropriate social behavior can often be modified by improving the quality of the curriculum and instructional procedures. However, teachers and other staff most often initially attend to these types of behavior problems. A lack of cooperative social behavior may make it very difficult for nonhandicapped persons in the community or nonhandicapped counselors at a job site to accept the individuals. The difficulties in social expression (Bates, 1980) may present the greatest obstacle in community acceptance for moderately and severely handicapped individuals. (Chapters 5, 6 and 9 specifically address these concerns.)

Communication Skills

Many severely and profoundly retarded and autistic children and adults are nonverbal. Furthermore, they may also be unable to communicate using manual devices such as communication boards or Bliss symbols. Signing systems may be an effective alternative. However, whatever the language program devised, the fact remains that communication skills are usually grossly delayed, further contributing to the problems in career and vocational progress. Higher functioning trainable mentally retarded students usually have more capacities in this area, although sentence structure and clarity of oral expression may significantly depress their vocational outlook.

Personal Care

The ability to care for oneself independently is often taken for granted. Independent grooming, eating, dressing, and toileting are presumed to be easily acquired skills at a young age. Proficiency in these skills is not easily attained for the moderately and severely handicapped. In fact, for many students these skills alone are major instructional objectives for long time periods (DeVore, 1979). Yet for independence in domestic and community environments, a high degree of ability must be achieved in this area.

Mobility and Ambulation Skills

Traveling within a school community, neighborhood, or home is a skill that is critical to being independent. One must have the physical ability to move about and also must have the cognitive understanding and memory to follow guidelines and instructions. Regrettably, most moderately and severely handicapped persons have not learned independent travel skills because they lack either of the abilities listed above. Educators frequently contribute to their deficit by providing training only within the classroom and not allowing practice sessions in the natural environment of a community. Vogelsburg and Rusch (1980) have aptly described many of the issues involved in travel training for disabled individuals.

Academic and Cognitive Behaviors

As one might expect, moderately and severely handicapped individuals usually exhibit very limited proficiency in reading, computation, and writing skills. Some controversy exists over the ability of these students to learn academic skills (Brown, 1973; Burton & Hirshoren, 1979). It seems that systematic instructional procedures can lead to fairly extensive reading and computational acquisition in trainable retarded individuals. The generalizability of these skills as well as their priority in community, domestic, and vocational environments is less clear. What is clear, however, is that there is substantial time involved in teaching these skills and often at the expense of higher utility nonacademic skills (such as crossing a street independently or blowing one's nose).

Vocational Skills

Although there is an increasing body of research literature that suggests otherwise (Bellamy, Horner, & Inman, 1979; Wehman, 1981), moderately and severely handicapped persons are generally not viewed as having vocational competence that is valued in the marketplace. Bellamy et al. (1979) note that over 80,000 to 100,000 moderately handicapped adults attend adult day programs that are typically *not* vocational in nature. Another 280,000 mentally retarded adults attend sheltered workshops (Whitehead, 1979) and, on the average, make only $400 annually. Clearly, the lack of widespread effective vocational training and job placement for this population has led to the common misperception of their lack of vocational potential.

Implications

It should come as no surprise that the major chapters in this book are aimed at describing curriculum and instruction procedures and guidelines for overcoming the lack of skills in the areas outlined above. There is an abundance of literature that is data-based and behavioral, yet with small subject samples. It is our intent in this book to provide an explanation, based on the most recent research, of how to develop functional skills in moderately and severely handicapped children and adults. Each of the characteristics above is addressed in subsequent chapters. This book has a programmatic orientation and stresses practical guidelines for program development and implementation at the secondary and adult level. The following section outlines major points that are important in any educational program for the severely handicapped. These points run through the entire text.

GUIDELINES IN PROGRAM DEVELOPMENT FOR MODERATELY AND SEVERELY HANDICAPPED YOUTH

The purpose of this section is to outline and briefly describe 12 points that are critical to developing and implementing an appropriate secondary school program. It is necessary to understand these points in order to feel comfortable with the remaining chapters.

Age-Appropriate Curriculum and Materials

A primary consideration in educational programming for moderately and severely handicapped learners is the development and utilization of curricular materials and activities that are consistent with a student's chronological age. For example, the use of a dart board could be encouraged as a recreational activity for 15-year-old moderately and severely handicapped students as opposed to the frequently used game of throwing a beanbag into Bozo the Clown's mouth. Both of these games require similar skills, but one is clearly more appropriate than the other.

> **A primary consideration in educational programming for moderately and severely handicapped learners is the development and utilization of curricular materials and activities that are consistent with a student's chronological age.**

Classrooms and other instructional settings should also reflect the chronological age of the students being served. The furniture, physical arrangement, bulletin boards, and other characteristics of the physical environment must be carefully evaluated according to the age-appropriate standard. Although Mickey Mouse and Peter Rabbit may be at home in preschool or primary classrooms, they should not adorn the walls or bulletin boards of secondary classrooms, regardless of the students' level of functioning. Both classroom decor and educational activities in a secondary classroom should reflect an emphasis on preparation for adult living in the least restrictive environment.

Interactions with moderately and severely handicapped students should be representative of interactions with any individual within a similar chronological age group. As we do not refer to nonhandicapped 18- to 21-year-olds as "kids" or children, neither should we refer to moderately and severely handicapped 18- to 21-year-olds as such. They, too, deserve to be referred to with dignity as "young man" or "young woman" or, at least, the somewhat ageless label "student." Similarly, the practice of delivering physical affection in the form of hugs and kisses or praise such as "good boy" or "good girl" is not appropriate for an adolescent or adult age group.

At all ages, an active effort should be made to identify chronologically age-appropriate objectives and materials. Although this emphasis may be extremely challenging for specific students, it is consistent with the philosophy of normalization (Nirje, 1969) and with our desire to promote community participation of moderately and severely handicapped individuals (Brown, Branston-McClean, Baumgart, Vincent, Falvey, & Schroeder, 1979).

If we choose to ignore the importance of age-appropriateness, consider the consequences. When parents, community residents, administrators, vocational rehabilitation counselors, and others view 20-year-old John playing with Tinker Toys during the middle of the day, what conclusion will they draw? Of course, they will surmise that John is a toddler and thus not *competent* enough to perform skills in the community, at home, or in a vocational setting. This mindset makes it exceptionally difficult to persuade these key individuals that John has viable training potential.

Specific Objectives

From a chronological age-appropriate curriculum, specific objectives should be selected for each student's individualized education plan (IEP). These objectives must reflect learning conditions, observable behavior, and a criterion for success. The accountability of educational programs for moderately and severely handicapped students continues to come under scrutiny, and precisely stated objectives are necessary to avoid the ambiguity that results from vague goals. Broadly-stated objectives (e.g., "Sally will improve her social interaction skills") do not promote consistency and accountability in educating moderately and severely handicapped students nearly as well as specifically-stated objectives (e.g., "When approached by a peer in the hallway within 10 feet, Sally will smile, nod, and wave on 4 of 5 occasions for 3 consecutive days"). See Chapter 10 for more specific examples.

The identification of specific age-appropriate objectives for each student is crucial to the development and implementation of an appropriate IEP. Unfortunately, many teachers of moderately and severely handicapped individuals select IEP objectives from developmental checklists, behavioral screening inventories, and standardized tests. As a result, teachers attempt to achieve broad developmental milestones rather than concentrate on the acquisition of those specific behaviors that cumulatively evolve into functional independence for the student.

Functional Activities

Once specific age-appropriate objectives are selected, functional teaching activities and materials should be developed. Functional teaching activities are instructional programs that involve skills of immediate usefulness to students and employ teaching materials that are real rather then simulated. For example, a student should be taught to match or sort colors by using different colored clothing items rather than by using different colored blocks. Additional examples of functional activities using real materials as contrasted to traditional nonfunctional activities are shown in Table 1.1.

Functional teaching activities are instructional programs that involve skills of immediate usefulness to students and employ teaching materials that are real rather than simulated.

An endless number of examples of nonfunctional activities frequently used in the classroom can be cited. This proliferation of nonfunctional activities can be traced to several possible origins. First, the deluge of commercial materials that have appeared in recent years has influenced teachers of moderately and severely handicapped students in their choice of materials and accompanying activities. Second, there is a belief among many educators that traditional nonfunctional activities are necessary for the child's "readiness" for more complex activities. This philosophy accounts, in part, for the reason that 20-year-old students have acquired isolated skills that have no apparent functionality, such as stacking rings on a post when they are unable to stack dishes properly.

Table 1.1. Nonfunctional and functional program goals

Goal	Nonfunctional	Functional
To tie shoes	Tie lacing board shoes	Tie real shoes
To increase fine motor skills	Place pegs in board and/or string beads	Assemble vocational products from local industry
To develop one-to-one correspondence	Place one chip on each colored circle	Place one cup with each place setting
To develop gross motor skills	Walk on a balance beam	Walk on bleachers or uneven sidewalk

Consistent Cue Hierarchy

When specific objectives and functional activities have been identified, instructional programs can be developed. An important goal of any instructional program for moderately and severely handicapped students is to teach the student to respond to natural environmental cues. However, educators cannot assume that learning will occur merely by exposing moderately and severely handicapped individuals to a task or an instructional setting. Instead, educators must systematically plan for skill acquisition as well as for the maintenance and generalization of newly acquired skills. A major component of a systematic instructional program is the application of specific prompting procedures that maximize student independence while minimizing errors.

Instructional cues or prompts are those extra stimuli that are provided in instructional sessions to facilitate a student's correct response. For example, when instructing a child to "Pick up the cup," a teacher may accompany the instructions with a gesture toward the cup. This gestural cue is an extra stimulus, or prompt, which facilitates the student's correct response.

The types of effective instructional cues or prompts can vary from individual to individual and from task to task. Instructional cues range from systematic waiting for independent performance to verbal prompts (providing extra verbal instructions) to gestural (e.g., a point or nod) or model prompts (i.e., demonstrating the skill for the student) to the most intrusive physical prompts, which involve manually guiding the learner through the desired task. A general rule for selecting prompts for an individual learner is to select the least intrusive physical prompts that involve manually guiding the learner through the desired task. Establishing an instructional cue hierarchy that emphasizes the use of the least intrusive prompt will foster independence and encourage success.

Instructional cues or prompts are those extra stimuli that are provided in instructional sessions to facilitate a student's correct response.

Regardless of the method of prompting, a teacher should specify in writing the procedures to be used. Time periods allowed for responding should also be specified to promote consistency in teaching. By carefully selecting and employing systematic prompting procedures, a teacher will effect the most rapid student change.

Data Collection and Charting

Data collection and charting of program results are important components of systematic instructional programs for moderately and severely handicapped learners. Data collection refers to the specific recording of student performance, and charting refers to the graphic display of this information. These practices are important to accurately determine a student's level of functioning prior to initiating an instructional program. Once a program has been initiated, data collection and charting enable the teacher to determine when to make program revisions and/or when a student has met an established criterion.

Prior to the initiation of an instructional program, a baseline assessment should be completed to determine each student's entry level skills for a particular program. Standardized assessments are insufficient in detail to provide a teacher with information on where to start a student in a given program. On the other hand, task analytic assessment (Knapczyk, 1975) is one method of data collection that has proved useful for this purpose. In order to complete a task analytic assessment, all component skills of a behavioral objective are identified and listed in serial order on a recording sheet. Situations are then structured in which the teacher systematically observes a student's performance on each of these component skills. This practice enables the teacher to pinpoint a student's specific competencies and those skills requiring instruction.

After a program is started, data collection and charting should continue on a regular basis, preferably daily. The frequent documentation of student performance enables the teacher to make ongoing program decisions. For example, if a student is not making progress, the teacher may decide to alter one of the following aspects of the program: 1) task presentation (e.g., teacher may need to break the task analysis into smaller component steps); 2) teacher instructions (e.g., teacher may need to use different verbal instructions, more explicit modeled demonstrations, and/or greater physical assistance); 3) response consequences (e.g., teacher may need to find an effective reinforcer).

Although continuous data collection is preferred, other less frequent arrangements (data probes) are still very useful. However, data collection and charting should be done regularly (e.g., once a week). At first, data collection and charting behaviors may seem like a cumbersome addition to one's teaching practice, but the benefits of more sensitive decision making, greater accountability, and visual recording of student progress should result within a short period of time.

Periodic Revision of the IEP

Although the law requires that an IEP be developed annually for each handicapped student, there are no provisions or guidelines regarding more frequent review. Thus, without these guidelines, many program plans are developed once a year without any formal review until the next year. This practice is inadequate for moderately and severely handicapped persons for several reasons: 1) learning rates of individual students are highly variable; 2) short-term objectives may need to be revised; and 3) program goals and priorities may change during a given school year.

At the beginning of each school year, an IEP should be developed for each student. This IEP should be formally reviewed and revised approximately every 3 months. With a student's recorded performance as the focal point of IEP review meetings, program changes can be made that facilitate student progress.

Classroom Schedule

To promote the consistency and structure necessary for an appropriate IEP for moderately and severely handicapped students, a specific written schedule should be posted in each classroom. A program schedule should provide a minute-by-minute record of student and teacher activities from the point of student arrival to student departure. The classroom schedule should be written to avoid ambiguity about who is responsible for which activity with which child. The following elements should be in the classroom schedule: 1) specific skill(s) being taught; 2) time that the skill(s) is to be taught; 3) child or group of children receiving instruction on a specific skill area; 4) adult responsible for instruction; and 5) setting for instruction (e.g., hallway, cafeteria, or outside). In many highly structured classes, schedules are developed for each student in the class. Table 1.2 provides a blank format for review.

Table 1.2. Sample classroom schedule

Student: Mark

Time of day	Specific objective being worked on	Staff person responsible	Location of training

> **To promote the consistency and structure necessary for an appropriate IEP for moderately and severely handicapped students, a specific written schedule should be posted in each classroom.**

Instruction Outside of the Classroom

As a part of each student's schedule, instruction outside the classroom should be included. Instruction on using the toilet, eating, community mobility, and countless other behaviors must be conducted in the environments in which these skills are typically expected to occur. If our goal is to see moderately and severely handicapped individuals function as fully in community life as possible, educators must seriously question the strict reliance on the "classroom only" training model. This model has been tried for several years, and has been found to be seriously lacking because it does not facilitate generalization of skills. As an alternative, the classroom/community service delivery model proposed by Certo, Brown, Belmore, and Crowner (1977) seems to be viable for moderately and severely handicapped students. In this model moderately and severely handicapped students are taught in a variety of different community settings, and skill acquisition is verified in the natural environments where the skills are required.

Clearly, extended instruction outside of the classroom often interferes with traditions of regular education as well as many special education programs for students currently in existence. Yet the alternative of continued situation-specific learning is no longer acceptable. By conducting instruction in a wide range of different environments, moderately and severely handicapped students will be better prepared to function as participating members of their home communities. More on this topic is continued in a later section.

Integrated Therapy

Additional components of a moderately or severely handicapped individual's program schedule may include a variety of ancillary services (e.g., physical therapy, speech therapy, and occupational therapy). The traditional method of delivering these services is to remove the individual from the ongoing classroom activities and provide the special service in an isolated therapy room. The individual therapy sessions typically last between 10 and 30 minutes and are conducted one to three times a week. With moderately and severely handicapped individuals, short therapy sessions that occur infrequently may be insufficient to effect significant behavior change.

The integrated therapy model or what has also been coined transdisciplinary model (Sternat, Messina, Nietupski, Lyon, & Brown, 1977) is an effective and efficient model for delivering special services to the moderately and severely handicapped students. In this model, the specialist is involved extensively in an inservice role, teaching classroom teachers, aides, and parents how to conduct and integrate therapeutic activities into regularly scheduled events. For example, a speech therapist may provide directions to classroom personnel and parents regarding how to encourage spontaneous requests during snack and meal time. By teaching a variety of persons to carry out needed special programs and by integrating these activities throughout a student's day, the skill development of moderately and severely handicapped students may be enhanced.

Whenever the specialist is involved in a direct therapy role, these attendant activities could profitably take place within the classroom. This practice maximizes the chance that other staff will learn how to carry out these special programs in the therapist's absence.

> **In the transdisciplinary model, the specialist is involved extensively in an inservice role, teaching classroom teachers, aides, and parents how to conduct and integrate therapeutic activities into regularly scheduled events.**

Instruction in Small Groups

Classroom program schedules should also include opportunities for small group instruction. Instruction in small groups increases the opportunity for observational learning. Although a teacher cannot assume or expect students to learn through observation or imitation alone, the opportunity exists in small group instruction, where it does not exist in one-on-one instruction. Furthermore, group instruction provides an opportunity for peer interaction and peer reinforcement. If children have been trained solely in one-on-one instructional sessions, they may be unable to perform adequately in a group setting, no matter how well they were programmed previously.

Group instruction requires that each group member learn to take turns, to wait and remain quiet while others respond, and perhaps, to raise his/her hand and wait for acknowledgment prior to responding. Without adhering to these basic rules, instruction in groups would become chaotic. Providing moderately and severely handicapped students with experiences in groups with direct teaching of the behaviors required of group members maximizes the chance for a successful transition into a less restrictive instructional setting.

Small group instruction does not necessarily imply that students within a group must be working on the same skill. Individualization within the group is most appropriate. Each student should have specific objectives, which may or may not be the same as those of the other students within that group. Although the development of effective group instruction activities may take time and careful planning, the resulting benefits should further the delivery of an appropriate education program for moderately and severely handicapped students.

Interaction with Nonhandicapped Individuals

Public Law 94-142 requires that all handicapped individuals be provided with an appropriate education in the least restrictive environment. The intent of this law was that handicapped persons must be educated with nonhandicapped individuals to every extent possible. For the mildly handicapped, this may involve mainstreaming into some regular classrooms, whereas for the moderately and severely handicapped students, this may involve the location of self-contained classes in age-appropriate regular public schools. This latter case is the rare exception in present service delivery models.

Interactions with nonhandicapped persons take many forms and are of varying degrees. Brown, Branston, Hamre-Nietupski, Johnson, Wilcox, and Gruenewald (1979) delineated the following levels of interaction: 1) proximal; 2) helping; and 3) reciprocal. At a minimum, moderately and severely handicapped and nonhandicapped students should be involved in proximal interactions. Proximal interactions are those that place moderately and severely handicapped·and nonhandicapped students together in common locations. For example, riding the school bus, attending school assemblies, and eating lunch are all activities that can be engaged in together when moderately and severely handicapped students are located in proximity to their nonhandicapped peers. Helping interactions are those in which the nonhandicapped students assist handicapped individuals in various activities such as moving to and from activities, feeding, dressing, and playing games. These helping interactions can be informal and unstructured or can be more systematic in nature (e.g., tutorial interaction). The third type of interaction identified by Brown et al. is the situation in which both the handicapped and nonhandicapped students receive some reciprocal benefit from being with each other. Playing a mutually enjoyable game and voluntarily attending a social event together are examples of reciprocal interactions.

Some of the most extensive writing related to the severely handicapped interactions with nonhandicapped peers comes from Stainback and Stainback (1982a; Stainback, Stainback, & Jaben, 1981). In one study, they found that nonhandicapped children held negative perceptions of severely handicapped peers (1982b). In another paper, three methods of promoting interactions were described in detail (Stainback, Stainback, Raschke, & Anderson, 1981). These included: 1) classroom organization, structure, and materials; 2) training severely retarded individuals in interactional skills; and 3) training nonhandicapped individuals to interact with the severely retarded.

Interactions between handicapped and nonhandicapped persons may benefit both participants in a variety of different ways. More inservice efforts should be directed toward preparing regular educators and students for increasing interactions with moderately and severely handicapped students. As school-based interactions are established, there will be greater opportunity for meaningful interactions to occur within neighborhoods and other community settings. The long-term impact of these interactions may result in significant improvements in the quality of life experienced by moderately and severely handicapped persons.

Family Involvement

It is imperative that educators of moderately and severely handicapped students establish strong relationships with their students' families. A few of the reasons in support of this position are as follows: 1) there is a need for a cross-environmental approach in instructional programming; 2) many functional skills are primarily used at home; 3) family involvement is required by P.L. 94-142. To promote family involvement, Turnbull et al. (1978) developed a list of questions that can be forwarded to a family in advance of the IEP staffing. These questions were designed to facilitate meaningful input from the family into the important process of program development. Active family involvement in IEP development can be used as a basis upon which to build cooperative program efforts.

Throughout all interactions with families of moderately or severely handicapped children, the teacher must convey a genuine respect for the family and its role in their child's education. With this as a basis, cooperative efforts are possible that may facilitate skill acquisition, maintenance, and generalization by moderately and severely handicapped students.

Family involvement, interaction with nonhandicapped students, and instruction outside of the classroom are extremely important elements of special education programs. They focus on *natural life environments*. In the section below we focus in more depth on this theme.

COMMUNITY-BASED INSTRUCTION

One of the points listed above, *instruction outside of the classroom,* is sufficiently important that we would like to call greater attention to it. As might be expected, this type of instructional service delivery will usually generate some questions and negativism from parents, educators, or administrators. There are numerous reasons for implementing this type of model, including:

1. Skill generalization
2. Reinforcer sampling
3. Awareness by nonhandicapped people
4. Appropriate role models
5. Elevated teacher expectations
6. Parent hope and interest
7. Demonstration of competence by severely handicapped students
8. Curriculum selection

Skill Generalization

The probability of a moderately or severely handicapped student performing a skill in a setting different from where it was originally learned is highly unlikely without sufficient practice (Stokes & Baer, 1977). Self-initiation of skills is also hindered through teaching that is limited to the classroom because the classroom provides an extremely limited array of discriminative stimuli. The teacher generally must create artificial discriminative stimuli, which usually take the form of verbal prompts. Under such conditions, skill development for students remains at a "prompted only" state; self-initiation of skills is clearly thwarted.

Consider, for example, the dilemma of teaching the use of picture communication cards of a student's favorite foods in the classroom. The teacher chooses cards based upon the parent's input of the student's favorite foods, and ice cream is included. After a long teaching process of associating picture card with the food item the student finally self-initiates showing the ice cream card at lunch, but no ice cream is available. An opportunity for greatly enhancing that skill has been lost.

Therefore, if generalization is to occur, it is imperative to provide sufficient opportunities for practice in real situations where all the variables cannot be controlled but where potential discriminative stimuli do naturally exist. It is usual for the student to practice a particular skill in two to three different environments before generalization is achieved. The greater the similarity between the original learning environment and the generalization setting(s), the quicker that transfer of training will occur. Skill generalization cannot be assumed to occur without instruction.

Reinforcer Sampling

Moderately and severely handicapped youths will never be aware of the reinforcing aspects of community living and facilities if they never have the opportunity to experience them. The pleasure of sitting in a park, bowling with one's family, going to a movie theater, or eating pizza in a local restaurant cannot be reinforcing until one has experienced it. Furthermore, many reinforcing aspects of community facilities are not reinforcing until one has developed some degree of proficiency within the environment. Therefore, one-time field trips are wholly insufficient, and systematic instruction must be provided.

Awareness by Nonhandicapped People

Shopkeepers, bus drivers, clergy, and people in the neighborhood need to be aware that moderately and severely handicapped individuals are part of the community. Moderately and severely handicapped youths and young adults must be present in the community and begin interactions with nonhandicapped people. Typical citizens in a community neighborhood will respond more positively to handicapped individuals *over time* if they are exposed to them more frequently (Voeltz, 1980).

Appropriate Role Models

Moderately and severely handicapped youths cannot be expected to develop more sophisticated behavior if they are only exposed to other severely handicapped youths. It is critical that other higher functioning and nonhandicapped role models be available for interaction. For example, some severely handicapped students who exhibit hand biting behaviors and stereotypical actions in the presence of each other reduce these actions when in the presence of higher functioning retarded persons who display more normal behavior. Although this is not always the case, it seems that a segregated environment of severely handicapped people supports maladaptive behaviors.

Elevated Teacher Expectations

One problem faced by teachers of moderately and severely handicapped students traditionally has been that their students rarely function in the community and usually do not advance into more sophisticated vocational, domestic, and leisure environments. The rate of teacher "burnout" grows and morale declines because limited progress is observed in students. Instruction in the community, however, is one excellent means of linking the real world with classroom instruction. Once this model is in place, a greater sense of relevance is attained and training takes on a more significant purpose.

Parent Hope and Interest

By the time severely handicapped students enter adolescence, parents' hopes may already be diminished for the probability of their child's integration into the community. *Living at home and rarely coming out of the house is not community integration.* A classroom-community model demonstrates to parents that staff are not afraid to take students into the community; it shows that staff believe students can acquire appropriate community living skills. Parents need to draw strength and support from teachers. In turn, teachers and other professionals must provide leadership in community skill training.

A classroom-community model demonstrates to parents that staff are not afraid to take students into the community; it shows that staff believe students can acquire appropriate community living skills.

Demonstration of Competence by Severely Handicapped Students

Community access is an ideal opportunity for students to demonstrate their abilities. It is an excellent means to illustrate the competence of handicapped individuals for nonhandicapped people and curious bystanders in different parts of the community. As noted earlier, it can also be very embarrassing for staff. The converse is true as well, however. Helping a handicapped student fit into a group of nonhandicapped people, wait in line appropriately, or make a purchase correctly are all signals to staff that instruction is proceeding effectively.

Curriculum Selection

Only after several failures and embarrassments in the community (e.g., student getting lost) will the most obvious and relevant skill priorities emerge for classroom instruction. The type of curriculum presently employed for many trainable retarded children and in classes for severely and profoundly handicapped students will begin to seem inappropriate when evaluated in the context of repeated problems that occur in community situations. At this point, the teacher and parent must identify more appropriate objectives to include in the student's IEP.

IMPLEMENTATION OF
COMMUNITY-BASED INSTRUCTION[1]

Although the previous section suggests reasons for adopting the classroom-community model, specific suggestions and guidelines for implementation were omitted. Because the chapters to follow are linked to this model, it is helpful to identify several specific strategies that can be utilized for providing training in natural environments and, subsequently, setting the stage for more social interaction between nonhandicapped peers and moderately and severely handicapped individuals.

Use of Other Local Public
Schools for Generalization of Skills

The first community access strategy to be described is the use of skill generalization in other public schools. Task-oriented skills that can be generalized include mealtime behaviors, kitchen utility or janitorial activities, intensive physical activities, and shop and art skills. Social skills that may be addressed include social interactions with peers in the hallways, maintaining eye contact, appropriate spectator behaviors during a seasonal play, and trying to walk more like an average teenager with hands in pockets. Previously minor or unnoticed inappropriate social responses immediately draw attention in a predominantly nonhandicapped environment. Other public schools are a good "try-out" before going directly into less controlled environments.

Use of Real Homes during the
School Day for Domestic Instruction

Another readily available community resource is the use of the student's home or community group homes for domestic instruction. The principal asset of this approach is the opportunity for simultaneous training of parents and students. In group homes there are added benefits of community worker inservice and exposure to potential future clients. The need for continued generalization training emerges clearly in these settings due to utilization of different equipment such as water faucets, toasters, and brooms.

Use of Community Facilities
Near Student's Home or Near School

Interviews with many parents of moderately and severely handicapped students reveal that the students generally do not accompany their parents or siblings on any type of community errand, trip, church activity, or social activity other than perhaps visits to a relative's home. The reasons commonly given are: 1) embarrassment due to inappropriate behavior; and 2) lack of acceptance on the part of the community (i.e., staring).

Although initially generalization training will prove more cost effective in community facilities that are close to the school program (e.g., a

---

[1]Janet Hill had major input in the development of this section through her efforts as former Project Coordinator of the Richmond (Virginia) Secondary Project.

nearby bowling alley for pinball generalization), the student's home community should be systematically approached if one intends to impact on parent and sibling behavior. For example, if school personnel initiate the first few training sessions in the mother's local grocery store and then gradually add the mother's presence and supervision, two previously restrictive forces are dealt with simultaneously (i.e., the low expectation of the mother and the inexperience on the part of grocery store staff and consumers). Demonstrating acquisition of skills such as pushing a grocery cart and waiting in line appropriately also will facilitate the mother's continued interest and efforts in having the adolescent accompany her on errands.

The challenge for continued generalization training during the school day will also require that the community surrounding the school be exposed to the student in a systematic fashion. The program should be described to store owners and managers. Utilizing several facilities on a repeated basis will prove positive in that managers and staff will become accustomed to the use of picture communication cards, response time delay, and scattered data sheets.

Use of Community-based
Recreation Classes and Scout
Troops for Nonhandicapped Individuals

City or county evening recreation classes, team sports for nonhandicapped youth and adults, and *regular* scout troop meetings provide another easily accessible resource for community integration of severely handicapped adolescents. A major advantage of this approach is that there is reduced resistance from the instructors, leaders, or participants because there seems to be a pervasive attitude that any person has a right to participate in these activities. To reinforce this attitude and to avoid disruption of the social group, mainstreaming of only one or two students per group should be attempted (Reynolds, 1981). These situations also provide the rare opportunity to integrate more profoundly handicapped persons who may be confined to a wheelchair or reclining type chair for partial participation purposes. This is especially true of many Girl Scout programs whose activities are largely sedentary and social in nature with limited motor requirements.

City and county evening recreation classes (e.g., ceramics and water color) that are usually only attended by nonhandicapped individuals also provide an atmosphere that may accommodate handicapped students with less refined social skill development. In general, the nonhandicapped participants are busily involved with their own projects and pay little attention to aberrant vocal behavior or mild physical stereotypes, yet social interactions and modeling can be orchestrated between handicapped and nonhandicapped participants.

Use of Local Sheltered
Workshops or Work Centers

Work generalization opportunities usually represent the most difficult area to penetrate in the integration process for moderately and severely handicapped students. Unless a privately funded sheltered workshop exists, state rehabilitation funds often do not subsidize the maintenance of the "hard-to-train" or slow worker on a short- or long-term basis. Thus, it is not profitable for workshops to accept many severely handicapped workers. In many geographical areas, the only means of enrolling a handicapped person in a workshop program is to pay approximately $15 per day in fees for "work adjustment" training. State grants from rehabilitation or mini-grants from service organizations such as the Council for Exceptional Children might be examined as alternative funding sources. However, depending upon the orientation of the workshop staff, a cooperative agreement could be established to allow neighborhoods, and vocational settings. This means of identifying skills for instruction will be referred to frequently in subsequent chapters.

ECOLOGICAL ANALYSIS

Throughout this text we refer to *ecological analysis*. Ecological analysis refers to a careful and systematic approach to identifying skills that are a high priority for the student to learn. With this approach a teacher does *not* quickly thumb through a standard curriculum guide or text and pick objectives that seem to be optimal for the student to know. Instead, the home and community environments are carefully assessed for important skills that the student needs to learn. Ecological analysis is a process that requires:

1. Focusing in on the primary home, community, recreational and potential work environments where the student spends or will spend his/her time
2. Visiting these environments and analyzing the skills that are essential for competence in each environment
3. Determining which of those skills the student can already perform
4. Prioritizing those skills that the student cannot perform in an order of the most important for instruction to less important
5. Validating that these skills are appropriate by double-checking with parents and significant others in the student's living environments

The key aspect of ecological analysis to remember is that it is a *process*, not a book of curriculum objectives. The strength of this approach is that it truly personifies *individualization* of educational programs for students and greatly influences the teacher to select only the highest priority life skills for instruction.

Let's take a close look at this process. Assume Sandra is a teacher of six autistic children. She decides to use ecological analysis to assess what skills she will select for Reginald, a new student in her class who was just placed in a group home. Reginald has recently returned from a state residential facility. Sandra first visits the group home and makes a list of necessary bathroom skills; she takes note that all children are expected to wash their hands before each meal and brush their teeth twice a day. She also observes that each student is encouraged to make his/her own snack after coming home from school. Numerous other activities in the home (e.g., hanging up clothes and doing household chores) suggest to her that there are several domestic objectives that require instruction.

Sandra also visits the local park and one or two of the most frequently visited stores, and assesses the travel requirements in the community. In addition, she inquires as to the church that Reginald attends. This "homework" begins to give Sandra a sharper picture of what objectives and activities she should focus on for Reginald. A trip to the local workshop, a survey of potential jobs available in the community, and visits with the school work experience coordinator also begin to help formulate selected prevocational objectives. In short, Sandra spends as much time, or more, on selecting functional curriculum as she does on writing instructional plans. Table 1.3 presents a sample worksheet for conducting an ecological analysis.

Several aspects of conducting an ecological analysis should be noted. First, direct observation is superior to phone interviews or secondhand information. Nevertheless, it may be necessary for the school social worker to help conduct the visits. Second, some of the visits (e.g., to a local drugstore) can be used for more than one student. Finally, there is no reason that home and community visits cannot and should not take place *throughout* the school year and not only at the end of the year before IEP development.

The ecological analysis approach is more time-consuming than the traditional approach to curriculum selection. However, it greatly increases the likelihood of selecting skills that are meaningful to a student.

Table 1.3. Ecological assessment worksheet

Instructions: Upon visiting the selected work setting or environment, you must determine three potential work subenvironments within the job site. (For example, in a cafeteria dishroom, one subenvironment might be working on emptying trays of dirty dishes. In a grocery store environment, one subenvironment might be bagging groceries at the cash register.) Once you have determined the three subenvironments you then must assess four to five vocational behaviors and the one or two *most important* non-work behaviors necessary for success. Please write one vocational instructional (short-term) objective for each subenvironment.

Job Site _____

Subenvironment #1	Subenvironment #2	Subenvironment #3
_____	_____	_____
Area	Area	Area
Vocational Skills:	Vocational Skills:	Vocational Skills:
a. _____	a. _____	a. _____
b. _____	b. _____	b. _____
c. _____	c. _____	c. _____
d. _____	d. _____	d. _____
e. _____	e. _____	e. _____
Nonvocational Skills:	Nonvocational Skills:	Nonvocational Skills:
a. _____	a. _____	a. _____
b. _____	b. _____	b. _____
Instructional Objective:	Instructional Objective:	Instructional Objective:

PURPOSE OF TEXT

This book is aimed at students preparing to work with moderately and severely handicapped individuals. It is also aimed at those vocational and special education teachers and rehabilitation personnel who are involved in career and vocational education programming for moderately and severely handicapped persons.

A major feature of this book is the focus on curriculum and instruction. In many other books, one can find information on behavior modification (Kazdin, 1975) and instructional methods (Smith, 1975; Wehman & McLaughlin, 1981). In this text, however, we concentrate exclusively on the major areas that are critical to the independent living and vocational habilitation of moderately/severely handicapped persons. We cover all content topics that are necessary for the independence of moderately and severely handicapped individuals. The sequence of chapters suggests that, initially, we must focus on the individual in his/her living environment. Therefore, the next two chapters are devoted to the continuum of living facilities available to handicapped people. Chapter 2 discusses the advantages and disadvantages of group homes, sheltered apartments, boarding homes, and foster homes. The associated programming requirements for successful living in these facilities are described. A logical outgrowth of this chapter is Chapter 3 in which necessary home living and domestic skills necessary for independent living are outlined.

From these chapters we then move to mobility training and how to travel independently. Chapter 4 discusses use of public transportation, crossing streets, and use of car pool arrangements to facilitate mobility. The next two chapters are concerned with the development of social and interpersonal skills (Chapter 5) and leisure skills and their importance in the individual's life (Chapter 6). Chapter 6 is aimed at discussing activities in the community that are chronologically age-appropriate.

Chapters 7 and 8 involve sheltered employment and competitive employment, respectively. Both of these broad categories of employment are principally concerned with future vocational placement of moderately and severely handicapped individuals. These two substantive chapters present a great deal of recent literature in the vocational area and translate it into practice.

Chapter 9 presents a detailed description of functional academic skills that moderately handicapped students may need to function independently. In Chapter 10 the importance of advocacy and community integration activities as they relate to special education programs is discussed. Undoubtedly, the direction of these efforts in the future will alter the success of career and vocational education for moderately and severely handicapped persons.

This book is punctuated with a number of the following characteristics, including:

Learning goals at the beginning of each chapter and highlighted sections throughout each chapter

Frequent references to current literature

Numerous case studies in many of the chapters to describe applications of research

Sample skill objectives

Discussions of optimal instructional procedures

Although the focus of this book is primarily on the school age population, we are equally concerned with the moderately and severely handicapped adult population. Much of the literature reviewed, in fact, has been drawn from the adult population.

CONCLUSION

This chapter reviews the purpose of the book and discusses the typical behavioral and learning characteristics of the moderately and severely handicapped. The following chapters are largely aimed at discussing how to overcome many of the perceived deficits of severely handicapped youth.

The classroom-community service delivery model and its application to education programming for secondary special education is described. Understanding this service delivery model is a major aspect of translating the information in this book into educational practice. Selected strategies for making this model work are highlighted.

Finally, numerous issues including data collection, intensity of career and vocational education programming, the role of the least restrictive environment, and individualizing program plans are discussed in the context of career and vocational education. These issues are important in understanding many of the concepts and philosophies espoused throughout the balance of the book.

COMMUNITY-BASED LIVING FACILITIES

*Contributed by: **Ernie Pancsofar, Ph.D.**, Assistant Professor, Bowling Green State University, Bowling Green, Ohio*

LEARNING GOALS

1. *Describe the relationship between normalization philosophy and residential placements for moderately and severely handicapped individuals.*
2. *Discuss the role of least restrictive alternative in community residential placement.*
3. *Identify major legislation and litigation that impacts on community residential placement.*
4. *Describe and explain the continuum of residential living options available to moderately and severely handicapped individuals.*
5. *Identify a strategy for establishing a range of community living options for moderately and severely handicapped persons.*
6. *List and discuss five barriers to developing residential facilities in the community.*

The rapid exodus of an increasing number of moderately and severely handicapped persons from large public residential facilities in conjunction with the development of locally provided public education for virtually all students has created an urgent need for communities to expand the range of residential options that currently exist. These trends have resulted in many individuals with unique needs being returned to their home communities and other similarly handicapped persons being maintained in these communities. Cumulatively, these concurrent trends have resulted in the average community being faced with an increasing number of individuals for whom nontraditional residential options need to be developed.

The deinstitutionalization movement and the Education for All Handicapped Children Act (P.L. 94-142) have combined to create a sense of urgency in many communities to further develop the range of community living options available to all its citizens. In particular, the deinstitutionalization movement has necessitated the need for the immediate expansion of community living arrangements for handicapped persons. In 1974 the concept of deinstitutionalization was articulated as the:

> prevention of admission by finding and developing alternative community methods of care and training, return to the community of all residents who have been prepared through programs of habilitation and training to function adequately in appropriate local settings, and establishment and maintenance of a responsive residential environment which protects human and civil rights and which contributes to the expeditious return of the individual to normal community living, whenever possible.
> (National Association of Superintendents of Public Residential Facilities for the Mentally Retarded, 1974, pp. 4–5)

The purpose of this chapter is to discuss several issues pertaining to the establishment of a range of community living options for handicapped persons. Before describing any other life activities such as work, recreation, and personal care, there must be an understanding of the types of residential options available to moderately and severely handicapped individuals. Furthermore, there are a number of issues, some of which are quite controversial, that must be considered in the context of residential planning. To develop appropriate curriculum and instructional programs without knowledge of such factors will lead to failure in the long run. These issues include *normalization, least restrictive alternative, continuum of residential options, administrative responsibility, barriers to community-based housing,* and *evaluation.*

The concepts of normalization and least restrictive alternative are the philosophical underpinnings of the deinstitutionalization movement. These concepts have appeared in litigation and legislation relevant to the need to establish a full range of community services for all handicapped citizens. In best meeting the residential needs of handicapped persons, a continuum of living options should be available. This continuum should include residential opportunities that meet a person's present as well as future needs. To establish such a continuum, administrative support must be generated at the local, state, and federal levels. Thus, an important issue confronting these administrative and planning groups will be the elimination of legal and attitudinal barriers to community living by handicapped persons. Finally, as efforts to establish more community living options increase, evaluation will play a prominent role. Evaluation must include needs assessment data and program effectiveness information. In the 1980s, human service organizations will be required to demonstrate accountability and cost-effectiveness. Program evaluation data will increase accountability and contribute toward a data base in support of the development of a range of community living options.

NORMALIZATION

The adherence to a philosophy of normalization has been an assumption held by most planners involved in developing community environments for handicapped persons. Although the majority of these planners verbalize a normalization philosophy, a smaller percentage actually reference one of the commonly accepted formulations of normalization (Wolfensberger, 1980). As a result, the public is told that a facility provides handicapped residents with "normalized life experiences" without explaining how these experiences enhance the individual's quality of life. Perhaps most clearly stated normalization refers to the

> use of culturally normative (familiar, valued) techniques, tools, methods in order to enable persons' life conditions (income, housing, health services, etc.) which are at least as good as that of average citizens, and to as much as possible enhance or support their behavior (skills, competencies, etc.), appearances (clothing, grooming, etc.), experiences (adjustment, feelings, etc.), and status and reputation (labels, attitudes of others, etc.). (Wolfensberger, 1980, p. 80)

The normalization principle has many tenets associated with it. Nirje (1977) presents eight of these tenets in a format that can easily be comprehended by citizens in the community. In poetic form, Nirje relates the essential ingredients for a faithful adherence to normalization.

> Normalization means . . . a normal rhythm of the day.
> You get out of bed in the morning, even if you are profoundly retarded and physically handicapped;
> you get dressed,
> and leave the house for school or work, you don't stay home;
> in the morning you anticipate events,
> in the evening you think back on what you have accomplished;
> the day is not a monotonous 24 hours with every minute endless.
> You eat at normal times of the day and in a normal fashion;
> not just with a spoon, unless you are an infant;
> not in bed, but at a table;
> not early in the afternoon for the convenience of the staff.
>
> Normalization means . . . a normal rhythm of the week.
> You live in one place,
> go to work in another,
> and participate in leisure activities in yet another.
> You anticipate leisure activities on weekends,
> and look forward to getting back to school
> or work on Monday.

Normalization means . . . a normal rhythm of the year.
A vacation to break the routines of the year.
Seasonal changes bring with them a variety of types of food, work, cultural events,
*   sports, leisure activities.*
Just think . . . we thrive on these seasonal changes.

Normalization means . . . normal developmental experiences of the life cycle.
In childhood, children, but not adults, go to summer camps.
In adolescence one is interested in grooming, hairstyles, music, boyfriends, and
*   girlfriends.*
In adulthood, life is filled with work and responsibilities.
In old age, one has memories to look back on, and can enjoy the wisdom of
*   experience.*

Normalization means . . . having a range of choices, wishes, and desires respected
*   and considered.*
Adults have the freedom to decide
where they would like to live,
what kind of job they would like to have, and can best perform.
Whether they would prefer to go bowling with a group,
instead of staying home to watch television.

Normalization means . . . living in a world made of two sexes.
Children and adults both develop relationships with members of the opposite sex.
Teenagers become interested in having boyfriends and girlfriends.
And adults may fall in love, and decide to marry.

Normalization means . . . the right to normal economic standards.
All of us have basic financial privileges and responsibilities,
*   are able to take advantage of compensatory economic security means, such as*
*   child allowances, old age pensions, and minimum wage regulation.*
We should have money to decide how to spend; on personal luxuries or necessities.

Normalization means . . . living in normal housing in a normal neighborhood,
Not in a large facility with 20, 50, 100 other people because you are retarded.
And not isolated from the rest of the community.
Normal locations and normal size homes will give residents better opportunities
*   for successful integration with their communities.*

Pieper and Cappuccilli (1980) formulated a series of questions designed
to determine how closely a community residential facility follows the normalization philosophy. Included in Table 2.1 are 15 of these questions. Perske (1980) has referred to negative responses to similar questions as

Table 2.1.   Questions about facilities and their residents to determine if normalization is
an operationalized concept

1. Did the residents choose to live in the home?
2. Is this the type of setting usually inhabited by people in the resident's age group?
3. Do the residents live with others their own age?
4. Is the residence located within a residential neighborhood?
5. Does the residence look like the other dwellings around it?
6. Can the number of people living in the residence be reasonably expected to assimilate into
    the community?
7. Are community resources and facilities readily accessible from the residence?
8. Do the residents have a chance to buy the house?
9. Do the managers of the facility act in an appropriate manner toward the residents?
10. Are the residents encouraged to do all they can for themselves?
11. Are the residents encouraged to have personal belongings that are appropriate to their ages?
12. Are residents encouraged to use community resources as much as possible?
13. Are all the residents' rights acknowledged?
14. Are the residents being given enough training and assistance to help them be competent, growing,
    developing individuals?
15. Would you want to live in the home?

"clangers." For example, if the answer to question 15, "Would you want to live in the home?" is no, it should sound a bell that something is wrong. If a community residential facility has policy statements that suggest a commitment to normalization, yet answers to the subsequent questions suggest otherwise, the practices of the facility need to be reevaluated.

LEAST RESTRICTIVE ALTERNATIVE

Biklen (1979) expressed the opinion that as a fundamental human right, all persons are entitled to live in the community in the least restrictive setting. In Table 2.2, this opinion is expressed more fully. The right to community living, as part of the least restrictive alternative philosophy, has strong grounds in recent court opinions and federal legislation. Further, these court opinions and legislation have been supported on the basis of constitutional rights. Specific litigation and legislation relevant to the concept of the least restrictive alternative are subsequently presented. This discussion is followed by specific references to the constitutional basis of a person's right to community living.

Litigation

The first time the notion of the least restrictive alternative surfaced as a legal concept was in the *Shelton* v. *Tucker* Supreme Court decision of 1960. In the majority opinion it was stated that "even though the governmental purpose be legitimate and substantial, that purpose cannot be pursued by means that broadly stifle personal liberties when the end can be more narrowly achieved" (*Shelton* v. *Tucker*).

The first application of the least restrictive alternative concept to the field of mental health did not occur until 1966 in a U. S. Court of Appeals decision. In this decision (*Lake* v. *Cameron*), the judges ruled that the burden of proof for finding alternatives to institutionalization rested with the state and not the individual (Mickenberg, 1980). Mrs. Cameron had a history of wandering away from her home, and as a result was committed to a mental institution. In the opinion of the appeals court, less restrictive

Table 2.2.   Community imperative:
A refutation of all arguments against deinstitutionalization

In the domain of human rights:
    All people have fundamental moral and constitutional rights.
    These rights must not be abrogated merely because a person has a mental or physical disability.
    Among these fundamental rights is the right to community living.
In the domain of educational programming and human service:
    All people are inherently valuable.
    All people can grow and develop.
    All people are entitled to conditions that foster their development.
    Such conditions are optimally provided in community settings.
Therefore:
    In fulfillment of fundamental human rights and
    In securing optimum developmental opportunities,
    All people, regardless of the severity of their disabilities, are entitled to community living.

means could have been employed by the state without resorting to commitment. Examples of lesser restrictive alternatives mentioned in this opinion included the use of an identification card, public health nursing care, and foster care.

The above two court decisions established precedent for the landmark civil commitment case of 1972, *Lessard* v. *Schmidt.* In this Supreme Court opinion, a specific sequence of steps was outlined to protect individuals from immediately being placed in institutions without alternative placements being investigated. Mickenberg (1980) describes the three-step sequence as: 1) identification of available residential alternatives; 2) documentation of alternatives that were investigated; and 3) justification for the determination that particular alternatives were unsuitable.

As the Supreme Court members were deliberating the *Lessard* v. *Schmidt* case an important development was occurring in Alabama. In 1971, Judge Johnson was presiding over the *Wyatt* v. *Stickney* court hearing. Wyatt was the landmark right to treatment case that developed standards for the physical-psychological environment, qualified staff, and the development of habilitation plans. Although the Wyatt decision is predominantly known for its right to habilitation declarations, important statements concerning the right to live in the least restrictive environment were also included.

> *No person shall be admitted to the institution unless a prior determination shall have been made that residence in the institution is the least restrictive habilitation setting feasible for that person.* (Wyatt v. Stickney)

Judge Johnson continued by defining that the least restrictive alternative included moving residents from:

1. more to less structured living
2. larger to smaller facilities
3. larger to smaller living units
4. group to individual residence
5. segregated from the community to integrated into community living
6. dependent to independent living

A further refinement of the least restrictive alternative concept is found in the Willowbrook Court (*New York Association for Retarded Citizens* v. *Carey*) opinion of 1975. In this opinion, a person's right to the least restrictive community living alternative cannot be limited by the available options in the service system, but must be viewed as the services needed from the individual's perspective. To assist in finding suitable alternatives, a Willowbrook Review Panel was formed to reduce Willowbrook State School from 5700 residents to 250 or fewer within 6 years.

In 1977 the Supreme Court resolved the issue of whether the search for a least restrictive alternative was an active or passive responsibility of the state. In the *Morales* v. *Turman* decision:

> *The state . . . must act affirmatively to foster such alternatives as now exist only in rudimentary form, and to build new programs suited to the needs of the hundreds of its children that do not need institutional care (e.g., group homes, halfway houses, home placements with close supervision).* (Morales v. Turman, 1974)

In one of the most closely watched court cases relevant to the least restrictive alternative, *Halderman* v. *Pennhurst State School,* the District Court's anti-institutional ruling was substantially modified at the U. S. Court of Appeals and U. S. Supreme Court levels. In the original court opinion, the judge declared that the very existence of Pennhurst was unconstitutional because it was incapable of providing minimally adequate habilitation (Ferleger & Boyd, 1980). An immediate closing of the institution was ordered. Additionally, a Special Master was appointed to oversee the plans of this deinstitutionalization order. The seven plans of this order are:

1. Specify the quantity and type of community living arrangements and community services needed
2. Specify the resources, procedures, and a schedule for individual evaluations and an individual exit plan and community program for each class member
3. Provide for the hiring and training of community staff to prepare plans for class members and assist in executing the responsibility to develop and monitor community services
4. Develop a continuing monitoring and advocacy system
5. Provide the class members themselves with information about implementation of the case
6. Provide parents and family of the class members with information about implementation of the case
7. Provide opportunities for alternative employment for each employee of Pennhurst, including employment in community programs and otherwise.

The U. S. Court of Appeals tempered the District Court's original decision by allowing Pennhurst to remain open, but to continue a planned phasing out of its use through community-based placements. Additionally, the Appeals Court judge ruled on the basis of existing Pennsylvania and federal statutes and did not rely on a constitutional right to live in the least restrictive environment. On April 20, 1981, the U. S. Supreme Court reversed the lower court's decision that there existed a "right to live in the least restrictive alternative possible" based on a federal statute. In a 6–3 decision the justices declared that it was not the intent of Congress to give mentally retarded persons a legal right to be treated in settings "least restrictive to personal liberty." The court took a conservative stand by not basing the opinion on constitutional grounds but upon their interpretation of Congress' intent in enacting the Developmentally Disabled Assistance and Bill of Rights Act of 1975.

The litigation of the 1960s and 1970s provided a strong support for the concept of the least restrictive alternative. The right of severely handicapped persons to live in community residential environments was being firmly established. The 1980s have begun with a more cautionary outlook as evidenced by the U. S. Supreme Court's Pennhurst ruling. The full impact of this decision is not yet known, but the momentum established during the 1970s will be felt in various degrees throughout the country.

Legislation

The litigation of the 1960s and early 1970s resulted in the passage of several federal laws. Three of these laws have had a significant impact on the need to develop community residential facilities for handicapped individuals. These laws are the Rehabilitation Act of 1973 (P.L. 93-112), the Education for All Handicapped Children Act of 1975 (P.L. 94-142), and the Rehabilitation, Comprehensive Services and Developmental Disabilities Amendments of 1978 (P.L. 95-602).

Rehabilitation Act of 1973 Section 504 of P.L. 93-112 is often cited as a mandate for the right of all handicapped persons to live in the least restrictive environment. Specifically, Section 504 states:

> *No otherwise qualified handicapped individual in the United States, shall, solely by reason of his handicap, be excluded from participation in, be denied the benefits of, or be subjected to discrimination under any program or activity receiving federal financial assistance.*

The language of Section 504, the committee proceedings concerning the law, the history of related enactments, its administrative construction, and the judicial decisions included in the previous section of this chapter are the basis for Laski's (1980) conclusion that Section 504:

1. Required that the segregation of disabled people be ended
2. Prohibited unnecessarily separate services and required that services be provided in the most integrated settings
3. Required that disabled people be admitted equally to all services and to the equal benefit of all services
4. Required that disabled people be provided services equally effective as those provided to the general population

Nonhandicapped persons are entitled to live in a variety of community residential settings, and based on Section 504 these same options must not be denied handicapped individuals solely by reason of their handicap.

Education for All Handicapped Children Act of 1975 In P.L. 94-142 Congress affirmed the right of all handicapped individuals to be educated in the least restrictive environment. This law has resulted in many communities developing educational services for many individuals who were previously excluded. As a result, more individuals are being maintained in local communities, contributing to the need to develop a range of community residential alternatives. Thus, the concepts of least restrictive educational environment and least restrictive living alternative complement each other and provide a vehicle for the total integration of handicapped individuals in the community.

Rehabilitation, Comprehensive Services, and Developmental Disabilities Amendments of 1978 As stated in Section 101 of P.L. 95-602, the intent of this act was to:

> *assist States to assure that persons with developmental disabilities receive the care, treatment and other services necessary to enable them to achieve their maximum potential through a system which coordinates, monitors, plans, and evaluates those services and which insures the protection of the legal and human rights of persons with developmental disabilities.*

Prior to the U. S. Supreme Court's opinion in the Pennhurst case, many proponents of community living for handicapped individuals cited this law as the legal basis for individuals to live in the least restrictive residential alternative. Because the Supreme Court did not feel that Congress was establishing such a legal right, advocates for the handicapped must view the law in a much less optimistic light.

Constitutional Rights

The formulation of the court opinions and public laws discussed in the previous sections has a strong foundation in the Constitution. In particular, the due process and equal protection clauses of the fourteenth amendment and the cruel and unusual punishment phrase in the eighth amendment are cited most often as a constitutional basis for the concept of a least restrictive alternative.

Due Process The due process clause of the fourteenth amendment states in part that no state shall "deprive any person of life, liberty, or property, without due process of law." Scheerenberger (1980) summarizes the provisions of due process as they pertain to the handicapped individual:

1. The right to at least an independent hearing and frequently to a full-jury trial
2. The right to participate fully in the decision-making process whenever possible, or to be appropriately represented by a parent, guardian, and/or counsel
3. The right to appeal
4. The right not to be institutionalized unless the individual is deemed harmful to others or to himself/herself

Due process enables an individual recourse to legal avenues to prevent a restriction of personal liberty by confinement in an institution. Both lay and professional advocates are exhorting the right of handicapped persons to question their current placement based on the due process section of the fourteenth amendment.

> **Due process enables an individual recourse to legal avenues to prevent a restriction of personal liberty by confinement in an institution.**

Equal Protection The equal protection clause of the fourteenth amendment contains the phrase "nor deny to any person within its jurisdiction the equal protection of the laws." Laski (1980) argues that "the segregation of retarded people and their classification for purposes of segregation and receipt of services offend and violate the equal protection clause of the fourteenth amendment" (p. 156).

Cruel and Unusual Punishment The entire eighth amendment consists of the statement, "Excessive bail shall not be required, nor excessive fines imposed, nor cruel and unusual punishments inflicted." Thrasher (1980) cites such factual information as "residents of mental retardation institutions (being) beaten by staff and other residents, unlawfully placed in solitary confinement, massively overdosed with psychotropic drugs for purposes of control, drowned in their bathtubs because there are not enough staff to watch them, sexually assaulted by staff, tied to their beds, etc. . ." (p. 104) as a factor in judicial decisions based on the cruel and unusual punishment amendment.

CONTINUUM OF
RESIDENTIAL LIVING OPTIONS

The concept of "least restrictive alternative" as applied to community living implies the existence of a continuum of residential options. A range of community living environments is delineated in Table 2.3. These options are generally listed in descending order along a continuum of least restrictive to most restrictive residential setting. By providing a range of residential options, the community living needs of handicapped persons can be met in a most appropriate manner. Unfortunately, residential opportunities for most handicapped individuals are restricted by community availability rather than provided according to individual need. In an attempt to more fully comprehend the living options that are needed to meet the individualized needs of handicapped persons, specific residential arrangements along the continuum of least restrictive to most restrictive are briefly described.

Highly Desirable Living Options

Independent living environments refer to those settings where handicapped persons are not reliant on external support beyond that which is normally obtained from generic community services. Sample settings that are in-

Table 2.3.   Continuum of residential living options[a]

1. Independent living
    Single-family homes
    Shared homes
    Individual or shared apartments
    Groups of individual apartments
    Dwellings in new apartment buildings
    Residential hotels
2. Natural or adoptive home (with in-home services)
3. Other relative's home
4. Friend's home
5. Foster family care
6. Developmental foster home
7. Group homes
    Small group home
    Medium group home
    Large group home
    Mini-institution
    Mixed group home
    Group homes for older adults
8. Nursing homes
    Community care facility (ICF)
    Convalescent home
    County home
9. Boarding homes
10. Hostels
11. Sheltered villages
12. Public residential facilities
13. Private residential facilities
14. Workshop-dormitories
15. Mental hospitals
16. Prisons

[a] Adapted from Heal, Novak, Sigelman, and Switzky (1980).

cluded within the independent living category include single-family homes, shared homes, individual or shared apartments, groups of individual apartments, dwellings in new apartment buildings, and residential hotels (Thompson, 1977). Each of these arrangements is briefly described below:

single-family homes: a free-standing single-family home in an average residential neighborhood

shared homes: two or more handicapped persons who prefer to share a single-family home and the cost of needed modification (often the sharing is between handicapped and congenial able-bodied persons)

individual or shared apartments: apartments (in large or small buildings) that are occupied by a single handicapped person or shared by two or more handicapped persons

groups of individual apartments: groups of apartments on one floor, scattered throughout the building, or scattered among several buildings in an apartment complex

dwellings in new apartment buildings: a percentage of living units in a large public or private apartment building that are designed for the handicapped

residential hotels: relatively large structures with private rooms and baths (not apartments) that are adaptable for the handicapped, with housekeeping and meal service available at commercial rates

The delineation of independent living environments is not meant to be looked upon as the most desirable to the least desirable view of options (e.g., single-family homes viewed as the ideal environment whereas a residential hotel is viewed as the least desirable). A variety of interacting factors account for why one option is selected over another as an independent living situation. Such factors include: 1) the availability of housing options; 2) the likes and dislikes of the individual; 3) the age of the individual; 4) proximity of residence to work, recreation, and a friend's home; and 5) the receptivity of neighbors. For example, an individual with the ability to live in a home alone but who wishes to share an apartment with a co-worker should not be pressured into choosing the single-family home option. The person's wishes should be respected. In this example, the single-family home may in fact be more restrictive than the shared apartment when the individual's desired interaction with a peer is limited.

> **For example, an individual with the ability to live in a home alone but who wishes to share an apartment with a co-worker should not be pressured into choosing the single-family home option.**

The previously mentioned residential options are intended for handicapped adults who are ready to live in an independent living environment. For children and adolescents, the first option of choice should be within the natural or adoptive home. Significant community efforts should be focused on providing parents with in-home services that counterbalance the factors leading to a decision to place the child in an out-of-home residential environment. If the natural or adoptive home cannot provide an adequate living environment, even with adequate community support services, the home of a resident's sibling, grandparent, aunt, uncle, offspring, or one who has befriended the resident or the resident's family might be considered.

> **Significant community efforts should be focused on providing parents with in-home services that counterbalance the factors leading to a decision to place the child in an out-of-home residential environment.**

The foster home is another residential option that may be appropriate for many children and adolescents. The usual foster home setting consists of "five or fewer retarded adults in a family's own home, families are not governed by a board of directors, and they collect monthly payments for the care of residents" (Baker, Seltzer, & Seltzer, 1977). For handicapped populations, Lensink (1980) has described a specialized foster home arrangement, the "developmental foster home." In a developmental foster home arrangement, the foster parents are chosen for their willingness to participate in training sessions. The purpose of these sessions is to extend the services of public school and other community agencies into the home environment. Thus, a contingency is applied to the receipt of monies allocated to foster home parents. This contingency stipulates that money will be provided for the foster family if they are willing to engage in cooperative programs with community agencies to ensure that skills learned in community environments are maintained in the home environment.

Another residential option includes the wide spectrum of facilities referred to as group homes. Included in this category are large homes (purchased, rented, or constructed) that usually house five or more residents who are supervised by live-in house managers or shift staff. Baker et al. (1977) divided the broad category of group homes into six subcategories:

small group homes: 10 or fewer residents
medium group homes: 11 to 20 residents
large group homes: 21 to 40 residents
mini-institutions: 41 to 80 residents
mixed group homes: including retarded adults and former mental hospital patients and/or ex-offenders in the same residence
group homes for older adults: including only older retarded people and often nonretarded people as well in group homes or rest homes

Because group homes can encompass such a wide variety of settings, one must be cautious when interpreting reports and documentation of resident functioning levels in group homes if the type of group home being described is not specified.

Less Desirable Living Options

Heal, Novak, Sigelman, and Switzky (1980) describe another group of living environments—nursing homes—as facilities that "include a variety of residential alternatives, all providing continuing medical care for anyone who needs it. Nursing homes are nearly always privately owned and are expected to make a profit for their owners." The authors describe three subcategories of nursing homes as:

community care facilities: a facility licensed as a nursing home, making it eligible for Federal Medicaid Support (Title XIX of the Social Security Act and its amendments). Two classes are distinguished according to size: 15 and under and 16 and over. The larger homes must have a nurse (LPN) on duty at all times, whereas the smaller homes need only have one on call.

convalescent homes: a nursing home whose residents are expected to stay for a reasonably short period of time for rehabilitation before they return to the community.

county home: a type of nursing home, usually for the elderly who are unable to afford private nursing home care. It was a much more common institutional alternative before Medicaid made nursing homes more readily affordable.

Boarding homes are another residential option. The resident is provided with room and board for a fee, but no other services are contracted. These homes house individuals of varying abilities. They are usually not classified as "group or family care homes" (Heal et al., 1980). Boarding homes are often found in larger communities, especially with individuals who are more mildly handicapped.

Hostels and sheltered villages are more unusual and seldom observed as residential options for handicapped persons. Their inclusion at this place on the continuum of residential living options is more for lack of a better placement than a justification of their present placement. Hostels are residential settings similar to the residential hotel, but usually are supervised by professional staff and placement is considered transitional or temporary (Thompson, 1977). For example, if a resident from an institution is targeted for independent living but needs a temporary adjustment period in the community, a hostel situation might be the residence of first choice. Baker et al. (1977) include sheltered villages in their classification of living alternatives. Sheltered villages provide "a segregated, self-contained community for retarded adults and live-in staff in a cluster of buildings usually located in a rural setting." Baker et al. (1977) describe Camphill Village as a prototype of this living arrangement.

The public residential facility is equivalent to the state run institution, whereas the private residential facility contains "a variety of privately owned and foundation-owned residential alternatives. Some of these are expensive, highly visible, multiple-treatment centers; some are largely custodial facilities; and some are communes that feature an idyllic life for handicapped and nonhandicapped co-residents" (Heal et al., 1980).

Workshop-dormitories are living options where the living quarters and work training program are associated administratively and at times housed within the same building. A relatively new concept, workshop-dormitories exist not to provide training for independent living in the community, but to provide an environment where individuals can be involved in a work program.

The mental hospital and prison are considered the most restrictive of the settings listed in this section. Although handicapped individuals without severe behavior abnormalities can still be found in mental institutions and prisons, their numbers are decreasing. Scheerenberger (1978) records that 5% of the discharges from public residential facilities are to mental hospitals, whereas 0.2% are discharged to prisons.

Establishing a Range of Living Options

All living options listed in Table 2.3 are not likely to exist in any one community. A major concern for advocates of community living for handicapped individuals is deciding which of the residential options is best suited for their community. Recommendations for facilitating the expeditious return to the community of presently institutionalized residents as well as maintaining handicapped persons presently living in the community have been made by Blatt, Bogdan, Biklen, and Taylor (1977), Neufeld (1977), and Scheerenberger (1974).

Blatt et al. (1977) outline a philosophy called "conversion" that represents a change in thinking toward the concept of deinstitutionalization. Conversion refers to "an orderly transition from an institutional to a community-based system of services, with concomitant plans to transform existing physical facilities, staff resources, institutional ideologies, community attitudes, and agency policies to alternative more humanizing uses and postures" (p. 41). Several principles must be adhered to in order for the conversion philosophy to occur. These include: 1) the delivery of services that are provided as a right of citizens, rather than a privilege; 2) services that are provided on a noncategorical basis; 3) services that constitute a continuum to ensure that each individual's needs are met in the most appropriate manner; 4) services that are provided under the least restrictive, most normalized circumstances possible; and 5) the agencies that provide services must be accountable to the consumer.

Neufeld (1977) and Scheerenberger (1974) present structural models that most closely approximate the deinstitutionalization philosophy outlined by Blatt et al. (1977). Scheerenberger (1974) describes five integrals that facilitate the deinstitutionalization process:

1. Establishing a local or regional agency or body with statutory authority to plan, implement, and coordinate programs for the retarded
2. Creating an independent standard setting and monitoring agency
3. Providing quality back-up services including technical consultancy
4. Obtaining substantial financial support
5. Establishing tough-minded, strong-willed advocacy programs in three areas: legal, agency, and citizen

Neufeld extends Scheerenberger's recommendations by specifying the responsibilities that should be established at the local, regional, and state levels to enable an efficient transition to occur from an institutional-dependent model to a community-based service delivery system. At the local level Neufeld recommends the creation of a human service board with jurisdiction over a small geographic area (i.e., county) or population area of 100,000 people. Within this size community, services can be developed to adequately meet the needs of its handicapped citizens and maintain as individual a relationship as possible. The primary purposes of a human service board are to ensure that a wide spectrum of services be available for handicapped citizens presently in the community and to be responsible for returning all institutionalized residents to their home communities. At the regional level, one would find residential facilities containing professionals responsible for providing technical assistance and training for personnel who are interested in working in smaller community residential facilities. Additionally, the provision of highly specialized medical care and treatment for the most severely handicapped individuals in the region would be the responsibility of the regional facility. The state agency would be responsible for administrative and political support to the local human service boards and regional facilities. Additionally, members of the state agency would be involved in human service research for the state legislature and develop statewide public education programs on the rights and needs of disabled citizens.

> **The primary purposes of a human service board are to ensure that a wide spectrum of services be available for handicapped citizens presently in the community and to be responsible for returning all institutionalized residents to their home communities.**

Based on the recommendations of Neufeld and Scheerenberger, local communities should have planning boards or human service boards to facilitate the integration of handicapped individuals in the community. To help accomplish this goal Bradley (1978) recommends that local agencies conduct a needs assessment of the community to determine the number and functioning level of handicapped persons in need of residential placement. A list of suggestions for inclusion in a needs assessment to be conducted by local agencies may include:

1. A review of the current institutionalized population in state facilities whose home community is under the jurisdiction of the local agency to ascertain the level of functioning, income levels, age, and potential for movement into less restrictive living environments
2. A survey of the community's handicapped persons residing in private institutional facilities to determine the appropriateness of ongoing placement and probable alternatives
3. A review of persons on waiting lists for public and private facilities whose families reside in the agency's community to determine the characteristics of such persons and the possibility of alternatives to the services applied for
4. Interviews with social and protective service workers to determine needs that they perceive among low income families with handicapped children
5. A survey of private proprietary and nonprofit agencies serving handicapped persons to determine the provider assessment of need
6. A canvass of other data sources including high-risk registers, school records, and vocational rehabilitation facilities (adapted from Bradley, 1978, p. 65)

After the needs assessment information has been collected, the local agency must determine what types of residential options are the highest priority and are feasible for its community. Initially, a primary emphasis might be to return all previously institutionalized residents to their natural families but with the establishment of adequate support services. Lensink (1980) has generated a list of support services that assist the family and provide incentives for the inclusion of a handicapped child and/or adolescent as a sustaining member of the family. Selected community support services include:

Trained baby sitters
Parent consultations
Training in speech, motor, and sensory development
Behavior management
Residential respite
Housekeeping assistance
Crisis medical and behavior problem assistance teams
Trained companions for handicapped teens and adults
Advocacy and assistance with generic health, education,
      and welfare agencies
Family counseling
Behavior therapy and psychotherapy for nonretarded family members
Direct subsidization of costs of caring for all handicapped persons

If the natural home or an independent living setting is not a feasible choice, alternative options need to be developed. Rather than merely choosing from the continuum of residential placements listed in Table 2.3, a sounder strategy would be to determine the level of assistance each person would need to adequately function in the community (Lensink, 1980). For example, from the list of returning residents, a determination of the number who are semi-independent or in need of minimal, moderate, or intense training to function successfully within the community should be made. Residential options should be sought that maximize the use of professional and paraprofessional staff for handicapped individuals of different functioning levels and degrees of need for supervision. With individuals in need of minimal supervision, periodic checks and assistance in the use of a community's generic services would take minimal effort for paraprofessional staff. Individuals in need of moderate supervision might need a residential option that includes a live-in staff component and paraprofessionals providing direct assistance under the guidance of a professional. Returning residents with intense training requirements may need the services of physical, occupational and speech therapists, an LPN living at the facility or on call, professional rehabilitation and/or special education staff, and well trained paraprofessionals. The actual physical structure of a housing option may not be as indicative of a more independent living environment than the amount of external assistance required by professional and paraprofessional staff. Therefore, when choosing residential options for handicapped individuals, the local agency needs to ask at least three questions: 1) What is the current functioning level of each returning handicapped person? 2) What amount of assistance will be needed for each individual to function successfully in the community? and 3) What housing option provides the optimal setting for the training to occur?

> **Residential options should be sought that maximize use of professional and paraprofessional staff for handicapped individuals of different functioning levels and degrees of need for supervision.**

In this section the functions of the local, regional, and state agencies responsible for establishing a range of living options were delineated. Much of the energy needs to be focused at the local level, following the suggestions of Lensink (1980) for providing home support services and Bradley's (1978) needs assessment recommendations. Even with careful planning by local agencies there may still exist legal and/or attitudinal barriers for establishing residential options for handicapped persons.

Barriers to the Establishment of Community Residential Facilities

Once a match is made between the handicapped person's functioning level and the living option that will best provide the environment for successful community experiences, there may exist barriers within the community that prevent the residential option from being established. Two barriers that have frequently presented difficulty are zoning regulations and negative public reactions. Both obstacles are subsequently discussed and suggestions are made to tactfully resolve their counterproductive influences.

Zoning Obstacles to Community Placement

One of the barriers often confronting community residential developers is the zoning restriction ordinance found in most communities. Zoning is defined as:

> Systematic regulation of the use and development of real property. Zoning restricts the ways in which a private owner can use his property by dividing a city into districts and then prescribing the uses to which real property within those districts can be put. This systematic regulation of land is designed to promote orderly and healthy community development through a comprehensive zoning plan which prohibits that which is harmful to health, morals, safety, or welfare. (Hopperton, 1975, p. 3)

Emmel (1980) describes the municipality's right to zone its property as originating from one of two sources: "a state zoning statute, which provides specific municipal authority over land regulation; or a state constitutional home-rule law, which allows the community sovereignty over many or all functions relating to the locality, including zoning" (pp. 175–176).

Many municipalities choose to restrict the types of residences allowed in "single-family dwelling" areas. By doing so, the town limits residential uses to single families with the definition of single family often narrowly defined as a "housekeeping unit related by blood, marriage, or adoption" (Knight, 1980, p. 124). In one court decision, *Village of Belle Terre* v. *Boraas* (1974), the community had a restricted ordinance that disallowed a group of six unrelated college students from living within a single-family dwelling area. The court upheld the ordinance and stated that the "ordinance bore a rational relationship to a permissible state objective." The question now arises: What does this mean for handicapped individuals being allowed to live in the least restrictive setting, namely, within a residentially zoned area of the community?

In addressing the above question, the majority of court opinions pertaining to unrelated mentally retarded and/or other handicapped individuals being allowed to live in "single-family dwelling" areas have used the following definition of family:

> So long as the group home bears the generic character of a family unit and is not a framework for transients or transient living, it conforms to the purpose of the ordinance.
> (*City of White Plains* v. *Ferraioli*, 1974)

Thus, the narrow interpretation of restricting occupancy based on marriage, blood-relationship, and/or adoption was replaced by a "home-like" environment that could not be denied handicapped persons. Court decisions similar to the White Plains opinion have "held that because a group home functions as a family does, with residents living as a single unit, participating in housekeeping, cooking, and other activities as a 'family' group, such a home fits within the definition of a family" (Mental Health Law Project, 1978).

Sensing the trend in court opinions such as the White Plains decision, states have begun enacting statutes disallowing restrictive zoning by local communities. In Virginia the state legislature passed such a law, which in part states:

> It is the policy of this State that mentally retarded and other developmentally disabled persons should not be excluded by county or municipal zoning ordinances from the benefits of normal residential surroundings. Furthermore, it is the policy of this State to encourage and promote the dispersion of residences for the mentally retarded and other developmentally disabled persons to achieve optimal assimilation and mainstreaming into the community. (Va. Code Section 15.1-486.2(A) Supp. 1978)

Restrictive zoning for the purpose of protecting the health, morals, safety, or welfare of a community has not been found sufficient reason to deny handicapped persons the opportunity to live as a family in an area zoned for single-family houses. However, even with the zoning obstacle removed as a barrier to community integration, the community's attitudes may still be ambivalent and create a second barrier.

> NARC's use of communications in the early years made a substantial impact . . . but that was an impact of awareness, or replacing a vacuum of ignorance with the substance of information. There is not yet evidence of fundamental changes in public attitudes toward the mentally retarded in the United States in areas of substantive importance such as acceptance of retarded persons as neighbors or as fellow workers. (Lippman, 1976, p. 100)

Because prejudicial attitudes may negate efforts to establish appropriate residential options within a particular community, efforts must be directed toward developing community acceptance.

> **Restrictive zoning for the purpose of protecting the health, morals, safety, or welfare of a community has not been found sufficient reason to deny handicapped persons the opportunity to live as a family in an area zoned for single-family houses.**

Community Acceptance of Handicapped Residents

The task of accurately determining the degree of community acceptance toward handicapped persons living in small residential environments is not an easy one. The extreme reactions that surface may not be indicative of the true feelings of the community. Such reactions have ranged from reports of community members setting a proposed group home site on fire (as seen on the CBS program *60 Minutes*) to neighbors interacting with handicapped persons in a mutually accepting manner (Perske, 1980). Usually, community members are surveyed to solicit their attitudes toward existing or potentially available living alternatives for handicapped individuals. Heal, Sigelman, and Switzky (1978) caution, however, that "the literature on attitudes appears to be an inadequate source of information about levels of community acceptance, characteristics of accepting neighbors, and the probability of active opposition." Even though the validity of results from attitude surveys may be questioned, members of local planning boards may still be called upon to describe the present level of community acceptance, predict the future probability of active opposition, and develop a profile of an accepting neighbor. The subsequent information in this section is intended to assist individuals in responding to the above issues.

Levels of Community Acceptance

There has been some evidence that people's attitudes toward community placement of previously institutionalized residents vary as a function of the perceived threat of contact or involvement by members of the community. In a no-threat situation, a Gallup poll, commissioned by the President's Committee on Mental Retardation, asked the following question: "Suppose mildly or moderately retarded persons have been educated to live in the general community. Would you object to six of them occupying a home on your block or not?" (Gallup Organization Report for the President's Committee on Mental Retardation, 1976). Eighty-five percent of the respondents replied that they would not object. Feeling that the Gallup survey might not be a true indicator of an actual perceived threat of having a mentally retarded person live on the same block as the respondent, Kastner, Reppucci, and Pezzoli (1979) conducted an additional attitude study. In this survey Kastner et al. compared the responses of "residents living near a house for sale (who) were told that the house might be appropriate for a group home and that the community mental retardation agency was interested in finding housing for retarded persons" to "a control group of community residents who were merely asked to participate in a neighborhood survey." There was a nine percentage point difference between the control and threat group responses. The actual threat of a house in the immediate neighborhood that might be used as a group home resulted in a lower acceptance response than the no-threat control group.

> **People's attitudes toward community placement of previously institutionalized residents vary as a function of the perceived threat of contact or involvement by members of the community.**

The findings of Kastner et al. support the earlier results of Rothbart (1973), who investigated one community's attitude toward a halfway house for ex-convicts. Persons living within a mile of the facility were less favorably disposed toward it than residents in the city who lived 3 to 5 miles away. Sigelman (1976) also found that a community in southwestern Texas was sharply divided on its willingness to permit a law to allow homes for retarded adults in areas with residential zoning restrictions. Again, the probability of actually having a group of deinstitutionalized residents living next door would be increased if such a law were enacted.

Probability of Active Opposition   One of the major preoccupations of community residence planning groups is the minimizing of active opposition to community placement of previously institutionalized residents. Should a well thought out public relations campaign be initiated, or should a quiet "take them by surprise" approach be employed? Is there some degree of opposition that may be more healthy than no reaction at all? Segal, Baumohl, and Moyles (1980), describing a community's reaction to mentally ill adults living in shelter-care facilities, found that "a moderate level of community reaction actually facilitated the social integration of sheltered-care residents" (p. 345).

Although predicting the probability of negative community reaction is tenuous, a guideline is suggested that may be of assistance to local agencies. If a housing option is being considered in a neighborhood composed of highly heterogeneous, transient, and liberal neighbors (e.g., near a university campus), there may be little need for an active campaign to solicit community support. These neighbors are used to seeing many people come and go within the neighborhood, and there is usually no unifying bond among neighbors. However, if a closely knit, stable, more conservative neighborhood is chosen for a residential site for handicapped persons, a more active, well thought out strategy may be desired. In this type of neighborhood everyone knows what is going on and block meetings are regular occurrences. In reviewing the literature on the previous two approaches, Heal et al. (1978) relate that "although the apparent unpredictability of community opposition reduces opportunities for the strategic placement of facilities in receptive neighborhoods, program planners can be heartened by preliminary evidence that opposition dissipates once the facility has been established" (p. 166).

Regardless of what initial approach may have been chosen by an agency, the probability of active opposition by community members may be reduced by following the suggestions of Stickney (1976) to:

1. Upgrade and maintain the facility and its grounds
2. Avoid putting a sign or label on the residence, so that the facility will look the same as the other houses
3. Provide needed nonresidential services to the community
4. Fill the residence gradually, and introduce residents one by one to local services
5. Always try to keep the public informed of the planning group's purposes and program, and do not surprise the neighbors
6. Encourage one-to-one sponsorship of a resident by community volunteers
7. Establish a program for the residents themselves to serve as volunteers
8. Encourage neighbors' support, not only as volunteers in some aspect of the program, but as donors of items for the home and its residents
9. Create opportunities for the individual residents to meet on social occasions with their new neighbors
10. Start a food cooperative or participate with an existing neighborhood food cooperative
11. Provide adequate supervision of residents, and make sure it is visible to the rest of the community

Characteristics of Accepting Neighbors One strategy to enhance community acceptance that is available to members of local planning agencies is to provide potential neighbors with accounts of the interactions of neighbors who have lived next to small residential facilities for handicapped persons. Perhaps the most ambitious undertaking to determine the characteristics of accepting neighbors has been by Perske (1980). After interviewing hundreds of neighbors and recording each interview on tape, Perske described 18 observations from neighborhoods that contained well-run small group residences. The in-depth interview process followed by Perske enabled him to develop a list of characteristics attributed to good neighbors:

1. More neighbors are for persons with handicaps than against them.
2. The presence of well-run, family-like residences for persons with handicaps has brought new zest to many neighborhoods.
3. Many neighbors are performing gracious acts on their own.
4. Many neighbors have a clearer understanding of how people became developmentally disabled.
5. Some neighbors can now look beyond diagnostic labels.
6. Many neighbors no longer view these people as an overwhelming army.
7. Neighbors can now recognize measureable development in persons with handicaps.
8. Some neighbors are not panicked over property values anymore.
9. Zoning laws are becoming fair for everyone.
10. Neighbors are appreciating these persons' needs to work harder.
11. Neighbors can now recognize courage and heroism in persons with handicaps.
12. Neighbors are learning that quality community-based programs are keeping these people busier than the average citizen.
13. Neighborhood children are powerful peer-group educators.
14. Neighbors are becoming natural reinforcers.
15. More and more, neighbors are feeling comfortable with these people.
16. Neighbors are recognizing that persons with handicaps must also be givers-to-the-community. ✓
17. Neighbors have come to see relationships with persons having handicaps as no big deal.
18. Healthy relationships between neighbors and persons with handicaps will lead to an improved civilization. ✓

> **One strategy to enhance community acceptance that is available to members of local planning agencies is to provide potential neighbors with accounts of the interactions of neighbors who have lived next to small residential facilities for handicapped persons.**

In summary, the advocates who are encouraging handicapped persons to live in community residential facilities need to answer the following questions:

What have been the past reactions of community members to atypical living
    arrangements in their neighborhoods?
What is the general profile of the neighborhood (i.e., closely knit, long-term
    residents or transient, uninvolved residents)?
How much exposure to the neighborhood will residents have?
What is the degree of handicapping conditions of the residents?
Is the location of the facility on the perimeter of the neighborhood or in the
    heart of the neighborhood?

The decision of how to approach community members about the prospect of
having handicapped neighbors will be guided by the answers to these questions.

CONCLUSION

Persons involved with obtaining suitable residential options for severely
handicapped individuals should be knowledgeable about the issues raised
in this chapter. The more knowledgeable a person is of these issues, the
higher the probability he/she has of securing the most suitable housing
option to meet the needs of each handicapped individual. The principle of
normalization and the concept of the least restrictive alternative form the
philosophical foundation for the assertion that all persons, regardless of
handicapping conditions, have a right to live in the community and enjoy
similar life-styles as their neighbors. Planning agencies must be able to
express this feeling in words the general public can comprehend and not use
professional jargon that easily scares potential neighbors.

    A variety of living environments that are included in the continuum of
residential options should be available within each community. With support from paraprofessional and professional workers, handicapped persons
can acquire greater independence over time. As residential options increase, agencies must have members who are skilled at evaluating the current needs of the community, the growth of residents within residential
placements, and the cost-effectiveness of each resident's placement. Careful
planning and adherence to the recommendations contained in the preceding
sections will increase the probability that professionals secure the best residential option for each handicapped member of their community.

DOMESTIC/HOME LIVING SKILLS

LEARNING GOALS

1. *Identify an array of domestic/home living skills that may comprise curriculum areas for instruction and explain the importance of these skills in the educational curriculum.*
2. *Describe how to assess home settings for identifying individualized target objectives for students.*
3. *Describe how to assess individual students' competency level in domestic/home living skills and how to prioritize which skills to teach.*
4. *Describe four instructional strategies that have been used to teach domestic/home living skills.*
5. *Explain the relationship between prompting techniques and the acquisition of domestic/home living skills.*
6. *Develop a program to teach domestic/home living skills that utilizes a self-instructional format.*
7. *Describe the importance and explain at least one method of socially validating domestic/home living skills.*

DOMESTIC/HOME LIVING SKILLS INSTRUCTION

Although much of the recent emphasis in programs for moderately, severely, and profoundly handicapped individuals has been on vocational training, an equal amount of attention must be placed on training those skills necessary for successful placement in a community living environment (Boyan, 1978; Cuvo & Davis, 1981). As it is important to work in the community, it is also important and perhaps basic to community work to live in a community-based setting. Placement in a community living setting without preparation is likely to result in failure and perhaps placement in or return to an institutional setting (Cuvo & Davis, 1981; Nihira & Nihira, 1975; Snell, 1981).

As described in Chapter 2, there are a number of different types of community living settings ranging from large group homes (or small community-based institutions) to regular apartment settings in which the apartment dweller is given supportive services when necessary. The type and quality of domestic skills necessary for successful placement likely will differ depending on the specific domestic setting. It has been documented, however, that a lack of domestic skills may result in an individual's failure to succeed in a community living placement (see, e.g., Crnic & Pym, 1979; Nihira & Nihira, 1975; Schalock & Harper, 1978).

Crnic and Pym (1979) surveyed independent living staff who were responsible for placing group home residents in independent living settings (e.g., apartments). One of the major variables identified by the independent living staff as responsible for the success of the group home residents in independent living was adequate basic living skills, which were expected only after training was provided. Similarly, Schalock and Harper (1978) evaluated the success or failure of 131 mentally retarded individuals who had been placed in independent living settings, all of whom had received instruction in daily living skills. Thirteen percent of these individuals failed to maintain their independent living status. The individuals who failed also demonstrated difficulties in money management, housekeeping, and meal preparation skills.

In a similar type of survey, Nihira and Nihira (1975) questioned the primary caregivers in foster and group homes to determine the factors that contributed to the residents' success in their community living environments. The ability to perform simple domestic tasks such as room cleaning, bed making, ironing, meal preparation, and yard work was frequently cited as important for success. In fact, Nihira and Nihira concluded that these skills were crucial for successful adaptation to community placement and further suggested that educators should develop preplacement training programs designed to teach domestic skills.

The majority of the individuals whose success or failure in community living has been evaluated have been mildly to moderately retarded. In fact, Eagle (1976) reported that only 1.3% of the individuals deinstitutionalized and placed in communities before 1960 had measured IQ's below 25. Because the failure of mildly and moderately retarded persons to maintain community living status has been attributed in large part to a lack of domestic skills, it seems logical to extend that problem, to an even greater degree, to severely and profoundly retarded individuals. Therefore, the need for training in domestic/home living skills before community placement becomes increasingly more important as the degree of handicap increases. Domestic skills training should be a large portion of a curriculum for moderately, severely, and profoundly handicapped students from a young age (Boyan, 1978). In addition, coordination of home, school, and community goals should be carefully planned so that training will not only facilitate success in a current home setting but also will facilitate movement into less restrictive community living environments.

DOMESTIC/HOME LIVING SKILLS

Domestic/home living involves a wide range of skills that can be defined as the activities that are engaged in within the home (i.e., the place where an individual lives either independently or supervised; Cuvo & Davis, 1981). Although many skills are used in other environments as well as in the home (e.g., toileting and communication), domestic/home living skills are defined as those skills that are not directly related to a specific vocational skill or job (Boyan, 1978) or community skills that only occur outside of the home (e.g., use of transportation, recreational facilities, and stores).

> **Domestic/home living involves a wide range of skills that can be defined as the activities that are engaged in within the home (i.e., the place where an individual lives either independently or supervised).**

One method of selecting domestic skills for instruction is to identify all of the rooms in a home setting and list the types of activities that are likely to occur in each room (Brown et al., 1979). For example, one room found in most houses is a bathroom. Some activities likely to be engaged in within a home bathroom are: 1) bathing; 2) washing hair, face, and hands; 3) brushing teeth; 4) shaving; 5) combing hair; and 6) using the toilet. In a kitchen, examples of activities are: 1) meal planning; 2) meal preparation; 3) sorting and putting away food; 4) washing dishes; 5) cleaning sink, table, and counters; and 6) mopping the floor. As stated previously, many of the skills used in the home will also be used in other settings. The way an individual uses the skill in a home, however, many times will differ from use in other settings. For example, bathroom use will cross environments, but rarely would an individual bathe or shave in bathrooms outside of the home. A list of activities and skills that may be appropriate to a home setting is provided in Table 3.1. Of course, for all students it is important to identify present and/or potential future home environments and teach only the skills relevant to those settings.

Table 3.1. Domestic/home living activities and skills

Safety skills[a]

1. Simple first aid
2. Use of phone for emergencies (e.g. fire, police, doctor)
3. Avoiding hazardous substances and activities
4. Requesting assistance when necessary

General housekeeping/maintenance skills[a]

1. Dusting
2. Vacuuming
3. Mopping
4. Sweeping
5. Emptying trash in appropriate receptacle
6. Cleaning windows
7. Changing light bulbs and fuses
8. Caring for/maintaining equipment

Clothing, care and use

1. Sorting, washing, and drying clothes
2. Ironing
3. Folding
4. Putting clothes in appropriate storage
5. Mending
6. Selecting weather-appropriate clothes
7. Selecting color/pattern-coordinated clothes
8. Selecting activity-appropriate clothes
9. Selecting age-appropriate clothes
10. Dressing

Bathroom activities

Personal care
1. Washing face and hands
2. Bathing and drying
3. Washing hair
4. Brushing teeth
5. Brushing hair
6. Shaving
7. Using deodorant
8. Menstrual care
9. Using the toilet

Cleaning
1. Washing tub/shower sink
2. Scouring toilet
3. Cleaning mirror
4. Mopping
5. Storing supplies

Bedroom activities/skills

1. Making bed
2. Changing bedclothes regularly
3. Engaging in solitary leisure activities
4. Dressing for bed
5. Sleeping
6. Cleaning room

Kitchen skills

Food preparation
1. Selecting appropriate foods
2. Following a recipe
3. Measuring
4. Using utensils (e.g. spatula, mixing spoon)
5. Using appliances
6. Using a stove
7. Setting the table

Kitchen organization
1. Identifying needed kitchen supplies for purchase
2. Categorizing food groups for storage (e.g. freezer foods, canned goods, refrigerator foods, etc.)
3. Storing dishes, pans, utensils, and supplies

Meal planning
1. Identifying food groups
2. Planning menus of nutritious combinations of food
3. Selecting appropriate recipes

Clean-up
1. Clearing table
2. Disposing of trash
3. Storing leftovers
4. Washing and drying dishes
5. Returning dishes to appropriate storage places
6. Scouring sink and cleaning counters
7. Sweeping
8. Mopping floor

Eating
1. Using utensils (e.g. spoon, fork, knife, cup)
2. Using napkin
3. Passing food dishes
4. Serving appropriate portions
5. Using table manners
6. Communicating food needs/preferences

Living room/family room activities/skills

1. Socializing with others
2. Engaging in leisure activities such as operating and watching television, operating record player, and operating radio
3. Cleaning (listed under General housekeeping)

Yard care skills

1. Grass mowing
2. Pruning
3. Shoveling snow
4. Planting
5. Weeding
6. Watering

a Used throughout the house.

PREPARING STUDENTS FOR
COMMUNITY DOMESTIC PLACEMENT

The need for domestic skills training at the elementary and secondary educational levels is well supported (e.g., Boyan, 1978; Crnic & Pym, 1979; Cuvo & Davis, 1981; Nihira & Nihira, 1975; Snell, 1981). As a result, a systematic method for preparing moderately, severely, and profoundly handicapped persons for community domestic living must be described. Figure 3.1 outlines the steps necessary for delivering services relevant to domestic/home living and pertinent to successful placement of handicapped persons in community living settings.

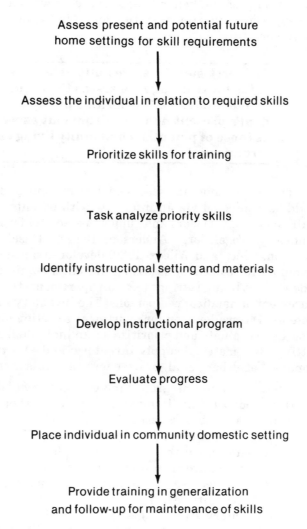

Assess present and potential future
home settings for skill requirements

↓

Assess the individual in relation to required skills

↓

Prioritize skills for training

↓

Task analyze priority skills

↓

Identify instructional setting and materials

↓

Develop instructional program

↓

Evaluate progress

↓

Place individual in community domestic setting

↓

Provide training in generalization
and follow-up for maintenance of skills

*Figure 3.1. Steps involved in domestic/home
living skills instruction.*

Assess Present and Future Home Settings

The number of skills associated with domestic/home living is very large (refer to Table 3.1), and the skill deficits experienced by moderately, severely, and profoundly retarded persons are vast. Therefore, expecting that every domestic/home living skill delineated in teacher-generated lists or available home living skills curricula (e.g., *Skills to Achieve Independent Living [SAIL]*, 1979) can be taught in the limited time usually available for instruction is unreasonable and inefficient.

Selectively choosing skills for training is necessary. The first step in systematic selection of skills for training is to assess the requirements and/or skill priorities of each student's present home environment as well as those of potential community living environments (e.g., a group home for a severely or profoundly handicapped student who currently lives with family or a supervised apartment setting for an individual who currently lives in a group home).

> **The first step in systematic selection of skills for training is to assess the requirements and/or skill priorities of each student's present home environment as well as those of potential community living environments.**

This environmental assessment of present and future living settings could be conducted via an interview with parents and family, group home staff, and/or supervisors and support personnel for individuals living independently. Vogelsberg, Anderson, Berger, Haselden, Mitwell, Schmidt, Skowron, Ulett, and Wilcox (1980) developed an Independent Living Skills Inventory to be used for assessing the skills required in specific community independent living settings (e.g., an apartment) that have been targeted for placement of handicapped persons. The inventory includes four major components: 1) consideration for apartment selection and set-up; 2) a checklist of skills to evaluate and prioritize for an individual student a specific living setting; 3) a material/supply inventory; and 4) a training model. The rationales Vogelsberg et al. provide for use of this inventory are:

1. There are many programs and curricula available that can be used to train independent living skills. However, there was no functional inventory available to cover the considerations necessary to complete a transition from dependent to independent living.
2. By focusing upon the delineation of factors in an independent living situation that are basic and vital to success in any one living situation, the process necessary to develop functional curricula for use in public schools was initiated.
3. The inventory strategy may make precise skills to teach handicapped individuals immediately apparent. Specific skills in the student's current repertoire are assessed, and the skills that must be taught are determined and prioritized for training.
4. The inventory can be the beginning of a longitudinal curriculum sequence to provide information for further development. Vital information on concrete skills necessary for later successful independent living may be provided to teachers of young handicapped students.

5. A precise inventory will help delineate specific criteria necessary for independent living, as opposed to the teacher's only "inferring" the performance that students will need when they attain a more independent living situation. (1980, pp. 40–41)

Johnson and her colleagues in Project PRIDE developed a Living Environment Needs Inventory (LENI) (Note 1, p. 282) that serves a purpose similar to The Independent Living Skills Inventory. The LENI was constructed to assist educators in identifying the requirements/needs of specific students' home environments so as to identify target skills for a student's individualized education plan (IEP). The LENI includes six sections that provide formats for: 1) identifying basic student, family, and medical information as well as information on ancillary services; 2) assessing family needs; and 3) identifying specific skill-related items for training.

The LENI is organized so that a student's previous and current living environments and needs can be assessed, and/or the instrument can be administered repeatedly over time to identify student progress and changing needs. This instrument provides a very useful format and listing of skills to conduct an environmental assessment and identify priorities for instruction. (Refer to Table 3.2 for sample items from the LENI.)

An alternative to the use of prepared home assessment inventories is to develop an informal teacher-made checklist. The skills and activities listed in Table 3.1 can be used to develop such a checklist. Through interviews and/or direct observation of a home setting, the behavioral/skill requirements for successful adaptation to present and future community living environments can be assessed and prioritized for instruction.

Assess the Individual Student

Once present and future domestic/home living settings have been assessed to determine the specific needs/skill requirements, the next step in the development of domestic goals is to assess the students to determine skill level. Domestic/home living skills can be assessed generally through the use of commercially available adaptive behavior scales or screening instruments (e.g., AAMD Adaptive Behavior Scale [Lambert, Windmiller, Cole, & Figueroa, 1975]; Camelot Behavior Checklist [Foster, 1974]; TARC Assessment Inventory [Sailor & Mix, 1975]; Independent Living Screening Test [Schalock, 1975]).

The AAMD Adaptive Behavior Scale, for example, includes a general assessment of independent functioning skills (such as toileting, cleanliness, and eating), economic activity, numbers and time, and domestic activities. Skills assessed within these categories are likely to relate, at least in part, to successful placement in domestic/home living settings. Even more pertinent to successful community domestic placement may be the skills assessed in the Independent Living Screening Test (Schalock, 1975). This screening instrument measures a student's skills in nine areas: 1) personal maintenance; 2) clothing care; 3) home maintenance; 4) food preparation; 5) time management; 6) social behavior; 7) community utilization; 8) communication; and 9) functional academic skills.

Table 3.2. Sample items from the Living Environment Needs Inventory (LENI)[a]

Student: _____ Date and time: _____ / / ____ (AM/PM

Informant: Name _____ (Relationship)

Interviewer: _____

Place: Address _____ & Directions _____

Phone Number (___)

First Administration or *Update?* (Circle one) If Update, fill in information for *previous* administration: Date _____ ; Informant: _____

Interviewer: _____

List all members of immediate family living at home (include pets)—Indicate name which student would use (e.g., "Dad")

Name _____ (Relation)

Name _____ (Relation)

Name _____ (Relation)

Name _____ (Relation)

Name _____ (Relation)

Medication:

Reported in Previous LENI   Current   Reasons

_____

_____

_____

List any Therapy Services or Recreational Programs in which student is participating outside of school:

_____

_____

Item	Support Level Previous	Support Level Current	Frequency Previous	Frequency Current	Comments
BEDROOM RELATED ITEMS					
1. Get up & start morning routine?					
2. Make own bed?					
3. Put away bed clothes/slippers?					
4. Get out clothes for day?					
5. Choose items of clothing to wear?					
6. Select clothing appropriate to weather & occasion?					
7. Communicate likes & dislikes re: clothing? (Score Mode)					
8. Dress himself/herself:					
a) Pull-on pants & socks?					
b) Pull-on shirts?					
c) Put on open-front shirts/coats?					
d) Put shoes on correct feet?					
e) Fasten: snaps?					
buttons?					
zippers?					
buckles?					
Velcro?					
9. If you help him/her dress, does he/she anticipate & cooperate (e.g. by holding out foot for shoe?)					
10. Interfering behavior when undressing?					

A. *Principal Concerns re: Student's Needs:* What are the skills you would most like to see worked on at school this year?

_____

_____

_____

_____

B. *Needed Support Services:*

—*Health-related* (OT, DDS, MD, etc.)

_____

—*Respite* (baby sitter, respite care, etc.)

_____

—*Recreational*

_____

—*Other* (transportation, etc.)

_____

Summary:

A. School commitments: Will provide the following information/assistance by:

_____ / /

_____ / /

_____ / /

_____ / /

B. Home commitments: Will provide the following by:

_____ / /

_____ / /

_____ / /

General Comments:

_____

aTable is from Project PRIDE (BEH Contract #300-77-0253).

> The AAMD Adaptive Behavior Scale, for example, includes a general assessment of independent functioning skills (such as toileting, cleanliness, and eating), economic activity, numbers and time, and domestic activities.

Although these general screening instruments and scales provide a standard method of measuring student adaptive skills, the skills measured may not be priorities for successful domestic placement. A method of assessment directly related to specific domestic skill requirements would be more useful for establishing individual student objectives. Evaluation of student skills in relation to the skill requirements/needs delineated by parents or guardians in a student's present home and by persons familiar with future community placements would provide this relevant information.

The priority skills identified through the environmental assessments should be used to devise a checklist for evaluating student skills. Skill level might be assessed through interviews with significant persons in the student's home environment or through direct observation of the student in the home setting. Following this general assessment of student domestic skills, a more specific assessment of skill priorities is needed to develop instructional programs. Specific skill assessment (e.g., task analytic assessment) is discussed in a subsequent section.

Prioritize Skills for Training

As discussed previously, moderately, severely, and profoundly handicapped persons frequently lack many skills necessary for living either independently or in supervised community settings. All skills cannot be trained at once due to time and logistical constraints (e.g., transportation difficulties). Therefore, skills that are considered important for community living must be prioritized for instruction.

A number of factors should be considered when prioritizing domestic skills for a particular student's IEP. In addition to interviews with parents, guardians, and community support persons to determine domestic priorities, the following questions should be answered about each identified skill:

1. Is the skill used frequently?
2. Can the activity/skill be used across situations or settings?
3. Is the activity/skill crucial for the student's placement in a community living environment?
4. Can the skill be taught efficiently?
5. Is the selected skill appropriate for the student's nonhandicapped peers?
6. Are the materials selected for instruction appropriate for the student's nonhandicapped peers?
7. Will the skill be maintained by natural environmental conditions?

Skills being evaluated for training should be ranked according to the number of these questions receiving a positive response. That is, skills for which all questions are answered with a definite "yes" are the highest priorities for instruction. In addition, the skills that are relevant throughout the day, regardless of the activities and settings in which they occur (e.g., toileting and expressing needs), are also among the highest priorities for instruction. Once priorities have been established, an instructional plan can be developed.

TEACHING DOMESTIC SKILLS

Analyzing Tasks

The complexity of many domestic tasks necessitates a systematic approach to instruction, and the use of task analysis is central to such an approach (Cuvo, 1978). Task analysis, or breaking a task down into discrete sequential steps, provides a format for assessing, teaching, and evaluating student progress.

Tasks such as dishwashing, bed making, meal preparation, and showering involve chains of discrete steps, many of which require very different types of skills. Tables 3.3 and 3.4, respectively, provide examples of task analyses of dishwashing, which consists of 42 steps, and bed making, which consists of 18 different steps. Successful demonstrations of the use of task analysis in evaluation and instruction of domestic skills have included teaching laundry skills (Cuvo, Jacobi, & Sipko, in press), clothes mending skills (Cronin & Cuvo, 1979), meal preparation skills (Johnson & Cuvo, in press; Robinson-Wilson, 1977), bathroom cleaning skills (Cuvo, Leaf, & Borakove, 1978), and bed making (Snell, in press).

Task analyses must be constructed prior to student assessment and program development. Although analyzing tasks into component steps would seem to be relatively routine, there are a number of steps educators should take to construct valid task analyses, (Cuvo & Davis, 1981; Cuvo, Note 2). A task should never be analyzed merely by sitting at a desk and mentally walking through the task components. In fact, a number of resources should be utilized, and the task analysis must be tested prior to using the steps in program implementation with handicapped students. Cuvo and colleagues (Cuvo, 1978) and Cuvo and Davis (1981) have suggested that validating task analyses should include the following steps:

1. Consult experts (individuals who are proficient in the task or who perform the task as part of their vocation, e.g., home economists for food preparation, tailors or seamstresses for sewing skills, janitors for cleaning skills)
2. Consult written documents (manuals that describe how to use equipment to complete a task, e.g., manuals that accompany washers and dryers or sewing machines)
3. Field test (pilot preliminary task analyses on experts)
4. Modify task analyses based on field tests
5. Field test task analyses on the target population (individuals with handicaps similar to those identified to receive instruction)
6. Modify task analyses to accommodate handicaps
7. Identify mandatory task steps (those steps crucial to task completion versus those extraneous to task completion, e.g., returning the salt shaker to the cabinet is not crucial to preparation of food for lunch)

Table 3.3. Task analytic assessment of dishwashing

Intervention Instructions: Give instructions, "(Name), wash the dishes." Allow 3 seconds for initiation of step 1. If correct, record (*). If incorrect or no response, proceed to verbal prompt. If correct, record (V). If incorrect or no response in 3 seconds, give model prompt. If correct, record (M). If incorrect or no response within 3 seconds, give physical prompt and record (P). Proceed through all steps in task analysis using these procedures.

Teacher: _____
Student: _Joe, Bob_____
Date: _____
Environment: _kitchen_____
Instructional cue: _____
_____ "Wash the dishes"

Washing dishes

1. S takes detergent from storage location and places on sink													
2. S lifts faucet to turn on water													
3. S picks up sponge													
4. S sponges out wash sink and rinses													
5. S sponges out rinse sink and rinses													
6. S puts sponge down													
7. S distinguishes between hot and cold water													
8. S adjusts water to appropriate temperature													
9. S places stopper so that rinse sink begins to fill													
10. S fills rinse sink to half full													
11. S places stopper so that wash sink begins to fill													
12. S picks up detergent													
13. S unscrews cap													
14. S measures detergent													

15. S pours detergent from cap into																
wash sink																
16. S replaces cap																
17. S puts detergent on sink																
18. S fills wash sink half full																
19. S places utensils and plates in																
wash sink																
20. S picks up each piece and scrubs																
with sponge until clean																
Knife																
Fork																
Spoon																
Plate																
21. S places each piece in rinse sink																
Knife																
Fork																
Spoon																
Plate																
22. S rinses each piece thoroughly																
Knife																
Fork																
Spoon																
Plate																
23. S places each piece in dish rack																
Knife																
Fork																
Spoon																
Plate																

24. S places glasses in wash sink																
25. S picks up each glass and scrubs with sponge until clean																
26. S places each glass in rinse sink																
27. S rinses each glass thoroughly																
28. S places each glass in dish rack																
29. S places remaining dishes and pans in wash sink																
30. S picks up each piece and scrubs with sponge																
Dish																
Pot																
31. S places each piece in rinse sink																
Dish																
Pot																
32. S rinses each piece thoroughly																
Dish																
Pot																
33. S places each piece in dish rack																
Dish																
Pot																
34. S manipulates stopper in wash sink so that rinse sink drains																
Dish																
Pot																

35. S manipulates stopper in rinse sink so that rinse sink drains																	
Dish																	
Pot																	
36. S rinses wash sink with sponge																	
37. S rinses rinse sink with sponge																	
38. S squeezes out sponge																	
39. S places sponge on sink																	
40. S empties debris from stopper into trash can																	
41. S replaces stopper in sink																	
42. S places detergent in correct storage location																	

Once this process is complete and a validated task analysis has been constructed, a specific assessment of student skills can be conducted. Task analytic assessment provides an instructor with a record of a student's performance on a task, which indicates the specific step on which instruction should begin. Table 3.3 provides an illustration of a data sheet for a task analytic baseline assessment of making a partially unmade bed. The instructions for baseline/probe assessment are included on the data sheet to ensure consistency across trials and trainers. The initial assessment should be conducted across trials over a few days to establish a stable record of performance. Once stability has been obtained, instruction should be initiated on the appropriate task step. The use of task analysis in instruction facilitates consistency and provides a systematic format for task completion.

Task analytic assessment provides an instructor with a record of a student's performance on a task, which indicates the specific step on which instruction should begin.

Throughout instruction a continuous record of performance should be maintained through regular probes that are conducted using the same pro-

Table 3.4. Task analytic assessment of bed making

Probe instructions: Place chair or bed along side, and start with partially made bed (sheet, blanket, and spread pulled down, wrinkled) and bed pushed into wall, pajamas under pillow.
Give instructions: "(Name), Make the bed." Allow 5 seconds for a response. If correct response, record (+). If incorrect response or no response, record (−) and complete the step for student, and proceed to the next step. Do not prompt or reinforce.

Teacher: _____
Student: _____
Date: _____
Environment: ___Home/School Bedroom___
Instructional cue: _____
___"Make the bed."___

Making Partial Bed

1. Pull bed from wall enough to walk around																
2. Place pillow and pajamas on chair, other bed, or dresser																
3. Pull top sheet with both hands to head of bed so it is straight																
4. Smooth																
5. Pull blanket with both hands to head of bed so it is straight																
6. Smooth																
7. Pull spread with both hands to head of bed so it is straight																
8. Smooth up to extra spread																
9. Grasp edge, spread both hands, and fold down from head to make a 10 to 17 inch space																
10. Smooth spread on other side																
11. Get pajamas, fold in half, and place in pillow space																
12. Get pillow, place in space, with lower edge on spread fold																
13. Smooth pillow																
14. Grasp spread edge with both hands and pull up over pillow																
15. Tuck up under pillow with edge of hand																
16. Smooth spread top and side on near side of bed																
17. Go to other side, smooth top and side.																
18. Push bed back against wall																

cedures that were used during baseline. This continuous record provides the teacher with a method for monitoring student progress. Once the student has met the program criterion as indicated by the regular skill probes, maintenance procedures can be implemented. On the other hand, if the student is failing to progress, the teacher will be able to detect such failure and modify the instructional program to facilitate learning.

Instructional Setting and Materials

Prior to initiating domestic skills training, decisions must be made regarding the instructional setting and materials. Should instruction be conducted in a classroom, a school kitchen or home economics room, an actual community home setting, or the student's present home environment? Should the instructor use a toy vacuum cleaner or a simulated stove or the real, usable appliance? Although these decisions depend largely on the types of facilities available, a number of variables should be considered prior to selecting materials and/or settings.

Cost efficiency is an important aspect of any training program. Cost efficiency refers to the amount of time, staff, and money required to teach a skill to criterion level. If the ultimate goal for a student is to use domestic skills in the family home, perhaps instruction may be more cost-effective if conducted in the student's actual home. Boyan (1978) suggested that practical experiences (instruction) should be provided in actual community residential facilities or apartments, and that these sites should function as "satellites" to the educational programs. This strategy would provide a smooth transition for students from their family homes as children to community living facilities as adults, and on a long-term basis may be more cost-effective.

As a general rule, instruction provided in the natural environment (the setting in which the behavior should occur) is more effective, maintains over time, and minimizes the necessity for training generalization (Brown, Nietupski, & Hamre-Nietupski, 1976; Kazdin, 1980; Stokes & Baer, 1977; Vogelsberg et al., 1980). Therefore, whenever possible, instruction should be conducted in the natural setting.

Martin, Rusch, James, Decker, and Trytol (1982) trained three moderately to severely retarded adults to prepare complex meals in their own apartments. Because all three subjects lived in different apartments, training was conducted daily in three different settings. Martin et al., however, suggested that the program was cost-effective in that training in the natural environments increased independence for each subject in daily living and minimized the need for future intervention or services in the trainers' home settings. Had the meal preparation skills been trained in a school or simulated setting, generalization to the actual home settings would have had to have been assessed, and most likely some training would have been necessary to facilitate daily use of the skills in the home environment.

> **As a general rule, instruction provided in the natural environment (the setting in which the behavior should occur) is more effective, maintains over time, and minimizes the necessity for training generalization.**

Due to lack of transportation, staff, and/or money, training in the natural setting may not always be feasible. If training in the actual home setting is not possible, training should be conducted in a setting that approximates as closely as possible the real home setting.

An alternative to training students in their present living environments is to train in potential future placements (e.g., the community group home or supervised apartments). As suggested by Boyan (1978), training in home living skills should be a cooperative effort involving teachers, parents, and community services personnel. Therefore, educators (school personnel) should seek out individuals responsible for community residential facilities and establish time on a regular basis, if possible, to train domestic skills in the actual residential settings. If training does not occur in a familiar residential setting, it is important to simulate as closely as possible the natural environments. Many of the successful demonstrations of teaching domestic skills have been conducted in simulated school settings and have included bathroom cleaning (Cuvo, Leaf, & Borakove, 1978), bed making (Snell, in press), laundry skills (Cuvo, Jacobi, & Sipko, in press), and food preparation (Johnson & Cuvo, in press).

Snell (in press), for example, taught four severely retarded males bed making skills including stripping and making a partially unmade bed and making a completely stripped bed. Training was conducted in a classroom with beds and bedclothes that were just like those used in the trainees' living settings. Once the bed making skills were learned, all skills were assessed on the trainees' actual beds at home to validate the use of bed making skills in the natural environment. If the skills were not at criterion level in the natural environment, training was provided.

Of equal importance to the selection of a training setting is the selection of instructional materials. In most instances instruction using real, usable materials would seem most appropriate and most likely to result in use of the skill over time (Brown et al., 1976; Brown et al., 1979; Kazdin, 1980; Stokes & Baer, 1977). For example, if vacuuming skills were targeted for instruction, the vacuum cleaner actually used in the student's home should be used to teach the appropriate skills. This eliminates the necessity for generalizing the skills acquired on one vacuum to the vacuum targeted for continued use. If, however, the student's home vacuum is not available, a vacuum that is as similar as possible to the home vacuum should be selected for training. This "rule of thumb" would apply equally to the selection of a stove to teach cooking skills (especially since the differences between stoves are so great), a mop for floor cleaning, and washers and dryers for laundering.

> **For example, if vacuuming skills were targeted for instruction, the vacuum cleaner actually used in the student's home should be used to teach the appropriate skills.**

There are, however, instances where simulated materials (materials that are not real or usable) or simulated situations would be appropriate and perhaps most cost-effective. For instance, teaching emergency skills such as using the phone to call the doctor, fire department, or police department (Risley & Cuvo, 1980), or teaching students how to behave in case of fire or injury (Matson, 1980) necessitate simulation. Risley and Cuvo (1980) used pictures to set the occasion for calling an appropriate emergency number. For example, a picture of a house on fire was presented to the student, and the trainer instructed, "Using this telephone and directory, show me what you would do if your house were on fire." The pictures were varied for each emergency (e.g., three different pictures depicting fire were used in training) so that responses were not limited to one specific situation involving a fire.

Similarly, Matson (1980) taught five moderately retarded persons to respond to home accidents (i.e., escape fire, treat cuts and seizures). Obviously, real fires could not be started, and cuts and seizures could not be provided for the purpose of training. Instead, Matson described the accidents in detail and taught appropriate responses through role playing and feedback. Although unavoidable, the potential problem with this sort of simulation is that trainers must infer that because the learners perform appropriately in simulated situations, they will also perform appropriately when the real emergency occurs.

Use of simulated instructional materials may also be more cost-effective in situations where the real materials are not available and access would require time, travel, and money. Nutter and Reid (1978) taught clothing selection skills to retarded women using a puzzle simulation of a woman. This permitted the trainers to provide a wide variety of clothing pieces to select from and to match. This wide selection would have been very difficult to provide if real clothing were required. In addition, the expense of gathering and/or purchasing the clothes likely would have been quite high.

Simulated equipment may also be used when training a skill that requires large, expensive equipment, such as washers and dryers for training laundry skills. Simulations should, however, require the same steps and movements required when using the real equipment. Furthermore, training should never be considered complete until the skills are verified on the real equipment in the natural settings.

Training Format

Because many domestic/home living tasks consist of complex chains of discrete steps (Cuvo, Note 2), the sequence for training each combination of steps must be carefully selected. Most demonstrations of domestic skills training have used a whole task approach or simultaneous instruction on all steps in a task (e.g., Cronin & Cuvo, 1979; Cuvo et al., in press; Cuvo, Leaf, & Borakove, 1978; Martin et al., 1982). Simultaneous instruction on all steps in a task involves beginning instruction on step 1 and proceeding sequentially through all the steps to the end of the task. This is considered one trial, and each trial should be conducted in this manner. Table 3.5 provides a sample instructional program for dishwashing, in which simultaneous instruction on all steps in the task is described. Because many of the steps in the dishwashing task are repetitions or quite similar, simultaneous instruction is appropriate.

> **Simultaneous instruction on all steps in a task involves beginning instruction on step 1 and proceeding sequentially through all the steps to the end of the task.**

For lengthy domestic tasks in which the majority of the steps are different, it may be necessary to use a forward or backward chaining format. Forward chaining involves teaching the first step in the task to a criterion level before chaining together the first and second steps, which are then

Table 3.5. Program format[a]

Time: 1:00–1:30 p.m.
Student(s): Joe, Bob, and Alice
Name of Program: Dishwashing

Specific Program Objective: Given dirty dishes, cleaning materials, and equipment in a natural setting, the student will clean the dishes leaving no visible residual food/drink for three consecutive daily probes with 100% accuracy according to a task analysis.

Rationale: Washing dishes is a required skill for independence in community living facilities. In addition, parents and guardians in the students' present environments consider dishwashing a priority.

Student Characteristics that:
1) assist: All students are ambulatory, have use of their arms and hands, and understand simple 1-step instructions;
2) hinder: Bob and Alice frequently refuse to comply with instructions when they do not wish to terminate an activity.

Baseline/Probe: Probe skill over a period of several days until a stable baseline is obtained. Continue to probe twice weekly after training has begun.
1. Give instructional cue, "(Name), wash the dishes."
2. Wait 3 seconds for response.
3. Record (+) for correct response.
4. Record (−) if step is incorrect or if there is no response within the three-second time period, and then complete the step for the student.
5. Proceed through all the steps using these procedures. Do not prompt or reinforce. Steps can be out of sequence and still be considered correct if the end result is satisfactory.

Behavior Change Procedures: Use simultaneous instruction across all steps of the task analysis.
1. Give instructions, "(Name), wash the dishes."
2. Wait 3 seconds for for self-initiation of step 1 in the task analysis.
3. If correctly self-initiated, record (+) and proceed to step 2 in the task analysis.
4. If incorrect or no response within 3 seconds, provide a verbal prompt (e.g. "(Name), get the detergent from the cabinet").
5. If correct, reinforce and record (V).
6. If incorrect or no response within 3 seconds, provide model and verbal prompt (e.g. "(Name), get the detergent from the cabinet like this. Now you try").
7. If correct, reinforce and record (M).
8. If incorrect or no response within 3 seconds of the model prompt, provide physical and verbal prompt (guide student through step with as little contact as possible while verbally instructing step), reinforce with social praise, and record (P).
9. Continue through all the steps in the task using these prompting procedures.

Data Collection Method:
1) Baseline/Probe: Record (+) for correct response (sequential or out-of-sequence step that results in satisfactory completion of the task). Record (−) for incorrect or no response after 3 seconds.
2) Intervention: Record (+) for correct response (in or out of sequence if appropriate), or prompt level needed for correct response (V, M, P).

Reinforcement—Type(s) and Schedule(s): Initially socially reinforce each step completed (e.g., "Great, you got the detergent"), regardless of the level of prompt required. Thin to a variable schedule of every 3 steps when the student has completed better than 75% of the steps independently for each trial across two days of instruction.

Maintenance and Generalization Procedures: Once criterion has been met, practice and record weekly and train student in other settings (e.g., private house or own home). Also, teach parents/guardians to maintain the skill in the home and provide parents with a simple checklist to monitor performance.

[a] Reprinted with permission of Adelle Renzaglia and the Community Based Instructional Program, University of Virginia, and Albermarle County Public Schools, Charlottesville, Virginia.

taught to criterion. These procedures are followed until all steps in the task are included.

Backward chaining is similar to forward chaining except the first step trained is the final step in the task. The final step is trained (trials are provided repeatedly on the final step) to a criterion performance level, and then the next to the last step is chained to the final step and taught to criterion. These procedures are followed until all steps have been included

Table 3.6. Program format

Time: <u>7:30 a.m. at home, 10:00 a.m. at school</u>
Student(s): <u>Mike</u>
Name of Program: <u>Bed making/Partial</u>

Specific Program Objective: Given a partially made bed, the student will make the bed with 100% accuracy according to a task analysis for that skill during probe conditions for three consecutive sessions.

Rationale: Bed making is a required skill for independent or supervised community living and has been identified as a priority in the student's present home setting. Also, bed making may be useful in a vocational setting (e.g., housekeeping).

Student Characteristics that:
1) assist:
2) hinder:

Behavior Change Procedures: Up to eight trials should be conducted daily. Use backward chaining procedure; complete all steps in task analysis but the final step.
1. Give the instructional cue, "*(Name)*, make the bed."
2. Wait 3 seconds for self-initiation of the final step in the task analysis (e.g., Push bed back against wall).
3. If correctly self-initiated, record (+).
4. If incorrect or no response within 3 seconds, provide a verbal prompt, (e.g., "*(Name)*, Push the bed back against the wall").
5. If correct performance follows the verbal prompt within 3 seconds, reinforce and record (V), and begin again.
6. If incorrect or no response within 3 seconds of the verbal prompt, provide a model plus the verbal prompt (e.g., "*(Name)*, push the bed back against the wall like this. Now you try").
7. If correct performance follows the model prompt within 3 seconds, reinforce and record (M), and begin again.
8. If incorrect or no response within 3 seconds of model prompt, provide physical and verbal prompt, reinforce and record (P), and begin task again.

When student has met criterion (three consecutive unprompted correct responses) on the final step in the task analysis, begin training on the next-to-last step in combination with the final step (e.g., Smooth other side's top and side, then push bed back against the wall) using the same prompting procedures. Reinforcement should be delivered *only* after completion of the final step regardless of the number of steps involved in the chain. A new step should be added when criterion is met on each combination of steps.

Data Collection Method:
1) Baseline/Probe: Probe at onset of each session.
  1. Give instructions, "*(Name)*, make the bed."
  2. Wait 3 seconds for response.
  3. Record (+) for correct response.
  4. Record (−) for incorrect or no response within 3 seconds and complete the step for the student.
  5. Proceed through all steps in the task analysis using these procedures.
2) Intervention: Record (+) for a correct response, or the appropriate symbol for the prompt level needed for a correct response (V, M, P). Run 1 to 8 trials per session, depending on step in task analysis being trained.

Reinforcement—Type(s) and Schedule(s): Social praise upon completion of each trial.

Criterion for Success: Three consecutive independently correct responses on steps trained will result in addition of a new step for training.

Maintenance and Generalization Procedures: Evaluate performance across settings and trainers. Maintain in his home through weekly contact with parents and provide parents with a simple checklist to evaluate performance.

---

a Reprinted with permission of Adelle Renzaglia and the Community Based Instructional Program, University of Virginia, and Albermarle County Public Schools, Charlottesville, Virginia.

in training. Table 3.6 provides an example of backward chaining in the instruction of bed making.

In instances where the student is a rapid learner or already has acquired some of the skills in a task, or the task consists of steps that are repeated over and over, simultaneous instruction on all steps is most efficient. However, for tasks that are very long in which the steps are, on the whole, different, the use of simultaneous instruction on the whole task may result in time for only one task trial per session, resulting in a slow learning rate. In this case, a chaining procedure may be more efficient. Chaining allows repeated practice on one step and then on a small chain of steps before adding new steps to be learned. An additional advantage of backward chaining is that the learner always ends a trial on the final task step, so the finished product is always evident.

A combination of simultaneous instruction and chaining may also be effective. Many domestic tasks can be separated into clusters of steps. For example, dishwashing could be divided into clusters of steps constituting: 1) filling the sink with soap and water; 2) washing glasses; 3) washing plates and bowls; 4) washing utensils; 5) rinsing; and 6) emptying and cleaning the sink. All of the steps in cluster one might be taught first using simultaneous instruction, and once the individual has reached criterion level, a second cluster of steps can be taught simultaneously and chained to the first cluster.

Although the majority of the demonstrations of successful domestic skills instruction have employed simultaneous instruction (Cuvo & Davis, 1981), no research is available that compares the different training formats. It is beneficial to compare these training sequences to identify the most effective approach. Student skills and task variables (number and difficulty of steps) should be evaluated to determine their interactions with the type of training format employed.

Prompting Procedures

Successful instruction of domestic/home living skills is dependent on identifying and implementing a systematic method of prompting correct performance of task steps in the selected sequence. A trainer must learn to be proficient at delivering consistent prompts in a predetermined manner. A range of prompting procedures/methods is available for instruction and includes: 1) verbal; 2) model; 3) gestural; 4) physical; and 5) stimulus or visual (modification of task materials) prompts. The selection of one or a combination of these procedures depends on student skills and task difficulty.

A variety of verbal prompting procedures has been used in successful demonstrations of domestic skills training (Cuvo & Davis, 1981). Verbal prompts have included: 1) directive instructions in which the action to be performed is described (e.g., "Pick up the dustcloth."); 2) details pertinent to the quality of the task being performed (e.g., "Wipe the *whole* table until clean."); 3) questions about task steps to cue correct response (e.g., "What do you do with the leftover food?"); 4) nondirective questions that provoke thought regarding the next step (e.g., "What comes next?"); and 5) confirmation of appropriate step performance (e.g., "That's right, put the leftover food in the refrigerator."). One or a combination of these different types of verbal prompts may be used for teaching a specific skill. An effective combination of verbal prompts is an initial nondirective cue (e.g., "What comes next?"), allowing the student to respond as independently as possible, followed by a directive verbal instruction (e.g., "Next, spread the butter on the toast.") as a backup prompt in the event that the student does not respond correctly.

Model and gestural prompts consist of a trainer demonstrating the task step or providing some type of nonvocal cue (e.g., a finger point) to prompt the student to perform the next step. Modeling can be provided by a trainer or a competent peer and can be ongoing or used only when a student is showing difficulty with a step. A group instructional format provides an optimal situation for peer modeling. Because most domestic tasks are long chains of behaviors, if groups of students are to be taught simultaneously, it is often necessary that they work side by side or take turns watching each other proceed through a task. In either case, there are many opportunities for each student to learn from the other.

> **Model and gestural prompts consist of a trainer demonstrating the task step or providing some type of nonvocal cue (e.g., a finger point) to prompt the student to perform the next step.**

Physical prompting or manual guidance is the most intrusive prompting procedure and involves physically guiding a student through a task step, usually with as little physical contact as possible. Physical prompts should be required only for the most difficult steps and should be faded as soon as possible to a less intrusive prompt.

Modifications of task materials can be made to provide, within the task, visual prompts that assist a student in task performance. For example, a visual cue can be added to the hot and cold water controls in a shower to cue a student to turn the handles to a particular point for appropriate water temperature. Schleien, Kiernan, Ash, and Wehman (1981) used color cues to prompt severely and profoundly handicapped individuals to turn stove controls to particular burner or oven temperatures. The use of color cues avoided the necessity for teaching number recognition for operating stove dials. Similarly, picture cues have been used to prompt food preparation (Johnson & Cuvo, in press; Martin et al., 1982; Robinson-Wilson, 1977), cleaning, bed making, and other daily living skills (Spellman, DeBriere, Jarboe, Campbell, & Harris, 1978).

> **A visual cue can be added to the hot and cold water controls in a shower to cue a student to turn the handles to a particular point for appropriate water temperature.**

Frequently, different prompts are used in combination from least to most intrusive (e.g., verbal, model, and physical). The least intrusive prompt is one that allows a student the greatest amount of independence in performing a task step. A system of least intrusive prompts utilizes a hierarchy of prompts that are presented in a least to most intrusive order, always allowing the student time to perform a task step with the greatest degree of independence. A least intrusive prompting system has been used to teach bathroom cleaning skills (Cuvo, Leaf, & Borakove, 1978), clothes laundering skills (Cuvo et al., in press), clothes mending skills (Cronin & Cuvo, 1979), and meal preparation skills (Johnson & Cuvo, in press). (Refer to Tables 3.5 and 3.6 for examples of a least to most intrusive prompting system for teaching dishwashing and bed making skills.)

Cuvo and his colleagues have also employed a most to least intrusive prompting system (e.g., physical prompts were used first and faded to model then verbal prompts). However, the most to least intrusive system was used only for those steps in a task that had been assessed prior to instruction as being difficult steps (e.g., Cuvo et al., in press; Cuvo et al., 1978, in press; Friend, Campbell, & Johnson, Note 2).

Regardless of the type or system of prompts employed, the ultimate goal of instruction is to help a student to become as independent as possible in performing a task. Therefore, a method for systematically fading teacher assistance in a task is necessary. The prompting systems described above build in a system for allowing student independence. An alternative method of fading a prompt is through time (Touchette, 1971). Progressively longer periods of time can be inserted between the general task instructions and the provision of a prompt until a student is successfully anticipating the correct response without assistance. Snell (in press) used a time delay system to teach bed making skills to three severely handicapped adolescents. Initially, physical and verbal prompts were progressively delayed, followed by model plus verbal prompts, which were then delayed until the students were performing the bed making tasks independently.

SELF-INSTRUCTION

Although in most instances direct, systematic instruction of domestic skills must be provided by a teacher, the sooner the teacher is faded out of the instructional interaction, the sooner a student will reach some level of independence. Strategies for facilitating self-instruction and self-management of appropriate home living skills provide desirable alternatives to teacher directed instruction.

The provision of picture cues or pictorial task analyses of domestic skills can provide a student with an interpretable step-by-step illustration of how to complete a task without teacher support. Pictorial task analyses have been used to guide severely handicapped students in completing cleaning chores, bed making (Spellman et al., 1978; Campbell & Johnson, Note 3) and meal preparation (Johnson & Cuvo, in press; Robinson-Wilson, 1977; Martin et al., 1982).

Initially it may be necessary, however, to teach the students how to use picture cues, but once this skill has been acquired any number of tasks can be guided to completion. Johnson (Note 6) developed a picture reading program in which picture-object matching and left-to-right sequencing skills were taught prior to using pictorial instruction. Once the picture reading skills were acquired, many daily living tasks were mastered via picture step-by-step instruction (Spellman et al., 1978). Figure 3.2 provides an example of a pictorial task analysis of the steps involved in window cleaning. Picture reading students should be able to follow independently the pictured steps to complete window cleaning in their own homes.

Robinson-Wilson (1977) taught severely handicapped students to follow simple picture recipes to make hot dogs, hot chocolate, and Jell-O. She also found that once the students were taught to use one recipe (regardless of the food item), they acquired the skills for the second and third recipes much more quickly. Johnson and Cuvo (in press) also taught cooking skills through the use of pictures, but instead of teaching specific recipes they taught mildly to moderately retarded subjects three general cooking techniques (broiling, boiling, and baking). Two food items were selected for each

1. Materials

2. Spray

3. Wash

4. Wipe dry

Figure 3.2. Pictorial task analysis of window cleaning.

cooking method and rotated for preparation (e.g., baking cornbread and biscuits was taught). All of the students acquired the food preparation skills rapidly using the picture cues, and two of the four students began to prepare food items in their homes that they had not been trained to prepare in the workshop setting.

Martin et al. (1982) also taught severely handicapped adults to use picture cues to prepare food. Their subjects, however, were taught to prepare five complex meals (e.g., one meal consisted of chuck roast, carrots, potatoes, and Jell-O with fruit cocktail) consisting of 48 to 76 steps or subtasks. Meal preparation via picture cues was dependent upon the participants' ability to perform basic cooking operations including frying, baking, broiling, defrosting, and peeling. All three participants successfully learned to prepare the meals independently in their own homes. These demonstrations of the successful use of pictorial task analyses reinforce the notion that pictures can be used as self-instructional cues at a very basic level as well as at the point where handicapped persons are performing complex domestic tasks.

Pictures can be used as self-instructional cues at a very basic level as well as at the point where handicapped persons are performing complex domestic tasks.

Visual cues can also be used as tools by severely handicapped persons for managing their own home settings. Frequently, domestic failure is the result of poor home management or failure to use domestic skills, even though an individual possesses the skills necessary for independence (Crnic & Pym, 1979). The development of a schedule of domestic activities that can be independently followed and maintained by the handicapped resident has been successful for facilitating home management. Bauman and Iwata (1977) taught two retarded men to manage their own apartment through the provision of a schedule for self-monitoring. Twenty-one housekeeping tasks (half were housecleaning and half were kitchen or meal related) were identified as necessary for home management, and a schedule for completing these chores was developed and posted for the two men. On a daily basis the men completed the assigned chores and checked them off on the schedule. No other instruction or feedback was provided. After becoming proficient at following the posted schedule, the men were asked to develop their own schedule and make task assignments. Consequently, they learned to manage their own home independently.

Frequently, domestic failure is the result of poor home management or failure to use domestic skills, even though an individual possesses the skills necessary for independence.

For individuals unable to read a written posted schedule, weekly picture schedules can be developed and posted for self-monitoring. Spellman et al. (1978) describe a weekly picture schedule for housekeeping (refer to Figure 3.3) that provides space for checking off tasks on a daily basis as scheduled. With continued investigations on the utility of self-monitoring strategies for domestic/home living, techniques for increasing independence of severely handicapped persons will continue to be developed and refined.

SOCIAL VALIDATION OF DOMESTIC SKILLS

As it is important to evaluate the skill priorities via community and home assessments and to validate task analyses of domestic tasks, it is also important to socially validate the performance quality of a skill (Kazdin, 1977). After students have acquired the component steps and independently performed a domestic task, it is important to evaluate the finished product. For example, a student may independently proceed through the steps involved in mopping and waxing a kitchen floor, but leave the floor dirty in spots or

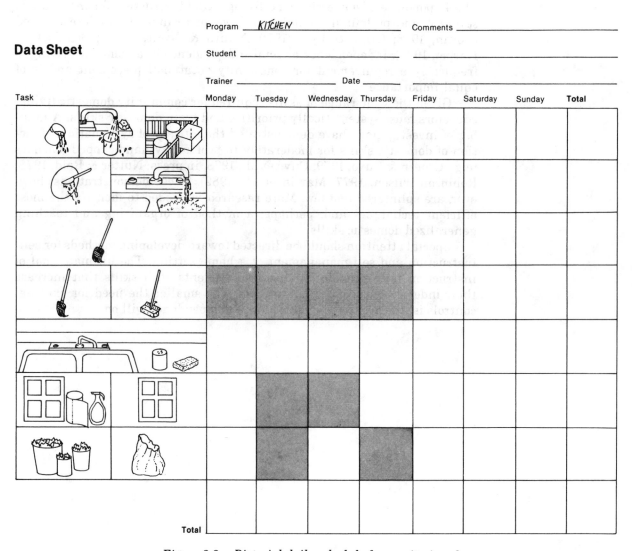

Data Sheet

Program ___KITCHEN___

Student _____

Trainer _____ Date _____

Comments _____

Task		Monday	Tuesday	Wednesday	Thursday	Friday	Saturday	Sunday	**Total**
Total									

Figure 3.3. Pictorial daily schedule for monitoring chores.

perhaps apply too much, resulting in wax buildup. The job quality, as a consequence, would not be acceptable.

Educators should build in a method for subjective evaluation of the completed task. Cuvo et al. (1978), for example, had naive observers evaluate the cleanliness of the bathrooms cleaned by the handicapped students. If the bathrooms were rated as clean, the student's performance was considered socially valid. Similarly, Johnson and Cuvo (in press) had independent observers rate food items that had been prepared by handicapped persons as appearing edible or inedible. These procedures for socially validating task performance emphasize a skill quality component, which, in the past, has been virtually ignored. However, if educators are attempting to train handicapped learners for a normalized living setting, attention must be given to subjective evaluation of skill performance.

SUMMARY

The importance of domestic/home living skills instruction for moderately, severely, and profoundly handicapped persons cannot be underestimated (Boyan, 1978; Crnic & Pym, 1979; Nihira & Nihira, 1975; Schalock & Harper, 1978). Independence or semi-independence in a domestic setting is frequently a requirement for community vocational placement and is of equal importance.

Given the wide range of skills required for community domestic living, educators must systematically prioritize and train domestic skills. A number of investigations have demonstrated the efficacy of systematic instruction of domestic skills for moderately to profoundly handicapped learners (e.g., Cronin & Cuvo, 1979; Cuvo et al., 1978, in press; Nutter & Reid, 1978; Robinson-Wilson, 1977; Martin et al., 1982). These demonstrations, however, are splintered and few. More research is needed to identify the most efficient techniques and, perhaps, a method of organizing and teaching generalized domestic skills.

Special attention should be directed toward developing methods for self-instruction and self-management of a home setting. The ultimate goal of instruction is to provide handicapped students with skills that increase their independence in daily adult life. The smaller the need for external controls is, the greater the individual's independence will be.

4

COMMUNITY MOBILITY

LEARNING GOALS

1. Describe the importance of mobility for moderately and severely handicapped persons.
2. Discuss the role that attitudinal barriers play in creating mobility problems.
3. Outline and briefly describe five types of mobility modes.
4. Analyze pedestrian behaviors and break them down into useful sequences that teachers and other practitioners can use for training.
5. Provide specific training recommendations for teaching public transportation skills.
6. Discuss the major sequential steps involved in developing and implementing a community mobility program.

The ability of an individual to participate independently or semi-independently in all aspects of community life is dependent on community mobility. Community mobility refers to movement from one place to another within a particular setting and travel between two community locations. The concept of community mobility was originally developed in program practice and literature related to working with visually handicapped individuals. In this context, community mobility is referred to as "orientation and mobility training." Orientation refers to a person's awareness of the environment in relation to space, objects, and other persons. According to Laus (1974), awareness of one's surroundings and one's relationship to those surroundings as they relate to everyday living is essential to independent mobility. If orientation training can be conceptualized as the cognitive component of community travel, mobility training can be conceptualized as the actual physical behaviors involved in movement from one place to another. Together these concepts refer to the complex set of behaviors that is required to ensure access to community activities.

For visually impaired individuals, orientation and mobility training has been a priority curriculum area for several years. As the rights of all citizens for participation in the least restrictive environment have been acknowledged, the concept of community mobility has received greater attention in curriculum planning for other groups of consumers (e.g., physically handicapped, mentally retarded, and seriously emotionally disturbed individuals). The importance of independent travel to a person's overall habilitation plan has been recognized by many sources. In 1971, the Joint Commission on the Accreditation of Hospitals (JCAH) required that all residents of institutions be given the freedom and training necessary for them to travel independently within the institutional grounds. A more global recommendation was advanced by the President's Committee on Mental Retardation in 1972. This recommendation encouraged all agencies and schools to provide training on travel skills such as street crossing, public transportation, and driver's education.

The lack of mobility skills is detrimental to the community participation of moderately and severely handicapped individuals residing outside of institutional settings. These skill deficits have resulted from limited travel opportunities and inadequate training programs. According to Saenger (1972), of 520 severely retarded adults surveyed in New York City, the majority had few or no independent travel skills. Consequently, these individuals were dependent on an expensive chartered bus system to take them to and from work. As stated by Tobias and Cortazzo (1963), "When retarded people are dependent on adult assistance for locomotion beyond the immediate environs of their home, the range of possible activities becomes very restricted and isolation becomes the rule" (p. 26). Bowe (1979) adds, "without means of transportation to educational, vocational, cultural, recreational, and commercial facilities in the community, it is virtually impossible for most severely disabled people to live outside of an institutional environment" (p. 484).

Given the integral relationship between community mobility and community functioning, a great deal of attention needs to be focused on the issues associated with preparing handicapped citizens to travel more independently. Program initiatives in this area must be concerned with increasing the handicapped individual's opportunity for community travel and with teaching specific mobility skills. In this chapter, increased opportunity for travel is discussed from the viewpoint of removing physical and attitudinal barriers to independent or semi-independent community mobility. This discussion is followed by the presentation of multiple mobility modes and training strategies that have been used successfully to teach handicapped individuals to travel more independently within their home communities. Specific examples of instructional programs in this area are cited for pedestrian travel and public bus transportation. In conclusion, several recommendations are presented for program practice and future research.

OPPORTUNITY FOR MOBILITY

The ability of a person to be independently mobile is dependent on several factors. One of the primary factors that influences the degree of mobility attained by handicapped individuals is the opportunity for travel from one place to another. Opportunity for mobility can be restricted by both physical and attitudinal barriers.

Physical Barriers

Physical barriers limit accessibility and consequently reduce a person's chances for full community participation. Physical obstacles include inaccessible transportation, lack of convenient parking, curbs, steep inclines, stairs, small doorway openings, and inadequate toilet facilities. There have been several developments in the past few years that have increased accessibility of transportation, public buildings, and community housing.

According to Bowe (1979), "accessible transportation serves both as a practical necessity and philosophical basis for independent living" (p. 474). Without accessible transportation, a physically disabled individual's opportunities for independent functioning are drastically reduced. In response to this problem, the Urban Mass Transportation Act (P.L. 88-365) was passed. This law was specifically designed to encourage "special efforts" to develop transportation systems that could be used by physically disabled citizens.

The federal commitment to increasing accessibility for physically disabled citizens extends beyond the transportation issue. As early as 1968, the Architectural Barriers Act (P.L. 90-480) was passed by Congress to ensure access to federally financed buildings and facilities. In establishing the regulations for this requirement, Congress used the specifications of the American National Standards Institute (ANSI) (1961) for making buildings and facilities accessible and usable by the physically handicapped (Standard A 117.1). Since the passage of the Architectural Barriers Act in 1968, several additional pieces of legislation have strengthened the movement toward improving the physical accessibility of community services and housing. These include the Rehabilitation Act of 1973 (P.L. 93-112) and amendments to this act in 1974 (P.L. 93-516). These developments were the first federal efforts to encourage uniform guidelines for physical accessibility.

> **Since the passage of the Architectural Barriers Act in 1968, several additional pieces of legislation have strengthened the movement toward improving the physical accessibility of community services and housing.**

The impact of barrier-free design and the movement to increase physical accessibility of transportation and other community services have been felt in all cities. In many communities extensive physical modifications have been made, including construction of ramps, widening of doorways, installation of elevators, cutting out of curbs, and purchase of lift buses. Although these modifications have removed many barriers to independent mobility, obstacles still exist. Realistically, many of these obstacles are not going to be eliminated. Some of these obstacles are outside the control of engineers and educators (e.g., weather conditions and natural terrain). Because mobility obstacles are likely to remain in every community, efforts must be directed toward teaching individuals to overcome these problems. For example, people may need to be taught how to:

1. Walk up and down stairs with and without using handrails.
2. Step up and down curbs.
3. Climb in and out of vehicles.
4. Use restroom facilities with narrow doorways and no railings.
5. Walk on uneven terrain and different textured surfaces.
6. Walk from place to place under inclement weather conditions.
7. Enter and exit buildings with a variety of doorway sizes and types.

By combining environmental changes with specific instruction programs, handicapped citizens are provided easier access as well as more skills for traveling independently within their communities. Community mobility programs should reflect this dual concern for improving physical accessibility and training skills that compensate for various environmental barriers. This combination of program emphases should result in maximal community mobility by all citizens.

> **In many communities extensive physical modification has been made, including construction of ramps, widening of doorways, installation of elevators, cutting out of curbs, and purchase of lift buses.**

Attitudinal Barriers

A person's opportunity for independent travel in the community is not only restricted by physical obstacles. Attitudinal barriers can severely restrict a person's chances for learning mobility skills. These barriers result from a combination of overprotectiveness and lowered expectations. Parents and professionals have contributed to this problem. According to Perske (1972), "such overprotection endangers the client's human dignity, and tends to keep him from experiencing the risk taking of ordinary life which is necessary for normal growth and development" (p. 29).

When independent community travel for severely retarded young adults was first discussed with one group of parents, Cortazzo and Sansone (1976) identified the most common concerns as fears regarding sexual molestation, kidnapping, injuries or accidents, getting lost, ridicule by others, failure to learn because of retardation, helplessness in emergencies, physical stress, danger in traveling in inclement weather, failure to recognize impending dangers or hazardous situations, and detriment to parents' health because of worry.

The above concerns were expressed by parents of mentally retarded adults. In all probability, these parents had encountered many professionals who had minimized expectations of independent or semi-independent living for their sons and daughters. The professional community has begun only recently to emphasize the concept of independent living and related skills instruction. Curriculum sequences for moderately and severely handicapped individuals have not typically included community mobility training. However, there is evidence that curriculum emphases are changing to reflect a greater concern for independent living skills training. As a result, independent travel is becoming an educational objective of higher priority to both parents and professionals.

To overcome problems related to overprotectiveness, the importance of community travel skills needs to be articulated to parents and other caregivers. Detailed programs for improving mobility skills need to be developed in a way that shows the relationship between supervised instructional activities and long-term goals of independent travel. If mobility programs are formulated in this manner, it may be possible to eliminate overprotectiveness barriers and raise expectations for independent community mobility. Such an approach demonstrates respect for each person's dignity by providing mobility opportunity with concurrent training activities. As individuals acquire independence in various mobility skills, supervision should be faded and the person's "dignity of risk" respected.

To enlist support of parents and professionals for travel training programs, Vogelsburg and Rusch (1980) suggest the use of a signed consent form that includes: 1) an explanation of the purpose and procedures of the program; 2) a description of potential discomforts or risks; 3) a description of benefits; 4) an offer to answer any program related questions; and 5) a provision that the trainee can withdraw from the program at any time. By working closely with the family in developing travel training programs, many fears can be alleviated and support can be generated for continued use of mobility skills following the initial training period. If parental fears persist, individual counseling has been used to reduce these concerns and generate program support (Cortazzo & Sansone, 1976).

Where community mobility programs have been conducted, the acquisition of independent travel skills by handicapped individuals has resulted in increased support from their parents for independent living training programs. According to Laus (1974), the public bus training program for moderately retarded students in the Pittsburgh school system resulted in parents viewing their offspring as young adults rather than as dependent children. The success of this program was an excellent demonstration for the parents of the overall purpose of the public school program (i.e., reducing dependency and promoting independence in all aspects of community life).

> **By working closely with the family in developing travel training programs, many fears can be alleviated and support can be generated for continued use of mobility skills following the initial training period.**

Overprotectiveness and lowered expectations can combine to present attitudinal barriers that severely limit a person's opportunity to acquire independent living skills. However, the development of responsible and effective community mobility training programs can alleviate fears and concerns regarding safety and consequently raise expectations of parents and professionals for independent living by handicapped individuals. The development of such programs will significantly increase the opportunity an individual will have to acquire independent travel skills.

MOBILITY MODES

The removal of physical and attitudinal barriers has increased community mobility opportunities for many individuals. To enable a person to take full advantage of these opportunities, a variety of mobility skills are necessary. Movement from one place to another in the community can be accomplished in several different ways and with varying degrees of independence. In Table 4.1, a matrix of mobility modes by potential destinations is presented.

Table 4.1. Community mobility matrix

	Mobility destinations				
	Home	Neighborhood	School	Community	Extracommunity
Mobility means Ambulation without assistance (e.g., walking)					
Ambulation with assistance (use of a prosthetic device such as a cane or crutches)					
Independent use of conveyance (use of wheelchair, bicycle, car, etc.)					
Dependent use of conveyance (passenger in wheelchair, car, van, or bus)					
Public transportation (use of elevator, car pool, taxi, bus, train, etc.)					

The travel modes identified in this matrix are ambulation without assistance, ambulation with assistance, independent use of conveyance, dependent use of conveyance, and public transportation. Each of these modes is discussed and specific examples within each mode are presented.

Ambulation without Assistance

Walking is the typical way in which people move from one place to another within a particular setting. Although most persons would have little difficulty finding their way between various locations within a community setting, severely handicapped persons may need to be specifically taught how to accomplish such tasks. These may include instructional programs to teach people to walk between the work floor and break area within a vocational setting and travel to and from the lunchroom or cafeteria at school.

Walking between community settings is usually referred to as pedestrian travel. In the literature, pedestrian travel has primarily referred to the behaviors of crossing streets and intersections. Because pedestrian travel has been the subject of several training studies involving handicapped persons, specific discussion of this topic is presented in a subsequent section.

Jogging and running are other means for moving from place to place within the community. Given the popularity of jogging as a recreational and physical fitness activity, increased involvement by moderately and severely handicaped persons should prove to be both normalizing and healthy.

Ambulation with Assistance

Due to sensory or physical disabilities, many individuals require assistance to ambulate independently. This assistance may be in the form of canes, crutches, seeing eye dogs, or sighted guides. For the most part, professional discussions in the literature regarding these ambulation aides have been restricted to individuals with normal intelligence who have visual or physical disabilities. However, because many mentally retarded persons have concomitant sensory and physical handicaps, these discussions need to expand to include the subject of teaching multiply handicapped persons how to use ambulation aides to travel functionally in their home communities.

Independent Use of Conveyance

A conveyance is a means of transportation in which one is carried from one place to another. Conveyances that can be used independently include manual wheelchairs, electric wheelchairs, tricycles, bicycles, mopeds, motorcycles, cars, and vans. The skills required to use these conveyances vary considerably in difficulty level, from the relatively simple set required to operate an electric wheelchair to the complex set needed to drive a van.

> **Conveyances that can be used independently include manual wheelchairs, electric wheelchairs, tricycles, bicycles, mopeds, motorcycles, cars, and vans.**

On the whole, very little programmatic research has been conducted to determine the practicality of training moderately and severely handicapped persons to use various conveyance means independently. As a result, there is uncertainty in the field regarding how realistic it is to teach specific means of mobility. However, as Gold (1976) has stated:

> The decision to teach or not to teach any task to the severely/profoundly handicapped must be based on whether or not that task can be analyzed into teachable components rather than some general feelings about the difficulty of the task. (p. 81)

Consistent with the above statement, Zider and Gold (1981) reported the results of a behind-the-wheel training program for two moderately retarded adults. As a result of this program, both subjects met criterion on the following skills trained in a simulator and driver training vehicle: 1) driver preparation by correct positioning of self and equipment; 2) starting and engaging in drive; 3) maintain speed and braking; and 4) turning and passing. Although the results of this study are encouraging, this area of instruction will undoubtedly remain controversial for mentally retarded persons due to the potential risks involved. It remains to be demonstrated that moderately retarded persons, such as those trained in this study, can make the necessary discriminations under ever-changing driving conditions that will enable them to maintain a reasonably safe driving record.

Although controversy will persist regarding the feasibility of teaching certain handicapped individuals to operate automobiles, the task analysis approach used in the Zider and Gold study could easily be applied to other conveyance means. For example, operation of a wheelchair and bicycle riding are mobility skills for which task analyses can be developed. By conducting detailed analyses of the necessary behaviors for using a variety of conveyances, innovative programs may evolve and the independent mobility of handicapped persons can be significantly advanced. Failure to conduct such analyses and related program development results in many individuals being unnecessarily dependent on attendant services for mobility within and between community settings.

By conducting detailed analyses of the necessary behaviors for using a variety of conveyances, innovative programs may evolve and the independent mobility of handicapped persons can be significantly advanced.

Dependent Use of Conveyance

Many handicapped individuals are transported from one place to another with the assistance of attendant staff. Frequently used conveyance means are wheelchairs, cars, vans, and buses. Although many individuals need assistance to travel, a large range of skills comprise the continuum from being totally dependent to independent in use of various conveyances. Unfortunately, little attention has been focused on this range of skills. However, the "principle of partial participation," as described by Brown, Branston-McClean, Baumgart, Vincent, Falvey, and Schroeder (1979), provides a rationale for giving dignity and respect to all skills along the continuum of dependence to independence.

The principle of partial participation contends that even if a person cannot independently perform an entire skill, this individual should be encouraged to participate as independently as possible. For example, if a person must be pushed from place to place in a wheelchair, he/she should be taught to assist as much as possible in the process. With certain individuals, this assistance might be as minimal as cooperating in a transfer from the chair to another location (e.g., bed or toilet).

Furthermore, there are several skills that may be required of individuals who are passengers in different vehicles. These include getting in and out, locking and unlocking doors, fastening and unfastening seat belts, remaining seated, keeping doors closed, and being socially appropriate during the trip. Failure to perform some of these basic skills may result in a person being denied the opportunity to participate in community activities.

Public Transportation

In addition to pedestrian travel, public transportation is the community mobility mode that has received the most research attention. Specifically, there have been several programs reported in the literature that have demonstrated the ability of mentally handicapped persons to use mass transit systems (i.e., public bus systems). Because there have been several studies on the topic of teaching bus riding skills, a separate discussion of these programs is subsequently presented.

Although numerous bus riding programs have been discussed in the literature, there have been few reports involving the instruction of handicapped persons to use other means of public transportation. Other public transportation means include use of escalators and elevators, participation in car pools, using taxi services, riding the subway, and traveling by train or airline. The lack of published program initiatives involving these mobility means probably reflects the fact that these means have been largely unavailable or unused by individuals with severe handicaps. As independent or semi-independent living and gainful employment become a reality for more of these individuals, the need to explore training techniques to maximize use of various public transportation alternatives is imperative.

MOBILITY DESTINATIONS

A person's mobility training needs are determined by the settings he/she must travel within and between. These settings can be referred to as potential mobility destinations. In developing individualized mobility training programs, a detailed analysis should be conducted of these destinations and the skills that are required to move within and between various settings. (Several mobility destinations are identified in Table 4.1.) These include home, neighborhood, school, community, and extracommunity settings. Based on the mobility requirements identified through the detailed analysis of mobility destinations, individuals should be assessed to determine specific training priorities. These specific training priorities may highlight needed environmental modifications to increase accessibility and alternative mobility modes that should be developed.

As indicated in Table 4.1, each person's mobility plan should reflect a dual concern for mobility mode and destination. This dual emphasis provides a concrete illustration of the functional value of community mobility. That is, community mobility should provide people with skills that enable them to participate more fully in community life. Independent mobility skills are essential to the goal of maximal community participation. Two mobility modes that have received considerable attention in the habilitation literature are pedestrian travel and public bus transportation.

> **Community mobility should provide people with skills that enable them to participate more fully in community life.**

PEDESTRIAN TRAVEL

Compared to other community mobility modes, pedestrian behavior has received considerable attention in the literature. Primarily this research has been focused on hazard perception and street crossing behaviors of normal grade school children and handicapped adults. The acquisition of independent pedestrian travel skills is important from the standpoint of ensuring a person's safety and from the perspective of increasing an individual's mobility range within the community. This dual concern is represented in the research literature.

An individual's perception of hazard or risk in a pedestrian situation affects how successfully he/she is able to cross streets and avoid injury. Heimstra and Struckman (1973) found that boys who scored as low hazard perceivers had significantly more accidents than did boys who were classified as high hazard perceivers. Although this study was concerned with a variety of accident behaviors, the implications regarding pedestrian safety are obvious. In a study related specifically to perception of hazard in a pedestrian situation, Salvatore (1974) investigated the ability of children (ages 5 to 14) to sense the velocity of oncoming cars. Results of this study revealed considerable differences associated with sex and age. For example, although males made more correct judgments over the whole speed range, females were more likely to classify correctly the dangerous, fast vehicles. In conclusion, these authors suggested that it would be desirable to determine if judgments of car speed and distance could be improved by training.

The need to pursue training techniques for improving safe pedestrian behaviors is given urgency by data associated with the pedestrian accident. According to Reading (1973), each year about 350,000 pedestrians are struck by vehicles and approximately 10,000 of these individuals die. From data collected in 1971 on fatal accidents involving pedestrians, 21% of these accidents occurred at intersections and 43% took place while pedestrians were crossing streets outside of an intersection (O'Brien, Note 5). Cumulatively these data reveal that 64% of pedestrian deaths are associated with street crossing behavior.

As early as 1961, Suchman suggested that accident investigators should begin to analyze injury producing behavior rather than accidents. In line with this suggestion, Jennings, Burke, and Onstine (1977) used behavioral observations in an attempt to better understand the behaviors that result in the pedestrian accident. As a part of their study, these investigators analyzed the records of 705 pedestrian accidents in the city of Portland, Oregon. This analysis revealed that 78% of the accidents were within 50 feet of the intersection and 60% of the accidents occurred on the near side of the street. Furthermore, 40% of these accidents occurred within the crosswalk on the near side of the street. On the basis of this analysis, behavioral observation activities were focused on pedestrian behavior associated with entering the street at the crosswalks. These authors concluded that development of direct observation techniques improves the opportunity to understand and reduce pedestrian accidents.

Direct instruction of pedestrian street crossing behavior will be necessary to ensure that many handicapped individuals are able to travel independently and safely in the community. With young children, often the victims of pedestrian accidents, appropriate street crossing behaviors have been established through systematic training procedures. Reading (1973) analyzed street crossing behavior and broke it down into the following three components: 1) come to a complete stop at the curb of the intersection; 2) make discrete observing responses of at least 3 seconds in all directions; and 3) proceed across the street within the crosswalk. Following a general demonstration of correct street crossing behavior in a school assembly, high school volunteers began reinforcing the students (ages 5 to 9) for appropriate street crossing behavior. As a result of this program, the percentage of correct street crossing responses increased for three groups of students from baseline levels of less than 20% to greater than 60% after instruction and reinforcement. A multiple baseline across groups of students and times of day was used to verify the effectiveness of the training program.

Direct instruction of pedestrian street crossing behavior will be necessary to ensure that many handicapped individuals are able to independently and safely travel in the community.

Yeaton and Bailey (1978) analyzed pedestrian behavior and further broke it down into six street crossing skills: 1) wait at the curb; 2) look all ways; 3) watch vehicle distance; 4) walk; 5) continue to look; and 6) use crosswalk. Using an instructional package consisting of explaining all safety precautions in crossing streets, modeling safe street crossing, asking questions relevant to street crossing behavior, and allowing students to cross with descriptive feedback for correct and incorrect responses, two groups of 12 students from different schools improved significantly in their street crossing skills. These gains were also evident at a non-training intersection, although the students' behavior was not as proficient as at the training setting. Of significance is the finding that those gains maintained or were easily recovered with minimal training after 1 year.

In the Yeaton and Bailey (1978) investigation, crossing guards were usually present at the intersections. As is evident from the students' low levels of correct street crossing behavior during baseline, these individuals functioned more to protect the children than to train them to cross more independently. However, given the simplicity of the instructional package, it seems quite feasible that the competencies of crossing guards could be expanded to include teaching as well as protecting young children, thus maximizing the safe passage of children all the way home from school.

In addition to normal grade school children, handicapped individuals have been involved in intensive instruction to establish independent street crossing behaviors. Page, Iwata, and Neef (1976) developed a task analysis for crossing streets that included several decision points. Based on this task analysis, five mildly retarded young adults were taught street crossing skills in the same classroom on a model simulation of four square city blocks. Generalization probes were conducted at three city intersections located within three blocks of the classroom. Training consisted of ten trials a day on one of five areas involved in street crossing: 1) intersection; 2) pedestrian light; 3) traffic light; 4) stop sign for cars going across the pedestrian's path; and 5) stop sign for cars going in the same direction as pedestrian. Each student was required to respond by moving a doll through the various intersections in the classroom model. Correct responses were praised and incorrect responses were followed by explicit feedback and modeling if necessary. As a result of this study, all subjects met criterion on the classroom training and generalized these gains to the community. An average of 21.2 sessions was required for the subjects to reach criterion. The authors emphasize that this study demonstrated the desirability of classroom training for teaching adaptive community behavior.

In an attempt to extend the initial findings of Page et al. (1976), Matson (1980) conducted a control group study of pedestrian skill training for moderately and severely retarded adults. Matson assigned 30 subjects to one of the following three groups:

1. No treatment control group (These subjects were not involved in pedestrian training, but were scheduled for 6 hours of training in other independent living skill programs.)
2. Classroom training (Each subject received 30 minutes of individual instruction on a daily basis for 3 months. Instruction was very similar to the classroom training described by Page et al. [1976]. A training session consisted of a trial on each target behavior.)
3. Independence training (The subjects in this condition were taught initially to recognize common pedestrian signs. This instruction was followed by 2 weeks of training in the classroom and the remainder of treatment at a mock intersection. At the mock intersection, a typical instruction session consisted of: 1) subject walking to the intersection; 2) trainer requesting one subject to perform each target behavior; 3) trainer using verbal and manual prompts to correct any errors; 4) trainer asking subjects to self-evaluate; 5) trainer verbally evaluating the subject; 6) trainer asking subjects to provide positive feedback; and 7) trainer asking other subjects to perform the targeted behaviors, repeating steps 3 through 7.)

The targeted pedestrian behaviors in this study were proper sidewalk behaviors, recognition of intersections, and crossing streets. Each of these targeted behaviors was taught by concentrating instructional efforts on a series of subobjectives. For example, crossing the street consisted of five subobjectives: 1) cross when lawfully appropriate based on traffic signal; 2) look in all directions; 3) cross within pedestrian crosswalk; 4) attend to traffic to avoid collisions; and 5) cross street without stopping.

Results of this study revealed that both classroom training and independence training were effective instructional strategies. However, independence training was more effective than classroom training for improving the live performance of pedestrian skills by institutionalized mentally retarded persons. With severely handicapped individuals, generalization from classroom training to actual performance in the community cannot be guaranteed. For these individuals, instruction may be most effective if it occurs in the natural environments where pedestrian behaviors are required.

With severely and profoundly retarded adolescents, several sources have emphasized the importance of instruction in the natural environment. Consistent with this emphasis, Vogelsburg and Rusch (1979) reported the results of a study that involved teaching three severely handicapped adolescents to cross partially controlled intersections. In this study, all instruction occurred in the community.

The targeted pedestrian behaviors consisted of approaching the intersection, looking for traffic, stepping into the street, and walking across the intersection. Instruction consisted of various combinations of preinstruction, instructional feedback, and selective repeated practice. Preinstruction involved verbally explaining all the steps of safely crossing streets. Instructional feedback was provided in various levels of assistance depending on student performance. These levels were verbal instruction, verbal instruction and model assistance, verbal instruction and partial physical guidance, and verbal instruction with total physical assistance. In Figure 4.1 the reader is provided an example data form that was used in this program to record levels of instructional assistance on each of the steps involved in crossing an intersection.

Selective repeated practice was used by Vogelsburg and Rusch to help clients learn particularly difficult behaviors. For example, after stopping at the curb each subject was required to complete a four-piece looking response (i.e., look behind, ahead, left, and right). If the subjects required physical assistance to perform this four-piece response, five repeated trials of these behaviors were given to each student. Of interest in this study was that the four-piece repeated practice did not facilitate acquisition. However, when this response was divided into two two-piece looking responses, repeated practice was effective and the students were able to learn the entire four-piece response.

At the conclusion of 70 training sessions, each approximately 20 minutes long, all three clients had acquired the basic skills for crossing partially controlled intersections. For these individuals, this acquisition provided a basis for them to acquire more advanced community mobility behaviors (e.g., crossing intersections with higher traffic density and using public transportation) (Vogelsburg & Rusch, 1979).

Most of the pedestrian travel research has been focused on street crossing behaviors. However, street crossing is one component of a complex continuum of pedestrian behaviors. For persons with profound retardation, independent walking from one location to another within a given setting may be a significant step toward more independent functioning. In a study reported by Gruber, Reeser, and Reid (1979), a backward chaining strategy was used to teach four profoundly retarded young adults to go from their residence to the workshop within the institution. After an initial baseline period, training began by escorting the subjects to within a few feet of the

Date: _____ Phase: _____ Session: _____

Trainer: _____ Trainee: _____

INSTRUCTIONAL ASSISTANCE

Code	Level of assistance	Specific physical assistance	Verbal cue
5	None	None	None
4	Verbal cue	None	"Listen"
3	Verbal cue and model	Point prompt	"Watch me"
2	Verbal cue and prompt	Nudges	"You do it"
1	Verbal cue and physical assistance	Total	"Do it with me"

	Tasks/trials	1	2	3	4	5	6	7	8	Total	Average
Approach	1. Walk to curb										
	2. Stop at curb										
Look	3. Look behind										
	4. Look in front										
	5. Look left										
	6. Look right										
Step	7. Wait for cars										
	8. Step off curb										
Walk	9. Walk quickly across street										
	10. Step on curb										

Figure 4.1. *Crossing uncontrolled intersection recording form. Reprinted with permission from Rusch and Mithaug (1980).*

workshop. At this point the instructor directed the clients to go to the workshop. Appropriate walking behaviors were praised, inappropriate behaviors were reprimanded, and edible treats were presented upon arrival at the workshop. By gradually having the clients walk further to school, it was possible to teach each client to walk the entire 1,000-foot distance between the dormitory and the work setting.

> **For persons with profound retardation, independent walking from one location to another within a given setting may be a significant step toward more independent functioning.**

In another demonstration of independent mobility instruction, a 12-year-old male with profound retardation was taught a sequence of three arrival behaviors associated with returning to his residence from school (Spears, Rusch, York, & Lilly, 1981). This sequence included walking to the building from the school bus, placing his school bag and coat in the bedroom, and walking to a playroom. Task analysis and use of pacing prompts (verbal preinstruction on previously missed tasks) resulted in independent arrival behaviors after 46 consecutive days of instruction.

Common to all successful pedestrian travel training programs has been a task analysis of street crossing behaviors and explicit feedback for performance. With normal youngsters and mildly handicapped individuals, classroom instruction has been an effective teaching strategy. However, for moderately and severely handicapped persons, community-based instruction may be necessary to ensure proficient performance under natural conditions. Still unresolved are the specific training techniques that may be needed to establish generalized pedestrian skills for performance under variable intersections and traffic conditions.

An emerging technology for facilitating generalization to untrained situations is called general case programming (Horner, Sprague, & Wilcox, 1982). Becker and Engelmann (1978) describe the general case as occurring when, "after instruction on some tasks in a particular class, any task in that class can be performed correctly" (p. 325) Regarding street crossing behavior, the general case is evident when a person demonstrates the ability to cross all variations of controlled and uncontrolled intersections. According to Horner et al. (1982), mobility trainers should identify the range of variability in pedestrian situations and provide instruction on multiple instances to represent this variability.

PUBLIC BUS TRANSPORTATION

In many communities public bus transportation is the most prevalent means of mobility. Consequently, several training programs have been directed at this transportation mode. Public transportation has been given a boost in the past few years as a result of an increased awareness regarding energy conservation. In most communities in which the population is over 30,000 some form of public bus transportation exists. With the new consciousness concerning excessive fuel consumption, the future of public transportation seems secure. It can be expected, then, that present public transportation systems will be maintained or expanded and that new systems will be initiated. These developments make public transportation opportunities more available to handicapped individuals than at any other time. Unfortunately, these increased opportunities have not necessarily been matched by increased ridership by handicapped citizens due to accessibility problems and lack of independent mobility skills. In this section, the results of several training programs to improve the independent use of public transportation by handicapped individuals are summarized. These studies have collectively demonstrated that under the appropriate instructional conditions most handicapped persons can learn to use public bus transportation to move about their communities.

As early as 1963, Tobias and Cortazzo were expressing the opinion that reliance on commercial bus systems was a disproportionately expensive mode of transportation for getting retarded adults to and from community-based programs. When a day services program for these adults was being planned, only 9 of 72 accepted applicants could reach the program without assistance. After 6 months of individualized tutoring and practice sessions, 31 clients were traveling independently. This eliminated the need for one chartered bus and resulted in a savings of $3,100.

In a follow-up article of this same program, Tobias and Gorelick (1968) provide more details on the travel/training techniques they found to be effective. The authors developed a general list of training recommendations that included:

1. Reduce parental anxiety by constantly reassuring them of the quality of staff supervision.
2. Provide positive feedback to parents on all trainee accomplishments.
3. Reward trainees' efforts by verbal reassurance and direct assistance. Use social praise for partial success and a "diploma" for final achievement.
4. Use landmarks (e.g., store signs) as substitutes for printed signs to point out cues that should have relevance for the trainees.
5. Provide special tutoring for specific mobility-related skills (e.g., pushing through turnstiles and identifying coins).

With the above training procedures, 60% of all trainees involved in travel training acquired the ability to use some form of public transportation. Of the 24 who were unable to travel independently, 14 were profoundly retarded, 6 were not allowed to travel by their parents, 2 had severe seizures, and 2 had incidents of socially unacceptable behavior during independent travel.

Additional data regarding the effectiveness of public transportation training for retarded adults were provided by Cortazzo and Sansone (1976). These authors summarized the results of travel training programs involving 378 adults. Of the 378 trainees, 199 learned to travel independently between their homes and the day program, with an average training time of 1½ months per trainee. Based on the success of this travel training effort, one program was able to reduce its annual budget for travel from $21,000 to $10,000 in 3 years.

The early demonstrations that persons with moderate and severe retardation could learn to use public transportation systems have been followed by more specific investigations regarding the effectiveness of various training procedures. For example, Kubat (1973) used experimental and control groups of 13 moderately and mildly retarded subjects to evaluate a training program consisting of: 1) discussion of appropriate bus riding behavior; 2) demonstration of the route by escorting the client in a private vehicle; 3) simulation of the bus ride in a private vehicle; and 4) opportunity for the trainee to ride the city bus with direct instruction from the trainer. For all experimental subjects, this training sequence resulted in acquisition of independent bus riding behaviors in approximately 12 hours of training.

Neef, Iwata, and Page (1978) conducted a comparative study of classroom instruction versus in vivo training of public bus transportation skills. This study consisted of classroom training for five retarded young adults and in vivo instruction for two other individuals. With both groups of subjects, a multiple baseline across subjects was used to demonstrate the effectiveness of the training procedures. Classroom instruction included: 1) manipulation of a doll through the steps of appropriate bus riding; 2) presentation of photographic stimuli (slides) for subjects to identify relevant and irrelevant cues for particular bus riding responses; and 3) training on a simulated bus with slides projected to show sequenced locations along a bus route. In vivo training involved a subject and trainer actually riding the bus on its daily route. The trainer contingently praised correct responses, provided explicit feedback for errors, and modeled correct responses. The bus riding behaviors targeted in this study were: 1) locating; 2) signaling; 3) boarding; 4) riding; and 5) exiting.

According to Neef et al. (1978), the results of this study strongly support the classroom training approach since the bus riding skills could be generalized to the natural environment. Average training time was 8.85 hours per subject in classroom training as compared to 33.25 hours for those subjects trained in vivo. The effectiveness of classroom travel training was maximized by using realistic simulations, minimizing distracting stimuli, and providing opportunity for repeated practice on difficult behaviors. Although classroom training was demonstrated to be extremely effective in this study, the subjects were primarily mildly retarded (mean IQ = 56). With a more severely handicapped population, generalization from classroom experience to community performance may be more of a problem.

> **The effectiveness of classroom travel training was maximized by using realistic simulations, minimizing distracting stimuli, and providing opportunity for repeated practice on difficult behaviors.**

In a study involving a 20-year-old woman with severe handicaps (e.g., limited speech and slow gait), Coon, Vogelsberg, and Williams (1981) examined the effectiveness of classroom and natural instruction for teaching independent use of a city bus. Examination of data from this program reveals that community performance was not significantly improved until natural environment instruction was provided. The equivocal nature of research findings involving classroom versus natural instruction suggest that researchers must further investigate the instructional conditions that are most efficient and effective with varying subject populations and target behaviors.

In the past few years, several public school programs for moderately and severely retarded students have initiated public bus transportation programs. These programs evolved out of an awareness that many individuals were completing their public school eligibility and were still lacking basic community survival skills. As a result, these individuals were so severely restricted in mobility that many were unable to participate in community activities.

One of the first published reports of public bus training for mentally retarded students of school age was presented by Laus (1974). Laus included 35 moderately retarded students (ages 14 to 21) in a mobility training program consisting of basic classroom activities, crossing intersections, and public bus travel. Classroom training activities were focused on identifying colors, numeral recognition, personal grooming, verbal communication, basic sign reading, counting, and exchanging money. Crossing intersections consisted of teaching students how and when to cross streets controlled by stop signs and other signs. Finally, public bus travel was taught on a one-to-one basis. During travel training instruction, the mobility trainer gradually withdrew his/her presence as trainees exhibited more independent behaviors. Approximately 2 weeks of daily instruction were required for independent acquisition of the bus route between home and school by each student. Once trainees were traveling independently, groups of 8 to 10 continued to meet on a weekly basis with the mobility instructor to discuss problems related to their daily travel.

As a result of this program all 35 students learned to travel by public bus transportation between their homes and school. These independent behaviors resulted in the Pittsburgh Public Schools accruing a savings of $20,000 per year in fees to leased conveyance services.

With another group of moderately retarded students, Certo, Schwartz, and Brown (1975) reported the procedures and results of an elaborate training program that was designed to teach 10 adolescents to use public bus transportation to obtain needed community services (e.g., food, clothing, recreation, and medical assistance). This program consisted of the following four phases.

Phase 1: Students were taught to ride a simulated city bus in the classroom.

Phase 2: Students were taught selected places in the community where specific services can be obtained and what buses were needed to reach those destinations.

Phase 3: Students were taught to ride actual buses to obtain specific community services.

Phase 4: Students were taught how to select appropriate buses to reach destinations not appearing on their route cards.

The results of this program support the position that moderately retarded individuals can acquire complex community mobility behaviors. Eight of the 10 participants in this program acquired several independent behaviors in all phases of the program. By directly programming for functional transportation use, this study has taken a major step toward maximizing community participation by moderately and severely handicapped persons.

Recently, more community mobility training programs have begun to emphasize the functional relationship between public transportation and one's access to community services. For example, Sowers, Rusch, and Hudson (1979) used systematic training procedures to teach a severely retarded adult to complete the following 10-behavior sequence to ride the city bus to and from work: 1) crossing controlled intersections; 2) crossing unmarked intersections; 3) using bus tickets; 4) walking to bus; 5) identifying the correct bus; 6) boarding; 7) riding; 8) departing; 9) transferring; and 10) walking to work. Further, Marholin, O'Toole, Touchette, Berger, and Doyle (1979) taught four moderately and severely retarded adults to use public bus transportation to travel between a public institution and various community locations for shopping and eating in a restaurant. In one of the more detailed transportation programs that has been documented, Carney, Menchetti, and Orelove (1977) reported the procedures and results of an effort to teach generalized use of a mass transit system to two moderately retarded adults. A goal of this program was that the subjects' community mobility skills would be maintained by the increased access that they would have to various community services.

According to van den Pol, Iwata, Ivancic, Page, Neef, and Whitley (1981), maintenance of community mobility is best accomplished by conceptualizing travel skills as intermediate responses in a chain that enables a person to engage in reinforcing activities (e.g., work to recreation to dining). These authors taught restaurant skills to retarded adults as primary reinforcers for community travel on a public bus system. By programming community activities as natural consequences for using public bus transportation, maintenance and generalization of both mobility and community living behaviors are maximized.

Several successful training programs have been documented for improving the public bus transportation skills of handicapped adolescents and adults. As with pedestrian travel training, common components of successful programs include task-analyzed skill sequences and explicit response feedback. Public transportation programs have primarily involved mildly, moderately, and severely retarded persons. As teaching techniques become further refined, the inclusion of profoundly retarded individuals and other difficult populations (e.g., autistic) in such training will likely occur. For all populations, the key to long-term use of public bus transportation is the establishment of community skills (e.g., shopping and library use) so that community mobility becomes a truly functional skill.

In addition to skill deficits, behavior problems may interfere with a person's successful use of public transportation. Disruptive school bus behaviors are frequently cited by bus drivers and public school officials as being prevalent and potentially dangerous. These behavior problems are present in handicapped and nonhandicapped student populations. Both group and individual management techniques have been used successfully to reduce these disruptions. For example, Greene, Bailey, and Barber (1981) reported the use of a "noise guard" and visual feedback to monitor sound frequencies above 500 Hz. When used in conjunction with specific contingencies for taped music and raffle prizes, this procedure resulted in group reductions in frequency of noisy disruptions and out-of-seat behavior. An individualized management program was reported by Chiang, Iwata, and Dorsey (1979). This study was conducted with a 10-year-old, moderately retarded male, who exhibited high rates of disruptive behavior on the school bus. A token system administered by the bus driver was used to reinforce the child for appropriate behavior at nine established distance intervals on the trip. With back-up reinforcement provided at home and school, this individualized program eliminated disruptive behavior on both the morning and afternoon trips during the last four sessions.

Although the above studies were successful, both were conducted under more controlled conditions than typically exist in other public transportation areas. Additional strategies may be necessary for behavior problems emitted in taxis and public buses.

RECOMMENDED PRACTICE
FOR MOBILITY TRAINING

The previous two sections of this chapter include several examples of effective mobility training programs for pedestrian travel and public bus transportation. Unfortunately, the focus of these efforts has been extremely narrow when compared to the broad range of mobility skills required by handicapped individuals. To assist the reader in developing community mobility training programs, several recommended practices are described below.

Assessment of Mobility Needs

The first step in developing mobility training programs is to conduct an ecological inventory of community environments in which a person is expected to function. This might include detailed analyses of the mobility requirements of school, vocational, domestic, and commercial settings. These analyses should reveal accessibility obstacles that need to be overcome, mobility modes that are available, and specific services that can be acquired by expanded mobility. This process should also include mobility needs of ambulatory and nonambulatory individuals.

Family/Guardian Support

At an early point in the development of community mobility training programs, family members or guardians should be consulted to determine priority objectives and enlist support for the program's goals. The long-term objectives of mobility training should be generally discussed and the short-term training activities should be carefully described. The program developer must be able to ensure adequate program supervision and safety precautions. The use of a program consent form is one method for formalizing the process of enlisting family/guardian support (Vogelsburg & Rusch, 1980a).

Task Analyses of Mobility Goals

Once mobility goals have been identified, these goals should be task analyzed. Several task analyses for pedestrian travel and public use have been presented previously. Additional task analyses are presented in Tables 4.2 and 4.3 for stair climbing and riding in an automobile, respectively.

Table 4.2.   Task analysis for stair climbing

Step   1.   Walk to foot of stairs
Step   2.   Place hand on handrail (slide up handrail as you proceed)
Step   3.   Lift right leg above first step (flex knee)
Step   4.   Place right foot on first step
Step   5.   Push off right foot (shift weight to right side)
Step   6.   Lift left leg above second step (flex knee)
Step   7.   Place left foot on second step
Step   8.   Push off left foot (shift weight to left side)
Step   9.   Lift right leg above third step (flex knee)
Step 10.   Place right foot on third step
Step 11.   Push off right foot (shift weight to right side)
Step 12.   Lift left leg above landing (flex knee)
Step 13.   Place left foot on landing
Step 14.   Push off left foot (shift weight to left side)
Step 15.   Lift right leg above landing (flex knee)
Step 16.   Place right foot on landing
Step 17.   Release handrail

Table 4.3. Task analysis for entering and riding in an automobile

Step 1. Locate car
Step 2. Find door handle that corresponds to riding position in car (passenger side)
Step 3. Grasp door handle with four fingers
Step 4. Put thumb on handle button
Step 5. Press button
Step 6. Pull door open (until it catches in open position)
Step 7. Walk up to car seat
Step 8. Lift left leg (bend knee) and swing it into car
Step 9. Twist trunk to right (90°)
Step 10. Sit down on seat (bend right knee)
Step 11. Lift right leg and swing into car
Step 12. Lean out of car
Step 13. Grasp inside door handle (right hand)
Step 14. Pull door shut
Step 15. Reach across body with left arm
Step 16. Locate lock with left hand
Step 17. Push lock down
Step 18. Grasp left seat belt attachment (left hand)
Step 19. Grasp right seat belt attachment (right hand)
Step 20. Buckle seat belt
Step 21. Maintain seated position throughout trip

Task Analytic Assessment

Task analyses of community mobility behaviors constitute the criteria for performance. Prior to developing training objectives, individuals should be directly observed and evaluated. To conduct a task analytic assessment, the task analysis for a mobility objective (e.g., uses elevator) is written in serial order on a recording form (Table 4.4). The instructor then provides the student with the opportunity to perform the skill and observes carefully what specific behaviors are accomplished independently and what behaviors require instructor assistance. Independent behaviors are recorded (+) and those requiring assistance are recorded (−). The instructor should continue assessment activities until performance has stabilized.

Community Mobility Objectives

After conducting task analytic assessment activities, individualized training objectives should be established. With handicapped individuals, these objectives should be specific, including details regarding the conditions, target behavior, and criterion for performance. Specificity in objective writing promotes *structure* and *consistency* in teaching practice, both conditions that maximize skill acquisition by slow learners. Example mobility objectives that reflect these properties are as follows:

When approaching a traffic light-controlled intersection, Jane will stop at curb, observe lights, watch for traffic, and cross safely within the crosswalk 100% of the time across 20 trials.

At 8:00 a.m. on school days, John will leave home and walk directly to the public bus stop on nine of ten consecutive school days.

When in Sears Department Store, Sally will appropriately use the escalator (see task analysis) to reach the second floor on three consecutive shopping trips.

When told to get into the automobile, Carl will open door, sit in passenger seat, close door, lock door, and fasten seat belt on nine of ten trips to the store.

Table 4.4. Task analytic assessment of riding an elevator

Teacher: Ernie Pancsofar Student: John J. Date(s): May '80 Environment: Apt. Bldg. Program: Independent use of elevator																
1. Walk to elevator area																
2. Push directional button																
3. Wait in front of elevator for elevator doors to open																
4. When directional button goes off, walk to open elevator																
5. Wait for people to leave elevator																
6. Enter elevator																
7. Push appropriate number button (floor desired)																
8. Step to the back of elevator (hold rail if necessary)																
9. Remain on elevator when doors open at undesired floors																
10. When elevator doors open and numbered light goes off, step off elevator																

Systematic Teaching Procedures

When specific training objectives have been delineated, instructional procedures should be detailed. With mildly handicapped individuals, classroom instruction may be an effective and efficient training strategy for a variety of mobility objectives. However, if this method is used, generalization should never be assumed and frequent evaluations should be conducted to demonstrate that classroom trained skills are actually used in other environments. For severely handicapped learners, most authors recommend that instruction should occur in natural environments as much as possible. Because generalization is less certain with this group of learners, instruction in natural environments provides individuals with skills where they can best be used.

After the teaching and generalization environments have been identified, instructor directions, correction procedures, and reinforcement contingencies should be specified. Instructor directions are those teacher behaviors that give the trainee information regarding what to do in a particular situation. These may include verbal statements, modeled demonstrations, and physical assistance. Correction procedures are those teacher actions that follow an error by the trainee. One frequently used procedure is to interrupt the trainee when an error is made and provide additional directions to facilitate correct performance. Another procedure is to reprimand the trainee verbally (e.g., "No!") and then provide information regarding how to perform correctly. Finally, reinforcing consequences for performance of mobility objectives should be specified. Most frequently social praise is used for successful performance of individual mobility behaviors and activity reinforcers are provided upon accomplishment of the mobility task. For example, individual bus riding behaviors may be socially praised by the instructor and the accomplishment of arriving at a destination reinforced by the activity of eating in a restaurant.

Systematic teaching procedures are necessary to promote skill acquisition by slow learners. These procedures need to be specified so that they can be used consistently by different instructors. By specifically identifying the teaching environment, teacher instructions, correction procedures, and reinforcement contingencies, optimal conditions for the acquisition of mobility skills are established.

Program for Maintenance and Generalization

The ultimate success of community mobility training programs is determined by the extent to which travel skills are maintained and used under a variety of different post-training conditions. Maintenance of mobility skills is best accomplished by systematically progressing toward a more intermittent reinforcement schedule and arranging for naturally occurring activity reinforcers to result from newly acquired mobility skills. For example, social praise for each response in the street crossing program should be reduced to occasional approval of appropriate pedestrian behavior. Further, crossing the street should provide the individual with access to something desirable (e.g., ice cream store).

> Social praise for each response in the street crossing program should be reduced to occasional approval of appropriate pedestrian behavior. Further, crossing the street should provide the individual with access to something desirable (e.g., ice cream store).

Generalization of community mobility behavior refers to the individual's ability to use different travel skills under a variety of stimulus conditions. Efforts to promote generalization must include direct instruction in the different transportation modes. As an example, several modes of public transportation may need to be included in a community mobility training program. In addition, handicapped individuals may need instruction on how to use specific mobility skills to travel within and between multiple community settings, to travel at different times of the day and week, and to travel in various weather, terrain, and traffic conditions. By systematically programming for maintenance and generalization, the overall purpose of community mobility instruction can be achieved. That is, handicapped individuals will be able to use a variety of mobility modes to participate in a full range of community activities.

SUMMARY

In this chapter, the importance of community mobility has been emphasized as it relates to independent or semi-independent functioning in all aspects of community life. Physical and attitudinal barriers were discussed as potential limitations to travel within and between various community settings. Many of these barriers have been reduced by accessibility legislation, community awareness, and parental involvement. The removal of physical and attitudinal barriers must be coupled with a broad conceptualization of the range of mobility modes available to handicapped citizens. These modes include ambulation without assistance, ambulation with assistance, independent use of conveyance, dependent use of conveyance, and public transportation. This conceptualization must also include potential mobility destinations such as home, neighborhood, school, community, and extra-community.

Furthermore, systematic training strategies must be tied to this conceptualization. Specific instructional sequences were described for pedestrian travel and public bus transportation. Components common to many of these instructional sequences are presented in the chapter as recommended practices. These components include assessment of mobility needs, family/guardian support, task analysis of mobility objectives, systematic teaching procedures, and programs for maintenance and generalization. By following these recommended practices, the mobility repertoire of moderately and severely handicapped persons can be broadened substantially. These skills should make possible a much richer and more independent life for many handicapped citizens.

5

SOCIAL-INTERPERSONAL SKILL DEVELOPMENT

LEARNING GOALS

1. *Discuss the importance of social-interpersonal development.*
2. *Describe the conceptualization of social-interpersonal competence that is presented in the chapter.*
3. *Identify six to eight categories of verbal and nonverbal social-interpersonal behaviors.*
4. *Describe how to use a normative analysis for determining social-interpersonal training objectives.*
5. *Describe four specific examples of instructional procedures that influence acquisition of social-interpersonal skills.*
6. *Define generalization and how it relates to social-interpersonal skill development.*
7. *Identify six programming techniques that can be used to generalize social-interpersonal skills for moderately and severely handicapped individuals.*
8. *Discuss four issues in social skills instruction.*

Social-interpersonal skill development of handicapped adolescents and adults is essential for successful integration and community adjustment. The importance of social skill development for mentally retarded persons, for example, is reflected in the historic distinction of mental retardation in terms of intellectual deficiency and inadequate social functioning (American Association on Mental Deficiency, 1977; American Psychological Association, 1968). According to Turner, Hersen, and Bellack (1978), intellectually deficient individuals are noted for their extremely limited social skill repertoire and excessive rates of socially unacceptable behavior. Follow-up studies conducted with mentally retarded adults have consistently revealed that social-interpersonal skill deficits interfere significantly with a person's vocational success and community integration (Goldstein, 1964; Stanfield, 1973). Skill deficits in this area are not limited to the mentally retarded population. For example, emotionally disturbed (Hallahan & Kauffman, 1978) and learning disabled (Bryan & Bryan, 1977) individuals have also been identified by the presence of social-interpersonal skill deficits. In some cases these skill deficits result in individuals being so unrewarding as social interaction partners that they serve as negative reinforcing agents whom others actively avoid (Kelly & Drabman, 1977; Kelly, Furman, Phillips, Hathorn, & Wilson, 1979).

The importance of social-interpersonal competence is widely accepted and the inadequacies of handicapped populations in this area are well substantiated. Unfortunately, too little attention has been given to the environmental conditions (segregated institutional settings) and instructional conditions (denial of public education) that have contributed to this perception. The increasing trend toward deinstitutionalization and integration of handicapped persons with nonhandicapped individuals in the least restrictive environment prioritizes the development of appropriate social-interpersonal behaviors (Brody & Stoneman, 1977; Strain & Shores, 1977). However, until recently few research efforts were directed toward the development of intervention strategies that promote this development (Strain, Cooke, & Appolloni, 1976).

DEFINING THE COMPONENTS OF SOCIAL COMPETENCE

One problem that has detracted from a more focused investigation of social-interpersonal behavior has been difficulty in defining the components of social competence. Whereas many can agree that handicapped persons lack appropriate social skills, few can agree on exactly what constitutes social behavior. Failure to arrive at specific definitions has precluded accurate measurement and evaluation of instructional procedures. These conditions have had a suppressing effect on curriculum and instructional technology development in the social skill area.

Where specific social-interpersonal skills have been defined, much of the research has centered on relatively discrete behaviors and has failed to tie these into a broader conceptualization. For example, studies involving younger students have been directed toward topics such as cooperative ball rolling (Morris & Dolker, 1974; Whitman, Mercurio, & Caponigri, 1970), pulling a peer in a wagon (Paloutzian, Hasazi, Streifel, & Edgar, 1971), block play (Whitman et al., 1970), and appropriate action on play materials (Hopper & Wambold, 1977). Older moderately and severely handicapped individuals have been involved in training programs designed to improve their table game-playing skills (Marchant & Wehman, 1979; Wehman, Renzaglia, Schutz, Gray, James, & Karan, 1976), greeting responses (Kale, Kaye, Whalen, & Hopkins, 1968), and use of the telephone (Nietupski & Williams, 1974). Recently, moderately and severely handicapped individuals have been involved in training programs that have included more complex target behaviors. For example, more effective conversational (Kelly et al., 1979) and job interviewing skills (Hall, Sheldon-Wildgen, & Sherman, 1980; Hill, Wehman, & Pentecost, 1979) have been successfully taught to moderately retarded adolescents.

One problem that has detracted from a more focused investigation of social-interpersonal behavior has been the difficulty of defining the components of social competence.

Despite the increasing sophistication of the training programs appearing in the literature, an overall *conceptualization* of social-interpersonal competence is lacking (Renzaglia & Bates, 1983). As a result, research has continued along many diverse lines of study and has failed to contribute toward the accumulation of a cohesive body of knowledge. Further, without such a conceptualization, the teacher has few guidelines to follow in attempting to promote the overall social-interpersonal competence of handicapped individuals.

In this chapter, social competence is conceptualized as those verbal and nonverbal behaviors that are emitted in an interpersonal context, which are perceived as socially appropriate by one's peers and/or significant others. This conceptualization conveys an emphasis on: 1) the need to coordinate the delivery of verbal and nonverbal responses; 2) the need to respond to unique aspects of particular interpersonal situations; and 3) the need to socially evaluate the effectiveness of specific interpersonal responses. Included in this conceptualization are social skills that require interaction with and without other people within a social context (i.e., a situation in which other people are present).

Tables 5.1 and 5.2 provide the reader with specific examples of verbal and nonverbal social-interpersonal skills. These skills are required in home, school, work, and other community environments. Key components in facilitating the development of these skills are: 1) identification of relevant content and standards for socially appropriate behavior; 2) selection of effective instructional procedures; and 3) incorporation of teaching methods that enhance maintenance and generalization. These components are described and numerous examples are presented to illustrate specific social

Table 5.1. Verbal social-interpersonal behavior

Social behavior	Nature of verbal interaction	
Verbal content	*Initiate (examples)*	*Receive (examples)*
1. Greetings	"Hello Tom."	"Hi, how are you?"
2. Praise	"That's a nice shirt you have on.	"Thank you."
3. Positive information	"I got paid today."	"That's nice."
4. Negative information	"I lost my glasses."	"I'm sorry to hear that."
5. Neutral information	"I watched TV last night."	"What did you see?"
6. Negative feedback	"You can't go to the store."	"Why?"
7. Criticism	"You're late for work."	"I'm sorry. I'll be here on time tomorrow."
8. Demands	"Please take off your hat."	"OK, I will."
9. Requests (questions)	"What would you like to drink?"	"I'll have a large 7-Up."
Verbal quality	*Description*	
1. Latency (time between social stimulus and response)	In conversation latency should be short (1–2 seconds). In hostile situations, longer response latency may help diffuse anger (e.g., count to 10 before responding).	
2. Volume (loudness of voice)	Volume of voice should be neither too loud nor too soft. Volume should also be geared to the situation (e.g., church or public park).	
3. Modulation (affect of voice)	Voice quality should fluctuate up and down rather than maintain a constant tone.	
4. Fluency (smoothness of verbal delivery)	The verbal delivery of a message should be smooth and not characterized by frequent interruptions (e.g., uh, um, etc.).	
5. Duration (length of response)	The duration of a response should be sufficiently long to deliver the intended message.	

skills training procedures. This discussion is followed by a summary of recurring issues in the social skills curriculum area.

DETERMINING SOCIAL-INTERPERSONAL OBJECTIVES

Behavioral objectives in the social-interpersonal curriculum area are best identified by analyzing the social expectations of specific settings (e.g., home, school, community, and work). Several different methods have been suggested for accomplishing this task. Williams, Hamre-Nietupski, Pumpian, McDaniel-Marx, and Wheeler (1978) referred to this process as a normative analysis. A normative analysis is accomplished by determining the social skills that are typically performed by nonhandicapped persons in a particular setting. This analysis may include the frequency and duration of specific social responses in relation to specific interpersonal contexts. For example, nonhandicapped adolescents may be observed at a school dance to identify the normal social expectations. The goals and objectives that evolve from this analysis reflect those skills that will enable a person to function as normally as possible. By teaching a handicapped individual to behave according to social norms, the chances of that person functioning successfully in community life are increased.

Table 5.2. Nonverbal social-interpersonal skills

Social behavior	Examples
1. Eye contact	Looks at person when talking or listening
2. Facial expression	Smiles when happy or hears good news; frowns when sad or hears sad news
3. Posture	Sits or stands upright; does not slouch
4. Interpersonal distance	Stands an appropriate distance from other person when speaking or listening
5. Physical appearance	Wears clothing that is in style and is appropriate for the occasion. Also has hair style that is similar to same age, non-handicapped peers
6. Hygiene	Maintains neat and clean appearance by bathing regularly, using deodorant, brushing teeth, shaving, and combing hair
7. Physical contact	Does not touch or hug strangers, shakes someone's hand when being introduced or saying good-bye, refrains from excessive hand shaking, and reserves more intimate physical contact (e.g., embracing) for close friends or relatives
8. Cooperative work and play	Participates willingly with other people in completing household chores and work assignments. Engages in cooperative and/or competitive social/leisure activities (see Chapter 6)
9. Social anonymity	Sits or walks within an interpersonal context without drawing undue attention to oneself. Sits in doctor's office waiting room and looks at a magazine. Walks through the park or mall on a Saturday afternoon with other nonhandicapped persons
10. Independent play/leisure	Attends spectator events in the community; plays solitaire game activities in the presence of other people (see Chapter 6)

A normative analysis is accomplished by determining the social skills that are typically performed by nonhandicapped persons in a particular setting.

Brown, Branston, Hamre-Nietupski, Pumpian, Certo, and Gruenewald (1979) suggested the use of an ecological inventory strategy to identify normal behavior standards. In this strategy, curriculum content is determined by an in-depth analysis of the individual in relation to his/her home community. This analysis includes the range of school, domestic, vocational, and community environments that a person is likely to encounter. As a result of this approach, specific social-interpersonal skills are identified that are required for an individual to function as normally as possible in the home community.

Figure 5.1 depicts the hierarchical procedures that are followed to generate specific skill inventories from this curriculum development strategy. By using this strategy, it is possible to identify a wide range of social situations that are likely to be experienced in various environments.

Because it is unlikely that moderately and severely handicapped persons can be taught to effectively respond to all possible situations, it is necessary to prioritize situations and skills that will most help a person to function successfully in an interpersonal context. Goldfried and D'Zurilla (1969) described a behavior-analytic model for prioritizing behavioral objectives related to social competence. Procedural guidelines from this model include: 1) situational analysis; 2) response enumeration; and 3) response evaluation.

Identify social environments within community functioning domains

School	Home	Work	Community (recreational)	Community (general)
1. Classroom	1. Kitchen	1. Work station	1. Movie theatre	1. Grocery
2. Hallway	2. Living room	2. Break room	2. Restaurant	2. Pharmacy
3. Lunch room	3. Recreation room	3. Locker room	3. Bowling alley	3. Bank

Describe social-interpersonal situations that occur within the social environment of the community functioning domains

Work

Work station	Break room	Locker room
1. Requests for help with work	1. Small talk/conversation	1. Greetings
2. Criticism about work performance	2. Social invitations	2. Discussion of weather, sports, etc.
3. Praise for work performance	3. Refuse requests	3. Requests for assistance (e.g., with clothes, locker, etc.)

Delineate specific social skills that are required in order to function effectively within various social situations

Figure 5.1. Strategy for developing community-referenced curriculum content including social-interpersonal skills. See Tables 5.1 and 5.2 for detailed listing of social-interpersonal skills that may be required in specific social-interpersonal situations.

Situational Analysis

As an initial step, a large sample of social-interpersonal situations should be identified. This sample could include general situations that have a high likelihood of confronting a large number of people and/or specific situations that are only experienced by a particular individual. For example, we all experience common situations (e.g., we are introduced to new people), and we experience unique situations that others are not likely to encounter in the same manner (e.g., criticism at work). The procedures for identifying interpersonal situations include: 1) self-observation; 2) direct behavioral observation; and 3) interviews or questionnaires involving persons familiar with the individual or group of individuals that is of concern.

Self-observation involving moderately and severely handicapped persons can consist of personal interviews and simplified self-recording procedures. Examples include direct questions ("When do you feel uncomfortable talking to others?") and use of a tape recorder diary to document good and bad experiences. Although the accuracy of information obtained through self-observation may be questionable, the potential usefulness of this information should not be excluded. If self-observation procedures are used, these procedures should be accompanied by direct behavior observation techniques. One behavior observation method is anecdotal recording of the frequency of particular situations (e.g., number of social greetings given and/or received). These observations should be conducted in a variety of different situations (e.g., home, school, work, community). Finally, interviews or questionnaires with significant others should be conducted. For moderately and severely handicapped persons, these significant others may be peers, parents, siblings, teachers, work supervisors, group home supervisors, or community sales personnel. Figure 5.2 provides a sample questionnaire that was designed to identify social skill program priorities. From such interviews and questionnaires with significant others, a comprehensive listing and description of commonly encountered social-interpersonal situations can be generated.

Functional Living Skills

We are working with groups of residents in an attempt to teach them more effective skills for getting along well with others and expressing themselves in a more appropriate manner. In setting group and individual goals we are very interested in what you see as their most crucial needs in this area. According to your knowledge regarding all the residents in your cottage, would you please rank the following eight social skills on the basis of which ones you feel are most in need of improvement. For example a "1" would indicate that skill area you feel is of top priority for your residents and an "8" would indicate the lowest priority. Any comments about the skill areas listed or any additional skills not included in this list would be most appreciated. Thank you so much for your help.

Rank

1. Turn down requests (borrow your radio, date, money, "pick-up")   _____
   Comments:

2. Express personal limitations (admit ignorance, admit confusion,   _____
   ask for help)
   Comments:

3. Initiating social contacts (conversation with a stranger, ask for date)   _____
   Comments:

4. Expressing positive feelings (compliment a friend, tell a girlfriend   _____
   or boyfriend you really like them)
   Comments:

5. Handling criticism (apologize when at fault, ask for constructive   _____
   criticism, ask whether you have offended someone, discuss
   someone's criticism)
   Comments:

6. Differing with others (express differing opinion, resist unfair demand,   _____
   tell friend you don't like what they are doing)
   Comments:

7. Assertion in consumer situations (resist sales pressure, request   _____
   service in restaurant, return defective items to a store)
   Comments:

8. Giving negative feedback (tell someone you don't like what they   _____
   are doing, ask person to stop blowing smoke in your face)
   Comments:

   Additional comments:

Figure 5.2. Sample questionnaire for identifying social skill program priorities.

Response Sampling

Once problematic or frequently encountered social situations are identified, Goldfried and D'Zurilla (1969) recommended that potential responses to these situations be listed. This procedure involves presenting the selected situations to a group of individuals and requesting that they respond. The individuals from whom the responses are sampled should be familiar with the target population of concern and/or be considered experts in the particular social-interpersonal skill area. As a result of this sampling process, a range of possible solutions can be identified for each social situation.

From interviews and questionnaires with significant others, a comprehensive listing and description of commonly encountered social-interpersonal situations can be generated.

Response Evaluation

For each interpersonal situation and range of responses, significant others should be consulted regarding the standards for effective behavior. Goldfried and D'Zurilla suggested that a rating scale be used to identify a rank ordering of responses to specific situations, from inferior to effective. The response that was ranked as most effective to a specific interpersonal situation would then be selected as a training objective. An example questionnaire for evaluating the effectiveness of specific responses is presented in Figure 5.3.

As a result of such a rank ordering, an objective scoring system for measuring social-interpersonal effectiveness can be developed. Based on the above example, Figure 5.4 is the resulting scoring system for evaluating how one introduces himself/herself to other people.

In this section, several strategies were suggested for generating socially valid objectives for social-interpersonal skills training. However, the teaching of socially valid behaviors does not in itself guarantee socially valid changes (Minkin, Brauckman, Minkin, Timbers, Timbers, Fixsen, Phillips, & Wolf, 1976). According to Kazdin (1977), the major criteria for evaluating behavior change is how well the client performs relative to others *and* how competently the client is perceived by others. Consequently, it is not only important to teach people to perform in a "normative" manner, it is also important to involve significant others in the evaluation of outcome. Instructional goals, training techniques, and outcome measures should be developed to reflect socially relevant and socially acceptable standards.

In large part the social relevance and acceptability of specific behaviors are determined by the social context. Because the socially competent person must perform appropriately under a variety of stimulus conditions, the individual must be able to perceive the critical aspects of specific situations and alter his/her response accordingly. Such social perception is extremely important when a person encounters social situations with different people in different settings. For example, it may be socially appropriate to act differently with close friends as compared with strangers. Similarly, social behavior standards are different in church compared to a local bowling alley.

Functional Living Skills

Several interpersonal situations have been developed which we would like you to rank order in regard to interpersonal effectiveness. Please read each of the situations and rank order each response grouping from 1 to 5. A rank of 1 would indicate that you feel the particular response grouping is the most appropriate and effective way of handling the situation. A rank of 5 would be the least appropriate and least effective of the response categories listed.

An appropriate and effective response is defined as clear and honest communication which a appropriate to the situation. an appropriate response should not involve a verbal attack on another person.

Based on your experiences with mentally retarded adults and/or assertiveness training your ratings of the responses will be very helpful in our setting appropriate goals for our classes. Thank you so much for your cooperation.

Situation: A new person starts work at your work table. You see this person for the first time and you say:

_____ Welcome.
I'm glad to meet you.
Hi.
Hello.

_____ Irrelevant comment
Nothing
I don't want to meet you.

_____ Hello, My name is _____. What's your name?
Hello, I'm _____. What's your name? I hope you like working here.
Hi, What's your name? My name is _____.

_____ Hi, I'm _____.
Hello, I'm _____. It's nice to meet you.
Hello, My name is _____.

_____ Well, hello. My name is _____. What's yours? Will you be my best
friend?
Hi, welcome. I'm _____. Who are you? I like you. Please be my friend.

Figure 5.3.   Content effectiveness questionnaire.

Behavioral objectives in the social-interpersonal skill area should reflect this sensitivity to social context. In developing social skill objectives, the conditions of performance should be spelled out very clearly to identify the relevant social stimuli. Two example objectives are presented to highlight the importance of social context in interpersonal performance:

When seated at a school play with peers, the student will watch the stage and refrain from talking during the play during 90% of the observation intervals.

When seated at an outdoor sports event with peers, the student will watch the field, talk with peers, and cheer appropriately during 90% of the observation intervals.

After objectives have been identified, instructional procedures must be developed. Procedures are described for teaching new social skills, maintaining previously acquired skills, and promoting generalization to more naturalistic situations.

```
Situation—Social Introductions

5—Must include: a social greeting (e.g., "Hi," "Hello," "Howdy"), inform person
    of name (e.g., "My name is _____"), and request other person's name
    (e.g. "What's your name?")
    Example: "Hi, my name is Paul. What's your name?"
    (Order does not affect the score. Additional comments such as "I hope you like
    it here," do not add to score.)

4—Includes two of above three
    Examples: "Hi. My name is Paul."
              "Hello. What's your name?"
              "My name is Paul. What's your name?"

3—Includes on one of above.
    Examples: "Hello."
              "Glad to meet you."
              "What's your name?"

2—Small talk response such as "How are you?" "How's it going?" "Are you new
    here?"

1—Introduction similar to any of the above three categories plus an overly friendly
    statement.
    Examples: "Hello, my name is Paul. What's your name? Will you be my best
              friend."
              "Hi. What's your name? Please be my friend. I like you."
```

Figure 5.4.   Verbal content scoring system.

INSTRUCTIONAL PROCEDURES

Several different teaching strategies have been used to facilitate the social-interpersonal skill development of moderately and severely handicapped individuals. These strategies are subsumed under the following instructional approaches:

1. Environmental arrangement
2. Response instruction
3. Consequence arrangement
4. Instructional combinations

The first three approaches have been used in isolation to promote social-interpersonal gains. The most common practice has been to combine two or three of these procedures.

Environmental Arrangement

The potential influence of planful environmental arrangements on social skill development of moderately and severely handicapped persons has received minimal attention in the research literature. These arrangements set the stage for students to perform socially effective or ineffective behavior. The lack of attention that has been given to these variables is surprising, given the importance that has been attributed to the social context in discussions of social-interpersonal behavior. Environmental variables that may influence social-interpersonal behavior are: 1) integration with non-handicapped persons; 2) physical setting; 3) materials that are presented; and 4) scheduling of activities.

Integration of Handicapped with Nonhandicapped Individuals.

The impact of P.L. 94-142 and Section 504 of the Rehabilitation Act has created an atmosphere that strongly supports efforts to integrate handi-capped and nonhandicapped persons in school and postschool settings. One of the arguments in support of integrated opportunities is founded on the basis of the assumed social benefits experienced by the handicapped person in these interactions. Exposure to more socially competent models is likely to enhance the social-interpersonal development of moderately and severely handicapped persons.

One study that demonstrated a positive influence of social integration involved handicapped preschoolers. In this study, the ratio of handicapped to nonhandicapped students present in free-play areas was systematically altered (Peterson & Haralick, 1977). The results of this investigation re-vealed that the handicapped youngsters engaged in more sophisticated play behavior when in association with nonhandicapped persons rather than when associating with only their handicapped peers. However, other re-search has demonstrated that significant changes in the social behavior of severely handicapped students does not occur strictly as a function of their being in association with nonhandicapped peers (Snyder, Appolloni, & Cooke, 1977). Snyder et al. further state that the degree of social benefit experienced by the handicapped individual may be increased by training activities directed at the nonhandicapped peers.

Recently, a variety of inservice materials has been developed for non-handicapped students to prepare them for involvement with moderately and severely handicapped individuals. Whether these materials and ac-tivities result in improved social-interpersonal performance remains to be demonstrated. However, the gains attained by nonhandicapped peers may provide sufficient support for integrated educational opportunities. For ex-ample, Voeltz (1980, 1982) found that integrated experiences were associ-ated with increased acceptance of severely handicapped students by their nonhandicapped schoolmates. These changes may contribute to a more fa-vorable environment for persons with severe handicaps as they work and live in their home communities with nonhandicapped peers.

Another integration arrangement involves interaction between higher and lower functioning handicapped peers. The social learning literature has documented the powerful influence of peer modeling (Bandura, 1969). How-ever, this research was conducted with nonhandicapped individuals. In re-search involving severely handicapped youngsters, Morris and Dolker (1974) documented the effectiveness of a higher functioning peer on the cooperative ball-rolling behavior of a profoundly retarded child. The poten-tial benefit of such an arrangement has not been investigated with older moderately and severely handicapped persons and other more sophisticated social skills.

Most integration studies have included preschool and elementary stu-dents in public school settings. There is a dearth of literature involving the integration of adolescent and adult handicapped persons with nonhandi-capped persons in nonschool settings. Future research must address the potential social benefit accrued by handicapped individuals interacting with nonhandicapped persons in vocational, community, and domestic settings.

Although the research evidence in support of integration is somewhat limited, there is *no* support that integration is harmful for moderately and severely handicapped individuals or for the nonhandicapped participants. This evidence argues against strict homogeneity of groupings on the basis of functioning level and suggests that integrated opportunities be provided for handicapped persons in school and postschool situations.

> **Future research must begin to address the potential social benefit accrued by handicapped individuals interacting with nonhandicapped persons in vocational, community, and domestic settings.**

Physical Setting   Different social-interpersonal behaviors may be required in different physical settings (e.g., public park, restaurant, or church). If moderately and severely handicapped persons are to develop their social-interpersonal repertoire fully, they must be given the opportunity to experience the unique situational demands of a wide variety of settings. By limiting one's exposure to various settings, a person's chance to learn more effective behavior is substantially reduced. Parents, teachers, and adult service providers must share responsibility for expanding the opportunities of moderately and severely handicapped persons to explore and experience their home communities fully.

Additional setting variables that may influence social-interpersonal behavior include background music, volume, number of people, size of room, type of lighting, and physical accessibility. Although researchers have investigated the effect of these conditions in relation to other behaviors (e.g., work productivity and hyperactivity), none of the work has specifically investigated the influence of these variables on the social-interpersonal development of moderately and severely handicapped persons.

Materials   Much of our social-interpersonal behavior involves manipulation of materials, particularly social/leisure materials. Most of these materials are manufactured and marketed with a certain age group in mind. In many cases, materials intended for nonhandicapped preschoolers have been provided for moderately and severely handicapped adolescents and adults. As a result, the moderately and severely handicapped person is often viewed as socially immature and incapable of adult-like behavior. For example, consider the different impressions that are generated from observing a person play with colored blocks versus a Rubik's Cube. Although the materials are similar, the Rubik's Cube is clearly more appropriate for adolescents and adults.

Availability and proximity of social/leisure materials are also contributing variables to the degree of social-interpersonal behavior evidenced by moderately and severely handicapped persons. At a minimum, these individuals must be given access to age-appropriate materials. Beyond increasing availability, the strategic location of these materials may encourage greater activity and allow for greater spontaneity in social-interpersonal behavior (Wehman, 1979). Wehman (1977) found that involvement with leisure materials was greatly increased for profoundly retarded persons by simply moving materials closer to them. Given the mobility and sensory deficits frequently associated with severe and profound retardation, it seems that adjusting the proximity of social/leisure materials and increasing exposure to these materials could promote more productive social-interpersonal behavior. Adaptive switches and wheelchair modifications have enabled persons with severe physical disabilities to interact more frequently and spontaneously with social/leisure materials. (See Chapter 6 for a more in-depth discussion of leisure skills instruction.)

> **Availability and proximity of social/leisure materials are also contributing variables to the degree of social-interpersonal behavior evidenced by moderately and severely handicapped persons.**

Scheduling of Activities   Planful scheduling arrangements can promote social-interpersonal development. These arrangements include scheduled opportunities for people to interact with others (e.g., social/recreation evenings), contingent access to preferred activities, and contiguous scheduling. Contingent access to preferred activities can be used to encourage individuals to participate in social activities that they otherwise might avoid. For example, access to dessert at a favorite ice cream shop could be made contingent on participation in a less preferred social-recreation outing (e.g., bowling). Contiguous scheduling refers to the planful sequencing of two or more events in an attempt to encourage prosocial behavior and discourage inappropriate behavior. Strain (1975) reported on such an arrangement involving retarded children. In this study, sociodramatic activities were scheduled prior to a free-play period. The sociodramatic activities involved reading stories to children, with each child acting out the various characters. In the free-play period that immediately followed, the frequency and appropriateness of the children's social play were increased.

> **Contingent access to preferred activities can be used to encourage individuals to participate in social activities that they otherwise might avoid.**

Systematic manipulation of environmental conditions may prove to be very effective and efficient instructional strategies for facilitating social skill development. A major advantage of procedures of this type is that the resulting social behaviors may be more spontaneous and not under the control of artificial reinforcers (Wehman, 1979). Far too often, these environmental arrangements are overlooked in instructional programming with handicapped individuals.

Response Instruction

Although careful arrangement of environmental conditions may facilitate more productive social-interpersonal behavior, moderately and severely handicapped persons frequently require more direct instruction. Task analysis, teacher instructions, and response chaining are instructional strategies that have been used successfully with this population to teach a variety of important skills. As these techniques have been applied to the social-interpersonal performance of moderately and severely handicapped persons, corresponding improvement in social-interpersonal performance has been observed.

Task Analysis Task analysis is one of the first steps in a more direct approach toward enhancing social-interpersonal development. With task analysis, the component behaviors of specific objectives are listed in serial order. These component behaviors are smaller behavioral requirements and are more easily attainable than the larger social-interpersonal objectives. Independent play, cooperative games, conversational speech, and interpersonal communication content are all examples of social-interpersonal objectives that have been task analyzed to facilitate skill acquisition by handicapped individuals. A sample task analysis for requesting assistance in a store is provided in Table 5.3. After objectives have been task analyzed, teacher instruction must be directed at the component steps. These steps must be chained together, and reinforcement delivered contingent on performance of the target behaviors.

Teacher Instruction If individuals do not independently perform component steps of the task analyses, teacher assistance is necessary. One method of providing such assistance is through verbal instruction. Verbal instructions include indirect suggestions (e.g., "It's free time"), general statements to perform an entire task analysis (e.g., "Tom, play a record"), and specific directions regarding component steps of a task analysis (e.g., "Tom, pick up a record"). In addition to verbal instructions, gestural prompts and model demonstrations may be necessary to ensure correct performance. Gestural prompts are usually provided by the instructor, who points out the correct action. In this example, a gestural prompt might consist of the teacher pointing to the record at the same time he/she is delivering the verbal direction. A model prompt would involve the instructor demonstrating the required action (e.g., picking up the record). As with gestural prompts, model demonstrations are usually provided in conjunction with verbal instructions.

Table 5.3. Task analysis of asking for assistance

Step 1 Get clerk's attention (e.g., "Excuse me")
Step 2 Make eye contact
Step 3 State what you are looking for (e.g., "I'm trying to find gloves")
Step 4 Request assistance (e.g., "Where are they please?")
Step 5 Thank person for assistance (e.g., "Thank you")

Alternative task analysis for nonverbal student
Step 1 Tap counter
Step 2 Make eye contact
Step 3 Point to picture of desired item
Step 4 Shrug shoulders
Step 5 Smile and/or sign thank-you

Verbal instructions include indirect suggestions (e.g., "It's free time"), general statements to perform an entire task analysis (e.g., "Tom, play a record"), and specific directions regarding component steps of a task analysis (e.g., "Tom, pick up a record").

Finally, if verbal, gestural, and model instructions are insufficient (i.e., do not result in correct performance), graduated physical guidance may be necessary. With graduated physical guidance, the instructor provides only as much physical assistance as is necesary to enable the person to successfully perform the targeted objective. In this example, some individuals may need to be touched at the elbow to initiate the action of picking up the record, whereas others may require hand-over-hand guidance. These two levels of graduated guidance are commonly differentiated as partial physical (PP) or total physical (TP) assistance.

Most commonly instructional sequences include combinations of these various prompt levels. One prompting system that combines each of the previously presented teacher instructions into a sequential ordering is the system of least prompts. This system requires the student to perform at his/her most independent level prior to the teacher providing assistance. Figure 5.5 provides a flow chart of the decisions that are necessary to properly use this system. By providing students with consistent instruction and systematic fading of teacher assistance, the system of least prompts has enabled moderately and severely handicapped persons to acquire a variety of functional skills.

Provide indirect instruction
("It's free time.")
↓
Provide general instruction
("Tom, play a record.")
↓
Wait 3 to 5 seconds for independence on step 1
(Pick up record)
↓
If step 1 is not done, provide specific verbal instruction
("Tom, pick up record.")
↓
If step 1 is not done, repeat specific verbal instruction
and point to record
↓
If step 1 is not done, repeat verbal instruction and
demonstrate picking up the record
↓
If step 1 is not done, repeat verbal instruction and touch
student's elbow to initiate picking up action
↓
If step 1 is not done, repeat verbal instruction and hand-over-
hand guide picking up the record

Figure 5.5. System of least prompts.

> **The system of least prompts requires the student to perform at his/her most independent level prior to the teacher providing assistance.**

Reinforcing Consequences

After a specific social behavior has been performed, its reoccurrence is dependent on the presence or absence of reinforcing consequences. Preferably, these reinforcing consequences are the natural result of performing socially appropriate behaviors. For instance, after requesting assistance in a polite manner, the store clerk reinforces the individual by being friendly and helping locate the item. This reinforcing response to a request increases the likelihood of that individual making similar requests in similar situations.

When naturally occurring events are not reinforcing enough to establish specific social skill behaviors, additional consequences must be arranged. These may include externally administered reinforcers and/or self-delivered reinforcement. Externally administered reinforcers are those events that are delivered by others (e.g., teachers, supervisors, parents) contingent on the occurrence of targeted social-interpersonal behavior. Reinforcers that are used with moderately and severely handicapped persons are food, drink, social praise, tokens, activities, and tangible items. By far, social praise is the most frequently used reinforcer. When social praise is not effective, highly individualized reinforcers must be selected and contingently delivered along with social praise. Eventually, these additional reinforcers are gradually faded until occasional social praise is sufficiently powerful to maintain the target behaviors. For example, social praise and tokens could be used to reinforce complimenting peers. Once this behavior is being performed consistently the tokens could be gradually eliminated until the behavior is maintained by occasional social praise from the teacher and a "thank you" from peers.

In addition to externally delivered reinforcement, self-reinforcement is another strategy that has been used to strengthen socially appropriate behavior. With self-reinforcement, moderately and severely handicapped individuals provide themselves with reinforcers for performing targeted social-interpersonal objectives. For example, attendance at an evening social club could be self-reinforced by the purchase of a soda at the completion of the evening. A recent study by Matson and Andrasik (1982) involving mentally retarded adults reported on the use of self-reinforcement for a variety of social-interpersonal objectives. The adults in this study used self-reinforcement to improve the following social skills: introductions, greetings, requests, asking favors, asking questions, sharing, complimenting, and talking politely.

> **Attendance at an evening social club could be self-reinforced by the purchase of a soda at the completion of the evening.**

Reinforcing consequences play a significant role in instructional programs involving moderately and severely handicapped persons. Every effort should be made to establish reinforcers that maintain behaviors for long periods of time. Naturally occurring consequences and self-reinforcement are methods that should be emphasized in social-interpersonal skill training programs. These two methods are further described in a subsequent section as generalization programming procedures.

Instructional Packages

Given the severe learning problems experienced by many persons who are moderately or severely handicapped, combinations of environmental arrangements, response instruction, and reinforcing consequences are usually necessary. Numerous instructional packages are possible from various combinations of the previously presented procedures. These combinations increase the probability that handicapped persons will acquire a more effective repertoire of social-interpersonal skills.

One specific combination of instructional procedures evolved directly from the work of Salter (1949) and Wolpe (1958). Salter's book, *Conditioned Reflex Therapy,* was the first published report of a direct instructional therapy for interpersonal relations inhibitions. In 1958 Wolpe popularized Salter's clinical technique by introducing the term *assertiveness training.* By using modeling and behavioral rehearsal, Wolpe arranged for his clients to engage in behaviors that previously had been sources of debilitating anxiety for them. The successful experiences that these clients had during assertiveness training served a deconditioning function for the previously associated anxiety. Wolpe's work was conducted with individuals who presumably had the necessary social skills in their repertoires, but were prevented from utilizing them due to maladaptive anxiety.

As the success of Wolpe's assertiveness training procedures became known, clinicians began to apply these techniques to a wider range of interpersonal behaviors and to more diverse subject populations. The modeling, rehearsal, and feedback components of assertiveness training have been found effective with virtually all social-interpersonal behaviors. However, as clinicians have begun to apply these procedures with chronic psychiatric and mentally retarded populations, some program adjustments have been necessary.

With chronic psychiatric patients and mentally retarded individuals, one cannot assume that relieving anxiety alone will enable them to function effectively. In these cases, instruction must be focused on teaching when to respond, what to do, and how to perform. These multiple objectives are met best by a multicomponent instructional package.

The instructional components that have been included in most interpersonal skill training programs are verbal instruction, modeling, behavior rehearsal, response feedback, and natural environment practice. Each of these components is defined and discussed in terms of its contribution to overall program success.

Verbal Instruction This component involves the trainer or teacher informing the client that he/she should engage in a specific behavior at a particular time. For clients who do not know when, what, or how to perform particular social-interpersonal behaviors, verbal instruction or coaching may be necessary for appropriate behavior to occur. This instruction may occur just prior to the social-interpersonal situation or during the actual situation. For example, before being introduced to a new person, the instructor may inform the client how to properly introduce himself/herself. During the introduction, the instructor may provide additional assistance as needed. This coaching enables the client to perform the targeted social objectives at the appropriate time and place.

Modeling   Often, verbal instruction is used in conjunction with modeling so that the client is not only told what to do, but is also shown what to do. With interpersonal skills training programs, videotaped, audiotaped, and live models have been used to demonstrate the targeted social skills. When response deficits exist, repeated exposure to the situation does not change behavior (Eisler and Hersen, 1973; Hersen & Bellack, 1976). In these cases modeling is necessary to facilitate skill acquisition. According to Hersen and Bellack (1977), modeling and verbal instruction produce a powerful treatment combination for teaching social skills to populations evidencing gross deficits in these areas.

With specific populations such as the mentally retarded, modeling has been effective as an educative procedure in dealing with conduct problems, aggression, withdrawal, hyperactivity, and classroom skills (Cullinhan, Kauffman, & LaFleur, 1975). In a review of modeling and the mentally retarded learner, Cullinhan et al. (1975) suggested that certain characteristics of many mentally retarded learners (e.g., highly dependent, low self-esteem) make them particularly sensitive to modeling influences.

Rich and Schroeder (1976) specified several potential aspects of the modeling situation that may facilitate its clinical value. These are the vividness of the model, the novelty of the demonstration, and the use of several peers of the same age and sex as models. Additional factors suggested as contributing toward the success of the modeling situation are the use of high-status, competent, and powerful models; the use of reinforcement following the model's performance; and the use of instructions for the observer to attend to the relevant cues of the model. As a general rule, moderately and severely handicapped persons should be instructed (coached) to observe the model, the modeling situation should be as realistic as possible, and the model's performance should be reinforced. In many cases it may prove advantageous to use nonhandicapped peers as models for effective social-interpersonal performance.

> **With specific populations such as the mentally retarded, modeling has been effective as an educative procedure in dealing with conduct problems, aggression, withdrawal, hyperactivity, classroom skills, and cognitive training.**

Behavior Rehearsal

Behavior rehearsal (or role playing) is a procedure that involves practicing positive responses to interpersonal situations under the supervision of a therapist or instructor (Eisler & Hersen, 1973). Because people learn best by doing, behavior rehearsal is a critical ingredient in interpersonal skills training approaches. In most training situations, behavior rehearsal follows verbal instruction and modeling. After being told and shown what to do, clients are given the opportunity to practice in simulated conditions. If a client was learning how to introduce herself, she might practice the response sequence ("Hi, my name is Jill") two to three times with different people within her class or group.

> **Behavior rehearsal (or role playing) is a procedure that involves practicing positive responses to interpersonal situations under the supervision of a therapist or instructor.**

Feedback

Verbal instruction, modeling, and behavior rehearsal are more effective when feedback is provided following the client's performance. Although response feedback is usually delivered verbally, videotaped and audiotaped feedback means have also been used successfully. The nature of response feedback has varied considerably. In some cases corrective feedback has been provided, and in others contingent reinforcers have been delivered. Corrective feedback includes statements such as "I like it when you look at my eyes while introducing yourself. Next time look right at me." Reinforcing feedback includes contingencies such as praise statements for polite requests and tokens for social initiations.

As part of social skills training with moderately and severely handicapped persons, response feedback is usually provided by the instructor, therapist, or counselor. However, it may be desirable to involve other clients in this process. For more severely handicapped clients, cue cards might be an effective method for assisting them to participate in the feedback process. An example cue card for eye contact and smiling is presented in Figure 5.6. This card might be given to peers as a means of focusing their attention on the importance of eye contact and pleasant facial expression in social-interpersonal situations.

Natural Environment Practice

Many interpersonal skill training programs have included homework assignments for clients to practice social skill behaviors in the natural environment. These assignments are designed to facilitate transfer from the instructional setting to the client's natural environment. Often these assignments are monitored by significant others in the client's environment such as the individual's spouse, parents, houseparent, or institution aide. By involving these individuals with the social skills program, the chances that the new social skills will be used and reinforced in the natural environment are maximized. Depending on the functioning capability of specific clients and cooperation of the significant others, the complexity of the individual homework assignments will vary. For example, Figure 5.7 provides homework assignments that were designed for moderately retarded adults and their group home parents. At a minimum these assignments serve as a communication link between the training environment and natural environment.

```
┌─────────────────────┐
│         EYE         │
│       CONTACT       │
└─────────────────────┘

   ┌─────────────────┐
   │                 │
   │      SMILE      │
   │                 │
   └─────────────────┘
```

Figure 5.6.   Feedback cue cards.

The above components have been combined into a powerful instructional regimen for teaching a variety of social-interpersonal behaviors. Verbal directives are used to inform the individual of the most important aspects of the target behavior. These directions are followed by a modeled demonstration of how to perform. After the verbal explanation and modeled demonstration, the person is given the chance to behaviorally rehearse (role play) the target behavior and receive feedback (i.e., reinforcement and constructive criticism). Finally, encouragement is given for the individual to perform the newly acquired social skills in more natural settings.

This instructional package has been used effectively with several different mentally retarded populations (Bates, 1980; Kelly et al., 1979; Matson & Andrasik, 1982; Rychtarik & Bornstein, 1979). Although the client populations in each of these studies acquired more effective social-interpersonal behavior, the question of long-term maintenance and generalization of skill gains remains.

GENERALIZATION PROGRAM PROCEDURES

The key to social-interpersonal program success is the degree of generalization that occurs. Stokes and Baer (1977) define generalization as: "The occurrence of relevant behavior under different, nontraining conditions (i.e., across subjects, settings, people, behaviors, and/or time)" (p. 350).

In the social-interpersonal area, we are interested in seeing individuals use newly acquired skills with different people in a variety of different places and across different time periods. Stokes and Baer (1977) conducted an extensive review of applied behavior analysis research studies and identified several strategies that have been used to facilitate generalization. Seven of these strategies are subsequently described.

NAME _Glenn_ DATE DUE _5-5-84_

Practice differing with a person who cuts in line in front of you in a store. Include: Get attention "Excuse me," tell him/her you were in line first, and ask him/her to wait until you've finished. Practiced with houseparent? Yes _✓_ Houseparent Signature _J. E. D._ Practice differing with someone who switches your favorite TV show off so that he/she can watch something else. Include: Get attention, tell what you were doing, ask person to change channel back, and suggest an alternative for the other person. Practice with Houseparent? Yes _✓_ Houseparent Signature _Jan E. Davidson_

Practice asking your houseparent for assistance to find a needed item (e.g., measuring cup for coffee). Practiced? _✓_ Practice asking for help to find an item in a store. Practiced? Yes _✓_ Houseparent Signature _Jan E. Davidson_

Please check which of the following that _Glenn_ did particularly well:
Good voice volume _✓_ Smooth talking _____
Good eye contact _✓_ Pleasant facial expression _____
Clear message _✓_

HOMEWORK
NAME _Joan H._ DATE DUE _5-19-84_

Practice introducing yourself to a new person who starts work at your work table. Include: Social greeting ("hi"), inform person of your name, and ask person his/her name.
Practiced? Yes _✓_ Houseparent Signature
Carol Byrne
Please check which of the following that
Joan did particularly well:
Good voice volume _✓_ Smooth talking _✓_
Good eye contact _✓_ Pleasant facial expression _✓_
Clear message _✓_
Comments: _KEEP UP THE GOOD WORK !!_

Practice initiating, sustaining, and terminating a "small talk" conversation regarding the weather. (Include nice social greeting, on-task discussion of today's weather, and a terminating response which acknowledges that it's been nice talking with the person, but you had better go.)
Practiced? Yes _✓_ Houseparent Signature _Carol Byrne_
OVER

Figure 5.7. Homework assignment cards.

Sequential Modification

If generalization fails to occur, the social-interpersonal skills training program may need to be implemented across every nongeneralized condition (i.e., responses, subjects, settings, or experimenters). For example, if you have taught an individual to play pinball, this person may need to be taught similarly to play other games in the arcade. If you have instructed a student to chat in the classroom with retarded peers, further training may be needed in different places and with different partners to promote generalization to these places and people.

Introduction to Natural Maintaining Contingencies

Skill selection, open communication, and exposure to natural contingencies are all factors that influence generalization. If the social-interpersonal objectives selected are behaviors that are commonly encountered in natural situations, there is a far greater chance that these behaviors will be reinforced in nontraining environments. The effect of functional skills selection can be accented by openly communicating with significant others who are in a position to reinforce newly acquired skills in a variety of community settings. Finally, planful exposure of a person to natural settings wherein newly acquired social skills are required may result in natural payoffs for these behaviors.

Train Sufficient Exemplars

According to Stokes and Baer (1977), generalization to untrained stimulus conditions or untrained responses can be programmed by training sufficient exemplars. For example, Stokes, Baer, and Jackson (1974) found that generalization of children's greeting responses was not evidenced after training by one experimenter. However, after receiving training from a second experimenter (a second exemplar), the children were able to greet over 20 members of the institution staff appropriately.

The possibilities of this method for improving generalization of social-interpersonal skills are infinite. Generalized toy play could be taught by providing instruction across multiple toys. Appropriate restaurant behavior could be promoted by exposing a person to a variety of different restaurants. This method for improving the generalization of social-interpersonal behavior seems viable and needs to be empirically documented. It remains to be demonstrated how many exemplars are needed to establish generalized performance for particular social skills and specific subject populations.

Train Loosely

Training loosely refers to the process of reducing the discriminative aspects of the instructional situation. By reducing these discriminative aspects, the training situation more closely resembles the post-training conditions. For example, rather than conduct conversational instruction in a classroom setting with token reinforcers, instruction may take place in a cafeteria setting with occasional social reinforcers. Although there are some advantages of training loosely from a generalization perspective, more consistent instruction may be necessary for lower functioning client populations to acquire social-interpersonal skills. Without acquisition, the issue of generalization is irrelevant.

Use Indiscriminable Contingencies

In the same manner that training loosely promotes generalization, the use of indiscriminable reinforcement contingencies makes program conditions more difficult to identify. Consequently, the post-training conditions are more similar to training conditions and generalization is enhanced. Two procedures that result in indiscriminable contingencies are: 1) intermittent schedules of reinforcement; and 2) delays in reinforcement delivery. Once new social skills have been established, the schedule of reinforcement should be gradually reduced until the newly established behaviors are maintained by natural reinforcers. If reinforcement (e.g., tokens) had been provided for each social greeting response during initial skill training, this schedule would need to be made less predictable to promote generalization. For example, the continuous schedule could be reduced to a fixed ratio of two schedule (FR-2). This schedule would result in reinforcement being delivered after every second greeting response. Further reductions in the discriminable nature of the contingency could be made by changing to a variable ratio schedule. A variable ratio of five schedule (VR-5) would result in tokens being delivered on an average of every five greeting responses. As the frequency of reinforcement becomes more intermittent and less predictable, the new social-interpersonal skills become less dependent on external reinforcement and generalization is enhanced.

> **Two procedures that result in indiscriminable contingencies are: 1) intermittent schedules of reinforcement; and 2) delays in reinforcement delivery.**

Kazdin and Polster (1973) examined the effects of a continuous reinforcement schedule versus an intermittent reinforcement schedule on the social interaction of two retarded individuals. The subject who received continuous reinforcement ceased to interact after the program, whereas the subject who was intermittently reinforced continued to interact with peers after the program was terminated.

The delay of reinforcement produces a similar effect on generalization performance as does the intermittent schedule. Specifically, if one were immediately reinforced for each greeting response, a delay in this reinforcer would result in a reduction in the dependency of the response on the external reinforcer. Consequently, generalization may be promoted by reducing the predictability of external reinforcement and allowing for naturally occurring consequences (e.g., a reciprocal greeting) to take on reinforcing qualities.

Program Common Stimuli

The training situation should contain stimuli that are encountered in natural settings where social-interpersonal behaviors are required. This procedure results in an increase in the range of natural stimuli that is associated with new social-interpersonal gains. In conducting social-interpersonal skills training, stimuli common to the natural environment can be programmed by: 1) conducting group training; 2) using peer tutors; and 3) developing realistic natural environment situations.

Group training usually involves individuals who will interact with each other in post-treatment settings. As a result, changes in social interaction patterns within the group are more likely to generalize. The use of peer tutors for social-interpersonal skill instruction serves a similar function as group training for facilitating generalization. Because the peer tutor may be present in the post-training environment, the occurrence of newly established social behavior is more likely. Finally, physical stimuli that are common to generalization settings can be arranged in a training setting to more accurately simulate the generalization environment. If an individual has difficulty resolving interpersonal conflicts over which television show to watch, a television and couch can be arranged in the training setting to simulate the natural situation. By making the training environment similar to the actual environment, generalization is enhanced.

Mediate Generalization

To promote generalization of social-interpersonal behavior from training to post-training situations, it may be advantageous to establish a response as a part of training that is likely to be used with other problems outside of training. This response may be referred to as a mediator. Language, self-recording, and self-reinforcement are all potential mediators that may be useful in promoting generalization. A person may be taught to self-direct a verbal statement (e.g., "good eye contact") to promote more effective performance in a social interaction. Self-recording can be used to monitor a variety of different social-interpersonal behaviors. The act of recording one's own behavior has been demonstrated to be an effective behavior change technique. Self-reinforcement in the form of providing positive consequences for oneself contingent upon a response has also been demonstrated to be a successful means for maintaining behavior after a training program has been terminated.

> Language, self-recording, and self-reinforcement are all potential mediators that may be useful in promoting generalization.

PROGRAM ISSUES AND RECOMMENDATIONS

In conclusion, several recurring issues in the social skill curriculum area need to be emphasized. These include, but are not limited to, the following: 1) curriculum development; 2) age-appropriate goals and materials; 3) antisocial behavior; 4) dependent behavior; 5) adaptations for physically handicapped individuals; 6) sex education; and 7) maintenance and generalization.

Curriculum Development

The development of a social skill curriculum should be a dynamic, ever-changing process. The school, home, and community environments should be assessed frequently to determine those social skills that are most functional for successful interpersonal performance. From such an ecological analysis, functional chronologically age-appropriate curriculum objectives can be identified and sequenced.

Age-Appropriate Goals and Materials

All goals and teaching materials for social skill instruction should be as chronologically age appropriate as possible. For example, play materials for a young severely handicapped child may consist of a spinning top, a jack-in-the-box, and a Big Bird puzzle. With older severely handicapped individuals, age-appropriate play materials might be playing cards, pinball machines, and simple table games. Although the selection of age-appropriate social skill objectives and materials may be difficult, it is necessary for educators to critically examine current practices regarding this standard. By ensuring that all goals and teaching materials are chronologically age-appropriate, the likelihood that severely handicapped persons will acquire useful social skills is increased.

Antisocial Behavior

In addition to an impoverished social skill repertoire, many severely handicapped students emit a variety of antisocial and inappropriate social behaviors. These may include behaviors such as physical aggression, public disrobing, and extreme withdrawal. With behaviors such as these, social skill instruction programs can be strengthened by developing contingencies for both increasing appropriate behavior and weakening inappropriate behavior. Behavior management procedures have proven very useful in reducing the antisocial and inappropriate social behavior of the severely handicapped (Renzaglia & Bates, 1983). It is recommended that less intrusive behavior management procedures (e.g., differential reinforcement) always be explored before resorting to more intrusive techniques (e.g., presentation of aversive consequences).

Dependent Behavior

It is a common observation that severely handicapped students seldom initiate social skill behaviors with each other and frequently direct most of their interpersonal behavior toward adults. Many of our program practices encourage these behaviors by not requiring initiating behaviors and by not arranging for reciprocal peer interactions. Instructors must actively program to promote initiated behavior and peer interaction. For example, during free time the program goal should shift from "plays game with instructor on verbal command" to "initiates game-playing activity with a peer."

Adaptations for Physically Handicapped Individuals

Physical disabilities are frequently associated with severe and profound retardation. In order to maximize the social skill development of these individuals, much attention must be given to the nature of instructional materials, location of these materials, positioning, and location in relation to other people. By positioning an individual properly with materials nearby the likelihood that social skill behaviors will be expressed and reinforced increases.

Sex Education

Social interaction behaviors with the opposite sex are essential social skills. For too long educators have failed to recognize the sexuality of severely handicapped individuals and have neglected to teach these important social skills. Because teachers infrequently teach sex education and the accompanying sexual behaviors, it is not surprising that some severely handicapped persons publicly masturbate and inappropriately display intimate affection. An excellent program designed to teach selected sex education and social skills to severely handicapped persons was reported by Hamre-Nietupski and Williams (1977). Additional programs such as this are needed if appropriate sexual behavior from the severely handicapped is to occur.

Maintenance and Generalization

As discussed previously, procedures to enhance the maintenance and generalization of social skill behaviors should be an integral part of every program. All programs should have provisions for individuals to engage in social skill behaviors in different places, with a variety of people, and with a variety of materials. A critical component of planned transfer of training is the involvement of the family and other community members in carrying out program contingencies. Once new social skill behaviors are established, the reinforcers should be faded and delayed until the person performs under natural stimulus conditions.

SUMMARY

The importance of appropriate social-interpersonal behavior is obvious in virtually all areas of a person's life. For handicapped persons, inadequate social behavior is often cited as the distinguishing feature that makes integration and assimilation into normal community activities more difficult.

This chapter provides a conceptualization of social-interpersonal behavior and a discussion of the major conditions that influence program effectiveness. Numerous references were provided to assist the reader in efforts to apply this material. As greater attention is focused on this curriculum area, the goal of community integration and participation by moderately and severely handicapped persons becomes more probable.

6

LEISURE SKILL INSTRUCTION

LEARNING GOALS

1. Provide four points that form a basis for including leisure skill objectives into the student's IEP.
2. Identify and describe the eight points that characterize an appropriate leisure skill training program.
3. Describe the concept of "age-appropriateness" and discuss how it relates to selection of leisure skill activities.
4. Relate the principle of normalization to recreation and leisure skill training.
5. Identify four different types of recreational adaptations.
6. Describe the major aspects of conducting home and community inventories of a student's leisure needs.
7. Relate the importance of teaching leisure skills in community settings.
8. Describe how a trainer-advocacy approach is related to facilitating community-based leisure for moderately and severely handicapped individuals.

Chapter 5 set the framework for social skill development. However, within the context of social-interpersonal skills are leisure skills, that is, activities in which individuals engage during their free time. Leisure activities may take place with other individuals or may occur in isolation. As more moderately and severely handicapped individuals are deinstitutionalized into the community (Gollay, Freedman, Wyngaarden, & Kurtz, 1978) as well as maintained in their natural homes, the need for *systematic* program inplementation of leisure skills increases (Stein, 1977; Wehman, 1978; Wehman & Schleien, 1981). The importance of recreational services has been observed frequently (Amary, 1975; Benoit, 1955; Stanfield, 1973; Wehman, 1977); however, the critical nature of systematic assessment, skill selection, and instruction for leisure skills has only recently been noted (Snell, 1978; Wehman & Schleien, 1981). Moderately and severely handicapped individuals usually include those with measured IQ's of between 0 and 50, and have been typically labeled as "trainable mentally retarded," "severely profoundly retarded," "autistic," "emotionally disturbed," "deaf-blind," or "multihandicapped." Most of these individuals exhibit substantial learning, behavior, and/or physical handicaps and therefore will not learn leisure skills without systematic instruction.

The purpose of this chapter is to provide guidelines for systematic leisure skill training of severely handicapped persons of all ages. First, a rationale for inclusion of leisure skill training into the educational curriculum is provided. Second, eight characteristics of an appropriate leisure skill program are outlined with supportive literature presented. Finally, guidelines for implementing a *trainer advocacy* approach to community-based recreation are delineated.

A RATIONALE FOR LEISURE SKILL INSTRUCTION

Abundance of Leisure Time

All too often, severely handicapped individuals have not developed the necessary skills to utilize their free time creatively or constructively. They will participate in an educational program for a relatively small part of their day and then have nothing to do during its remainder. Unoccupied time must cease to be the dominant quality of an individual's life-style. Constructive activities must be offered to fill this void. The development skills must be encouraged and systematically programmed as the free time problem is critical. The student's use of leisure time and attitude toward recreation may determine the degree of success he will experience through the educational efforts. Constructive use of free time has become a vital aspect of healthy and normal living, especially since leisure time has become increasingly available for all people.

Limited Engagement in Appropriate Leisure Unless Systematic Instruction Is Provided

Without systematic instruction in leisure skills programming, severely handicapped individuals will not learn the skills necessary to play appropriately (Wehman, 1977). Even after the child has acquired the skill, without systematic instructional strategies (see Snell, 1983, for detailed description of systematic instruction), he/she may never maintain, self-initiate, or generalize the skill for use in other environments. Besides emphasizing the provision of activities that build on the present capabilities of the youth and prevent further disability, systematic instruction must be provided to foster engagement in appropriate leisure activity. Instruction of this sort may include assessing the leisure skill competencies of the individual, careful selection of materials and skills for instruction, and implementation techniques or specific training methods to assist in the acquisition, maintenance, and generalization of the skills.

> **Without systematic instruction in leisure skills programming, severely handicapped individuals will not learn the skills necessary to play appropriately.**

Reduction of Inappropriate Social Behaviors

Severely handicapped children often engage in seemingly inappropriate, unacceptable social behavior. Children that are constructively using their leisure time do not exhibit such behaviors (e.g., body rocking, head banging, violent actions, and social withdrawal), which are typically characteristic of these individuals. Research has clearly indicated that there is an inverse relationship between acquisition of play skills and self-stimulatory, abusive behavior. Recreational activity of a social nature provides opportunities through which the participant can learn to adjust to the social demands of society.

Means of Teaching Social, Domestic, and Communicative Skills

The development of leisure skills in severely handicapped individuals may enhance social, cognitive, domestic, language, and motor skill development. Involvement in leisure and recreational activities offers some of the most effective means for individuals to acquire and develop these skills.

The facilitation of social skill development is acquired through group activity. Children who fail to develop these necessary skills are considered handicapped. The development of cooperative leisure behavior and participation in social activities will lead to making friends, getting along with others, learning to share, compete, cooperate, and take turns, and a more satisfactory social adjustment. An adequate social adjustment is required for successful daily living, including time on the job, in the community, and with friends and family.

Recreation is also a vehicle by which gross and fine motor skills are developed. Inactivity usually results in poor eye-hand coordination, cardio-vascular endurance, agility, dynamic and static balance, manual dexterity, and muscular strength. Because physical development is essential for a healthy body and self-concept, it is critical that severely handicapped students be given every opportunity to experience play and develop physically (Moon & Renzaglia, 1982).

Constructive leisure also contributes to cognitive development. During play and creative activity, individuals will communicate with each other and learn concepts related to language, arithmetic, and other forms of learning that foster academic capabilities. Even for the nonverbal individual, vast amounts of facial and bodily communications are facilitated during play, developing cognitive abilities and broadening the range of knowledge and personal involvement of participants.

Being able to prepare a snack or eat appropriately in a fast-food restaurant is also an example of domestically oriented leisure activity. One of the most frequent social activities enjoyed by a family is eating[1]; therefore, it is easier to participate with the family if the severely handicapped students have appropriate eating skills.

> **Because physical development is essential for a healthy body and self-concept, it is critical that severely handicapped students be given every opportunity to experience play and develop physically.**

A BRIEF REVIEW OF LEISURE PROGRAMS

Leisure skill studies in the past 5 to 10 years have been increasing in the professional literature. A brief review of special education, psychology, recreation, and physical education journals indicate that little attention was given to systematic instruction of age-appropriate skills for severely handicapped youths and adults. Table 6.1 lists over 30 papers that provide a chronology of leisure programs published. Most of these papers documented behavior change through carefully collected data.

A perusal of Table 6.1 indicates several overriding characteristics or trends. These trends include:

1. An emphasis on programs for children more than youth or adults
2. Little or no home-based leisure programs, with institution environments predominating in the earlier part of the past decade
3. At times, marginal emphasis on age-appropriateness of materials

It is noteworthy that few studies are available that emphasize home-based leisure instruction or demonstrate generalization to the home or community. It is perhaps symptomatic of center or school-based instruction that

---

[1]A Harris poll conducted in 1978 documented eating as the most popular form of leisure activity by Americans.

so little attention has been given to showing how leisure can be taught in natural environments where leisure skills will, in fact, be practiced.

In sum, it is the studies in Table 6.1 that form the basis for much of the information in this chapter. The following sections draw as much as possible on these types of data-based articles and papers.

Characteristics of an Appropriate Leisure Skills Program

Once education and recreation professionals begin more regularly to include recreation and leisure instructional objectives into a moderately and severely handicapped student's IEP, then the question turns to: What is an appropriate leisure skills instructional program? Stated another way: What characteristics or attributes should run through an optimal leisure skill program? Eight characteristics of an appropriate leisure program are:

1. A philosophical base that reflects normalization theory and chronological age-appropriateness in curriculum
2. Integration of handicapped with nonhandicapped individuals in recreation settings
3. An opportunity for all handicapped individuals to participate to some degree with the assistance, if necessary, of material, skill, or facility adaptation
4. A behavioral approach to training and instruction
5. A commitment to task analysis and instruction by objectives
6. A commitment to the collection and evaluation of objective data in support of leisure programs
7. The need for leisure instruction to take place in natural community settings with the opportunity to have a trainer-advocate for assistance
8. The need for independent use and access to community-based recreation facility

The Role of Normalization and Integration in Leisure Program Planning

The philosophy of normalization (Wolfensberger, 1972), when applied to leisure skill programming, suggests several major concepts that need to be considered when planning a program. For example, the notion of *chronological age-appropriateness* as a criterion to be used in skill selection (Brown et al, 1979; Wehman & Schleien, 1980) is derived from normalization theory. Contemporary thinking suggests that severely handicapped persons should be allowed the opportunity to engage in leisure activities that are comparable to those engaged in by nonhandicapped peers. Wehman and Schleien (1980) have described procedures for selecting skills in this manner, and Johnson, Ford, Pumpian, Stengart, and Wheeler (1980) have developed a manual that lists numerous chronologically age-appropriate leisure activities as well. This important concept is discussed later. The items below highlight several major aspects of the normalization and leisure interaction.

Table 6.1. Papers and programs related to leisure skills instruction for the severely handicapped

Empirical articles	Category of severe handicap	Child/adolescent/adult	Leisure Activities	Age-Appropriateness	Settings
Whitman, Mercurio, & Caponigri (1970)	Severe retardation	Child	Block passing	Marginal	Institution
Favell (1973)	Severe/profound retardation	Child	Putting pegs in board	Marginal	Institution
Morris & Dolker (1974)	Severe retardation	Child	Ball rolling	Yes	School
Wehman, Karan, & Rettie (1976)	Severe retardation	Adult	Multiple leisure activities	Marginal	Adult day program
Kissell & Whitman (1977)	Profound retardation	Adolescent	Toy play	No	Institution
Wehman & Marchant (1977)	Severe retardation	Child	Playground equipment	Yes	School
Day & Day (1977)	Moderate/severe retardation	Child/adolescent	300 leisure activities	Yes	School
Johnson & Bailey (1977)	Moderate retardation	Adult	Puzzles/card games/clay/painting/weaving/rug-making	Yes	Community half-way house
Wehman (1978)	Severe/profound retardation	Adolescent/adult	Multiple leisure activities	Marginal	Institution
Hopper & Wambold (1977)	Severe retardation	Child	Free play with toys	Yes	School
Wehman, Renzaglia, Berry, Schultz, & Karan (1978)	Severe/profound retardation	Adolescent/adult	Fitness training/table games	Yes	Institution
Wehman & Marchant (1978)	Severe retardation	Child	Free play with toys	Yes	School
Ferrara & Hill (?)	Autistic	Child	Automated and nonautomated toys	Yes	School
Wambold & Bailey (1979)	Severe/profound retardation	Child	Free play with toys	Yes	School
Marchant & Wehman (1979)	Severe retardation	Child	Table games (lotto)	Yes	School, home
Walters & Watters (1980)	Autistic	Adolescent	Physical fitness	Yes	School
Wehman, Schleien, & Kiernan (1980)	Multihandicapped	Adult	Use of instamatic camera	Yes	Adult developmental center, community
Matson & Marchetti (1980)	Moderate/severe retardation	Adult	Operating a stereo	Yes	Institution

Reference		Age	Activity	Marginal	Institution
Adkins & Matson (1980)	Moderate retardation	Adult	Potholder	Yes	School
Tiegerman & Primavera (1981)	Autistic	Child	Object interaction with toys	Yes	School
Donder & Nietupski (1981)	Moderate retardation	Adolescent	Playground skills	Yes	School
Arakaki (1981)	Multihandicapped	Child	Free play with toys	Yes	School
Schleien, Kiernan, & Wehman (1981)	Moderate retardation	Adult	Multiple leisure activities	Yes	Community-group home
Odom (1981)	Moderate/severe retardation	Preschool child	Free play with toys	Yes	School
Horst, Wehman, Hill, & Bailey (1981)	Severe/profound retardation	Adolescent	Frisbee/electronic bowling/cassette player	Yes	Community
Hill & Wehman (1981)	Severe/profound retardation	Adolescent	Electric pinball/fast food restaurant/regular girl scouts	Yes	Community
Schleien, Wehman, & Kiernan (1981)	Severe/profound retardation	Adult	Darts	Yes	Adult development center, community
Hill (1982)	Multihandicapped	Child	Automated toy	Yes	School, home
Bates & Renzaglia (1982)	Profound retardation	Adolescent	Table game	Yes	Institution
Day, Powell, Dy-Az, & Stowitscheck (1982)	Severe retardation	Child	Free play with toys	Yes	School
Nietupski & Svoboda (1982)	Severe retardation/autism	Adult	Lotto game	Yes	Nursing home
Hill, Wehman, & Horst (1982)	Severe/profound retardation	Adolescent	Electric pinball	Yes	School and community
Arakaki (1981)	Profound retardation	Child	Toy play (musical thing, 12 blocks, bean bags)	Yes	School
Graham (1981)	Severely retarded	Adolescent	Lego, Lite Brite, Target, Musical Thing	Marginal	School
Voeltz & DeLong (1981)	Severely retarded	Adolescent	Free leisure activity	Yes	School

[a] This listing also includes unpublished instruments and other sources, which are not listed among the references in the back of this book. Interested readers should contact the senior author for further information on these materials.

> **Contemporary thinking suggests that severely handicapped persons should be allowed the opportunity to engage in leisure activities that are comparable to those engaged in by nonhandicapped peers.**

Normalization as a Multifaceted Process Adherence to the normalization principle involves a variety of practices that are designed to reduce both the "differentness" in appearance and performance of disabled persons while simultaneously expanding the public's degree of acceptance for differentness. Key responsibilities for leisure education service providers include utilizing "culturally normative" techniques with clients, which facilitate acceptance on the part of the public with whom the client will be interacting. For example, recent techniques described by Wehman and Schleien (1980) involving recreational adaptations including material, skill sequence, procedural, and facility modifications have enabled severely disabled adults to participate in such normative leisure activities as bowling and photography (see Participation in Recreation Programs section). Such interventions have the combined effect of developing leisure skills that may be generalized for use in other community settings, enabling the general public to observe developmentally disabled persons participating *successfully* in normal leisure pursuits.

Integration in Recreational Settings Depends on the Involvement of Small Groups Central to this principle is the notion that handicapped people will be accepted more readily by their nonhandicapped counterparts if their numbers in a particular setting do not exceed a proportion which could reasonably be expected to occur through normal interactions. Often cited examples of special camps, large numbers of mentally retarded persons occupying several bowling lanes, and the inclusion of masses of handicapped individuals in swimming pools illustrate the negative effect that such practices may have in leisure settings. It is important to keep the numbers of handicapped individuals small because nonhandicapped individuals will then be more likely to exhibit a greater tolerance.

Grouping Individuals with Different Disabilities Together Successful involvement of disabled persons with nondisabled individuals, not other disability groups, is the ultimate goal of the normalization process. Therefore, instructional or purely recreative pursuits such as horseback riding programs and special event days catering exclusively to disabled members of a community and leagues and tournaments for handicapped participants do *not* achieve the ultimate goal of providing normative recreational environments. It serves no meaningful purpose, other than administrative convenience, to mass handicapped individuals by their presumed category.

> **It is important to keep the numbers of handicapped individuals small because nonhandicapped individuals will then be more likely to exhibit a greater tolerance.**

Involvement in Appropriate Activities in the Community The techniques and procedures described in a later section may be implemented directly with handicapped persons in community leisure service settings in many instances. For example, leisure skill instruction should be conducted in settings and time frames typical of society at large. Also related to the concept of appropriate recreation is the motivation underlying participation. As the ultimate impetus for leisure skill instruction, techniques presented are designed to provide progressive success and achievement on the part of the learner.

Involvement of Handicapped Persons in Community Settings Is Best Achieved by a Cooperative Approach Potential resource persons who can exert a significant influence on the leisure life-style of a disabled person include family members, education and recreation personnel, volunteers, advocate association staff, and municipal recreation and social service personnel. Each of these individuals has an important role to play in developing the skills and abilities necessary for the disabled individual to maximize free time. The approach to leisure skill development illustrated by this text provides for meaningful involvement from *all* persons concerned with this process. Although the assessment procedures and certain adaptation techniques lend themselves to formal education/recreative settings, family members, peers, and others could become readily involved in supplementing and reinforcing leisure skill instruction in home and community settings.

Participation in Recreation Programs

Another major characteristic of an appropriate recreation program for severely handicapped individuals is *participation*. Brown et al. (1979) have advocated the principle of partial participation (i.e., the need to modify or adapt materials or activities to allow the individual to enjoy some degree of participation). A major problem with many leisure activities for the severely handicapped has been that the activities are too passive in nature and do not require participation.

Fortunately, there are a number of adaptations that can be utilized to facilitate partial participation by severely handicapped individuals. Wehman and Schleien (1980) have categorized these into *material, procedural, skill sequence,* and *facility* adaptations. The section below describes examples of each of these adaptations in more depth.

Material Adaptations Materials and equipment used in a recreational activity are frequently barriers to participation because the equipment usually has been designed by and for nonhandicapped individuals. Materials and equipment may be adapted. For example, equipment may be modified to permit bowling by individuals with difficulties in fine and gross motor coordination, balance, and muscular strength required to lift and roll a bowling ball down an alley. The bowling ball may be placed on top of a tubular steel ramp. The bowler then "aims" the ramp at the pins and releases the ball. A bowling ball pusher similar to a shuffleboard stick may also be used to push the ball down the alley. The pusher may be adjusted to various lengths, allowing ambulatory, nonambulatory, short, and tall individuals to play. Another adapted device that can be used by a person unable to lift a conventional ball is a handle-grip bowling ball. Simple palmar grasp and basic gross motor arm movements are required to manipulate this device. Once released, the handle snaps back flush into the bowling ball, allowing the ball to roll toward the pins. These adaptations for bowling can permit many severely physically handicapped persons to enjoy bowling.

Procedural Adaptations Most games or activities have a standard set of procedures, or rules. If an individual's physical condition makes following a particular rule difficult, it may result in the potential participants becoming spectators. Rules can be modified or simplified when teaching a game, and then later shaped to conform to the rules used by nonhandicapped peers. These difficulties need not be insurmountable and may be overcome by changing the original rules.

Basketball requires a player to bounce or dribble the ball every time a step is taken. A change permitting one dribble for several steps may permit an individual with difficulty in eye-hand-foot coordination to become an active member of the team. Perhaps with practice, coordination will improve.

Pool can also be made more accessible to a person who has difficulty discriminating striped from solid balls during a game of eight-ball. Instead of the usual practice of designating certain balls to each participant, players may take turn shooting at any ball on the table, and the individual with the most balls pocketed wins.

> **Rules can be modified or simplified when teaching a game, and then later shaped to conform to the rules used by nonhandicapped peers.**

Rule changes in card games may also be made. For example, concentration requires the players to draw two cards consecutively with the object being to draw the greatest number of pairs. In order to decrease the difficulty of discriminating between numbered and picture cards, all "picture cards" (i.e., jacks, queens, kings) could be assigned the same value.

Modifications in procedures and rules can turn a seemingly impossible task into an enjoyable recreational pursuit. Changing the rules of a complex activity may allow an adolescent or adult to participate in an age-appropriate game or sport, rather than forcing an individual to resort to playing with an age-appropriate toy or participate in a child's game.

Skill Sequence Adaptations One of the most effective ways to teach a severely handicapped individual a recreational activity is to break the skill down into small component steps. These actions are identified through an analysis of the task itself and subsequently sequenced in a logical order. However, often a sequence of steps applicable to a nonhandicapped individual may prove too difficult or impractical for a severely handicapped person to follow.

A hobby such as cooking can provide a clear illustration of the problem. When boiling an egg, a nonhandicapped person may place the egg into a pot of boiling water. It is obvious that this could be a hazardous problem for an individual with physical and/or intellectual limitations. A remedy to this problem is to rearrange the sequence of the component steps of the skill by training the cook to place the egg into the saucepan initially and then fill the pot with cold water. Then bring the water to a boil. This procedure does not alter the final results, but facilitates a safe and practical method of performing this worthwhile leisure pursuit.

A modified skill sequence applicable to the manipulation of a camera can also be implemented. Typically, an individual will first raise the camera to eye level and then places an index finger over the shutter release button. However, individuals lacking sufficient fine motor coordination could initially be trained to position their finger over the shutter release button prior to lifting the camera. In this way, the individual would merely have to depress the button once the camera was appropriately positioned (Wehman, Schleien, & Kiernan, 1980).

Community-based Facility Adaptations The community itself offers many age-appropriate recreational facilities that nonhandicapped individuals regularly use. A local swimming pool, museum, restaurant, library, and church are all public facilities available to handicapped people. Unfortunately, many severely handicapped individuals are denied access to these places and subsequently cannot utilize their leisure time in these environments. This problem is most evident for nonambulatory individuals who are unable to enter public buildings because of narrow doors, inadequate toileting facilities, and absence of access ramps. In addition, transportation to many of these facilities is inadequate. Many of these architectural barriers, however, have been overcome by the installation of wheelchair ramps leading to buildings, enlarged doorknobs, extended handles on drinking fountains, and other equipment adapted for those with severe motor impairments.

Although these physical modifications reduce barriers to utilization, there is one principle that must be seriously considered: interaction of handicapped and nonhandicapped individuals. The handicapped person utilizing the adapted equipment or facility must not, at the same time, be separated from interacting with the community in general. Those modifications should blend in with the standard equipment so not to make any person stand out as being too different. For example, pier fishing could be made accessible to severely physically impaired individuals and retain its normal qualities. Guidelines require:

1. An access walk to the pier of at least a 5-foot width to allow for turning of the wheelchairs
2. The provision of a handrail around the entire pier (which, according to the Virginia Commission of Outdoor Recreation, must be 36 inches high and have a 30-degree angle sloped top for arm and pole rest)
3. A kick plate to prevent foot pedals of wheelchairs from going off the pier
4. A smooth, non-slip surface should be provided on the access walk as well as on the pier

---

The handicapped person utilizing the adapted equipment or facility must not, at the same time, be separated from interacting with the community in general.

The four types of adaptations described above represent the primary ways in which a creative teacher or therapist can reduce failure and frustration for severely handicapped persons. Although it is imperative that these adaptations be individualized (i.e. not provided for the group as a whole) and temporary, it is certain that without these modifications recreational involvement by many handicapped individuals would be nonexistent or minimal at best. A later section presents an illustration of how systematic instruction principles may be applied in conjunction with material and skill sequence modifications to develop and generalize an age-appropriate leisure skill in a severely handicapped person.

> **Although it is imperative that these adaptations be individualized (i.e. not provided for the group as a whole) and temporary, it is certain that without these modifications recreational involvement by many handicapped individuals would be nonexistent or minimal at best.**

Age-Appropriateness of Leisure Activities

Consistent with normalization theory and community integration, it is necessary to identify leisure skills that are age-appropriate. It is essential to ascertain the motor ability level of the student and then match that skill level to age-appropriate activities. Consider the example of a profoundly retarded youth who is taught the baby skill of pulling a plastic frog on a table. An alternative activity might be pulling a level for a pinball or vending machine. Similarly, Wehman et al. (1980) taught a severely multiply handicapped woman how to operate an adapted automatic camera as a substitute activity for placing pegs in a pegboard. The chapter appendix in this chapter has a resource list of age-appropriate leisure activities.

Behavioral Training

The methods component of instructional programs refers to the procedures used to train the desired skills. The most important aspect of this component is that it be understood that training and specific leisure skill instruction must take place in order for the severely handicapped to learn. It cannot be assumed that individuals with severe behavior and/or learning deficits will simply "pick up" leisure activities. Leisure skills must be trained.

Numerous training procedures have been used with moderately and severely handicapped individuals. For example, specific reinforcement strategies have been used to develop cooperative leisure actions with severely retarded children (Favell, 1973; Morris & Dolker, 1974; Wehman & Marchant, 1978). Reinforcement has also been used in a changing criterion strategy that emphasized the behavior shaping of dart throwing skills with severely retarded adults (Schleien, Wehman, & Kiernan, 1982). An extension of this shaping strategy was used in combination with weekly leisure counseling sessions with high-functioning retarded adults in a group home (Schleien, Kiernan, & Wehman, 1981).

Other training arrangements that emphasize manipulating antecedent events have also been designed for the successful implementation of leisure skill programs as well. Modeling and physical prompting (Hopper & Wambold, 1977; Hill, Wehman, & Horst, 1982; Bradtke, Kirkpatrick, & Rosenblatt, 1972; Cuvo, 1978), have been the primary forms of teacher assistance in the initial stages of instruction. Breaking a leisure skill down in a task analysis format has also been helpful (Wehman & Marchant, 1977). As the individual becomes more competent and learns to enjoy the leisure skill more, the more intensive prompts can be faded to verbal instructions. Eventually, the presence of the leisure material should serve as a cue to the individual to initiate constructive actions. The simple presence of more leisure materials may, in fact, lead to an increase in leisure activity by severely retarded individuals (Reid, Willis, Forman, & Brown, 1978; Wehman, 1978).

With very low-functioning, nonambulatory, profoundly retarded persons it may be necessary to develop a special material. Hill (in press), for example, demonstrated how the use of a specially designed cartoon box, which required minimal motor behavior to activate, could increase purposeful arm movements, head control, and positive affect in a profoundly retarded boy.

Tables 6.2, 6.3, and 6.4 provide sample instructional programs for isolated and cooperative leisure activities. The format includes instructional objectives, materials, task analysis sequences, and instructional procedures. The reader who desires more of these materials is referred to Wehman and Schleien (1981).

In sum, the most important features of a leisure skill training program are:

1. To provide an enjoyable activity or atmosphere
2. To provide for participation by the individual in some way
3. To provide no more training or assistance than necessary
4. To provide for a *repertoire* of leisure activities that the individual can utilize with minimal supervision

As important as specific training techniques are, the guidelines above must be followed in any conceptual model of leisure skill programming.

Measurement

Measurement refers to the methods used to systematically and empirically verify skill acquisition (e.g., number of correct responses; responses/trials to criterion, rate, latency, duration, frequency, and intensity of responses) and sampling procedures. Evaluating in an objective (quantitative) way the progress made by handicapped students in a leisure program is an important component of the program. Without this component it is difficult to document the effectiveness of training procedures or demonstrate the positive leisure behavior change.

Some of the measurement tactics employed in research on recreation with moderately and severely handicapped individuals include pre-test/post-test percent of correct/incorrect responses (Newcomer & Morrison, 1974), number of responses (Johnson & Bailey, 1977; Morris & Dolker, 1974), task analytic assessment (Hamre-Nietupski & Williams, 1977; Wehman & Marchant, 1977; Wehman & Schleien, 1980), interval recording (Hopper & Wambold, 1977), and time sampling (Favell & Cannon, 1977; Wambold & Bailey, 1979). In addition, Wehman (1977b; 1979a) and Williams, et al. (1978) have suggested various measurement tactics for use in a recreation/leisure skills program for severely handicapped persons.

Table 6.2. Instructional program

Type of activity: Physical Activity — Arm Wrestle

Instructional objective: Given an opponent, the participant will pull the opponent's hand from a perpendicular position to a horizontal position on the table top (against the opponent's force pulling participant's hand in opposite direction), 50% of the time.

Materials: Another player

Verbal cue: "Jerry, have an arm wrestle."

Task analysis	Activity guidelines/special adaptations
1. Sit facing opponent at table	Make sure that participant and opponent are evenly matched in size and strength to avoid injury.
2. Extend dominant arm to midline of body	Instruct participants to hold dominant upper arm with nondominant hand to help stabilize the dominant arm.
3. Bend dominant arm at elbow until arm is perpendicular to table	
4. Place elbow on table in front of body	A rubber substance or towel could be placed under participants' arms to avoid elbow sliding.
5. Extend dominant hand toward opponent's hand (who has positioned arm in same manner)	It is recommended, whenever possible, to have participants arm wrestle with each arm to build forearm and biceps strength equally on each limb.
6. Place palm of dominant hand against opponent's dominant hand	
7. Grasp opponent's hand using palmar grasp	Isometric contraction (force against force) is an excellent means to build body strength. Arm wrestling utilizes this exercise concept.
8. Place dominant arm against opponent's dominant arm	
9. On "go" command, apply downward pressure to opponent's hand, pulling it toward nondominant side of body	
10. Continue applying downward pressure against opponent's arm until one player weakens	
11. Pull opponent's hand downward until it is horizontal to table top to win arm wrestle	

Evaluating in an objective (quantitative) way the progress made by handicapped students in a leisure program is an important component of the program.

Two of the most frequently used means of measurement have been task analytic assessment and time sampling. Task analysis assessment is aimed at evaluating the degree of proficiency which an individual has in performing leisure skill. The number of steps in the task analysis that the individual completes independently are recorded. With these data the teacher can then identify which steps to begin teaching. Table 6.5 presents a task analytic assessment for throwing a frisbee.

The time sampling measure, on the other hand, allows the teacher to assess at different intervals of the day for brief time periods (30 seconds to 5 minutes) the individual's leisure activity. Assume the teacher is interested in documenting how much constructive leisure activity is taking place and how much self-stimulatory stereotyping is occurring. The strategy would involve defining each behavior and then observing the occurrence or nonoccurrence of each behavior at designated time periods throughout the day. The time sampling approach has been described in detail by Kazdin (1975) and is an efficient way to assess play and leisure activities.

Table 6.3. Instructional program

Name of activity: Cast Baited Fishing Line

Instructional Objective: Given a pole with a line and a baited hook, the participant will cast the line 5 feet into the water, 80% of the time.

Materials: Fishing rod, fishing line, fishhook baited with worm, fishing area

Verbal cue: "Kathy, throw your line into the water."

Task analysis	Activity guidelines/Special adaptations
1. Stand 2 feet away from and facing water, feet parallel and 6 inches apart	The casting motion should be practiced initially with any stick or a yardstick ruler. This will be lighter and easier to manipulate.
2. Bend knees, lowering rear toward ground	
3. Extend dominant arm outward toward pole, palm faced down, fingers extended	Handle of fishing rod can be built up with foam padding and tape.
4. Lower dominant arm until palm makes contact with pole 1 foot from bottom end	A light stick or head pointer can be used with a participant having minimal use of arms and hands. This should only be used when fishing for small fish and participant should be accompanied.
5. Curl fingers around pole	
6. Wrap thumb around opposite side of pole	
7. Apply inward pressure between thumb and fingers to grasp pole firmly	Pier fishing can provide relaxation for all individuals. Those in wheelchairs who would like to participate should choose a pier with these qualifications: 1) access walk to pier from shore must be a minimum of 5 feet wide to allow for turning of wheelchairs; 2) handrails must be provided around the entire pier and according to the Virginia Commission of Outdoor Recreation, must be 26 inches high and have a 30 degree angle sloping top for arm and pole rest; 3) a kick plate must be provided to prevent foot pedals of wheelchairs from going off the pier; and 4) a smooth, non-slip surface must be provided on the access walk and on the pier.
8. Bend elbow, bringing pole to waist level	
9. Extend knees, raising body to upright position	
10. Rotate wrist 90 degrees clockwise so that pole is perpendicular to front of body, parallel to ground	

Leisure Instruction in Community Settings

A popular setting for teaching leisure and recreation skills for special educators is the classroom. There is an implicit assumption made that severely handicapped students will automatically *generalize* the skill to home or community environments. Yet we know that this inference is not usually accurate (Stokes & Baer, 1977). Therefore, it is necessary for leisure instruction to actually take place in the community (i.e., in recreation centers, movie theaters, fast food restaurants, parks, and scout groups). Programming must also occur in the individual's home environment.

Johnson and Bailey (1977) and Schleien et al. (1981) both taught chronologically age-appropriate leisure skills to mentally retarded adults in group home settings. Hill, Wehman, and Horst (1982) provided training for severely retarded youths to use an electronic pinball machine in several community settings on a weekly basis. In each of these efforts, the participants learned the skills and generalized them more quickly because of their functional nature.

The concept of training leisure skills, or for that matter any skills, outside of the classroom does not always jibe with administrative concerns and the traditional public school service delivery system. Yet teachers and administrators must adapt their usual means of service delivery to accommodate the needs of severely handicapped students. It is vital that students receive specific instruction in settings other than the classroom if parents are to consider these instructional efforts truly credible. Furthermore, the

Table 6.4. Instructional program

Name of activity: Plant Care — Plant Seed

Instructional Objective: Given a flower pot, potting soil, spoon, and potting rocks, the participant will put the rocks and the potting soil in the pot, and plant the seed, 80% of the time.

Materials: Flower pot, potting soil, potting rocks, spoon, newspaper, seed

Verbal cue: "Elise, fill the flower pot with soil and plant a seed."

Task analysis	Activity guidelines/special adaptations
1. Kneel or sit opposite pot and soil.	Because filling a pot with dirt can be somewhat messy, scattering layers of newspaper beneath the pot and soil will make clean-up easier.
2. Extend dominant hand downward to rocks, palm faced down	
3. Grasp handful of rocks with dominant hand using palmar grasp	Potting soil and pebbles are commercially available, but it is not absolutely necessary to use them. Small rocks or pebbles can be gathered outside and soil from a garden can be used.
4. Position dominant hand holding rocks directly above pot	
5. Drop rocks into pot by extending fingers	Tape or paint can be used on the inside of the pot to indicate rock level and soil level.
6. Continue filling pot with rocks until bottom is covered	If participant has difficulty grasping a spoon, a larger spoon with the handle built up can be used, or a child's beach shovel would be handy. The participant could also use her hands to scoop the soil and fill the pot.
7. Grasp spoon with dominant hand using palmar grasp	
8. Position scoop end of spoon directly above open bag of potting soil	
9. Lower arm and spoon into soil by extending at elbow	For participants having difficulty grasping seeds, place single seed in small Dixie cup and have participant pour seed into flower pot.
10. Raise arm up by bending at elbow, scooping soil with spoon	Initially, seeds can be dumped onto aluminum tray, making it easier for participant to grasp single seed.
11. Position spoon directly above pot	
12. Rotate wrist downward, emptying soil into pot	Many times, several seeds will need to be planted in order to get one plant growing. Therefore, to enhance potential for successful performance, it is recommended that several seeds be planted.
13. Continue scooping and emptying soil into pot until it is filled to rim	
14. Extend dominant hand downward toward pencil, palm faced down	
15. Grasp pencil	
16. Position pencil directly above filled flower pot	
17. Lower pencil 3 inches into center of soil by extending at elbow	
18. Rotate pencil back and forth to form small hole in soil	
19. Raise pencil out of soil by bending at elbow	
20. Release pencil onto ground by extending fingers	
21. Extend dominant hand downward toward plant seed, palm faced down	
22. Grasp plant seed with dominant hand using pincer grasp	
23. Position seed directly above hole in soil	
24. Drop seed into hole by extending fingers	
25. Push top layer of soil into hole	
26. Pat top layer of soil down by applying gentle pressure onto soil with fingertips	

Table 6.5. Task analytic assessment for tossing a frisbee

	M	T	W	Th	F
1. Extend hand downward toward frisbee	+	+	+	+	+
2. Curl fingers underneath frisbee	+	+	+	+	+
3. Position thumb on top edge of frisbee	+	+	−	+	+
*4. Apply inward pressure with fingers and thumb to grasp frisbee firmly	−	−	−	+	+
5. Bend at elbow, raising frisbee to chest	−	−	−	−	−
6. Hold frisbee parallel to ground	−	−	−	−	−
7. Bring frisbee inward toward nondominant side of body	−	−	−	−	−
8. Quickly extend elbow outward away from body	−	−	−	−	−
9. Snap wrist outward and extend fingers to release frisbee	−	−	−	−	−
10. Toss frisbee 2 feet	−	−	−	−	−
11. Toss frisbee 3 feet	−	−	−	−	−
12. Toss frisbee 4 feet	−	−	−	−	−
13. Toss frisbee 5 feet	−	−	−	−	−

*Instruction should begin on step 4. Verbal cue: "[Name], throw me the frisbee."

inclusion of *generalization objectives* on the student's IEP should also be planned when appropriate. Once teachers have established a routine for teaching leisure skills in the community, there will also be a greater sensitivity as to what behaviors the community will not tolerate in severely handicapped students. This finding will help shape future curriculum selection.

INITIATING A LEISURE PROGRAM: EVALUATING THE HOME AND COMMUNITY

Many, if not all, of the characteristics listed in the previous section will be facilitated when the student's leisure program is determined through a sequential assessment process. This process should heavily emphasize input from the client (Voeltz, Biel-Wuerch, & Wilcox, 1982), the home, and the community. There are five major steps in the recreation/leisure assessment process. This process assumes an approach that begins by evaluating the community and home where the student lives or will live for appropriate leisure activities. The assessment activities are briefly described below.

Step 1: Preliminary Screening

A brief overview of the student's background and behavior is summarized initially before moving into the next phases of the assessment process. The purpose of this screening is primarily to acquaint the teacher and adaptive physical educator or recreation specialist with the student and help in the initial inventory of the community. Often this information is readily available from other more detailed reports (i.e., occupational and physical therapy evaluations). It is not usually necessary to conduct separate motor assessments.

Step 2: Home/Community Inventory of Leisure Skills

An inventory of leisure activities and patterns available in the home should be provided through questions given by the teacher or possibly school social worker. These answers provide input to selecting relevant skills for assessment. An inventory of available community recreation facilities should also be completed. This assessment may be done in conjunction with local park and recreational personnel. Tables 6.6 and 6.7 provide sample inventories that can be utilized. The inventories provide information that helps the teacher narrow down the focus from potentially hundreds of leisure activities to a smaller, more manageable number.

Table 6.6.   Home living inventory

Student name _____

Student age _____

Type of current residence _____

Target date for programming _____

1. What leisure materials are currently available in the home (or living unit) (e.g., frisbee, yo-yo, cards)?

   _____

   _____

2. Do other members of the family (or living unit) engage in leisure activities at home regularly? Specify the nature and frequency of these activities.

   _____

   _____

   _____

   _____

3. Do the parents or caregivers have the funds or willingness to purchase necessary leisure materials?

   _____

4. Are the parents or caregivers willing to carry through leisure activities program in the home?

   _____

   _____

5. What types of leisure activities are currently provided in the home (or living unit) for the student?

   _____

   _____

   _____

   _____

   _____

   _____

Table 6.7. Community leisure inventory

Student name _____

Student age

Name of community being assessed _____

1. Identify the major recreational facilities used by most community members.

    _____

    _____

    _____

2. Are the leading recreational facilities accessible for those with physical impairments and sensory impairments, as well as those who need public transportation? Explain.

    _____

    _____

    _____

3. Evaluate, if possible, the recreational facility director's attitude toward mentally handicapped consumers.

    _____

    _____

    _____

    _____

4. Describe the availability and nature of parks in the child's neighborhood.

    _____

    _____

    _____

5. Identify the community agencies currently providing or operating recreational/leisure programs for the handicapped individuals (churches, youth agencies, etc.)

    _____

    _____

    _____

6. Do these agencies provide transportation?

    _____

7. Describe the availability and nature of aquatic facilities.

    _____

    _____

    _____

Table 6.7. (continued)

8.   Are handicapped individuals encouraged to participate in organized community activities, such as little league baseball, adult softball, and volleyball? If so, how?

_____

_____

_____

9.   Do community schools address leisure time activities? If so, describe.

_____

_____

_____

_____

Step 3: Identify Pool of
Leisure Activities for Assessment

From the inventory of the student's home and community, a pool of leisure activities is selected for assessment. These may be categorized into indoor, outdoor, home, and community. The activities represent a group of leisure skills that the teacher and parents have decided will be assessed for eventual instruction. In Table 6.8 is an example of such a pool or group of activities that might be selected for student assessment and subsequent instruction.

Table 6.8.   Sample of group of leisure activities for student assessment

These activities were selected for student assessment from an inventory of possible leisure activities in the home and community in which the students live or will live. This pool of activities should be small enough so that students will realistically be able to attain competence and enjoyment with them over a 3-year period.

1. Tic tac toe	1. Pinball	1. Use of playground	1. Softball
2. Cards	2. Movie	2. Bicycle riding	2. Fishing
3. Tape recorder	3. Bowling	3. Plant care	3. Camping
4. Photography	4. Church activities	4. Pet care	4. Badminton
5.	5.	5.	5.
6.	6.	6.	6.
7.	7.	7.	7.
8.	8.	8.	8.
9.	9.	9.	9.
10.	10.	10.	10.

Step 4: Student Assessment

The major focus of the client assessment is to do behavioral assessments of the client's ability level on the leisure activities identified in the leisure pool. The results from this assessment—in addition to analysis of pertinent existing data relevant to communication, medical, educational, and motor assessments—form the basis for which objectives should be established. One illustration of the type of assessment that is commonly used to pinpoint the proficiency level of the student is the task analysis assessment presented in Table 6.4.

Step 5: Select High Priority Leisure Objectives

This component of the assessment process involves identifying guidelines for selecting leisure objectives. For example, student choice and chronological age-appropriateness of the activity are important influencing factors in selecting objectives. The teacher and/or recreation specialist must experiment in identifying those activities that the student enjoys most and that can be used the most often. The following questions summarize the major *student assessment* questions that may need to be addressed.

1. How proficient or competent is the client at performing the principal components of the activity?
   Mode of Assessment: Task analysis of activity (steps recorded).
2. How able is the client at performing leisure activities independent of supervision and for *sustained* periods of time?
   Mode of Assessment: Frequency recording (seconds/minutes) of appropriate leisure activity, time-sampling also acceptable.
3. How appropriate is the client's use of the leisure material?
   Mode of Assessment: Teacher evaluation of social acceptability of use of materials.
4. What social interaction skill level does the client exhibit in different activities?
   Mode of Assessment: Frequency of social interaction between peers; time-sampling also acceptable.
5. What activity/objective does the client consistently prefer or choose over other activities/objectives?
   Mode of Assessment: Present different activities/objectives and record choices on checklist.

It is expected for a client's functioning level to influence which and how many of these initial assessments are necessary to be performed. Behavioral recording forms are used for each mode of assessment.

A TRAINER-ADVOCACY APPROACH TO COMMUNITY-BASED RECREATION

Having discussed the components of a leisure program, we now move to an approach (or a service delivery system) for helping moderately and severely handicapped persons participate in community-based recreation programs. The focus is not on the specific details of how to teach a leisure skill, but rather how to assist the integration of severely handicapped and nonhandicapped participants.

A trainer-advocacy approach is suggested for facilitating this integration. Such a service delivery system requires: 1) instructional guidance by a staff person for the handicapped client at the place where the recreational activity is occurring; and 2) advocacy on behalf of the client from the group leader and the nonhandicapped participants in the group. Once the individual has received a reasonable degree of acceptance by the members of the group (i.e., some people in the group take a special interest in the student), the trainer and advocate can reduce their involvement at the setting. There are six aspects of this approach that highlight its utility.

1. Number of handicapped participants should be small for individualization
2. Emphasis is on social acceptability and enjoyment by client
3. Social feedback from nonhandicapped participants
4. Parental involvement in planning activity
5. Ongoing nature of activity
6. Appropriate matching of client leisure interest to program

Small and Individualized

As a general rule, one to three severely handicapped individuals is sufficient for integration into a nonhandicapped group of eight to ten. With this ratio the staff person can directly help in the initial adjustment process. Usually nonhandicapped people are somewhat uncomfortable during their first encounters with the severely handicapped. A small group makes it easier for the staff person to individualize the effort and help the nonverbal client communicate and thus be accepted easier. This approach is an obvious contrast to those in which large groups of severely handicapped people are bussed to the activity site.

Social Acceptability

The social acceptance of the individual plays a *major factor* in how well that individual adjusts. For successful participation in community recreation programs, the emphasis must be on social acceptability and not necessarily a high degree of leisure skill proficiency. The essence of leisure is to participate and have fun; different individuals, whether handicapped or not, can enjoy an activity in spite of limited ability.

> **For successful participation in community recreation programs, the emphasis must be on social acceptability and not necessarily a high degree of leisure skill proficiency.**

It is important for the student to minimize antisocial or inappropriate and bizarre behaviors (i.e., self-stimulatory motor actions or strange verbalizations). These types of behaviors tend to make most nonhandicapped individuals very uncomfortable, and hence exclude the severely handicapped person from participation in the activity. In a community activity such as going to a fast-food restaurant, inappropriate social behaviors will effectively "turn off" clerks and other consumers in the restaurant. Therefore, it is imperative that a goal of social acceptability is paramount in leisure program planning. It should be remembered, however, that these social skills are often best taught in the real setting; hence there will probably be some initial adjustment problems.

Social Feedback

The trainer and advocate must establish a dialogue with the nonhandicapped participants or consumers in the area. In order to facilitate participation in a formal social group, it is vital to receive regular social feedback as to how the student is being accepted. Ongoing evaluation throughout the activity lets the staff and student know how the rest of the group feels. Evaluation can take the form of verbal communication or written survey forms (Hill & Wehman, 1980; Martin et al., 1982).

Parent Involvement

Because participation in a predominantly nonhandicapped group may be threatening to parents of severely handicapped individuals, it is crucial whenever possible to involve parents in the planning of the activity. Issues to consider include:

1. Transportation
2. Location of setting
3. Type of activity
4. Age, sex and race of nonhandicapped participants
5. Student's interests and preferences

When parents can observe their son or daughter participating in an enjoyable group with nonhandicapped peers, there is a greater likelihood that they will encourage further involvement in normal community recreation programs. Without parent support it is highly improbable that the program will work.

Ongoing Nature of Community Activity

One feature of a trainer-advocacy approach is that the community activity be ongoing in nature. The activity should be a repeated event unlike a field trip which has a singular impact. For optimal learning and experience for both the severely handicapped and nonhandicapped participants, repeated exposure is a very important facet.

Matching of Client
Interests to Community Activities

The individual's specific strengths and preferences must also be carefully considered in designing a community recreation program. Bates and Renzaglia (1978) have outlined several points that address the importance of matching the individual's interests with selected recreational activities available in the community. An initial assessment of a client's strengths and weaknesses must be made initially. (See Wehman & Schleien, 1981, pp. 16–17, for a listing of about 20 assessment tools.)

CASE STUDIES OF
LEISURE SKILL TRAINING

In order to demonstrate a number of the guidelines and principles discussed so far in this chapter, it is helpful to highlight two case studies that were conducted with severely handicapped youths.[2] The leisure skills presented have been selected to demonstrate how the timely procedures and advocacy techniques can be used with severely handicapped individuals. In the subsequent case studies, students were taught use of a frisbee and how to operate a cassette recorder.

Case 1: Use of a Frisbee

Participants and Setting The two participants, Ron and Ralph, are males ages 21 and 19, respectively. They have been classified severely retarded, with IQ's measuring below 30. Their expressive vocabulary is very limited (i.e., Ralph exhibits echolalic speech; however, Ron is presently in a picture communication program). Both participants engage in high rates of inappropriate activities during free time. The setting is a public school for severely and profoundly handicapped students in Richmond, Virginia.

Rationale for Skill Selection Frisbee playing was selected as an activity for several reasons. First, it is portable and can be played a number of places. Second, it is inexpensive. Third, the motor actions required are quite simple to perform once they are carefully coordinated. Finally, frisbee playing can be a two-person skill; the interdependent nature of the activity was viewed as desirable because the participants engaged in minimal cooperative leisure.

Task Analysis The task analysis was initially drawn from the leisure curriculum developed by Wehman and Schleien (1981). It was then modified by the instructor for use with the participants in this program (i.e., catching and throwing skills were both utilized). The task analysis formed the basis for initial assessment and instruction. It can be found below.

Throwing the Frisbee

1. Hold the frisbee in throwing position, fingers curled on the underside, thumb topside, index finger on edge.
2. Raise dominant arm, lifting frisbee to shoulder level.
3. Bend elbow, bringing frisbee inward toward chest.
4. Continue bending elbow until rim of frisbee makes contact with non-dominant shoulder.
5. Quickly extend elbow outward away from body.
6. When elbow is fully extended, release grasp on frisbee.
7. Throw frisbee 3 feet (keeping underside of frisbee parallel to ground).
8. Throw frisbee 6 feet (keeping underside of frisbee parallel to ground).
9. Throw frisbee 10 feet (keeping underside of frisbee parallel to ground).
10. Throw frisbee 15 feet (keeping underside of frisbee parallel to ground).

---

[2]Portions of these case studies were presented in the year-end report *Instructional Programming for Severely Handicapped Youth* by P. Wehman and J. Hill.

Catching the Frisbee

1. Stand away from (at least 5 feet) and face other player.
2. Extend both arms outward toward other player, palms outward, fingers extended.
3. Follow path of frisbee through air (using eyes and hands).
4. When frisbee approaches, grasp in hands firmly.

Teaching Procedures From the initial baseline data, a step was selected for instruction. Ron began instruction on step 1 of throwing frisbee and Ralph's training started on step 4 of catching. These steps were the target behaviors that each individual was unable to complete independently.

A staff person initially modeled the entire skill prior to a 15-minute training session. Instruction was then begun on the specific training step in the frisbee throwing task analysis. A four-step hierarchy was used for purposes of training and subsequent data collection: 1) independent response, 2) verbal prompting, 3) modeling, and 4) physical guidance. The trainer initially provided a verbal cue to Ron and then Ralph to complete the step. If the student performed it correctly, he was socially reinforced. If not, then the verbal cue was repeated and a model was presented. If the response was correct, then social reinforcement was provided. This sequence of graduated guidance was repeated throughout the training session. Training trials were alternated between the two students, and took place inside and outside the school.

Behavior Observation Five training trials on the target steps were given during 15-minute instructional sessions daily. Data were collected dependent upon which step of the cue hierarchy was necessary for performance by the student. Weekly nonreinforced probe data were then collected on the skill to monitor progress. These data were collected when a trainer gave the general cue (i.e., "Ron, throw the frisbee"). At a later point in the program it was decided to collect nonreinforced probe data at the end of each session instead of weekly. This was done for more regular feedback on student progress.

Results Baseline data in Figure 6.1 indicate that Ron did not exhibit any frisbee skills whereas Ralph's data showed a minimum of steps he was able to complete independently (i.e., Ron functioned at a 0 proficiency level on throwing, Ralph averaged 61% on catching). Once systematic instruction was provided, both participant's frisbee playing skills increased to 100%. After criterion was met a maintenance program was initiated so Ron and Ralph would sustain this particular skill and, when given the opportunity, generalize playing frisbee to different settings. The maintenance program provided intermittent reinforcement for Ron and Ralph to throw the frisbee for gradually extended lengths of time.

Case 2: Operating a Cassette Player

Participants The participants, Terry, Troy, and Gary, ages 16, 10 and 21, respectively, have been classified as severely and profoundly retarded with multiple handicaps (i.e., Gary is also classified as legally blind with an IQ measuring below 30). Gary has a limited expressive vocabulary, and Terry and Troy are nonverbal, with only Troy using the signs for eat and drink. Terry and Troy also exhibit a high rate of self-abusive, inappropriate

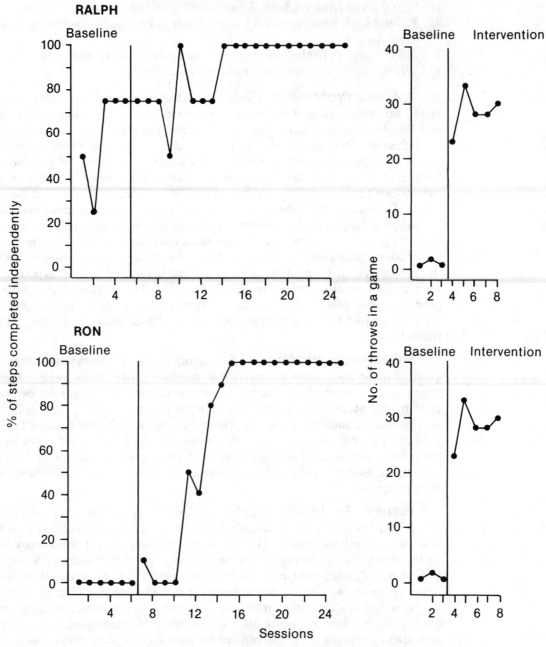

Figure 6.1. *Frisbee playing skills for two students.*

behaviors such as head banging. It was observed by the staff, however, that all three of the participants appeared to enjoy music. Therefore, operating a cassette player was viewed as an age-appropriate leisure activity.

Rationale for Skill Selection Manipulating a cassette player requires a simple set of motor behaviors (i.e., bar pressing) and yet results in an immediate positive consequence. This activity is a good leisure skill for individuals with extremely limited motor repertoires and visual impairments. It is also an activity that may facilitate increased family acceptance because it is a common domestic leisure activity. Finally, there is a large range of different music reinforcers that can be employed.

Task Analysis The task analysis below was used for the initial assessment and instruction:

1. Sit/stand in front of cassette player.
2. On cue, reach toward cassette player.
3. Extend index finger toward buttons.
4. Place finger on appropriate (play/on) button.
5. Push "play" button down.
6. Listen to music for 1 minute.
7. Listen to music for 2 minutes.
8. Listen to music for 3 minutes.
9. On cue, reach toward cassette player.
10. Extend index finger toward buttons.
11. Place finger on appropriate (stop/off) button.
12. Push "stop" button down.

Teaching Procedures and Observation The baseline assessment data revealed that Terry should receive instruction on step 2, Troy on step 6, and Gary on steps 3, 4, and 5. The instructional procedures were implemented systematically using continuous social reinforcement. They were identical to the procedures used in the previous study.

Adaptations Because Gary was blind, the following adaptations were made on the cassette player for him:

1. The three buttons not necessary for turning the machine on and off were covered with a small piece of cardboard and tape.
2. The play button (on) was covered with Velcro (a rough-textured material).
3. The stop button (off) was covered with felt (a soft-textured material).
4. Small pieces of felt were also placed on both sides of the individual cassette tapes opposite the end inserted into the recorder.

Behavior Observation Nonreinforced data probes were collected once a week which examined whether the student completed each step appropriately and independently. A percentage of steps completed independently was calculated for each weekly probe.

Results Examination of baseline data indicated all three participants were unable to operate a cassette player fully, with Terry averaging 23%, Troy 62%, and Gary 50% proficiency. Through consistent, systematic instruction, however, all participants increased their ability to operate the cassette player independently with 90 to 100% accuracy during nonreinforced probe sessions and maintenance probes. Figure 6.2 provides the data for this program.

SUMMARY

The purpose of this chapter is to provide information related to leisure skill instruction for moderately and severely handicapped youths. After briefly outlining previous studies that have occurred in the past decade, characteristics of an appropriate leisure program were described. These eight characteristics formed the foundation for the balance of the chapter. An assessment strategy and accompanying forms were also provided. Finally, two descriptive case studies were presented as illustrations of how age-appropriate leisure skills might be taught to severely handicapped youths.

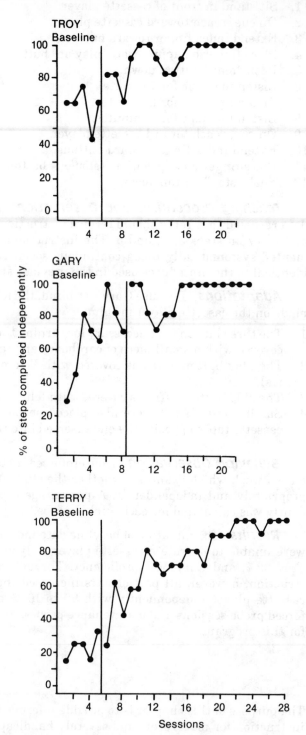

Figure 6.2. Operation of a cassette player for three students.

APPENDIX
Selected Leisure Activities for Moderately and Severely Handicapped Children and Adults

I. OBJECT MANIPULATION

Beanbag

C*   Stack beanbags
C   Underhand beanbag throw
C   Overhand beanbag throw
C   Toss beanbag from hand to hand
C   Balance beanbag on head

Blocks

C   Arrange blocks horizontally
C   Stack blocks vertically
C   Build block tower
C   Hit block tower over
C   Load blocks into toy truck

Camera

C/A   Look through camera
C/A   Press button on camera
C/A   Wind camera

Cracker Jack

C   Open Cracker Jack box
C   Eat Cracker Jack
C   Find prize in Cracker Jack box
C   Close Cracker Jack box
C   Shake Cracker Jack box

Etch-A-Sketch

C   Turn Etch-A-Sketch dials
C   Draw a line on Etch-A-Sketch
C   Draw a square on Etch-A-Sketch
C   Shake Etch-A-Sketch to erase design

Glider Plane

C   Assemble glider plane
C   Color glider plane
C   Throw glider plane
C   Throw glider plane through target
C   Catch glider plane

Hula-Hoop

C   Walk through hula-hoop
C   Roll hula-hoop
C   Spin hula-hoop on floor
C   Swing hula-hoop on arm
C   Twirl hula-hoop around waist

Medicine Ball

C/A   Roll medicine ball
C/A   Pick up medicine ball
C/A   Throw medicine ball
C/A   Catch medicine ball
C   Lie on medicine ball and roll on floor

Vending Machine

A   Locate vending machine
A   Select item
A   Place coin in machine and pull lever/push button
A   Consume item

Yo-Yo

C   Put yo-yo string on finger
C   Flick yo-yo down
C   Pull up yo-yo and catch it
C   Wind yo-yo
C   Tie string onto yo-yo

II. GAMES

Board and Table

C/A	Bingo
C/A	Checkers
C/A	Crossword puzzle
C/A	Darts
C/A	Foozball
C	Jacks

Motor

C/A	Arm wrestle
C	Dodge ball
C	Hopscotch
C	Tag
C/A	Tug of war

Cards

C/A	Mix cards
C/A	Deal cards
C/A	Hold cards in hand
C/A	Arrange cards in hand
C/A	Taking turns
C/A	Draw a card
C/A	Play a card
C/A	Identify colors
C/A	Identify suits
C/A	Identify numbers
C/A	Identify winning hand
C/A	Concentration
C/A	I Doubt It
C/A	Old Maid
C/A	Slap Jack
C/A	War

III. HOBBIES

Books and Magazines

C/A	Take book/magazine off shelf
C/A	Turn pages in magazine
C/A	Find seat in library
C/A	Check out book/magazine
C/A	Acquire library card

Cooking

C/A	Pour liquid
C/A	Stir ingredients
C/A	Mix liquids
C/A	Chop ingredients
C/A	Operate stove
C/A	Operate toaster
C/A	Spread ingredients
C/A	Boil water
C/A	Use can opener
C/A	Use bottle opener
C/A	Use blender
C/A	Make Kool-Aid
C/A	Make peanut butter and jelly sandwich
C/A	Make caramel apples
C/A	Pop popcorn

Cycling

C/A	Get on and off bicycle
C/A	Peddle bicycle
C/A	Steer bicycle
C/A	Balance bicycle
C/A	Brake bicycle

Nature

C/A	Walk through woods
C/A	Collect rocks
C/A	Collect leaves/flowers
C/A	Press leaves/flowers
C/A	Look through binoculars
C/A	Catch butterfly
C/A	Rake leaves
C/A	Collect seashells
C/A	Skip stone into water
C/A	Plant/tree identification (smell, touch)

Pet Care

C/A	Walk dog on leash
C/A	Put collar and leash on dog
C/A	Pet dog
C/A	Brush dog
C/A	Feed dog
C/A	Use "pooper-scooper"
C/A	Feed goldfish/turtle
C/A	Feed hamster
C/A	Clean hamster cage
C/A	Take hamster out of cage
C/A	Pet hamster

Photography

C/A Load film in camera
C/A Look through camera
C/A Press button on camera
C/A Wind camera
C/A Position object/person to take picture
C/A Use pinhole camera
C/A Make photograph album
C/A Use Viewmaster

Plant Care

C/A Put dirt in pot
C/A Plant seed
C/A Water and mist plant
C/A Position plant in sun
C/A Root plant
C/A Trim plant
C/A Put plant hanger on and hang plant
C/A Pick flowers
C/A Arrange flowers in vase

Spectator Leisure/Community Events

C/A Purchase ticket
C/A Hand ticket to doorman
C/A Locate seat
C/A Buy refreshment from vendor
C/A Use vending machine
C/A Go to restroom
C/A Attend to event
C/A Leave facility
C/A Attend church
C/A Go to movie theatre
C/A Attend social dance
C/A Go to ball park

Spectator Leisure/Home

C/A Use radio
C/A Use record player
C/A Use headphones
C/A Select record
C/A Use television
C/A Use Viewmaster

Table Game Hobbies

C/A Place coin in machine
C/A Operate machine
C/A Take turns during game
C/A Demonstrate knowledge of game completion
C/A Play foozball game
C/A Play pinball
C/A Play electric bowling game
C/A Play pool

IV. SPORTS

Bowling

C/A Select bowling ball
C/A Pick up ball from ball return
C/A Approach foul line
C/A Roll ball down alley
C   Reposition pins (if toy set is used)

Fishing

C/A Dig for earthworms
C/A Pull worm out of pile of dirt
C/A Bait hook
C/A Cast baited fishing line
C/A Wait for fish to bite
C/A Pull in fish
C/A Take fish off hook

Golf

C/A Place ball on ground
C/A Hold golf club
C/A Swing golf club
C/A Putt golf ball
C/A Drive golf ball
C/A Follow through

Handball

C/A Put on glove
C/A Bounce ball
C/A Serve ball
C/A Run toward ball
C/A Hit ball against wall

Horseshoes

C/A Select horseshoes and walk to stake
C/A Grasp horseshoe
C/A Throw horseshoes
C/A Pick up horseshoes surrounding stake

Playground Equipment

C/A See-saw play
C/A Sliding board play
C/A Swing play
C/A Twirl-a-round play
C/A Monkey bars play

Swimming

C/A Enter swimming pool
C/A Adjust to water
C/A Walk through water
C/A Breath control
C/A Back float
C/A Back float with kick
C/A Backstroke
C/A Prone float
C/A Prone glide with kick
C/A Rotary breathing
C/A Crawl stroke

Weight Training

C/A Put weights on dumbbell
C/A Identify amount of weight
C/A Underhand grip and lift
C/A Curl
C/A Lift weight over head
C/A Benchpress

Winter Sports

C/A Put on gloves
C/A Make a snowball
C/A Throw snowball
C   Build snowman
C   Decorate snowman
C/A Sledding
C/A Pull sled up hill

---

*C, chronologically age-appropriate skill for children.
 A, chronologically age-appropriate skill for adolescents and adults.
 C/A, chronologically age-appropriate skill for children, adolescents, and/or adults.

7

SHELTERED EMPLOYMENT

LEARNING GOALS

1. Describe the function of the variety of sheltered work settings available.
2. Discuss briefly the advantages and disadvantages of these different work settings.
3. Identify and describe how to assess the community for relevant work tasks.
4. Detail the major aspects of an individual habilitation plan for sheltered work.
5. Discuss the role of task variables in job acquisition.
6. Discuss the role of setting variables in job acquisition.
7. Describe the role of a teacher in facilitating job acquisition.
8. Outline and describe four strategies for accelerating slow production rates in moderately and severely handicapped workers.

The previous chapters have marginally discussed the importance and role of work in the lives of moderately and severely handicapped individuals. In this chapter and the next, sheltered workshop training and (nonsheltered) competitive employment training are presented in depth. It is important to understand that both of these major forms of vocational opportunities for moderately and severely handicapped individuals can be presented in a continuum of most restrictive to least restrictive. Students are expected to have choices from this continuum.

Initial efforts to provide vocational services for many handicapped individuals were in sheltered work settings. Sheltered workshops were established primarily as training facilities rather than as long-term employment for handicapped workers (Hansen, 1980). In fact, sheltered workshops were most frequently viewed as temporary placements for handicapped individuals with the purpose of providing training in the work adjustment skills necessary for moving into competitive jobs.

In the past decade, however, increased emphasis has been placed on providing vocational services for severely handicapped adolescents and adults. The most influential piece of legislation to result in increased services for severely handicapped persons was the Rehabilitation Act of 1973, which established services to severely handicapped individuals as a priority regardless of their potential for competitive placement. As a result, sheltered workshops have rapidly grown in number and size (Greenleigh Associates, 1975; Whitehead, 1979). Even though there has been rapid growth in sheltered workshops, the majority of persons served in sheltered workshops have been individuals functioning in the mildly to moderately handicapped range (e.g., IQ's above 50) (Greenleigh Associates, 1975). Whitehead (1979) reported that although over 280,000 severely handicapped adults are being served in sheltered workshops, 30 times that number are being served inappropriately or not at all. Consequently, educators of moderately, severely, and profoundly handicapped students must be aware of: 1) the services and employment opportunities in sheltered settings; 2) the training strategies that have been successful in providing persons with similar handicapping conditions with the skills necessary for placement in sheltered settings; and 3) the training strategies that have been demonstrated successful in maintaining work skills at adequate levels for continued placement in sheltered settings.

SHELTERED WORK SETTINGS

Sheltered work facilities provide a number of services, including transitional placement, extended employment, and work activities programs. The provision of each of these services depends on the workshop obtaining the appropriate licenses from the U.S. Department of Labor.

Transitional Employment

A transitional employee is placed in a sheltered setting on a temporary basis with the long-range expectation of competitive employment. Individuals referred to a sheltered setting for transitional placement may be referred for extended evaluation, work adjustment, or training in a specific vocational skill area (Flexer & Martin, 1978). Transitional employees are usually referred to sheltered workshops by state vocational rehabilitation counselors for the refinement of skills necessary for obtaining work in the competitive job market.

Extended Employment

Extended employment options may include sheltered employment and a long-term work adjustment status. Severely handicapped persons, when accepted into sheltered work settings, are usually given extended employment status.

A *sheltered employee* is usually an individual who is placed in the workshop as a terminal employee. The sheltered employment status provides the opportunity for remunerative work to handicapped persons who are considered unable to compete in the competitive job market (Flexer & Martin, 1978). Sheltered employees are usually those individuals who work steadily but may lack speed. They require very little staff time and/or few ancillary services, but the decision usually has been made that the sheltered employee is not likely to move into a transitional status or a competitive job.

Frequently, workshops establish a sheltered industry within the workshop facility to employ the sheltered workers. Sheltered industries are self-employed. That is, the items are produced and sold directly to the public or to merchants in the community rather than being subcontracted to local industries, which in turn sell the items. A number of different commodities have been and are presently being produced by self-employed sheltered industries. These include refinishing or repairing items (e.g., furniture and appliances), the manufacturing of items (e.g., decorative candles), and salvaging materials (e.g., scrap metals). Maintenance of self-employed sheltered industries is dependent upon production and sales large enough to subsidize the employees and to furnish the industry with materials for continued production. Obviously, the success of a sheltered industry is subject to the demand for the items being produced and the state of the economy.

> **Sheltered industries are self-employed. That is, the items are produced and sold directly to the public or to merchants in the community rather than being subcontracted to local industries, which in turn sell the items.**

A *long-term work adjustment status* is usually given to those handicapped persons who have been assessed to have numerous behavioral/skill deficits but are still considered capable of acquiring the skills necessary for obtaining either a sheltered or a transitional status. A long-term client usually requires considerable amounts of staff time and supervision. In addition, ancillary services such as vocational or behavioral counseling, academic instruction, and/or other services including speech, occupational, and/or physical therapy are frequently required for the long-term clients. Unlike the sheltered employees, long-term work adjustment clients usually do not produce enough to pay for the many ancillary services they receive. Therefore, long-term clients are usually referred by community agencies (e.g., vocational rehabilitation, public schools), which pay for the services required to habilitate or rehabilitate these individuals.

Work Activities Programs

Although long-term work adjustment programs serve many individuals who do not qualify for sheltered or transitional work programs, the majority of severely and profoundly retarded persons are accepted, even as long-term work adjustment clients. Instead, many severely handicapped adolescents and adults are considered unemployable and unable to contribute to the economy as productive employees. As a result, work activities programs were established to serve those persons considered to be nonproductive workers (Rusch & Schutz, in press). Whereas extended employment and transitional programs must pay workers a certain percentage of the hourly minimum wage, a work activities status allows the program to pay the worker per project for the amount of work completed and no more (Flexer & Martin, 1978).

Between 1968 and 1977, work activities centers grew by 600% (Whitehead, 1979), reflecting the increased emphasis on severely and profoundly handicapped adolescents and adults. These centers usually provide exposure to a variety of skills and activities, including domestic/daily living skills, social skills, leisure/recreation skills, and some vocational skills training. Work activities programs are frequently viewed as providing prevocational skill training, and it is not unreasonable to expect some individuals to advance to a long-term adjustment or a sheltered work status in a rehabilitation facility.

Frequently, rehabilitation facilities provide a continuum of services within a sheltered setting. Work activities, long-term adjustment, sheltered work, and transitional services may be housed within one facility, allowing for movement from one service to another when appropriate.

PREPARING A STUDENT FOR SHELTERED WORK

Educators cannot assume that a simple referral of a handicapped student to a sheltered facility will result in a successful placement. The student must have the skills necessary to be accepted and to become a successful, productive worker within the sheltered setting.

Prior to referring a severely handicapped student for sheltered work, educators must be aware of the sheltered settings available within the particular community. There should be a direct link between instruction prior to referral and the potential job placements (Mithaug, Hagmeier, & Haring, 1977; Rusch & Mithaug, 1980; Wehman & McLaughlin, 1980). Target skills selected for vocational instruction should be those skills required to perform specific jobs in the workshop setting. If employer requisite skills/behaviors are not present prior to placement in a work setting, a severely handicapped student is likely to fail on the job (Rusch & Mithaug, 1980). In addition, the development of skills that do not have relevance to a particular community placement would seem to be an extremely inefficient use of instructional time (Wehman & McLaughlin, 1980).

Target skills selected for vocational instruction should be those skills required to perform specific jobs in the workshop setting.

Assess Community Sheltered Settings

In order to develop the link between prevocational programs or vocational preparation and sheltered settings, vocational educators should actively assess each client's community to determine the type of sheltered settings available for placement. Initial community assessment may be for the purpose of merely identifying the options for placement in sheltered work settings. A checklist indicating: 1) the location of the workshop; 2) the contact person; 3) the type of client served; 4) the services provided; and 5) the type of work performed may provide an educator with enough information to indicate which workshops may be appropriate for particular clients. Table 7.1 provides an example of a general assessment instrument and how it might be used to survey a community's sheltered settings.

Once a general assessment of potential sheltered placements within a community has been conducted, a more thorough survey of specific sheltered workshops is necessary. Surveying the entry-level behavior/skill requirements of specific sheltered settings assists in establishing vocational program goals and student objectives (Mithaug et al., 1977; Rusch & Mithaug, 1980). Mithaug et al. (1977) developed a survey instrument designed to assess entry-level skill requirements for sheltered work settings. This survey was used to assess entrance requirements of sheltered settings in five northwestern states and its use was replicated in a midwestern state (Johnson & Mithaug, 1978). The results of these surveys led to the development of the *Prevocational Assessment and Curriculum Guide* (Mithaug, Mar, & Stewart, 1978). This instrument provides a method of assessing entry-level skill requirements and establishing a curriculum for students that is relevant to sheltered vocational placement.

Another example of a survey instrument designed to assess entry-level skill requirements of sheltered work settings is provided in Table 7.2. The survey was developed to assess entrance requirements for transitional and/or extended employment programs in community sheltered work settings (Renzaglia, Note 6). The survey rates skill areas as: 1) irrelevant; 2) minimally important; 3) important; and 4) mandatory. This rating allows workshop personnel to distinguish between those behaviors/skills considered necessary for admittance into a work facility and those behaviors/skills that are important but not necessary. After completing such a survey, the behaviors/skills assessed can be ranked in order for instruction, with the mandatory items being top priority for training.

When using a survey instrument such as those developed by Mithaug et al. or Renzaglia (refer to Table 7.2), the information is usually obtained through interviewing workshop staff or self-administration of the survey.

Table 7.1. General checklist for assessing sheltered employment

Types of services/ programs	Type of work	Necessary entry skills (indicate survey items)
Work activities, sheltered work, long term, transitional	Circuit boards, packaging playground equipment, assembly of electrical lights	
Work evaluation, transitional, sheltered work	Furniture refinishing, clothing repair, appliance repair	
Work activity, speech therapist, adult education	Clerical jobs, domestic activities, recreation activities, arts and crafts	

Where	Contact person	Level/disability/ age accepted
Sheltered workshops 1. Sheltered businesses (city)	Mr. Jones	Mild-severe ED, MR 18 years and older
2. Goodwill Industries (City)	Ms. Smith	Mild-moderate Mostly ED, some MR 16 years and older
Activity/work/day centers 1. ARC adult activity center (county)	Mr. Brown	Moderate-severe mental retardation 18 years and older

Therefore, vocational educators who use these surveys to prioritize skills for instruction must rely on the verbal report of sheltered workshop personnel. Mithaug, Mar, Stewart, & McCalmon (1980) found a high correlation between the verbal report of workshop staff on skills important for entrance into sheltered settings and the actual skills of successful employees. The results of this investigation provided support for the assessment and establishment of specific client objectives based on structured surveys.

In addition to assessing the relevance of specific work skills (e.g., use of tools, assembly, packaging), the survey should include an assessment of the importance of work-related skills to success in sheltered work settings. Many times the lack of transportation, appropriate social or language skills, proper grooming, and other non-work behavior is the reason for exclusion from a particular job placement. Consequently, work-related behavior may be as crucial to job success as specific work skills training. Table 7.3

Table 7.2   Survey of entrance criteria for sheltered workshops

Facility _____
Personnel involved in completing this form (position titles will be satisfactory):

_____

Your facility is considered primarily to be (check one):
Transitional workshop _____   Permanent work activity center _____
Other (specify): _____
Number of clients served on a daily basis: _____
Major disabling condition of clients seen by your center: _____
Population of the area your facility serves (check one):

Under 10,000 _____
10,000 to 25,000 _____
26,000 to 50,000 _____
Greater than 50,000 _____

Instructions:
Please rate the skill areas as they apply to an individual being considered for placement into your facility. First, rate the areas as they would apply to the entrance behaviors necessary for a DVR funded client who will be placed into your evaluation and training or transitional workshop. Use the second scale for rating the entrance skills necessary for a client being considered for extended programming, including sheltered work or work activities in your facility. Use the following response measures (1 to 4):

1. Irrelevant: Is *not* considered when evaluating an individual for admittance into the program; does *not* apply.
2. Minimally Important: Is considered when evaluating an individual for admittance into the program but would not be considered a deciding factor.
3. Important: Is heavily weighed in the evaluation of an individual for admittance into the program and could be a deciding factor.
4. Mandatory: Is necessary, without exception, for admittance into the program.

Skill areas	DVR funded client				Client being considered for extended programming			
1. The individual demonstrates independence in the following self-help skills:								
a. Toileting	1	2	3	4	1	2	3	4
b. Eating	1	2	3	4	1	2	3	4
c. Dressing	1	2	3	4	1	2	3	4
d. Personal hygiene	1	2	3	4	1	2	3	4
2. The individual demonstrates independence in the following basic survival skills:								
a. Use of public transportation	1	2	3	4	1	2	3	4
b. Use of the telephone	1	2	3	4	1	2	3	4
c. Money management	1	2	3	4	1	2	3	4
d. Time telling	1	2	3	4	1	2	3	4
e. Following a schedule	1	2	3	4	1	2	3	4
f. Caring for personal belongings	1	2	3	4	1	2	3	4
3. The individual demonstrates receptive language skills such as responding to his/her name and following directions.	1	2	3	4	1	2	3	4
4. The individual demonstrates imitation skills.	1	2	3	4	1	2	3	4
5. The individual demonstrates expressive language skills such as communicating needs and interpersonal communication.	1	2	3	4	1	2	3	4

Skill areas	DVR funded client				Client being considered for extended programming			
6. The individual demonstrates problem solving skills in response to work-related situations as well as social situations.	1	2	3	4	1	2	3	4
7. The individual demonstrates functional reading, arithmetic, and spelling skills.	1	2	3	4	1	2	3	4
8. The individual demonstrates basic discrimination skills such as color, shape, and size.	1	2	3	4	1	2	3	4
9. The individual demonstrates the ability to move from location to location without assistance.	1	2	3	4	1	2	3	4
10. The individual demonstrates full use of shoulders, arms, and hands.	1	2	3	4	1	2	3	4
11. The individual demonstrates the ability to attend to, concentrate on, and persist at a task until completed.	1	2	3	4	1	2	3	4
12. The individual demonstrates the ability to engage in his/her own work for an entire workshift.	1	2	3	4	1	2	3	4
13. The individual demonstrates the ability to perform a task of good quality and at a consistently high rate.	1	2	3	4	1	2	3	4
14. The individual demonstrates the ability to interact appropriately with others and make appropriate use of leisure time.	1	2	3	4	1	2	3	4
15. The individual demonstrates the ability to express the appropriate degree of emotion in the appropriate situations.	1	2	3	4	1	2	3	4
16. The individual demonstrates the ability to complete a task without constant direction and support.	1	2	3	4	1	2	3	4
17. The individual demonstrates compliance and is nonaggressive in social and work-related activities.	1	2	3	4	1	2	3	4
18. The individual demonstrates the ability to attend work on a regular basis.	1	2	3	4	1	2	3	4
19. The individual demonstrates respect for the property of others.	1	2	3	4	1	2	3	4
20. The individual demonstrates situation appropriate behavior and does *not* engage in the following nonfunctional competing behaviors in work-related or social functions.								
a. Stereotyping	1	2	3	4	1	2	3	4
b. Self-mutilation	1	2	3	4	1	2	3	4
c. Compulsive rituals	1	2	3	4	1	2	3	4
d. Excessive fantasy	1	2	3	4	1	2	3	4
e. Masturbation	1	2	3	4	1	2	3	4
f. Bizarre speech	1	2	3	4	1	2	3	4
21. The individual demonstrates the ability to cope with all the components of the environment including the demands and reprimands made by his/her supervisors and peers.	1	2	3	4	1	2	3	4
22. The individual demonstrates the ability to cope with changes in his/her environment including the people with whom he/she is interacting.	1	2	3	4	1	2	3	4
23. The individual demonstrates tolerance for frustrating events such as the delay of reward, conflict, and failure.	1	2	3	4	1	2	3	4
24. The individual demonstrates the ability to accept and complete the type of work assigned regardless of his/her job interests.	1	2	3	4	1	2	3	4
25. The individual demonstrates acceptance of his/her placement within a group of peers for work or leisure activities.	1	2	3	4	1	2	3	4
26. Please add any other skill areas evaluated when your agency considers an individual for work placement and indicate the level of importance (1, 2, 3, or 4)								

provides a list of work-related skills that may be important to success in a work setting. This list can be used to develop a checklist that is relevant to a specific community sheltered work setting.

In addition to assessing the relevance of specific work skills (e.g., use of tools, assembly, packaging), the survey should include an assessment of the importance of work-related skills to success in sheltered work settings.

Establish a Work Training Site

The information obtained through surveying specific sheltered work settings provides the structure for establishing a vocational training site with the intent of preparing students for sheltered placement. Once the survey information has been gathered, the vocational trainer must evaluate the facility available for conducting vocational instruction. The amount of space, length of the work training session, type of room, and number of students to be trained must all be considered when deciding upon the type of vocational preparation program to be offered.

If a variety of jobs are being performed in the community sheltered work settings, selection of specific jobs for vocational skills preparation might be based on the amount of space available for instruction and the amount of space required for the particular jobs. If limited space is available for training and a large number of students are involved in instruction, then the job selected for training should be one that requires little movement on the part of the workers and as little space as possible. Regardless of the amount of space, number of students, or length of the work training day, the jobs selected for training in preparation for sheltered work must be directly related to (if possible, the same as) the jobs being performed in the community sheltered setting.

In addition, once the work training setting has been established, it is best to restrict the activities conducted in that setting to work. Especially when instructing moderately and severely/profoundly handicapped students, educators must maximize the environmental cues as much as possible. Therefore, restricting the activities in the training room to work or work-related activities will minimize conflicting environmental cues, which signal that off-task or non-work-related activities are permissible.

Develop an Individual Habilitation Plan

Individual student habilitation plans should emerge from a comparison of the information gathered through community assessment and individual student skill levels. This comparison should point out the discrepancy between student skills and the skills required for obtaining work in a sheltered setting.

Traditional methods for evaluating work skills attempt to predict the likelihood of successful employment of those individuals being evaluated (Flexer & Martin, 1978; Revell, Kriloff, & Sarkees, 1980). Predictions are usually made on the basis of the use of a number of evaluation techniques

Table 7.3. Additional vocationally related behaviors that may be important to securing and maintaining a job

I. Transportation
    A. Job in walking distance
        1. Client can walk to work alone
            a) during good weather
            b) during bad weather
        2. Client walks with companion to work
            a) during good weather
            b) during bad weather
    B. Job not within walking distance
        1. Client can arrange for his own transportation to and from work
            a) taxi
            b) special bus (ride system)
            c) personal ride/driver arrangements
        2. Client uses bus system to and from work
            a) alone
            b) with companion
        3. Client participates in a carpool

II. Clothing Selection
    A. Selects clothing with some assistance
    B. Selects clothing without assistance
    C. Selects appropriate clothing
        1. Work clothes
        2. Social clothes
        3. Weather appropriate
    D. Neatness of appearance

III. Communication and Interpersonal Relationships
    A. Communicates needs
    B. Communicates social "niceties" (i.e., "good morning," "I'm fine, thanks")
    C. Communicates with supervisor
    D. Communicates with peers on the job
    E. Responds to supervisory requests/instructions

IV. Work Attendance and Punctuality
    A. Arrives at work on time or early
    B. Does not leave work station early for lunch or end of day
    C. Attends regularly (few absences)

V. Use of Vending
    A. Identifies appropriate money
    B. Selects appropriate machine
    C. Selects item
    D. Retrieves change (if applicable)

VI. Telephone Behaviors
    A. Uses pay phone
    B. Uses regular phone
    C. Dials number
    D. Locates number in book
    E. Uses operator assistance (to find number)

VII. Self-initiated Care of Work Area
    A. Acquires new materials when out
    B. Keeps work area neat and clean
    C. Prepares work area at the beginning of each day
    D. Closes out work area at the end of each day

VIII. Functional Academics
    A. Money management
    B. Time telling
    C. Following a schedule
    D. Reading
        1. Functional sight-words
        2. Pictorial instructions

IX. Parental Cooperation
  A. Supplemental Security Income (SSI)
     (accepting of reduction if client becomes productive in labor market)
  B. Parents willing to let son/daughter try to work
     1. Will give permission for training/placement
     2. Will support son/daughter in new placement
        a) encouraging in difficulties
        b) willing to make son/daughter go to work during adjustment period
     3. Supportive of work staff
X. Interfering Behaviors
  A. Individual does not excessively engage in the following nonfunctional competing behaviors:
     1. Stereotyping
     2. Self-mutilation
     3. Compulsive rituals
     4. Excessive fantasy
     5. Masturbation
     6. Bizarre speech
  B. Responds appropriately to interruptions or visitors

including: 1) a clinical assessment of the potential worker; 2) laboratory work samples; 3) work experience evaluation; and 4) work tryouts (Revell et al., 1980).

A clinical assessment involves the use of norm-referenced evaluation instruments. Standardized intelligence, aptitude, academic, and personality tests are frequently used to obtain scores that can be compared to a norm group on the same instruments. In addition, interest inventories and norm-referenced manual dexterity tests are frequently administered for the purpose of making predictions regarding job success. Although high scores on many of these instruments may positively correlate with job success, clinical assessment instruments are generally inadequate for *predicting* future performance and success (Flexer & Martin, 1978). Standardized assessments are especially limited when evaluating severely handicapped persons who have had limited experience and no training in work skills.

> **Although high scores on many of these instruments may positively correlate with job success, clinical assessment instruments are generally inadequate for predicting future performance and success.**

Laboratory work samples are usually a part of a standardized system for evaluating performance on specific work tasks (e.g., Vocational Information and Evaluation Work Samples [VIEWS], The Tower System). Although work samples evaluate skills more relevant to actual work tasks than clinical assessment, they are still quite limited for evaluating the skills or work potential of severely handicapped persons. Laboratory work samples are rarely normed on a severely handicapped population, and without such norms it is difficult to make predictions regarding this population. Furthermore, standardized work samples rarely provide for an instructional period in which the worker is given training on the evaluation task. Therefore, those individuals who have difficulty learning or who have had no previous experience with work may perform poorly on the work samples, but this performance may not represent what could be accomplished with systematic instruction.

Work experience evaluation that involves job sampling or replication of actual community job tasks (Revell et al., 1980) and work tryouts are more valuable than the other traditional assessment techniques for evaluating severely handicapped learners. Because these evaluation techniques involve performance in a work setting on relevant tasks, the information obtained is likely to be more pertinent to performance on a real job.

Even though work experience evaluation and job tryouts yield information that seems more relevant to job performance than other traditional techniques, they rarely provide opportunities for the severely handicapped worker to develop new skills (Gold, 1973). In addition, traditional techniques do not identify the specific step(s) in a task at which the learner's skills break down, nor do they evaluate the learner's skills in relation to specific community job requirements as identified by potential employers. Therefore, *alternatives to traditional work evaluation procedures* should be employed.

If a *survey instrument* has been used to identify the entry-level skills for specific community sheltered settings (refer to Table 7.2), the items identified as mandatory or important for obtaining work in specific sheltered settings can be used to assess individual student skill levels. That is, student skills can be compared to a specific job's entrance requirements. If a student meets all of the requirements for obtaining employment, then he/she will likely succeed on the particular job. If specific required skills are not in the individual's repertoire, then those skills should be taught in a vocational preparation program. Therefore, the results of the community assessment survey serve as an initial assessment instrument of an individual worker's skills.

A more in-depth analysis of student skills can be conducted through the use of *direct observation* techniques. Direct observation consists of evaluating a student's skills on specific tasks by observing him/her performing the task. This allows the instructor to pinpoint the step in the task at which the student's skills break down. Through the use of systematic instructional techniques in evaluation, the instructor is able to identify techniques most successful for instructing the individual being evaluated. In addition, learning rate and work production rate can be evaluated and the optimal learning environment for facilitating an individual's acquisition of work skills and work production rate can be identified.

COMPONENTS OF SPECIFIC WORK SKILL TRAINING

Although a number of work-related skills (e.g., language, social skills, use of public transportation) may determine eligibility for placement on a job, the primary focus of this chapter is on instruction of specific work skills. The two major components of work skills instruction are: 1) *acquisition training*; and 2) *increasing work production rate*. Acquisition refers to learning how to perform accurately the steps in a work task. Acquisition of work skills may be hindered due to poor discrimination skills or sensory impairments such as vision or hearing problems (Wehman, Renzaglia, & Schutz, 1977). In such cases, specific instructional techniques designed to facilitate acquisition should be employed. Work production rate becomes a focal point only after the work task has been mastered and refers to the rate at which the task is completed. Slow work production rates may be the result of a number of factors including slow motor behavior and/or the presence of nonfunctional interfering behavior (Wehman, Renzaglia, & Schutz, 1977).

The instructional strategies designed to facilitate acquisition of specific work tasks and work production rates have involved environmental variables antecedent to task performance, specific task variables, and performance consequences available within the work setting.

JOB ACQUISITION

Task Variables

Task analysis, or breaking a task into component parts and sequencing the steps for training (refer to Table 7.4), is a central component of work skills instruction (e.g., Bellamy, Horner, & Inman, 1979; Clarke, Greenwood, Abramowitz, & Bellamy, 1980; Crosson, 1969; Gold, 1972; Bates, Renzaglia, Robertson, Brereton, & Clees, in press). Task analyses have been used successfully to *assess* individual student's skill levels in relation to a work task (e.g., Gold & Pomerantz, 1978), to *teach* the component steps required in a work task (e.g. Crosson, 1969; Gold, 1972), to *identify potential problem steps* in a task, and to *evaluate student progress.* In fact, Gold (1972) suggested that a work skill that cannot be task analyzed into teachable components may not be worth the time and cost required to teach that task to handicapped learners. Different tasks, however, may be appropriate for particular populations, and a task may be analyzed in different ways to accommodate a variety of handicapping conditions.

Table 7.4. Task analysis of booklet binding using spiral binder

1. Stand in front of hole punch machine
2. Place handle in upright position
3. Place plastic binder on binding head so that plastic rings are between vertical "fingers" (to far left) and tips of plastic rings point away from you
4. Pick up 12 to 15 sheets of paper
5. Align by tapping them on table
6. Insert in hole punch with left edge against paper guide
7. Hold in place with left hand
8. Pull down handle with right hand
9. Push back (away from you) slowly on operating lever as far as it will go
10. Take paper out
11. Place punched paper vertically into the area of open rings (front cover facing out)
12. Align holes with tips of plastic rings
13. Swing book down so rings enter the punched holes of the book
14. Continue steps 3 to 12 until all pages of the book are on the plastic binder
15. With right hand return operating lever to the upright position
16. Lift up bound book to remove
17. Stack to one side

As an *assessment tool,* a task analysis provides the framework for evaluating student skills. With a task analytic assessment, the exact steps on which an individual's skills break down can be identified, indicating where to begin instruction (Gold & Pomerantz, 1978). By systematically observing the student attempting to complete the steps in a task, the instructor is able to mark the performance (correct or incorrect) of each step in the task analysis. Through repeated trials across instructional sessions, a consistent measure of the steps in the task that the student has mastered and those requiring further instruction will be obtained.

> **By systematically observing the student attempting to complete the steps in a task, the instructor is able to mark the performance (correct or incorrect) of each step in the task analysis.**

Once the initial assessment (baseline) has been obtained, continued task analytic assessment in the form of probes conducted prior to instruction on a regular basis facilitates *program evaluation.* Regular task analytic probing provides a record of student mastery of new steps in a task, as well as indicating those steps that need further instruction and, perhaps, the necessity for program changes to increase learning.

Task analyses provide a structure for training specific work skills. The most frequently demonstrated use of task analysis in training is through teacher step-by-step instruction. A task analysis indicates the discrete steps required for task completion and, therefore, provides the teacher with a description of the behaviors requiring systematic instruction.

The use of task analysis for self-instruction of work skills may be as effective and in many cases more efficient than teacher step-by-step instruction. For individuals who are capable of reading, a written task analysis may be enough to help the learner to acquire a task. As noted in Chapter 3, however, those students who cannot read may find that picture cards (Wehman, 1979) or pictorial sequences of the steps required for job completion (e.g., Robinson-Wilson, 1977; Spellman et al., 1978) may facilitate job acquisition, performance, and independence. Vocational skills ranging from janitorial duties to task assembly can be represented in a series of pictures (line drawings or actual photographs) that the worker is able to follow to job completion. Through the use of simple self-monitoring techniques, even a severely handicapped worker may be able to identify his/her work station, complete individual components of the work task (Wehman, 1979), and self-monitor work quality. As each component of the job is completed, the worker can check off that step on a self-monitoring sheet, or a flip chart depicting the steps in a task could be provided for sequencing skills.

Autoinstructional Equipment has also been used as a training device for individual learners. Screven, Straka, and Lafond (1971) used coordinated slides and tapes to train students to plug solder. Blackman and Siperstein (1967) suggested that presenting task analyses through a visual and auditory mode without direct supervision of the trainer was successful for task acquisition. Such techniques, although time-consuming in preparation, have facilitated the acquisition of work tasks with minimal direction from a trainer or supervisor.

Arrangement of the task materials for acquisition and efficiency has been identified as an important variable (e.g., Bellamy et al., 1979; Gold, 1972; Levy, Pomerantz, & Gold, 1976). Sequencing the order of the parts to be assembled should aid in greater independence in industrial jobs (Gold, 1972). The task materials should be lined up such that the worker can move in a left-to-right progression, selecting parts from each successive position, and assembling the product in an orderly fashion. Other suggestions include minimizing the number of different manipulations of a task, sequencing the task such that exceptions can be taught after the general case, maximizing the distinctiveness of cues that are provided by the task, avoiding manipulations requiring precision, and maximizing the use of skills the client has already acquired.

Fixtures, automated equipment, or *jigs* may also be employed to facilitate the acquisition of vocational tasks (e.g., Bates et al., in press; Bellamy et al., 1979). Jigs or fixtures can be used for a variety of reasons. They may aid in counting (e.g., Renzaglia, Wehman, Schutz, & Karan, 1978) and/or measurement (Clarke et al., 1980). A worker with insufficient counting skills may be required to bundle work units in packages of ten. Instead of counting ten units, he/she may place one unit on each of 10 trays and then bundle them together. Similarly, a worker may be required to cut dowels into 2-inch sections, but rather than measuring each piece, he/she is merely required to place a dowel in a device that indicates a 2-inch piece for cutting.

A jig can aid a physially or motorically involved worker in operating a piece of equipment or completing any other work task that requires manipulation skills that are not physically possible for the individual. For example, a worker who has the use of only one hand may be unable to use a screwdriver while holding the required work materials. Therefore, a device that is designed to brace the material would allow the client to use the screwdriver with his/her functional hand and complete the project.

When constructing fixtures or jigs, it is important to consider the intrusiveness of the added equipment. Although in many circumstances a worker is unable to complete a task without an aid, an intrusive or cumbersome jig may not be acceptable in the sheltered setting. If preparation of the jig requires effort, or the amount of space required is unreasonable for the work station, a sheltered employer may not accept the task modifications. It is, therefore, important to minimize the size and preparation time required for use of a jig.

When constructing fixtures or jigs, it is important to consider the intrusiveness of the added equipment. If preparation of the jig requires effort, or the amount of space required is unreasonable for the work station, a sheltered employer may not accept the task modifications.

Setting Variables

The *setting* in which vocational skills are trained may affect the acquisition and maintenance of specific work skills (Bellamy et al., 1979; Wehman &

McLaughlin, 1980). When possible, training should occur in the natural work setting. However, many times this is impossible because of space and personnel limitations and the logistical concerns of many sheltered work settings.

In the early stages of acquisition, training may be conducted in an isolated or simulated work environment. Role playing, behavioral rehearsal, and task simulation can help to prepare a student for work (Brown, Bellamy, & Sontag, 1971; Lynch, 1979). However, once skills are acquired in the artificial setting, it is important to verify that the student can perform the skill in the actual work setting. Potential workers must be exposed to and learn to react appropriately to distractions, loud conversations, aggressive or verbal attacks, and criticism that may occur on the job.

Competent co-workers (Clarke et al., 1980), and *peer models* (see, e.g., Bellamy, Peterson, & Close, 1976) have been used successfully to facilitate the acquisition and maintenance of specific work skills in an actual work setting. Handicapped workers can learn from competent co-workers. In addition, the use of co-workers as models may assist with fading the presence of and necessity for outside vocational instructors.

Training Format

Prior to establishing a systematic instructional program for teaching a specific work task to a handicapped learner, an instructor must select one of the following training formats for instruction: 1) simultaneous instruction on all steps in the task; 2) forward chaining of the task steps; or 3) backward chaining of the task steps. (See Chapter 3 for further examples of these techniques.)

Simultaneous instruction on all steps in a task involves proceeding through the task from beginning to end using training techniques on any steps requiring instruction. Bellamy et al. (1979) advocate the use of simultaneous instruction over backward or forward chaining of vocational skills. They suggest that instruction on all steps facilitates the speed of acquisition and maintains the rhythm of a task and the task momentum. Table 7.5 provides an example of an instructional program using systematic instructional procedures through simultaneous instruction on all steps of the booklet binding task. Simultaneous instruction involves teaching on each of the 17 steps of the task analysis (refer to Table 7.4) from beginning to end on each training trial.

Forward chaining techniques involve training only the first step in the task that has not been mastered and teaching that first step to a criterion level. Once the first step is mastered, instruction will begin on a chain of the first plus second steps in the task (refer to Figure 7.1). Each combination of steps is trained to criterion before another succeeding step is added to the chain. This method is used until the entire task is completed from beginning to end without assistance. An example of the use of forward chaining in teaching the booklet binding task is provided in Table 7.6.

Backward chaining techniques involve training only the last step in the task to criterion levels and then adding each preceding step as criterion is met (refer to Figure 7.1). To utilize a backward chaining procedure, the task must be initially completed to the last step. This can be accomplished by either completing the task to the last step before presenting the task to the learner (e.g., Walls, Zane, & Thuedt, 1980) or by guiding the learner

Table 7.5. Sample instructional program using *simultaneous instruction* on all steps of booklet binding task

Time of Program: _____   Student Name: _____

Date: _____   Program Initiator: _____

1. Specific Program Objective (describe behaviorally):
   The client will use the spiral hole punch to punch and bind five consecutive booklets, with 100% accuracy (following enclosed task analysis).
   Rationale:
   Preparation for actual contracted job and may lead to future subcontracts requiring same skills.

2. Student Characteristics that:
   1) assist:
   2) hinder:

3. Behavior Changes Procedures:
   Simultaneous instruction all steps:
   1. Give instructions to client, "(*Name*), bind a booklet."
   2. Allow 3 seconds for independent initiation of step 1.
   3. If correctly self-initiated, record (+) and proceed to step 2.
      If incorrect or no response within 3 seconds, provide verbal prompt (e.g., "(*Name*), stand in front of the punch machine"), and if correctly completed, reinforce and record (V).
   4. If incorrect or no response within 3 seconds of verbal prompt, provide model and verbal prompt (e.g., "(*Name*), stand in front of machine like this"), and if correctly completed, reinforce and record (M).
   5. If incorrect or no response within 3 seconds of model prompt, provide physical and verbal prompt (e.g., guide client through step with as little contact as possible while saying "(*Name*), stand in front of the machine"). Reinforce with social praise and record (P).
   6. Proceed through all steps in the task analysis using these procedures.

4. Reinforcers (include type and schedule):
   Social praise on a variable schedule of approximately every third response, and for prompts reinforce final prompted step. Individual payment plans and systems will be used depending on client (e.g., tokens, graphs, money, etc.).

5. Data Collection Method:
   Probe:
   Prior to each training session a probe will be administered in which a (+) for correct responses and a (−) for incorrect or no response within 3 seconds will be recorded. If an incorrect or no response is made, *perform the step for the client* and proceed to next step. Do not prompt or reinforce.
   Training:
   Record the level of assistance necessary for successful completion of each step in training (i.e., +, V, M, or P).

6. Criterion To Be Met for Success:
   Five consecutive independently correct completions of steps in task analysis with 100% accuracy.

7. Maintenance and Generalization Procedures:
   Evaluate performance across settings and vary trainers.

through the task to the last step, which is then trained (e.g., Spooner & Hendrickson, 1976). One advantage of backward chaining is that reinforcement is always delivered after task completion, so the trainee learns to anticipate the positive results of the completed product. Walls et al. (1980) found backward chaining to be more effective than simultaneous instruction on all steps of assembly tasks. The backward chaining technique used in this study consisted of completing the task for the student to the step that was being trained. In fact, the task was assembled out of the trainee's sight. Refer to Table 7.7 for one example of the use of backward chaining in teaching the booklet binding task. Comparison of the training formats presented in Tables 7.5 through 7.7 permits a comparison of the three different formats for instruction of vocational skills.

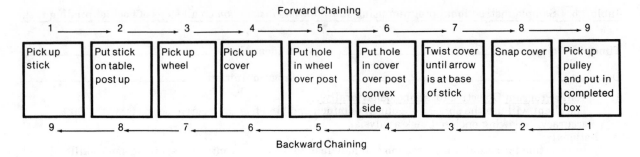

FORWARD CHAINING: Begin with the first step in the task. Reinforce step 1 to criterion, then steps 1 and 2 to criterion, etc.

BACKWARD CHAINING: Provide information only after completion of the final step in the task. Begin instruction on the last step (step 9) and teach to criterion. Then teach the chain of steps 8 and 9 to criterion, etc.

Figure 7.1. The use of forward versus backward chaining in a pulley assembly task.

Although there are no definitive data indicating the superiority of one training format over the others, there are a number of variables that may affect the successful use of the training format selected. Student characteristics may interact with effective instruction. If a student has successfully learned vocational tasks in the past or has already acquired a number of the skills required for the task to be trained, simultaneous instruction on all steps may be most effective and efficient. However, if a student has never been instructed in vocational tasks and/or has very few skills related to the task selected for instruction, it may be more effective to use a chaining technique. Similarly, if a student has a very short attention span and requires frequent reinforcement, perhaps chaining techniques would be most appropriate. In addition to student characteristics, task length and complexity may interact with the successful use of specific training formats.

> **If a student has never been instructed in vocational tasks and/or has very few skills related to the task selected for instruction, it may be more effective to use a chaining technique.**

Teacher Behavior

In addition to arranging task and environmental variables for optimal acquisition of vocational skills, the teacher must be proficient at prompting and reinforcement strategies if he/she is to be successful at teaching vocational skills to handicapped learners (Bellamy et al., 1979). Systematic use of instructional or response prompts in a training interaction is basic to effective instruction. The type of instructional prompts can range from unintrusive verbal to more intrusive gestural and model prompts to the most intrusive physical prompts or manual guidance.

An instructor may choose to use only one type of prompt in the instructional session (e.g., a verbal prompt). If only one type of prompt is used, the instructor must be sure that the type of prompt selected is *functional* for the

Table 7.6. Sample instructional program using *forward chaining* of steps in booklet binding task

Time of Program: _____   Student Name: _____

Date: _____   Program Initiator: _____

1. Specific Program Objective (describe behaviorally):
   The client will use the spiral hole punch to punch and bind five consecutive booklets, with 100% accuracy (following enclosed task analysis).
   Rationale:
   Preparation for actual contracted job and may lead to future subcontracts requiring same skills.

2. Student Characteristics that:
   1) assist:
   2) hinder:

3. Behavior Changes Procedures:
   Forward chaining procedure:
   1. Give instructions to client, "(*Name*), bind a booklet."
   2. Allow 3 seconds for independent initiation of step 1 (or first step client did *not* perform consistently correctly during baseline).
   3. If client correctly performs step 1, reinforce and record (+). This is considered completion of one trial, so start at the beginning of the task for trial 2 (e.g., give general instructions for task and teach step 1).
   4. If client was incorrect on step 1, or did not respond within 3 seconds, provide a verbal prompt for step 1 (e.g., "(*Name*), stand in front of punch machine"). If correct response to verbal prompt, reinforce and record (V) and go back to the beginning again.
   5. If incorrect or no response to verbal prompt, model step while repeating verbal prompt (e.g., "(*Name*), stand in front of punch machine like this"). If correct response after model, reinforce and record (M) and go back to the beginning.
   6. If incorrect or no response within 3 seconds after model, physically guide client through step (as little physical contact as possible) while repeating verbal prompt. Reinforce and record (P) and go back to the beginning again.
   After criterion (five consecutive unprompted correct responses) has been met on step 1, begin training on the 2-step chain of steps 1 and 2.
   The prompting procedure described above should be followed for each step in the chain, and the level of assistance required should be recorded (i.e., +, V, M, or P). However, reinforcement will *only* be provided *after the completion of the chain of steps* (e.g., after step 2).
   Each step in the task analysis will be added in this manner. After criterion has been met on the previous chain of steps, a new step will be added and taught until all steps in the task analysis are being trained from start to finish of the binding task.

4. Reinforcers (include type and schedule):
   Social praise for completion of a trial (the steps included in the chain). Individual payment plans and systems will be used depending on the client (e.g., tokens, graphs, money, etc.).

5. Data Collection Method:
   Probe:
   Prior to each training session a probe will be administered in which a (+) for correct responses and a (−) for incorrect or no response within 3 seconds will be recorded. If an incorrect or no response is made, *perform the step for the client* and proceed to next step. Do not prompt or reinforce.
   Training:
   Record the level of assistance necessary for successful completion of each step in training (i.e., +, V, M, or P).

6. Criterion To Be Met for Success:
   Training:
   Five consecutive independently correct responses on the steps being trained will result in the addition of a new step for training.
   Mastery:
   Five consecutive independent completions of all steps in the task analysis with 100% accuracy.

7. Maintenance and Generalization Procedures:
   Evaluate performance across settings and vary trainers.

Table 7.7. Sample instructional program using *backward chaining* of steps in booklet binding task

Time of Program: _____   Student Name: _____

Date: _____   Program Initiator: _____

1. <u>Specific Program Objective (describe behaviorally):</u>
   The client will use the spiral hole punch to punch and bind five consecutive booklets, with 100% accuracy (following enclosed task analysis).
   <u>Rationale:</u>
   Preparation for actual contracted job and may lead to future subcontracts requiring same skills.

2. <u>Student Characteristics that:</u>
   1) assist:
   2) hinder:

3. <u>Behavior Changes Procedures:</u>
   <u>Backward chaining procedure:</u>
   1. Complete all steps except last step while client is watching (or last step client *did not complete consistently correct* during baseline.
   2. Give instructions to client "(*Name*), finish binding a booklet."
   3. Allow 3 seconds for independent initiation of last step (or appropriate step).
   4. If client correctly completes last steps, reinforce and record (+). This is completion of task, so begin again.
   5. If client was incorrect on last step or did not respond within 3 seconds, provide a verbal prompt (e.g., "(*Name*), put the booklet on the finished pile"). If correct response to verbal prompt, reinforce and record (V). Begin task again.
   6. If client was incorrect on last step or did not respond within 3 seconds of verbal prompt, model step while repeating verbal prompt (e.g., "(*Name*), put the booklet on the finished pile like this"). If correct response, reinforce and record (M). Begin task again.
   7. If incorrect response or no response within 3 seconds of model, guide client through last step (as little physical contact as possible) while repeating verbal prompt. Reinforce and record (P) and begin task again.
   After criterion (five consecutive unprompted correct responses) has been met on the last step, begin training on the next-to-the-last step *in combination with* last step (you will be instructing on a 2-step chain, e.g., steps 16 and 17.).

   The prompting procedures described above should be followed for each step in the chain, and the level of assistance required for each step should be recorded (i.e., + , V, M, or P). However, *reinforcement will be provided only after the last step in the task* (regardless of the number of steps included in the training). Each step will be added in this manner. After criterion has been met on the chain of steps in training, a new step will be added (working back toward the beginning of task) until all steps are being taught from start to finish of the binding task.

4. <u>Reinforcers (include type and schedule):</u>
   Social praise for completion of a trial (the steps included in the chain). Individual payment plans and systems will be used depending on the client (e.g., tokens, graphs, money, etc.).

5. <u>Data Collection Method:</u>
   <u>Probe:</u>
   Prior to each training session a probe will be administered in which a (+) for correct responses and a (−) for incorrect or no response within 3 seconds will be recorded. If an incorrect or no response is made, *perform the step for the client* and proceed to next step. Do not prompt or reinforce.

6. <u>Criterion To Be Met for Success:</u>
   <u>Training:</u>
   Five consecutive independently correct responses on the steps being trained will result in the addition of a new step for training.
   <u>Mastery:</u>
   Five consecutive independent completions of all steps in task analysis with 100% accuracy.

7. <u>Maintenance and Generalization Procedures:</u>
   Evaluate performance across settings and vary trainers.

individual with whom it is to be used. In other words, if a verbal prompt alone is selected for assisting an individual student in task performance, the instructor must have predetermined that verbal cues are understandable (functional) to that person. Similar consideration must be made if model prompts are selected as the sole assist for task performance; the learner must have imitation skills in his/her behavioral repertoire.

An alternative to selecting only one type of prompt for instruction is to use a range of prompts within any one instructional session. A least-to-most intrusive prompt system has been used successfully in teaching janitorial skills (Cuvo, Leaf, & Borakove, 1978), wood-working skills (Bates et al., in press), and assembly tasks (Spooner & Hendrickson, 1976) to handicapped workers. A least intrusive prompt system allows the learner to perform each step in the task with the greatest degree of independence. This is accomplished by first allowing a specified period of time (e.g., 3 seconds) for self-initiation of a task step. If the student does not self-initiate, a verbal prompt would be given. If the verbal prompt was not successful, then a model or gestural prompt might be given, and, if unsuccessful, a physical prompt would be used to step completion. Reinforcement would be delivered upon step completion regardless of the level of prompt required for success. Refer to Tables 7.5 through 7.7 for examples of the use of a least intrusive prompting system in teaching the booklet binding task.

An alternative to the least intrusive prompt system is a system that begins with the most intrusive prompt (e.g., manual guidance) and fades to less intrusive prompts (e.g., physical to model to verbal). Cuvo, Leaf, and Borakove (1978) suggested that a most-to-least intrusive prompting system may be most effective with the steps in a work task that have been identified as difficult to acquire. For difficult steps, beginning with manual guidance and fading to less assistance may ensure success with a near errorless pattern of learning.

Regardless of the type and/or system of prompts used for vocational skills instruction, it is important to be consistent in the type and delivery of each prompt from trial to trial. In addition, the system of prompting should be described in detail, including the time allowed before prompts, and the type and frequency of reinforcement for completion of task steps. This promotes consistency from trial to trial and replication between staff persons.

Modifying Stimulus Materials

For work tasks that require difficult discriminations, modifications of task materials that make initial discriminations easier may be necessary. *Redundant cues* are additional or extra task cues that are added to task materials but have no relevance to the natural task cues. The most frequently used redundant cue for aiding in the acquisition of individual tasks is color coding (e.g., Gold, 1972; Irvin & Bellamy, 1977). Gold (1972) used color coding to facilitate moderately and severely retarded workers in the acquisition of a complex bicycle brake assembly. Color was added to the side of each part of the brake assembly that was to face the worker. Individuals who were trained on the task with the color codes acquired the skills in half the time of those who were trained without the color cues.

> **Redundant cues are additional or extra task cues that are added to task materials but have no relevance to the natural task cues.**

Lights, pictures, and tactile stimuli can also serve as redundant cues for task acquisition. It is, however, very important to fade, systematically, the redundant cues once the task has been acquired, until the learner is responding to the natural cues of the task alone.

Easy-to-hard instructional sequences also require modifications of task materials, but consist of maximizing the relevant cues within the task so that the initial discrimination is easy and gradually becomes more difficult (e.g., Gold & Barclay, 1973; Irvin & Bellamy, 1977). Unlike redundant cues, easy-to-hard sequencing techniques do not involve the addition of cues that have no relevance to the discrimination. Instead, easy-to-hard sequences intensify the relevant cues of the task (Bellamy et al., 1979). For example, if a worker were being taught to identify a dirty versus clean restaurant table, initial discriminations may involve a very clean, clear table and an extremely dirty, dish-filled, messy table. The differences between clean and dirty are magnified initially and would then be gradually reduced across training trials until the learner is able to make subtle discriminations between clean and dirty tables.

> **Easy-to-hard sequences intensify the relevant cues of the task. For example, if a worker were being taught to identify a dirty versus clean restaurant table, initial discriminations may involve a very clean, clear table and an extremely dirty, dish-filled, messy table.**

Gold and Barclay (1973) used easy-to-hard sequencing in teaching moderately and severely retarded learners to sort 1-inch bolts from ⅞-inch bolts. Because bolt *length* was the relevant dimension of the task, initial discriminations were made easy by maximizing the differences in length of bolts (e.g., 1½ inch versus ¾ inch). After criterion level performance was achieved on this easy discrimination, the bolt lengths were gradually altered until 7/8-inch bolts were being successfully sorted from 1-inch bolts.

Although there is little empirical evidence to suggest that the use of redundant cues is superior to easy-to-hard sequencing or the reverse, a number of factors might be considered in selection of the technique. The type of task, time required to modify task materials, and cost of materials preparation may indicate that one strategy is more desirable than the other. In any case, the use of stimulus prompts may be necessary for task acquisition.

WORK PRODUCTIVITY

Once vocational skills have been acquired, the emphasis in vocational training shifts to proficiency of task performance or work production rate. The importance of production rate as a variable influencing success of handicapped individuals has been documented in sheltered employment. In sheltered employment settings, production rate usually provides the basis for paying workers (i.e., piece rate payment) and is frequently associated with workshop admission standards and levels of employment within the workshop labor force. For example, individuals performing at less than 25% of the competitive production rate are considered unproductive and are assigned a work activity or long-term status. Persons performing at higher production rates are classified as sheltered or transitional employees and are paid according to their productivity.

> **In sheltered employment settings production rate usually provides the basis for paying workers (i.e., piece rate payment) and is frequently associated with workshop admission standards and levels of employment within the workshop labor force.**

The effectiveness of a variety of intervention procedures for improving work productivity of handicapped individuals is well documented (Bellamy et al., 1976). These intervention procedures have included the manipulation of a range of antecedent, performance, and consequence variables.

Arrangement of the Antecedent Environment

Arrangement of antecedent variables involves manipulating task or environmental variables prior to actual work skill instruction and includes: 1) physical arrangements; 2) interpersonal constellations; and 3) supervisor instructions.

Physical Arrangements Physical aspects of the work environment include noise levels, background music, work station design, equipment, charts, and location of the work station. Schroeder (1972) developed individual booths with automated production recording equipment for mildly and moderately retarded sheltered workshop participants. These physical arrangements in combination with individualized incentives resulted in production rate increases. In another investigation, Martin, Pallotta-Cornick, Johnstone, and Goyos (1980) used environmental engineering in combination with other antecedent and consequence events to reduce distractors in the work setting.

However, research specifically directed at evaluating the relative contributions of various physical arrangements to productivity of handicapped individuals has not been conducted. For example, productivity as a function of different styles and tempos of background music has not been investigated in the vocational literature with handicapped workers.

Interpersonal Constellations The interpersonal constellation refers to the number and characteristics of co-workers and staff in the work area. In a sheltered employment situation, virtually all co-workers are handicapped, and the supervisor-to-worker ratio is often less than 1 to 10. Work productivity should be investigated under various supervisor-to-worker ratios and with different mixes of handicapped and non-handicapped workers. Identifying the arrangement of staff and workers that maximizes efficiency and minimizes staff demands facilitates increased services to larger numbers of handicapped persons.

Supervisor Instructions A supervisor's instructions prior to work can range from general statements (e.g., "It's time to work.") to explicit statements regarding work productivity goals (e.g., "Your work quota is 500 today."). Although most programs include supervisor instructions, the contribution of these instructions to overall productivity has not been thoroughly examined.

Gold (1973) documented production rate increases made by groups of moderately retarded persons after they were provided with a relatively complex task (i.e., bicycle brake) and given a general instruction (e.g., "Work until the bell goes off."). Although these increases were witnessed in the absence of a conventional reinforcement system, the study only lasted 10 days and did not control for practice effect.

Several studies have been reported that have used supervisor instructions to indicate specific production contingencies (Bates, Renzaglia, & Clees, 1980; Bellamy, Inman, & Yeates, 1978; Cohen & Close, 1976; Gordon, O'Connor, & Tizard, 1955; Horner, Lahren, Schwartz, O'Neill, & Hunter, 1979; Jackson, 1979; Jens & Shores, 1969). These verbal instructions have frequently been strengthened by directing the client's attention to additional cues for information regarding the acceptability of a particular speed of production. Behavioral graphs (Jens & Shores, 1969), cueing lights (Jackson, 1979), and timers (Bates et al., 1980) have been used to augment verbal directions. Verbal instructions from a supervisor have also been used to direct independent, cooperative, or competitive production (Gordon et al., 1955; Huddle, 1979). Although successful use of verbal instruction has been documented, it may be as effective for many individuals to provide instructions in the form of written messages, pictures, or modeled demonstrations. These potential alternatives to verbal instructions may be less demanding of staff time and therefore more efficient.

Behavioral graphs, cueing lights, and timers have been used to augment verbal directions.

Performance Variables

Performance variables are task-related cues, supervisor prompts, and co-worker characteristics that may exert an influence on work productivity. Several studies have introduced task-related redundant cues into the work routine that are intended to stimulate higher production rates. These have included timers (Bellamy et al., 1978), cueing lights (Jackson, 1979), and tape on a wrist watch (Horner et al., 1979). These cues were intended to provide constant reminders to the workers regarding the importance of high productivity.

Supervisor prompts during the production period are often a natural and necessary component of vocational programming with severely handicapped populations. The schedule of supervisor prompts has seldom been consistent. Martin et al. (1980), however, provided "get to work" prompts on a variable interval schedule of 5 minutes. This procedure in combination with other antecedent and consequent events resulted in substantial work production increases.

Co-worker's competencies and co-worker reinforcement are additional variables that have influenced productivity. Kazdin (1973) and Brown and Pearce (1970) demonstrated that vocational productivity in sheltered settings is influenced by supervisor reinforcement of co-workers. Kazdin, however, attributed this influence to the cueing qualities of reinforcement rather than to imitation of a co-worker's reinforced behavior.

Ideally, vocational productivity is controlled by the natural cues in the situation. For example, the dishwasher in a restaurant experiences times of high volume and times of low volume. During high volume, work productivity should increase in response to the sight of more dishes. Unfortunately, many handicapped persons have not been taught to interpret such natural productivity cues, and as a result their performance suffers.

Consequence Arrangement

Most researchers in the vocational area have emphasized the contingent relationship between production behavior and environmental consequences. This is the only instructional area in which tangible rewards are considered a natural and necessary consequence for sustained performance. In fact, numerous laws have been written to guarantee a person's right to receive compensation for work productivity.

The "work ethic" is a respected value in our society. According to Martin and Morris (1980), this value is evidenced when individuals perceive work as a viable means to an end. A person's perception of this relationship cannot be directly measured, but can be inferred by demonstrating a functional relationship between vocational production and consequence arrangement. A frequently encountered vocational contingency in our culture is the weekly paycheck.

In sheltered employment, thousands of handicapped individuals receive a paycheck every week that is based on their productivity. However, for many severely handicapped individuals, this consequence arrangement is too delayed and too abstract to have an enhancing effect on productivity. A variety of more immediate consequences have been applied to enhance productivity, including performance feedback, external reinforcement, and self-reinforcement. In addition to positive consequences, a few aversive procedures have also been applied to decrease "off-task" behavior and to discourage slow production behavior.

> **In sheltered employment, thousands of handicapped individuals receive a paycheck every week that is based on their production. However, for many severely handicapped individuals, this consequence arrangement is too delayed and too abstract to have an enhancing effect on productivity.**

Performance Feedback Performance feedback refers to the procedure of providing objective information to workers regarding their work production rate. Feedback can be provided through verbal report, graphic displays, viewing videotape, use of automated devices, and redundant cues. In virtually all of the studies that have used feedback strategies, it is difficult to isolate the relative contributions of supervisor instructions, specific incentives, and the objective performance information. For example, in the Jens and Shores (1969) investigation, three moderately retarded adolescents were shown their graphed performance of previous work at the beginning of each work period and again at the end of the work day. As a result, it is impossible to determine whether the improved performance is attributable to an antecedent goal incentive or to the feedback consequence.

Performance feedback has been provided during task performance and at the end of a workday. DeRoo and Haralson (1971) videotaped vocational production behavior of mildly retarded young adults on an assembly task. When inappropriate behavior occurred, performance was halted and individuals were required to view the tape. This procedure resulted in performance gains of at least 59% by all persons involved.

Ongoing performance feedback has been provided to workers with cueing lights that are maintained "on" by continuous attention to a production task (Jackson, 1979). Bates et al. (1980) provided ongoing feedback to a profoundly retarded worker by indicating visually the number of pennies earned in relation to the number of pennies required to purchase a snack for break. Prior to each 1½ to 2-hour work period, the trainer calculated the number of drapery pulleys the worker was required to complete to make a predetermined production quota. After determining the quota, the trainer placed penny boards (2-inch x 4-inch boards with slots for pennies) on the table next to the worker's station (see Figure 7.2). The worker received one penny for every two drapery pulleys assembled. Therefore, as the worker progressed toward the criterion work requirement, fewer penny slots were exposed providing continuous feedback as to fulfillment of the quota. These procedures, in combination with a changing criterion technique (raising the quota as each preceding quota was met) increased the worker's production rate from a completely unacceptable rate for a sheltered work setting (approximately 1% of the norm for nonhandicapped) to approximately 50% of the norm for nonhandicapped workers (or twice the rate required for sheltered employment).

In a study with severely retarded adults in a sheltered workshop, Flexer, Martin, and Friedenberg (1977) attempted to bridge the gap between daily earnings and purchasing power by providing the workshop clients with an earnings chart. This procedure, in conjunction with gradual changes in the reinforcement schedule, resulted in approximately a 66% increase in productivity. Furthermore, daily earnings were charted as savings toward future purchases, thus demonstrating that severely retarded persons are capable of high production under conditions of delayed gratification.

Reinforcement Contingencies A variety of different types of reinforcement and reinforcement schedules has been used with handicapped workers in vocational settings. These have been variable interval schedules (Bellamy et al., 1975), fixed interval schedules (Schroeder, 1972), and fixed ratio schedules (Martin et al., 1980; Schroeder, 1972). According to Schroeder (1972), frequent fixed interval schedules or schedules based on

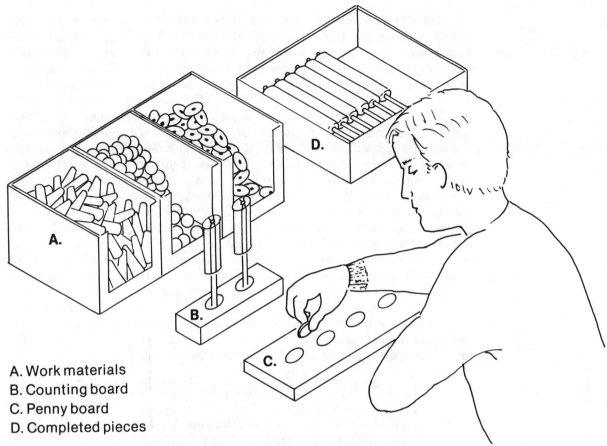

A. Work materials
B. Counting board
C. Penny board
D. Completed pieces

Figure 7.2. Use of continuous feedback and a self-reinforcement strategy to increase production rate.

the passage of a specific interval of time (e.g., payment every 30 minutes) resulted in more performance than frequent ratio schedules and payment based on the completion of a specific number of work units (e.g., payment for every 5 units of work completed). This result, however, was reversed as the interval and ratio became greater.

In a study involving sheltered workshop employees, performance under the schedule of a paycheck every 2 weeks was used as a comparison for future schedule changes. By gradually increasing interval reinforcement schedules from 5 minutes to 60 minutes, production increased 41% above baseline levels. Another study was reported by Martin & Morris (1980) that demonstrated the superiority of fixed ratio schedules of reinforcement over infrequent interval schedules. Both of the above studies were conducted in sheltered settings and involved severely retarded workers.

Finally, a frequently encountered production contingency in the vocational production area is the use of goal setting. In goal setting, a production goal is established and a worker is provided different consequences for exceeding the goal. The criterion goal is changed according to the worker's productivity, thus providing a changing criterion demonstration of the goal contingencies. These procedures have been used successfully in sheltered settings (Bates et al., 1980; Bellamy et al., 1978) and allow for a gradual step-by-step increase in production rate, which is frequently more feasible than a drastic increase in expectation for production.

Self-reinforcement Because supervisor-to-client ratios in vocational settings are less than ideal and because handicapped individuals may need individualized contingencies, an economical means of reinforcer delivery is needed. Self-reinforcement, the process of providing oneself with rewarding consequences contingent upon a behavior, is a method that requires minimal supervision and has been effective in changing behavior.

Wehman et al. (1978) reported a series of three experiments that compared the effectiveness of external reinforcement, self-administered reinforcement, and self-determined reinforcement on the vocational production rates of severely disabled adults. In these studies the self-administered reinforcement conditions resulted in production performance that was equal to or better than external reinforcement. In one study that was designed specifically to investigate the effectiveness of self-administration of reinforcement as compared to external delivery, Horner et al. (1979) found self-administration of tokens to result in substantially greater improvements in the work production rate of a severely retarded adult than did externally administered tokens. The worker was taught to self-administer a single token for every adapter assembly completed. The self-reinforcement was an alternative to signaling a supervisor to deliver the token. Performance in the self-administration condition was approximately equal to the competitive production rate on the same task, as opposed to a 50% performance rate during external reinforcement conditions.

> **In one study that was designed specifically to investigate the effectiveness of self-administration of reinforcement as compared to external delivery, self-administration of tokens resulted in substantially greater improvements in the work production rates of a severely retarded adult than did externally administered tokens.**

Zohn and Bernstein (1980) reported a study in which four moderately retarded adults were taught to self-record the number of hospital kits that they assembled in 15-minute work periods. Two subjects demonstrated improvements in both production rate and attending to task as a function of the self-monitoring activity.

Finally, Bates et al. (1980) taught a profoundly retarded adolescent to self-administer pennies for completion of drapery pulley assemblies. A counting block was used to cue the person to self-reinforce after the completion of two pulleys (refer to Figure 7.3).

Self-reinforcement procedures have been successfully applied to sheltered work with severely disabled workers and provide a viable alternative to frequent external delivery of reinforcers. Because many severely disabled workers require frequent reinforcement (many times more frequent than nonhandicapped), the use of strategies of self-reinforcement provides an efficient method (less demanding of staff time) of increasing and maintaining acceptable work production rates.

Negative Consequences Many handicapped individuals continue to perform inadequately even after antecedent and reinforcement procedures have been systematically altered. Frequently, this is due to a high rate of interfering behavior (Wehman, Schutz, Renzaglia, & Karan, 1977). Reminders to get back to work (Bellamy et al., 1976), positive practice in working fast (Wehman et al., 1976), and isolation-avoidance procedures (Zimmerman, Overpeck, Eisenberg, & Garlick, 1969) have been used contingent on off-task and/or slow working behavior. Each of these techniques has resulted in production rate increases. The use of negative consequences to increase production rate should be considered, however, only after other positive techniques have been explored. It is most desirable to teach the worker to respond to the benefits of work rather than to teach him/her to avoid the negative consequences.

SUMMARY

With the push for deinstitutionalization and the emphasis on normalization of handicapped learners, it is not surprising that vocational skills instruction has become a focal point for many educators. If severely handicapped persons are to succeed in community living settings, it is increasingly important that they have a vocation (Bellamy et al., 1976; Gold, 1973).

Community sheltered employment settings provide viable employment options for moderately, severely, and profoundly handicapped persons. Even though sheltered settings have been in operation for a number of years, it has not been until recently that sheltered work settings have accepted severely handicapped employees. Therefore, vocational educators must be aware of entry-level skill requirements for obtaining and maintaining employment in sheltered settings. With this information, vocational educators are able to prepare students for successful placement in specific sheltered work settings.

Through the systematic application of learning principles, moderately, severely, and profoundly handicapped persons have been able to acquire complex vocational skills (e.g., Bellamy et al., 1976; Gold, 1972) and produce at adequate rates (e.g., Bates and Harvey, 1979; Bellamy et al., 1979; Flexer et al., 1977). Educators must, therefore, incorporate the procedures developed by vocational researchers into educational programs, which should result in increased vocational competence and successful sheltered employment for severely handicapped persons.

8

COMPETITIVE EMPLOYMENT

LEARNING GOALS

1. Identify the points involved in a rationale for placing moderately and severely handicapped individuals into competitive employment.
2. Describe five reasons why public school programs do not adequately prepare moderately and severely handicapped individuals for competitive employment.
3. List and describe the sequence of activities involved in the job placement process; and identify several types of problems and solutions that occur during job placement.
4. Discuss the range of problems and solutions that is encountered in competitive employment programming.
5. Describe the role and process of fading staff from client supervision at a job site.
6. List the problems and solutions involved in the staff fading process, as well as the types of follow-up that can be provided to students already employed.
7. Identify and describe five major problems and solutions for improving job placement in public school systems.

Competitive employment is the placement of an individual into a job that usually pays the minimum wage in which nonhandicapped persons predominantly work. Most moderately and severely handicapped individuals have rarely been employed competitively, and it has only been in recent years that some efforts have been made at helping this population enter gainful employment (Rusch & Mithaug, 1980; Wehman, 1981).

As was described in the previous chapter on sheltered employment, there has been tremendous development in the application of behavioral technology to sheltered workshop training of the moderately and severely handicapped. However, in the continuum of vocational placements, a competitive employment setting may be optimal in terms of opportunities for greater wages, advancement, and working with nonhandicapped peers. It is incumbent upon teachers and counselors not to close the door on competitive employment for moderately and severely handicapped individuals (Brolin, 1982).

It is the purpose of this chapter to discuss the importance of competitive employment for handicapped individuals. Also, we review in depth the problems involved in linking secondary special education programs to competitive employment in adulthood. The placement process, job site training, client advocacy, and client evaluation are each discussed. Selected case studies are provided as a means of highlighting the concepts presented in this chapter.

WHY COMPETITIVE EMPLOYMENT?

Wages and Benefits

The first and most obvious point in favor of competitive employment placement is the increased opportunity for greater wages and benefits. With the tremendous cost of maintaining handicapped individuals in centers that are nonvocationally oriented or that rarely lead to competitive employment, it is apparent that those clients who can earn competitive level wages will be most favorably viewed. These clients will require less Supplemental Security Income (SSI) assistance from the federal government and, perhaps equally important, will clear the way for other more severely handicapped clients.

Competitive wages will increase the independence of severely handicapped individuals. The benefits may include insurance policies, medical insurance, dental insurance, and retirement. Of course, not in all cases will this range of benefits be available. Compared with the offerings of developmental centers and most sheltered workshops, however, there is a much greater likelihood of this type of fringe support.

The most obvious advantage of competitive employment, wages and benefits, may also be the most profound in the long run. Working all day for four to five dollars is not a particularly dignified remuneration for one's daily vocational pursuits. It is only natural that the individual eventually comes to look upon himself/herself as inferior to those without disabilities. Furthermore, nonhandicapped persons who visit sheltered centers may leave with a perception that the handicapped worker's economic value is only worth four to five dollars a day. This is an insidious and unfair conclusion.

Integration with Nonhandicapped Persons

Closely linked in importance to wages and benefits is the opportunity to work among nonhandicapped people and not be segregated with disabled individuals. This issue also includes the opportunity to serve nonhandicapped consumers and directly see these consumers daily. Similarly, the likelihood of meeting new individuals and making friends with nonhandicapped persons is enhanced.

Working with nonhandicapped peers provides opportunities for handicapped workers to learn to accept criticism and ridicule to which all individuals must adjust. Continual insulation and protection from real work obstacles is a false panacea in the habilitation of severely disabled individuals.

The increased visibility of handicapped workers in community settings also cannot be discounted as a major advantage of competitive employment. In order to elevate the expectations and perceptions of employers toward severely disabled individuals, direct contact and observation of their work abilities is a primary means of ensuring continued hiring practice and retention.

Working with handicapped peers provides opportunities for handicapped workers to learn to accept criticism and ridicule to which all individuals must adjust.

Normalization

Working for a real company or organization, one that is not organized necessarily for the purposes of therapeutic rehabilitation of its employees, is a normal event that comprises a substantial part of nonhandicapped persons' lives. The opportunity to go to work regularly and to not be subjected to the vacillations of contract and subcontract orders for work is one that should be available to all disabled people. Although layoffs and seasonal work are certainly evident in competitive work, if one has a history of competitive employment, the likelihood of obtaining other competitive jobs in the off-season may be better.

Wolfensberger (1972) and Bellamy et al. (1979) point out that work is a socially equitable activity that should be available for severely disabled individuals. From work comes a feeling of fulfillment and improved self-concept (Brolin, 1982).

Greater Opportunity for Advancement

Whitehead (1979) has observed that, regrettably, very few of the clients in workshops leave for competitive employment. According to a U.S. Department of Labor report (1977), only 12% of regular workshop clients are placed in competitive situations, and only 3% are retained after two years of such a placement. This suggests that segregated work centers are not usually able to place significant numbers of clients in the real world. Consequently, the possibilities for increased wages and job responsibilities seem remote for many severely disabled persons.

On the other hand, a competitive placement may generate an opportunity for greater advancement. This may take the form of a better work shift, more regular work hours, a more pleasant job, supervisory work, or better wages. Such advancements are not guaranteed by any means and an advocate may well be necessary; however, it may be easier to move to a different job with another company from a competitive placement as opposed to coming from a sheltered workshop or work activities center.

Improved Perceptions by Family and Friends

Parents play a major and ever-critical role in facilitating the advantageous aspects of competitive employment. By helping to overcome transportation problems, working out SSI limitations, and providing strong moral support to their son or daughter in the job placement, parents can make a competitive placement successful or completely block it. It is our contention that increased competitive placements of severely handicapped individuals will lend greater credibility to their work potential. These demonstrations of competence will begin to reduce the fears of parents about their son or daughter working in the real world. Parents of handicapped persons are in touch with each other regularly, frequently follow each other's advice, and will often take the counsel of parents before professionals. Hence, it is necessary to increase the number of successful competitive placements of severely handicapped individuals.

THE PLACEMENT PROCESS[1]

The process of placing a moderately or severely handicapped person in a job can be very difficult. It requires perseverance and careful planning of a sequence of events starting with a job search. Figure 8.1 outlines the major points involved in making a placement from start to finish. The major components are reviewed briefly below.

The first step involves *searching for a job*. This can include reviewing classified advertisements in the local newspapers, utilizing personal contacts, and checking with the local employment commission and National Alliance of Businessmen chapter. Once a job is located and a placement made, frequently, other jobs will be made available from this placement.

While searching for a job, it is imperative to *analyze the different work environments* according to their respective physical and social interaction requirements. For example, it may be that a job is located for a student but

---

[1]This section was prepared with the assistance of Patricia Goodall and Paula Cleveland.

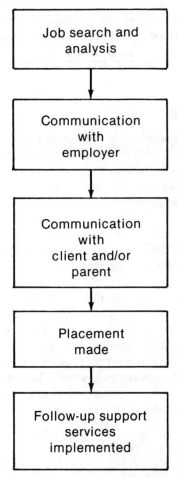

Figure 8.1. The placement process.

that the specific environment is not conducive to his/her abilities. Belmore and Brown (1978) have carefully performed a detailed job analysis of typical dishwasher job environments, which is useful.

The third step in the placement sequence is employer communication. This step refers to talking with the appropriate supervisors and explaining the individual client's capabilities, discussing the federal tax credit available and any other information the supervisor may need to know.

Once the employer decides to consider hiring the client, then serious discussions can begin with the parents and client. A work schedule can be reviewed, transportation systems worked out, and concerns about the possible loss of SSI payments discussed (Wehman & Hill, 1979). If these discussions are successful, then a job interview, the next step in the placement sequence, can be set up. Before this interview, appearance, eye contact, and appropriate handshaking behavior should have been taught and rehearsed (Hill et al., 1979).

The final step in the placement process is the actual hiring of the client. In addition to possibly filling out a job application or any other forms necessary, the teacher or counselor must work out a job site visit and follow-up schedule. Ideally, weekly records can be kept of the client's job progress, wages earned, and rates of absenteeism. (See Rusch & Mithaug, 1980, and Wehman & McLaughlin, 1980, for more on record keeping in this area.)

> **The process of placing a severely handi-
> capped person requires perseverance
> and careful planning.**

Responsibility for Job Placement

There are a number of beliefs as to who should carry out the duties of job placement. Some steadfastly maintain that the rehabilitation counselor alone is responsible, whereas others in the field would like to see specialists recruited from the business and sales world. Bruyere (1976) notes that as the debate of generalist counselor versus placement for the severely disabled continues to grow and expand, we will benefit from the broad range of experiences of those who utilize the various approaches.

Bruyere (1976) aptly suggests that the resolution to this debate may lie in reorganization of program structure that maximizes the use of existing staff. Obviously, a rehabilitation professional who has the *skill* and *interest* to do job placement would be most effective. Forcing reluctant counselors to place clients will only result in a higher number of unsuccessful placements. Making a job placement is not an extremely difficult task; however, making a good placement—one in which the client is most likely to experience long-term successful employment—requires skill and judgment on the part of the placement counselor. The counselor must be committed to placement because it can be a tedious, time-consuming process of job analysis and client assessment.

Characteristics of an Effective Placement Specialist

Those professionals involved in the job placement of severely handicapped individuals agree that effective placement is not an easy task. Wehman (1981) has said that it requires tremendous perseverance and patience. Olshansky (1977) stated that placement work is characterized by daily traumas that are overwhelmingly distressing. Others mention that a placement specialist needs to have a certain kind of durable and outgoing personality. What then, does it take to be an effective placement specialist?

In general, the placement specialist must possess a thorough knowledge of the characteristics and abilities of the clients to be served, as well as an awareness of the current trends in vocational opportunities for the targeted population (i.e., the severely disabled). A strong commitment to the belief that handicapped workers *do* make valuable employees may be the most important attribute of a placement counselor.

Knowledge and commitment alone, however, do not distinguish the placement specialist; it is the ability to actively convey the employability of the severely disabled to a wide variety of individuals (employers, parents, clients, and other professionals) that is the hallmark of the placement specialist. It appears, then, that a good placement specialist is not only a competent rehabilitation professional, but is also able to function comfortably and effectively in a public relations role.

On a more specific level, placement counselors should exhibit specialized skills in the various task areas that comprise the placement process. To aid in identifying some of these necessary skills, Table 8.1 describes the major components of the placement process, as well as the important skills needed to perform each step of the process.

The placement process as outlined in Table 8.1 is comprised of three major areas: *job development, client assessment,* and *placement.* Each of the areas is of equal importance in the placement process; they are, in fact, interdependent. A weakness in one area may result in a problem-ridden or unsuccessful placement. The tasks involved in each phase must be performed with knowledge and skill in order to produce a placement that is most likely to be successful.

The placement process can be viewed as a simultaneous, ongoing execution of the component steps involved in each phase. The actual placement of a client into employment is accomplished through the synthesis of information that is obtained during job development and client assessment activities. Therefore, the placement specialist must have the ability to focus and coordinate all parts of the placement process toward the goal of job placement.

Job development involves employer contact, job analysis, and negotiation for a placement. The placement counselor must be assertive, enthusiastic, and able to communicate effectively with a wide variety of employers. The counselor should be adept at relating to an employer's needs and concerns in terms that are meaningful to the employer; detailed explanations of the rehabilitation process or an aggressive, "hard sell" approach will only serve to alienate the employer.

If the employer is interested and there exists the potential for a job opening that a handicapped worker could fill, a thorough job analysis should be completed. This phase of job development is crucial in order to determine, as objectively as possible, whether or not a disabled client would be capable of performing the job duties. Usually there is a significant variance in job requirements for similar positions among different companies (e.g., the job duties for a dishwasher vary greatly from company to company).

The placement process does not exist without the job development stage. It is essential, therefore, that the placement specialist be willing to commit a great deal of time and energy to this task area. The art of placement involves the nurturing of company contacts that have been established during initial canvassing of employers; the placement counselor must continuously engage in canvassing activities if placements are to be made.

The placement specialist must also be able to determine how much time and effort to expend on a potential employer. It is necessary to recognize the point at which it becomes frustrating and unproductive to continue to actively pursue a placement that is not forthcoming; maintaining contact with the employer on a periodic basis would be more appropriate. The distinction must be made between a possible placement and a probable placement.

Client assessment entails evaluating all client referrals in terms of employability in the competitive job market. The placement counselor must be able to understand and interpret the various vocational and educational assessment tools that are commonly used in the rehabilitation process. A vast amount of client information must be gathered and evaluated, including social, medical, vocational, educational, and environmental factors that may influence successful competitive placement.

Table 8.1. Placement competencies

Components of the placement process		Skills needed by placement specialist
1. Job Development		
a.	Contact employers to screen for potential job openings	1a. Knowledge of area businesses and industries (type of business, location, number of employees, hours of operation, etc.) Ability to judge the type and time of initial contact (letter, phone call, personal visit) Possession of good verbal (telephone communication) and written (letter writing) skills Professional appearance (neatly dressed and well-groomed) Possession of valid driver's license and reliable means of transportation
b.	Provide employers with an understanding of placement goals, including services and benefits to company	1b. Knowledge of and commitment to competitive employment capabilities to the mentally retarded Knowledge of services offered to employers: active pool of job-ready clients, initial full-time on-site client training, follow-up and consultation services for handicapped employees Knowledge of financial incentive for hiring disabled workers (e.g., Targeted Job Tax Credit, National Association of Retarded Citizens On-The-Job Training Funds) Ability to convey information to employers in an interesting, helpful, and sincere manner. Flexibility to communicate meaningfully on various levels with a wide variety of employers
c.	Provide information to employers regarding the abilities of mentally retarded workers	1c. Knowledge of the characteristics and abilities of mentally retarded individuals Knowledge and experience in the successful competitive employment of the mentally retarded Ability to actively convey the concept of employability of handicapped individuals in terms that will be of interest and concern to potential employers Ability to relate the work abilities of mentally retarded individuals to the specific needs and concerns of the employer (i.e. productivity, loyalty, long-term reliability, etc.)
d.	Locate appropriate job openings within company for handicapped workers	1d. Knowledge of the type of work performed at businesses or industries contacted Knowledge of the characteristics of job duties that have been successfully performed by mentally retarded workers Ability to recognize and identify positions within a company which could be filled by a mentally retarded worker (e.g., entry level positions requiring low level skills and having a structured routine).

e. Analyze the requirements of a job opening through preplacement observation and communication with employer

1e. Ability to gather general information about the position: number of hours per week (full-time or part-time); weekly schedule (weekend work, fixed or variable schedule); permanent, temporary, or seasonal work; rate of pay; fringe benefits (insurance, sick leave, vacation, salary increases)

Ability to gain a detailed description of job duties from the employer and/or co-workers by asking questions of a specific nature (e.g., Is the employee responsible for rotating the stock as well as putting it up? How many cleaning solutions are used to mop the floors?)

Ability to determine specific requirements of the job in terms of a handicapped worker through observation and questioning: orientation skills needed, reading and writing requirements, physical stamina necessary, availability of supervision, volume of work performed, routine or variable schedule of duties, number and type of decisions to be made by employee, general atmosphere and layout of company, amount of public contact, number and nature of co-workers, etc.

f. Arrange job interviews

1f. Ability to coordinate schedules and appointments to effectively accomodate employers' needs

2. Client Assessment
a. Evaluate client referrals in terms of employability in the competitive job market

2a. Educational background and experience in mental retardation
Understanding of standard vocational and educational assessment tools
Understanding of social, medical, vocational, educational, and environmental factors that may influence successful competitive job placement
Ability to secure all necessary client information through coordination with all persons and agencies involved
Knowledge of essential functions of specific jobs of interest and relevance to the client
Knowledge of transportation systems available to clients

b. Provide counseling to parents, guardians, and, in some cases, agencies that do not view competitive employment as a realistic objective for clients

2b. Educational background in mental retardation, as well as expertise in individual counseling techniques
Awareness of current trends and vocational opportunities available to mentally handicapped persons
Ability to communicate facts and evoke understanding in reference to competitive employment for mentally retarded individuals while empathizing with parent and/or agency concerns and expectations
Awareness of disincentives to competitive employment for the handicapped (such as fear of losing SSI benefits) and ability to offer viable solutions or alternatives

Components of the placement process	Skills needed by placement specialist
3. Placement a. Match job requirements to client abilities in order to make an appropriate placement	3a. Ability to evaluate job analysis data and client assessment information to determine client's suitability and potential for a particular job opening Ability to match job duty requirements with working skills of client, including social and communication skills required Ability to match other essential aspects of job to client's needs such as location, transportation, hours, potential for long-term employment, parental attitudes, fringe benefits, etc.
b. Arrange job interviews and starting dates	3b. Ability to coordinate schedules and appointments to accommodate the needs of the employer, as well as the client, client's family, and other agencies involved
c. Identify and remediate barriers to competitive employment	3c. Awareness of potential barriers to employment of mentally handicapped workers, such as transportation problems or lack of proper work attire Ability to work with clients, families, agencies, and employers to coordinate efforts to remediate employment barriers by offering alternatives or solutions

Often, standard information that is received from agencies can be dated or vague (e.g., "This client is hopelessly retarded"); the placement specialist should not rely too heavily on this type of reporting to arrive at a final decision concerning employment for the client. The personal interview with the client will produce a wealth of relevant information: the client's communication and social skills will be a reflection of how the client will probably perform during a job interview. This is also an opportunity to determine the client's likes and dislikes, as well as establishing vocational goals.

If possible, the placement specialist should attempt to observe the client in a work situation. If this is not feasible, contact workshops and/or training center personnel who are familiar with the client to elicit feedback on the client's work habits and general degree of success.

Meeting with parents or guardians is an important part of the total client assessment. Parental support is a crucial factor in the success or failure of the client's employment; nonsupportive or uncooperative family situations can make it difficult for the client to achieve a satisfactory employment situation. This is also the time to discuss parental concerns and fears about competitive employment for their son or daughter.

The placement specialist evaluates all pertinent information, along with personal observations, to determine, as objectively as possible, the client's general ability and potential to enter the competitive job market. The client's social skills, behavior, transportation needs, and demonstrated work skills all serve as indicators of the readiness of the client to work competitively.

Once a client has been evaluated as work ready, the actual placement of the client into competitive employment can take place. The job analyses that were performed during the job development stage provide objective guidelines as to what specific work skills the client needs to possess or develop for particular jobs available in the community.

Job development and job analysis is a continuous process; therefore, an appropriate job lead may not exist for a particular client at the time the client is determined to be ready for employment. During the ongoing process of job development, the placement specialist remains attuned to the abilities and skills of clients in reference to specific job requirements.

When a job seems appropriate for a particular client or clients (i.e., skills and abilities of the client match the specific requirements of a job), a job match has been accomplished. The placement specialist arranges a job interview for the client; if the employer seems interested, the counselor negotiates for a work start date for the client. Thus, a client has been placed into competitive employment.

Problems Encountered During the Placement Process

Throughout the placement process, there are barriers and problems that can impede a successful placement. Attitudinal barriers may halt the placement process at the point of initial employer contact. The President's Committee on Employment of the Handicapped (1981) listed "idea barriers" as a major problem in the placement process. Three idea barriers cited in the survey were:

1. Negative public reaction to retarded people
2. Nonacceptance by fellow workers

3. The belief that mentally retarded people are more prone to job related injuries

It has been shown that these beliefs will decrease or disappear once the mentally retarded worker is employed (Hill and Wehman, 1980; Cohen, 1953). However, the placement specialist faces the difficult task of overcoming these barriers *before* a client can be placed into competitive employment.

Without employers who are willing to hire handicapped workers, placement cannot exist. It follows, then, that the major problem encountered during the placement process is in locating cooperative employers and in reeducating reluctant employers about the value of handicapped workers. The placement specialist must be prepared for, and able to counter, the stereotypical views held by many employers. It is in this situation that the placement counselor must function effectively in a public relations role. Addressing the fears and concerns of the employer while providing facts about the successful employment of disabled persons will reassure the employer and, it is hoped, result in a positive change in attitude.

> **Once a client has been evaluated as work ready, the actual placement of the client into competitive employment can take place. The job analyses that were performed during the job development stage provide objective guidelines as to what specific work skills the client needs to possess or develop for particular jobs available in the community.**

The job training component of a vocational program will prove to be an important advantage when contacting employers. Employers who are initially hesitant about hiring a handicapped worker find it reassuring to know that a job trainer will accompany the new worker, full time, onto the job site to assist with the initial training and adjustment of the client. The trainer not only ensures that the job will be done satisfactorily during the early period of employment, but functions as a role model for supervisors and co-workers who may be unsure of how to interact with the handicapped worker. Also, the job trainer's role of advocate for the client is often crucial in the beginning when problems may arise in regard to job duties, relationships with co-workers, and other areas.

The incentive of the Targeted Jobs Tax Credit (TJTC), coupled with the availability of free project supervision for the client, often sways an interested but fearful employer to try a disabled worker. Our long-term commitment to follow-up services also earns the respect of employers who feel that rehabilitation is truly sharing in the cooperative venture with business to help severely handicapped persons become employed. The TJTC is federal legislation that allows the employer to gain a tax credit for 50% of the wages of the handicapped or disadvantaged worker's first year of employment, with 25% in the second year.

Clients themselves can also be problematic during the placement process, although the problems they present can usually be resolved through counseling and intervention. During the client assessment period, the placement counselor determines if there are any serious obstacles to the client's employment. Areas such as motivation to work, vocational goals, transportation, communication skills, medical conditions, and social behavior are examined in order to evaluate the client's readiness for competitive employment. A serious deficit in any area will, of course, affect the client's potential for employment. If the client seems motivated to work, has realistic job expectations, and exhibits acceptable behavioral standards, the placement counselor may determine that the client is competitively employable. Further investigation into the work habits and the abilities of the client (demonstrated or potential) guide the placement counselor in focusing in on the most feasible areas of employment for the client (e.g., the client expresses a strong desire to perform janitorial work, but will need a great deal of supervision with little public contact).

The client's family or living situation is a strong influence during the placement process. Family attitudes may range from overprotective to uncooperative. The placement specialist must be able to understand and offer facts and reassurance to the family or other persons involved with the client prior to placement. If the family seems hesitant about competitive employment for the client, this must be addressed immediately, not when the client has been offered a job. This can often be avoided by being as straightforward as possible during the initial meeting with the family.

This section is not intended to be an exhaustive analysis of the problems that may arise during the placement of handicapped persons into competitive employment. Every professional involved in job placement has certainly experienced a myriad of problems that are unique in nature. However, the three basic problem areas (related to employers, clients, and families) that have been discussed represent the most frequently encountered problems in the job placement of severely disabled individuals. Table 8.2 has been prepared to summarize specific problems within these three areas and to offer effective responses for the placement specialist when faced with a different situation.

THE ROLE OF TRAINING AND ADVOCACY IN EMPLOYMENT

Once a placement is made, the program is really just beginning. Systematic instruction and advocacy are two critical elements to job site training and retention for moderately and severely handicapped individuals. Vocational training is an important factor in elevating the level of worker competence on the job (Bellamy et al., 1979). Advocacy (i.e., acting on behalf of the client) is often directed toward positively changing the attitudes of nonhandicapped individuals in the client's work and community environments (Biklen, 1979). A more detailed discussion of advocacy is provided in Chapter 9.

In order for a handicapped individual to succeed in competitive employment over a long period of time and with a minimum amount of professional assistance or support, job skill alone is probably insufficient to maintain employment. For example, individuals with no verbal skills or limited motor behavior will frequently require special provisions or consideration by nonhandicapped co-workers and employers. It is important that the feelings and attitudes of co-workers be taken into account. If co-workers feel a

Table 8.2 Placement problems and solutions

Presenting problem	Response of specialist
1. Employer	
a. During initial contact (either by telephone or in person), employer is reluctant to meet with placement specialist.	1a. Send or leave program information with employer; follow-up with phone contact at a later time. (As a general rule after two direct contacts by phone or in person and a written contact, it is best at this time to leave the employer with the option to respond.)
b. Employer holds stereotypical views of the characteristics and abilities of handicapped persons.	1b. Provide examples of the types of jobs that various handicapped workers perform successfully, as well as the different personalities of the workers (e.g., alleviate the employer's spoken or unspoken fears about communicating with a handicapped worker, incidents of violence, bizarre sexual behavior, occurrence of seizures, etc.). Treat all employer concerns as legitimate and seek to reassure the employer of the long-term support of the project staff.
c. Employer does not view handicapped persons as a feasible source of labor.	1c. Provide factual information about the successful employment of handicapped workers that relates specifically to the employer and the type of business (e.g., the administrator of a nursing home may be interested in the successful employment of a client who works in the housekeeping department of a local hospital). Financial incentives, such as the Targeted Jobs Tax Credit, may sway the employer to try a handicapped worker on a "trial" basis.
d. Employer has unrealistic expectations concerning handicapped workers.	1d. Provide the employer with concrete examples of what can realistically be expected from a handicapped employee (e.g., a client may be able to unload stock from a truck, but even after many months on the job he may not be able to drive a forklift or fill out inventory forms). The employer should be led to understand the individual variability of each handicapped person: one client may need a very structured routine on a permanent basis, whereas another may be able to adapt to changes in schedule after a period of time on the job.
e. Employer seems interested, but vacillates in regard to setting up a client interview or specifying a starting date for hire.	1e. Given the investment of time that has been made up to this point, the placement specialist must try to determine as objectively as possible whether the employer is genuinely interested or if an attempt is being made to avoid further involvement. If there seems to be genuine interest, perseverance and patience (not harassment) on the part of the placement counselor usually leads to a placement. When the employer seems to be avoiding further involvement, it may be best to leave future contact up to the employer (if the employer does, in fact, call you later, you can be sure of genuine interest).

f. Employer is able to provide only a vague description of job duties or subsequently changes job duties between the time of the client interview and the starting date of employment.

1f. A thorough description and analysis of the job duties should be obtained before any client is taken to the job interview. The placement specialist should also attempt to observe the job duties being performed before placement; in this way, any discrepancies between what is supposed to be done and what the job actually entails can be discussed with the employer. If an agreement cannot be reached in terms of the client's capabilities and the requirements of the job, there are several alternatives: 1) arrange for another client, who is capable of performing the job, to be interviewed; 2) suggest job modifications in which specific job duties could be traded and/or shared with co-workers (perhaps the handicapped worker could wipe down tables for a co-worker while the co-worker rotates stock, which requires reading skills); 3) if arrangements cannot be made to place a client in a position at this time, ensure the employer of your continued interest in working with him/her in the future and maintain contact on a periodic basis.

2. Client

a. Client has unrealistic or undefined vocational goals.

2a. Provide the client with information about a variety of jobs that are available in the community, based on an assessment of the client's interests, qualifications, and past work or training experience. Counsel the client regarding employment opportunities that are realistically within his/her capabilities (e.g., a client who states that he wants to be a singer can be directed toward a more practical job and encouraged to sing as a hobby only).

b. Client has low social and/or communication skills or exhibits poor hygiene habits.

2b. The placement specialist should note during the client interview any problem areas. This information should be shared with the family and referring agency in a straightforward manner. Prior to a job interview it may be necessary to involve the family in making sure that the client is appropriately groomed. If the client has poor social skills, the placement specialist may review important parts of a job interview with the client (e.g., practice shaking hands, how to sit properly during the interview, answers to questions that may be asked). In many cases, the placement counselor should take on a more aggressive role during the actual interview and try to focus the employer on the client's capability to perform the job.

c. Transportation to and from work is a problem for the client.

2c. If the client lives near a bus system, but does not know how to ride a bus, bus training can be arranged. The family and/or referring agency may also be able to provide assistance with bus training. Other alternatives for transportation are: 1) arrange transportation to a bus line; 2) arrange carpools with co-workers or persons working near the client's job site (such as neighbors or relatives); 3) the client may be able to ride a bicycle to work; 4) search for possible employment within walking distance of the

Presenting problem	Response of specialist
	client's home; 5) companies that provide transportation for the handicapped can be contacted; 6) the client may take a taxi to and from work.
3. Family	
a. The family (or guardian) of the client has unrealistic vocational goals for the client.	3a. Provide factual examples of the types of jobs that various handicapped workers perform successfully, relating this information specifically to the client. For example, it may be of interest to them that another client who was in the same vocational center is working at a local restaurant as a dishwasher. Counsel the family regarding employment opportunities that are realistic in terms of the client's abilities (they may not be aware of the specific job requirements necessary in certain occupational areas).
b. The family (or guardian) is overprotective regarding competitive employment.	3b. Provide examples of the types of jobs that various handicapped workers perform successfully. Empathize with the family while attempting to alleviate the fears they may have about competitive employment. Treat all family concerns as legitimate and seek to reassure the family of the careful job match that is made, as well as the long-term support of the school staff. Gentle confrontation is sometimes appropriate, and the family may also be persuaded to allow the client to work on a "trial" basis.
c. The family (or guardian) is nonsupportive of competitive employment.	3c. Reinforce the importance of all family members to the success of the client's employment. Stress the advantages of the client being employed (contribution to household income, independence of client, more time alone for family members, etc.). It may be necessary to increase the amount of project involvement with the family before, during, and after placement if the family seems reluctant to cooperate on its own. In extreme cases, the support of other agencies, relatives, or neighbors may be recruited, and the client can be successfully placed even though the family is nonsupportive.
d. The family is overly dependent on the security of monthly public support payments.	3d. Provide factual information concerning Supplemental Security Income payments that may alleviate the family's fear of losing a stable monthly income (e.g., the initial trial work period and automatic re-entitlement to benefits for 2 years). Convey to the family the reality of the paycheck, in terms of number of dollars, which the client will be earning compared to the amount of the SSI check. In some instances, the family may force a client to resign just before SSI payments are to be cut off. It may be appropriate, particularly if the client has been a productive and stable employee, to inform the family that the Social Security office may investigate the circumstances surrounding the client's resignation from employment.

disabled individual is not "pulling his/her load" or is receiving unfair privileges, it may negatively affect morale and lead to social exclusion of the client. More importantly, the client loses what might be a critical ally for assistance in strange or unfamiliar situations where a nonhandicapped person might function more quickly or capably (Hill & Wehman, 1980).

It must be recognized that training techniques have not reached the degree of sophistication for preparing handicapped citizens for *all* possible situations that may arise in complex heterogeneous work and/or community environments (Rusch & Mithaug, 1980). The inadequate amount and quality of career and vocational education that has been provided to many handicapped individuals in school must also be taken into consideration.

The purpose of the following section is two-fold. First, specific learning problems that arise in on-the-job training situations with severely handicapped workers are described. The second part of this section involves how to provide training assistance that will help remediate the problem outlined.

PROBLEMS ENCOUNTERED IN ON-THE-JOB TRAINING

Listed below are several problems that frequently surface once an initial job placement of a severely handicapped individual is made. Of course, problems may be more frequent and/or diverse in nature as the functioning level of the person decreases. For example, moderately and severely handicapped individuals (those in the general IQ range of 20 and 50) are likely to present fewer motivational deficiencies and more work proficiency problems (i.e., speed, quality). Higher functioning individuals seem to present more off-task and noncompliant behaviors, although they usually grasp job requirements quickly. Below are listed five major problem areas that must be addressed across all functioning levels of handicapped workers when placed in competitive employment.

Broadening the Range of Jobs a Client Can Perform

Traditionally, severely handicapped persons receive employment training that is limited in scope and that does not sufficiently prepare the individual for the local job market. Frequently, training is given for nonfunctional skills that purportedly help the client become "ready" for work (i.e., sorting colors or shapes). Yet the range of job competencies required—even in unskilled food service or custodial utility positions—can be far-reaching, depending on the size and location of the cafeteria or hotel. Teaching to criterion levels competence in sweeping, dishwashing, tray sanitizing, and busing tables is fine until the foreman introduces the industrial vacuum cleaner, which must be operated before closing. If the client cannot quickly learn new jobs, his/her overall value is diminished substantially to the supervisor. Because of the high turnover and absenteeism in many unskilled or semiskilled positions, workers must be able to fill in and perform absent co-workers' job duties.

Improving Job Quality

Each place of employment has certain standards and methods by which a job must be done. These standards vary within every company and organization. It is critical that teachers and placement specialists be able to analyze *job requirements* and *employer expectations* for different jobs. Both aspects must be analyzed. If a supervisor feels that a client has been "pushed" on him/her by the personnel director, the requirements of the job may be more stringent. For example, picking up trash on the grounds could be a very difficult job to accomplish if the supervisor is rigorous in what is accepted as clean or not clean. The severely handicapped worker must avoid appearing incompetent on the job or unable to maintain a level of quality equivalent to nonhandicapped co-workers.

Increasing Work Rate

Even if one's performance is errorless, speed is also considered. The worker who picks up every piece of trash but takes 3 days to do it will be terminated from the job. What is critical in this situation is analyzing *why* the person is slow. By assessing what factors are interfering with rate, an eventual strategy can be devised to improve rate. Here are several possible reasons for diminished or inconsistent rate:

1. Lack of reinforcement or positive consequences associated with job
2. Physical or health-related problems that make it difficult to perform at an adequate speed
3. Frequent distracting factors in job areas
4. Poor memory by the client (thus requiring continual repetition of earlier parts of task)

An analysis of the trainee's work characteristics and the job setting over a period of several consecutive days usually yields information, such as the points above, which facilitate program planning.

Working without Supervision: Self-Initiated Performance

Probably one of the most frequently heard complaints from employers about severely handicapped workers who are mentally retarded is that they cannot work independently over sustained periods of time. The lack of self-initiated work performance can partly be attributed to educational programs that foster dependence on the teacher by students. Limitations in self-initiated work can also be traced to the initial problem noted (i.e., the ability to perform only a limited number of jobs).

These workers who do not self-initiate performance limit their employability in three significant ways. *First,* the probability of advancement to more stimulating work is greatly diminished. *Second,* the perceptions of co-workers of the handicapped worker may be negative. *Third,* the client may lose the job if the employer gets tired of continually reminding him/her what has to be done.

> One of the most frequently heard complaints from employers about severely handicapped workers who are mentally retarded is that they cannot work independently over sustained periods of time.

Fading Trainee Assistance

Most on-the-job training programs that are effective with severely handicapped individuals provide for direct trainer assistance and guidance. Helping the individual adjust to the job is an important part of the supervisor's job. This form of intervention is usually welcomed by the company's supervisor, who is looking for assistance as well. Unfortunately, the worker will become dependent on the trainer unless there is a systematic effort to fade (reduce) the amount of assistance. The number of hours and minutes provided in training should be recorded thereby yielding a daily or weekly benchmark of guidance. The fading process is described in considerably more detail in the following section.

TECHNIQUES FOR OVERCOMING ON-THE-JOB TRAINING PROBLEMS

There are several basic instructional techniques that may be used to overcome the problems described above. These techniques are not complex, yet when provided in an orderly sequence can facilitate behavior change (Alberto & Schofield, 1979; York, Williams, & Brown, 1976). They are discussed below.

Verbal Instructions

The initial form of assistance offered should be a verbal cue or instruction to correct the problem or lack of appropriate behavior. A verbal cue may also be used to increase speed or prompt a sequence of self-initiated work behaviors.

Verbal instructions are the most natural form of cue or assistance provided in work settings. With severely handicapped workers instructions should be short, direct, and minimize extraneous (not necessary) words. Inservicing of employers and co-workers in the trainee's work environment should include the type of verbal cueing that is optimal for the trainee.

Gestural Assistance

Pointing is another effective means of eliciting behavior from severely handicapped workers. Pairing a verbal cue with a gesture or looking in the desired direction is another acceptable format of communication in most work establishments. Gestures frequently are more effective than verbal cues alone with clients who have difficulty in processing what the supervisor is asking. Gesturing is also a more universal form of communication, which allows nonverbal clients to initiate and receive social interactions. In order for gesturing to be effective, the client must pay attention to the supervisor or co-worker giving the gesture.

Modeling and Demonstration

Showing a client how to do a job is a more involved form of instruction and is time-consuming in busy work settings. Ideally, preemployment training should already have taken place so that job proficiency is not a question. Also, for modeling to be a successful instructional strategy, the client should be able to imitate. Inservicing of employers in modeling techniques should reflect the necessity of demonstrating skills in small steps or clusters. As with gesturing it is necessary to have the client's attention before modeling the behavior.

Physical Guidance

Some clients require hands-on assistance and manual guidance in completing portions of a skill. Fast-paced work environments are not usually the ideal places for this type of training, which requires precision instruction. However, it may be that a new piece of equipment is introduced or the client's job role is expanded to include new tasks; if so, then physical assistance may be necessary.

Practice

Establishing a work routine that provides substantial practice and repeated trials on a task(s) is the surest way of increasing work proficiency, even though extended practice is probably not possible while on the job. However, it is a good practice to start in a job with few tasks initially (i.e., running a freight elevator, cleaning pots, wrapping silverware).

Feedback

Providing information to a client as to how he/she is doing on a job is *feedback*. Feedback lets the individual know that the work being completed is not correct or that it is very well done. In either event, it is good instructional strategy to inform the trainee as soon as possible, especially a new trainee.

Social Reinforcement

Social reinforcement includes praise, approval, attention, and compliments. Social reinforcers can come from parents, co-workers, training staff, employers, or even from the worker. To be effective social reinforcement should be *contingent* (i.e., immediately follow the target behaviors being developed). When a severely handicapped client is new on the job, *immediacy* of reinforcement helps him/her understand the relationship between the special attention that is being received and the job just completed. Labeling, or telling why reinforcement is being given ("Ted, nice job of scraping all the plates!"), also helps the client understand.

Once a severely handicapped worker is hired, it is a good practice to start in a job with few tasks initially (i.e., running a freight elevator, cleaning pots, wrapping silverware).

IMPROVING THE WORK PRODUCTIVITY OF A MENTALLY RETARDED WOMAN IN A CITY RESTAURANT: A CASE STUDY

As an illustration of the training techniques described in the previous section and previous chapter, a case study is presented (Wehman and Hill, 1980).

Rose is a 28-year-old black female classified as moderately mentally retarded. She is verbal and exhibits extremely compliant and passive behavior. Rose had no history of previous employment, but received 5 months of work adjustment training at a local sheltered workshop for production efficiency. She was assigned to a rehabilitation counselor's caseload, but no placement had been made. Rose currently resides with relatives in the city and is working at a local cafeteria.

The program took place at a local city cafeteria in the downtown area. The cafeteria serves approximately 800 people per day and is considered to be a fast-paced operation. Rose was assigned to wrap silver Monday through Friday and on Sundays from 10:30 to 3:00. The job involved taking silver from a bus pan, sorting the silver into containers, and wrapping the silver. Object and visual discrimination were necessary. The finished roll consisted of one knife, one spoon, and two forks, each of which had to be clean. Rose's station was located approximately 10 to 15 feet away from other employees, and she had no direct contact with the supervisor of the cafeteria. Project staff, during training, were within 2 feet of the trainee.

Program Objective

After receiving an ample amount of clean silver, Rose had to wrap six rolls in 1 minute over three consecutive sessions. The criteria were enforced throughout each day she worked. Rose's baseline data showed low production rates. It was decided that her work behavior could be shaped by the selection of a 5-minute work interval in which she had to produce four rolls per minute; eventually six rolls were required per minute.

Training Procedure

A baseline of rate data was taken to assess Rose's level of production. During the baseline Rose was shown a model and given verbal prompts on how to wrap silver. Her baseline data indicated rates of production considerably below the employer's criterion for that position. It was observed that Rose spent too much time in positioning the pieces of silver before wrapping them, and she only used one hand to obtain the silver to be wrapped. In order to increase production, supervisor intervention was necessary. The program used to increase production was a changing criterion/design with a fading process of supervisor intervention. The technique of intervention used was a teaching strategy and a point system. The strategy consisted of using both hands to obtain the silver to be wrapped, paired with placing the silver on the napkin without neatly positioning the silver, and then wrapping the silver as fast as possible. The teaching strategy was enforced throughout the day *except when* the supervisor was recording. During the first phase of the program, Rose had to produce four rolls of silver per minute during the observation periods. Two 5-minute time samples were taken daily. If the target number was reached during the observation periods, a point was given. Rose had to earn at least one point per day for three consecutive days before reinforcement was given. During the observation periods, Rose was told when to begin and stop. She reached criteria easily during the first phase of the program and reinforcement was given. The same procedure was used for the second phase of the program. The second phase was more difficult for Rose because she had to produce six rolls of silver per minute and the 5-minute observation period was only once a day. The trainee had to work faster and she only had one chance per day to earn a point. Although the second phase was far above the baseline, it was believed that this criterion could be obtained. Rose was able to produce six rolls of silver per minute for three consecutive days.

A choice of three outings was offered to Rose as reinforcement. When the first criterion was met, she chose a trip to the movie; when the second criterion had been obtained, Rose chose a trip to a restaurant.

After the second criterion had been met and reinforcement given, supervisor intervention was eliminated. The teaching strategy and point system were stopped. One observation period was taken daily to see if the trainee was able to maintain performance. Rose was not told when the sampling observation was beginning or when it had ended. It was observed that Rose continued the strategy taught through the sampling and was able to maintain her production rate, never falling below 5.4 rolls per minute during an observation sample. The supervisor then faded the observation periods to one per week. It was observed that Rose was still able to maintain her rate of performance.

Program Results

Results of this behavioral program indicated that Rose's rate of silverware rolling increased by over 100%. Figure 8.2 shows that the mean number of rolls per minute was under three during baseline and increased to over six. At the same time Rose's wages accumulated to a total of $624; she had four absences and was late two times for work. Furthermore, Rose's on-task behavior was recorded and revealed 100% time on-task for 16 of 18 observation sessions over a 3-month period.

Evaluation of Rose's work behavior in this *changing criterion design* clearly reveals a significant change in her behavior and, in all probability, facilitated her continued employment. Because the design did not allow for verifying which element, the *teaching strategy* or *token system*, was more critical in Rose's increased work, it is not possible to say which was more important. However, it seems that the teaching strategy was the greater contribution than the point system in increasing Rose's rate of silverware rolling. Figure 9.2 indicates that even after the point system was faded, Rose's rate of production was maintained. The acquisition of skill played a significant role in the program for Rose in that she was able to respond to the request for silver. This in itself appeared more reinforcing for Rose than the point system.

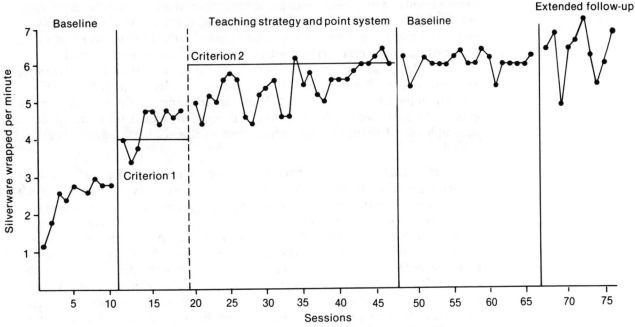

Figure 8.2. Rose's increase in rate of wrapping silverware.

REDUCING TEACHER ASSISTANCE AT THE JOB SITE

When a trainer-advocacy type of model is used in job placement programs for moderately and severely handicapped individuals, an important consideration is reducing the amount of time that a trainer must spend with a client who is new to a job. As noted earlier, in order to help many individuals adjust to a competitive employment placement, it is frequently best to provide intial training and advocacy support at the job site (Rusch & Mithaug, 1980; Wehman, Hill, & Koehler, 1979). What this usually involves is having a trained staff member (i.e., from a special education or rehabilitation discipline) present as often as possible in the early stages of the placement and gradually decrease the amount of time available over a period of several weeks or even months.

Problems in Fading Staff from the Job Site

Although the presence of trained staff will influence the work adjustment and job retention of handicapped individuals, it may be an expensive price to pay in terms of staff withdrawal. A number of problems can arise in an intensive job site training program. These problems include: 1) *financial expenditure;* 2) *staff reluctance;* 3) *real supervisor dependency;* 4) *client and parent dependency;* and 5) *rate of fading.*.

Financial Expenditure The cost-effectiveness of a job site training model is only borne out once a certain number of placements are made and retained. For example, if a $10,000 per year job teacher or counselor must spend 6 months with two severely retarded persons in a cafeteria every afternoon, then the cost of his/her salary is probably not warranted. On the other hand, if this supervision is necessary for 4 weeks and then gradually reduced while new placements are added, then the cost may be more competitive. The cost would also be competitive if *six to eight* moderately or severely handicapped persons who had never worked before were adjusted into a competitive employment situation within a six-month period.

Thus, the first problem related to fading is the cost invested in training and maintaining handicapped clients. It is especially difficult to fade when certain individuals with extended on-site training would probably make excellent employees in the long run. This problem argues for more effective preemployment training and preparation in the student's earlier years in school.

Staff Reluctance to Withdraw

A second difficulty in reducing staff assistance is that trainers often become personally involved in a client's progress and feel it necessary to be continually present. This is a laudable goal in terms of ensuring the trainee's work performance to the employer; however, it does not foster independence on the job. Although it is a natural emotion to not wish to leave the individual alone, the daily presence of a familiar staff member may, in fact, cultivate a client's dependency on the trainer. One solution to this problem that merits some consideration is the regular rotation of different trainers into work sites. This allows for interaction with all clients who have been placed. Such a strategy should help to diminish the close attachments that staff members gain with clients.

> **Although it is a natural emotion to not wish to leave the individual alone, the daily presence of a familiar staff member may, in fact, cultivate a client's dependency on the trainer.**

Client/Parent Dependency on Staff

Closely related to the above problem is that of clients and/or families of clients who become so dependent on the availability of daily individualized attention that the quality of their performance is reduced significantly with the removal of staff. Parents may need staff assurances initially in order to feel sufficiently comfortable to let their son or daughter go to work; eventually, however, parents must be "weaned" from these assurances. One way of coping with this problem is having parents visit the work establishment from time to time and view their son's or daughter's job competency. Additionally, dependent clients can be involved with co-workers at lunch or breaks while the trainer gradually becomes less accessible.

Supervisor Dependency on Trainers

Another fading problem that may occur is that some managers will not want the trainer to leave. If no systematic efforts have been made to have the disabled worker interact with and/or take orders from the job supervisor, the trainer will unwittingly become a necessity for the client's job retention.

Consider a case where the real supervisor directs all orders to the trainer, who in turn directs them to the client. Although this may be appropriate for a few days initially, in the long run this will be disastrous for fading the trainer from that site. Obviously what happens in this extreme situation is that the supervisor is in no way prepared to cope with the client and may not even want to interact with him/her. Consequently, the supervisor will continually request assistance and daily on-site supervision from the trainer.

Rate of Fading A fifth issue to be considered is how quickly to withdraw staff assistance. Is it appropriate to assume that all clients will initially require daily supervision and 2 weeks later 3-day-a-week supervision, culminating in weekly checks for 60 days? In short, at what point can the amount of staff time be reduced? These questions cannot be answered for all clients, but rather should be considered on an individual basis with each client's data serving as the basis for decision making. The use of on-off task performance, amount and type of prompts, and supervisor's evaluations will quickly provide feedback to the trainer as to the rate at which fading can occur.

There are two primary areas to remember when determining the rate of trainer fading. First, rapid withdrawal of staff assistance may very well result in complete loss of any behavioral gains established earlier. Second, fading that occurs too slowly leads to two of the problems discussed above: *client/parent dependency* and *supervisor dependency*. The next section provides a discussion of techniques which may be employed to attack several of the problems which surround the dilemma of fading staff assistance.

Strategies for Solving the Staff Fading Problem

There are a variety of techniques that can be used, which are based on operant training (i.e., generalization and response maintenance literature). These techniques are described below. It is important to remember, however, that at this point limited data are available to support these strategies. Empirical studies done in real work settings are necessary.

Transferring Verbal Control from Staff Trainer to Supervisor Initially all training, prompts, and job requests may be filtered from the supervisor through the trainer to the client. This is especially true for nonverbal clients, who might normally inhibit employer communication. As the number of trainer prompts approaches that normally required of a supervisor to direct a nonhandicapped worker, the trainer begins involving the supervisor in the worker prompts. This is done initially by modeling worker prompts while the supervisor is nearby. The trainer can later explain to the real supervisor what prompts have been necessary to ensure the client does the job. In addition it must be restated that the trainer will not always be able to remain on site full-time. The supervisor's directives must be redirected to the client.

Reduction of Supervisor and Client Accessibility to Trainers A second technique for overcoming employer and client dependence on staff is to systematically reduce the trainer's presence. This promotes the number of supervisor-client interactions and transfers the focus of control to the supervisor. The initial periods of trainer absence should be during a time when the operation is at a slower pace and when the supervisor is not under pressure, and consequently more likely to offer additional time. Eventually the trainer's presence is reduced over more days and during higher pressure times. Each client requires differing trainer reduction schedules. In addition, some minimal assistance may be necessary on a continuing basis for clients with more severe disabilities, whereas less disabled clients may be maintained with little or no follow-up services.

The initial periods of trainer absence should be during a time when the operation is at a slower pace and when the supervisor is not under pressure, and consequently more likely to offer additional time.

Transferring Reinforcement of Client to Supervisor Early in training the client is frequently prompted and reinforced by the trainer. In some cases, the client may even receive his/her paycheck from the trainer, who can help the client with the check cashing and depositing process. Once the client realizes the significance of the paycheck, however, it is important for the supervisor to present the client's check. Modeling verbal reinforcement while supervisory staff is present and explaining to the supervisor the benefits of reinforcing client on-task behavior must be initiated as the trainer begins to fade out. Changing project staff during training facilitates easier generalization from trainer to supervisor.

Teaching Self-Reinforcement Teaching the client the significance of the paycheck and producing a chart showing daily earnings facilitates one basic self-reinforcement technique. The following example utilizes self-reinforcement. One client's job is to remove and stack dishes, pots, and silverware as it comes through the dishwashing machine. If the client is not fast enough, the machine will stop until the worker can catch up. The client has been taught to self-monitor and self-reinforce with language by making statements to himself/herself such as: "Good job, the machine has only stopped two times this morning." Another self-reinforcement technique is matching high levels of behavior with reinforcement such as short breaks when the worker gets caught up or works ahead of criterion. Self-reinforcement techniques can be utilized to help maintain criterion levels of performance as the trainer begins fading out.

Use of Co-workers Enlisting nonhandicapped co-workers in the training process will, in the long run, facilitate job retention. It must be recognized that once a trainer begins to withdraw from the work site, the co-workers are the peer group with which the client must interact acceptably. If these individuals are helpful and supportive, then the client's disability may very well be minimized. On the other hand, if the individual is not accepted, then complaints to the supervisor will probably result in eventual termination. A recommended practice for having co-workers become involved is for the trainer to gain rapport with them explaining a little about the client's disability, background, and related behavioral characteristics.

The fading process from the job site is important. However, it is our contention that follow-up will be necessary even after the client seems to be functioning independently. This process may include helping a client overcome temporary problems with a new supervisor, or work out different transportation arrangements, or learn how to complete tasks newly added to the job. This type of infrequent but periodic support can be crucial to long-term job retention. Therefore, the following section briefly addresses the following points: 1) factors influencing client need for follow-up; 2) types of follow-up that can be provided; and 3) the staff efficiency necessary to promote the follow-along function.

FACTORS INFLUENCING THE NEED FOR FOLLOW-UP

The need for client/employee follow-up is usually evident soon after the training period ends and the presence of the job trainer is minimal. While the trainer is present the client gets a great deal of individualized attention and positive reinforcement. The individual learns to enjoy work, and to carry out the job tasks in a conscientious manner. In spite of the gradual nature of the trainer fading process, problems can develop after this period. Just as the handicapped worker has learned good work habits while the trainer was present, bad work habits from co-workers or even supervisors may be acquired as well. For instance, a mentally handicapped worker may see co-workers stealing merchandise. The client learns to steal, but fails to be as discreet as his/her co-workers, and subsequently is singled out as the culprit. Other problems may develop if the supervisor fails to discipline the handicapped worker as he/she would other workers. Poor work habits will be learned and resentment from co-workers could result.

Once the initial excitement about the job and the extra attention subside, the client/employee may lose enthusiasm and a conscientious attitude, and at the same time be exposed to new pressures and have difficulty coping with his/her feelings. Independent functioning alone is responsible for success at work. The support of a trainer-advocate staff person is crucial at this time.

As stated earlier, the purpose of ongoing follow-up is to assist the severely disabled worker in maintaining his/her job. Staff can teach job skills through on-the-job training; however, problems are likely to occur after the job skills have been learned. Problem solving and self-advocacy have, unfortunately, been difficult skills for these individuals to acquire.

The purpose of ongoing follow-up is to assist the severely disabled worker in maintaining his/her job.

Severely handicapped employees typically gain employment in jobs that are routine and repetitive. Regardless of the routine nature of the job, the work environment cannot be completely stabilized. It is constantly changing, and the client may require follow-up intervention in order to successfully cope with certain changes. Changes in management or a new supervisor or even co-worker may, for many different reasons, affect work performance. The job training specialist may be able to prevent this problem from developing by assisting the client in self-advocacy or by simply talking with the persons involved. Changes in work schedules or job tasks may necessitate on-site intervention and retraining in order to ensure job retention. Similarly, changes in the home environment can also hinder job performance and require follow-up services with the involvement of the parents or guardians. Through periodic questionnaires and talks with parents and guardians, the job training specialist learns of changes before they occur and is able to prevent serious work-related problems. Even a change in medication may require increased follow-up services as the changes may initially elicit mood swings or even seizures. Because parents are not usually able to see their son or daughter on the job, it is important to inform them of his/her progress and address their concerns as well.

On-Site Visit

After the initial training has been completed, follow-up can be accomplished in several ways. A visit to the job site maintains personal contact with supervisors, co-workers, and the client. Many times talking with co-workers elicits the most useful information. They work directly with the client and may be more willing to discuss the client's performance with staff. This on-site visit also can enable trainers to spot firsthand potential problems or ways of improving performance.

Telephone

If site visits are not always feasible and/or necessary, a telephone call may be sufficient. Although the trainer may be likely to notice potential problems from a visit, some employers may talk more candidly over the telephone. In many cases this is especially true of parents or guardians. Many parents are very protective, even overprotective, of their sons or daughters working independently. A monthly call to parents may help to relieve their anxieties concerning the placement of their son or daughter into competitive employment.

Supervisor Evaluations

Supervisor evaluations and employee progress reports are more tangible forms of follow-up. When filling out an evaluation form, some employers provide information not broached during personal contacts. Supervisor evaluations are given bimonthly for the first 2 months, monthly for the next 2 months, and quarterly thereafter, keeping in mind appropriate fading of staff intervention.

Progress Reports

Using information received from the supervisor evaluation form, a progress report is completed and sent to the client and parents or guardians. This indicates how the client is performing in the eyes of the employer as well as how he/she compares to fellow co-workers. The progress report serves to reassure parents that the teacher or counselor is still involved in the placement of their son or daughter, and it also gives staff an opportunity to make suggestions as to what can be done at home to improve performance at work.

Parent Questionnaire

A parent questionnaire is also sent home with the progress report. The form is designed to assess the client's development and attitude at home since his/

her employment. The form has room for written comments by parents or guardians. Learning of problems at home that could affect the client/employee's job performance is an important preventive follow-up measure.

Follow-up services when used in conjunction with each other ensure the best possible feedback, whether through a visit, a call, a questionnaire, or an evaluation form. Each employer and co-worker has their own idiosyncratic style of communicating, and by using a variety of techniques, effective elucidation of the client's situation can be obtained.

Locus of Follow-up Control

As the client's employment condition stabilizes and program staff are able to fade out significantly, long-term maintenance strategies should be transferred to local case management personnel when possible. The case manager will most likely, however, need inservice training in dealing with the business community. Insensitivity to the demands associated with operating a profit-oriented business might alienate an otherwise supportive link in the client's ecological environment.

After reviewing visits, phone calls, and evaluation/questionnaire forms the experienced case manager can elect to contact the job specialist should more intensive intervention be required. The local community's level of commitment in assuming a share of the follow-up service needs indicates their attitude toward competitive job placement of their disabled citizens. A lack of commitment and/or consistent application of follow-up services would likely result in many job terminations. The locus of control then cannot be transferred without appropriate case management training and local administrative support.

STAFF TIME EFFICIENCY IN FOLLOW-UP SERVICES

Follow-up strategy must be carefully planned in order to be both effective and cost-efficient. In planning the follow-up strategy, the job training specialist should consider such factors as the intervention purpose, the intervention technique to be used, the timing of technique application, and the intervention's duration. Because effectiveness and efficiency in follow-up services both contribute to improved intervention, the trainer must ask the question: How can my intervention best be implemented? Spending too much time at a job site, for instance, can be expensive as well as foster dependence of the client and/or supervisor. Alternatively, as job counselors have unfortunately experienced too often in the past, not enough time spent with clients will ultimately end in job termination.

Trainer time management must be looked at in two dimensions. First, what intervention is to be provided? Second, who will provide that intervention? In deciding what intervention should be provided, observation, site visitation, evaluative forms, anecdotal records, behavioral baseline, and ultimately staff experience are used to formulate the intervention strategy. In developing a strategy to determine who will provide intervention, a team concept must be developed and flexibility among co-trainers established. Too often the amount of time available to the vocational counselor dictates the amount of follow-up work provided. Additionally, the vocational trainer/

counselor with a rigid caseload may not be available for crisis intervention because of, e.g., vacation or illness. Job specialist staff must work in pairs; here the team members brief each other on their individual caseloads. Frequent exchange of clients receiving follow-up services helps familiarize staff with their partner's clients. This "buddy" system is especially important when a trainer-advocate places a new individual into a competitive job. During full-time initial training, the trainer is not available, sometimes for weeks, to provide the imperative maintenance follow-up services for other clients. The caseload partner can, however, provide crisis intervention services and monitor other follow-up needs.

Telephone communication and mailed supervisor evaluation forms with periodic site visits are sufficient follow-up services for clients who are well stabilized. The trainer must be sensitive during visits and phone conversations with employers to possible cues for problems needing direct contact. Also, close scrutiny of the supervisor evaluation form may indicate the need for a site visit.

Direct observation may never be completely replaced by the phone conversation or evaluation forms because supervisors often do not identify problems in their early stages of development. Furthermore, the client may refrain from exhibiting inappropriate behaviors in front of the supervisor, yet through unobtrusive observation or when conferring with co-workers these behaviors may surface.

The trainer must be sensitive during visits and phone conversations with employers to possible cues for problems needing direct contact.

Subtle training of supervisors, co-workers, and parents in the use of learning principles and management techniques is more cost-effective than continual provision of direct client training. Utilizing the time management technique of arranging client-parent meetings at the *staff's* home base must be viewed in terms of the meeting purpose. When the meeting's outcome is not affected by the meeting place, then the home base is more cost-efficient. Excessive job specialist travel may promote an unrealistic view of the project's staff availability to parents, counselors, and clients.

Perhaps the most cost-efficient strategy for follow-up centers around prevention rather than intervention. For example, the job training specialist must be aware of the many factors affecting each client's job performance. When any of these influencing forces pose a threat, it is necessary to be alert to the effect this may have on the client and provide whatever follow-up services are needed. For instance, should a client's work schedule be changed, the job training specialist may need to retrain the client for the first few days on a new bus schedule. If not, the client may be late for work and late returning home. Thus, the employer would be upset as well as his/ her parents or guardians. Not only could the client be fired for being late, but he/she could also be emotionally upset by the trauma of the whole situation. Any change in a client's work situation and/or home environment poses a threat to job performance. Planning follow-up services to prevent further development and complication of problems is a most effective and cost-efficient strategy.

When planning a site visit or even a phone call, the job training specialist should schedule a time that will not inconvenience or interrupt the normal business operation. For example, if the purpose of the visit is to talk with a cafeteria manager, the best times to talk would be early morning or mid-afternoon, not during the lunch rush.

Job sites that are located within a reasonable distance of each other should be assigned to the same job training team. Site visits should be orchestrated to minimize travel time. This reduces travel between job sites and increases cost-effectiveness of follow-up visits. Ongoing consistent follow-up services must be provided to facilitate the severely disabled population's entrance into competitive work. A flexible, dynamic trainer maintenance format is the most cost-effective application of follow-up services.

THE RELATIONSHIP OF PUBLIC SCHOOL PROGRAMMING TO COMPETITIVE EMPLOYMENT

To this point, we have not discussed the specific delivery problems unique to the public schools that can occur in job placement and job site training. There has been an assumption, albeit implicit, on the part of some investigators and practitioners that similar conclusions about the procedures and results taken from studies involving adults to the public school based adolescent population could be drawn. Regrettably, this is not true; the public school system is markedly different in terms of service delivery than adult day programs that sponsor activities for mentally and physically handicapped adults in this country. The training and orientation of teachers and administration, the length and composition of the school day, the lack of career-oriented curriculum, and the inadequacy of definitive linkage with outside agencies such as local vocational rehabilitation offices are but some of the problems that often impair the nonsheltered job placement of which many moderately and severely handicapped youths are capable.

In order to solve these problems we must first understand what the specific problems are. Furthermore, it is necessary to explore the reasoning and historical perspective behind these obstacles. There is very little research that analyzes these difficulties; this is probably because there are remarkably few intensive job placement and job site training programs based in school systems for the moderately and severely handicapped. (The paucity of empirical vocational research available for the intermediate and adolescent age level attests to this as well.) This section is aimed at isolating several main problems that we view as impairments in most school systems for job placements. In the context of problem identification, we make suggestions for improvement.

Inadequacy of Current Curriculum

Perhaps the single greatest problem in linking secondary programs with competitive employment placement is the inadequacy of the current special education curriculum. Teachers and other support personnel do not look at the work environments in which students will ultimately work and live for curriculum objectives. There is an extensive reliance on curriculum guides, which all too often hold no close relationship to the competencies necessary for independence vocationally. The IEP objectives reflect contexts that the teacher feels comfortable with, not objectives that are crucial for eventual placement into nonsheltered employment.

Consider for example, Ron, a trainable retarded 16-year-old, who receives instruction on improving balance by walking on a balance beam. The 15 minutes daily expended on this activity with the help of the occupational therapist may lead to higher scores on a developmental checklist; it does not, in any way, however, show a necessary link to the skills required in most competitive employment positions. The balance beam skill would be considered *nonfunctional* (i.e., low in utility or in its immediate or future use). Yet we continue to see a multiplicity of these types of activities in secondary special education classrooms.

> **Perhaps the single greatest problem in linking secondary programs with competitive employment placements is the inadequacy of the current special education curriculum.**

A major reason for the continued existence of nonfunctional skills probably stems from the fact that teachers do not usually participate in job placement or job site training. Therefore, they do not know what skills are high in utility; when teachers examine relevant work environments carefully for curriculum selection, they engage in ecological (job) analysis. The inventory by Belmore and Brown (1978), which was discussed earlier, can be completed for behaviors necessary for success in a dishwasher's job, a landscaper's job, a farmer's job, or a clerical assistant's job. However, one must go to the job sites and carefully analyze the behaviors that are required for completion. These behaviors then must be formulated into objectives that are taught to students in preparation for eventual job placements. Until this approach is adopted more widely, adult service providers will continue to face serious difficulties in job placement for the handicapped.

Organizational Weaknesses in Vocational Programs at the Secondary Level

A second major weakness in many secondary-level vocational programs for handicapped students is that they are often placed in separate programs from nonhandicapped students. This arrangement contributes to the situation of a worker who can do his/her job, but not relate to co-workers, most of whom are nonhandicapped. We know that the social aspect of any job may contribute enormously to the sense of satisfaction derived from it. This is especially true in settings such as large cafeterias, where many individual tasks are in themselves not particularly rewarding. Many retarded workers find jobs in these settings, and therefore it is important that in their training they be stimulated to interact appropriately with their more normal peers. The reverse of this is equally true. Normal workers who are accustomed to and comfortable with handicapped persons can be invaluable in easing placements. The most natural means to this end is to integrate all students in training as much as possible.

A second benefit of increased integration in training is to ensure that the handicapped workers are trained to realistic goals and skill levels. It may be too easy to modify or eliminate an objective that all members of a special population find difficult when they are the only ones in the program. If, however, they are training alongside students who do succeed at, for example, using a time-clock, there is increased motivation to both teachers and slower students to find a way for them to adapt or practice until the skill is learned. Quite often there are big gaps in the job competencies that handicapped persons bring with them on referral, and each missing link seriously undermines their perceived value in the eyes of many employers. For example, one employee who could operate automated dishwashing machines could not appropriately mop the floor. Holding handicapped workers to the same standards in training as their nonhandicapped peers would help reduce this problem.

Normal workers who are accustomed to and comfortable with handicapped persons can be invaluable in easing placements.

As touched on above, a broad focus on the subject of job skills is needed by those who would truly prepare handicapped persons for competitive employment. Basic job skills need to be augmented by related competencies, and the secondary level is the right place to do this. Examples of considerations that cannot be avoided at placement time, and are best addressed much earlier, include:

How will the person conduct himself/herself in an interview? Basic skills can and should be taught.

How will the person get to work? Can they use the mass transit system? Adding bus training onto a full day of job training makes it rough for the student and trainer.

Can the person maintain the uniform of work clothes required? Good appearances are important.

How will the person handle the money earned? Basic knowledge of budgeting and prudence are essential.

Many high school vocational programs for the severely disabled deal too little with questions such as these. Our experience indicates that without some of the support skills described above, good job skills may not stand alone. With the competition for jobs and the minimum time many caseworkers have for each client, those who are lacking these attendant skills may never get a chance to demonstrate their specific job skills.

Another organizational weakness is that many vocational instructors who know their area of specialty do not know how to teach mentally retarded individuals efficiently. What they know but cannot communicate is not going to help their students. This leads to students not developing their full potential, which is especially tragic with the special population. Special education teachers can act as consultants to vocational trainers to help maximize the impact on their students. In addition, inservice training is mandated for all those who work with exceptional children, and should help if done well.

Lack of Parental Support

One recurring obstacle to the placement of handicapped youths is lack of parental support. This is the result in most cases of parents' concern for the welfare of their offspring, rather than resistance to personal inconvenience. We have found such concern to be based on legitimate fears and doubts, which have festered too long without benefit of offsetting information. These exaggerated fears and doubts can result in qualified persons being denied an opportunity or only receiving lukewarm support, which may increase the chance of failure.

It is important to appreciate parents' fears and doubts, and to have a genuine sensitivity to them in order to help set these concerns in their proper perspective. Given that parents know their children best and have probably given ample demonstration over the years of holding their best interests in mind, to the extent professionals fail to credit these points, they deserve parents' skepticism. There is some chance of severely disabled workers' being abused or embarrassed in a work situation; of course their parents are concerned. Given the maze of regulations governing SSI payments, there is need for caution to avoid disqualifying a person prematurely; fiscal responsibility is always in order. Added to factors such as the trouble involved in helping a person prepare for a job, and the big letdown for all concerned when it does not work out, these points justify parents in adopting a "show me" attitude with respect to the question of whether their retarded offspring should plan on being competitively employed. Only information that specifically addresses these questions can be expected to allay the uneasiness they generate.

> **It is important to appreciate parents' fears and doubts, and to have a genuine sensitivity to them in order to help get these concerns in their proper perspective.**

If parents receive more ongoing positive input regarding the work potential of their retarded children from an earlier time than is now the case, more healthy attitudes would result. Secondary-level vocational educators could do much to help in this regard.

The first thing vocational educators can do to help develop family support is to make certain they themselves are well-informed on the points at issue. There are increasingly numerous examples in professional literature of successful placements of severely retarded workers. Familiarity with these examples enables educators to speak with authority in advising parents and students on realistic expectations. If educators will in general take every opportunity to convey their own positive feeling about vocational potential, they will do much to overcome parental hesitation and misgivings. One way in which the importance of looking toward employment can be communicated to students and families is by including vocational objectives in IEP's. In some situations, students are spending time in school workshops without any related objective being in their educational plan.

Any activity that can serve to demonstrate learned job skills to family members will increase their belief in students' potential. Inviting them to visit technical centers and other training sites would be good. Further exposure could be created through competition between students in training, or by having students volunteer to apply their developing skills in certain community settings. One excellent function that teachers might perform is putting the parents of successful program graduates in touch with those who are uneasy about their own children's futures. Such mutual support by parents might be the best single means toward raising expectations regarding the work potential of their severely disabled sons and daughters.

IGNORANCE AND RESISTANCE BY THE PUBLIC AND EMPLOYERS

In seeking to place disabled workers into competitive community employment, one major obstacle is resistance by the public and employers. There is law prohibiting day-to-day help. Some jobs such as busing tables in a restaurant have high visibility, and if customers are discomforted by the appearance and behavior of the bus-person, a manager must take that into consideration for the sake of his/her business. It is a fact that many people are made uncomfortable by the sight of a handicapped worker. We feel this is largely a result of ignorance, of the natural tendency to feel uneasy when reminded of anything we do not understand, especially when most of its associations in our minds are with sadness and injustice. In addition to these factors, many employers have real doubts about handicapped workers' abilities and the adequacy of their training. These are difficult to allay quickly, and such general misgivings often prevent specific applicants from receiving a chance to display their talents. Again, such misgivings are largely the result of ignorance. We believe secondary-level vocational programs can and should assist more in making the general public better informed of the truth about students' potentials.

Generally speaking, more exposure to the public of facts about good training programs, proven success stories, and handicapped persons in general is needed. To that end, mainstreaming and all other normalization efforts are the hope of the future. But in the short term, other steps are possible and much needed.

Having potential employers actually observe good training programs is one way of educating them. This could be done by approaching persons who manage large food service operations, for example, and asking them to observe and advise on possible ways of upgrading current programs. The hint of flattery involved might help create a positive attitude toward what they would see. To the extent these advisers saw a program and students already doing well enough, they would be impressed. Challenging them to make suggestions would help reinforce the good image they might have.

Staging competitions in which students use vocational skills they have learned and inviting businessmen to judge is another way of creating exposure. Such events could be within a school, between schools, or between school systems. Secondary benefits of such competitions would lie in providing students a good intermediate objective and in possibly attracting media attention.

One way to broaden the general public's awareness of the disabled population and their abilities might be through arranging for students to volunteer their services for the sake of training opportunities. There are women's clubs, for example, that would be glad to have students serve at a luncheon where otherwise members would do it themselves. Other persons would welcome the exercise of janitorial or grounds maintenance skills on their property by students seeking practical experience. Parents of students can be of great assistance in arranging such opportunities. Perhaps higher functioning students could be given supervisory responsibility on such field trips, thus avoiding a drain on teachers' time.

> **One way to broaden the general public's awareness of the disabled population and their abilities might be through arranging for students to volunteer their services for the sake of training opportunities.**

One excellent idea we have seen used by a school's vocational coordinator is the preparation of a brief filmstrip telling of his school's training program. This is mounted in a portable, self-contained screening device that he takes with him on community contacts. This well-done presentation is an excellent supplement to his verbal description, in effect proving that what he says about training received is true.

Recently, one local school system initiated an Adopt-a-School program in which certain local businesses are each matched with one school. The business then arranges some activities for their adopted school, drawing on their practical knowledge to enhance classroom experiences. This is an example of the sort of opportunity that must be seized upon by special educators to ensure that their students are included in a relevant way. By so doing, they can raise the awareness of the community and foster acceptance of exceptional students.

SUMMARY

This chapter has outlined why competitive employment opportunities for moderately and severely handicapped people are important. We have discussed job placement techniques in depth because this process is crucial to accessing community-based employment. Training, advocacy, and ongoing follow-up by teachers and/or counselors were also described as essential components to a comprehensive vocational program. Finally, the role of parents and other significant people in the life of the handicapped worker was outlined. We believe that the information contained in this chapter, as well as the previous chapter, forms the basis for appropriate vocational programs for moderately and severely handicapped persons.

9

FUNCTIONAL ACADEMICS

LEARNING GOALS

1. *Discuss a generalized approach to teaching academics versus a task specific or functional task approach to teaching academic skills.*
2. *Describe a variety of reading and math curricula designed to teach generalized skills and discuss appropriate use of these curricula with severely handicapped learners.*
3. *Develop task analyses and skills sequences appropriate for teaching specific functional academic skills.*
4. *Describe how to assess individual student's competency levels in functional academic skills and how to determine on which skills to begin instruction.*
5. *Discuss the considerations related to teaching academic skills in a classroom versus a natural, community-based setting.*
6. *Describe two types of prompting procedures that can be used to teach functional academic skills.*
7. *Discuss the use of prosthetic aids to assist students in successful performance of daily living tasks requiring the use of functional academic skills.*

Traditionally, educational programs for handicapped as well as nonhandicapped students have emphasized the acquisition of academic skills (e.g., reading, writing, and arithmetic). For those students who are not quite ready for instruction in the academics, prerequisites are usually taught. For example, sorting colors and shapes and matching pictures have often been and still are taught as prerequisite to math and reading skills. Due to vast skill deficits and a slow learning rate, severely handicapped students frequently do not progress beyond this prerequisite skill instruction. As a result, it is not unusual to see severely handicapped adolescents being taught color and shape sorting, matching, and labeling, or alphabet reciting and labeling, to the exclusion of functional skills that may facilitate independence in adult life (Langone, 1981; Wheeler, Ford, Nietupski, Loomis, & Brown, 1980).

Instruction based on a developmental curriculum—a sequence of skills that gradually builds from prerequisites to generalized skill levels—is the approach educators usually take with nonhandicapped students beginning in the early grades. This approach may also be appropriate for young handicapped children who have many years left in public education (Wheeler et al., 1980). However, educators should carefully monitor progress to prevent a situation where students grow older while the skills taught remain at the prerequisite or nonfunctional level. Although functionality is an important issue at all ages, as students grow older, their instructional programs should include an increasing number of skills that are immediately usable, skills that are crucial for independence in the natural environment (Langone, 1981; Wheeler at al., 1980).

Most commercially available academic programs are based on a developmental progression from prerequisites to generalized skills. However, these programs frequently are not applicable to moderately and profoundly handicapped students. Therefore, teachers must modify or adapt commercial materials for use with handicapped students. If adaptations are made, special attention should be given to making the target skills of the curriculum immediately usable for severely handicapped students.

The skills included in the category of functional academics are vast in number and vary greatly. Unlike the other skill areas discussed in this book, functional academic skills comprise a traditional curricular area rather than a life skill domain (e.g., the vocational, domestic, leisure/recreational, or community domains). The skills included under the functional academic category cross life skill domains and are used in different environments and subenvironments and at different times with a variety of people. For example, time telling skills, which fall into the functional academic category, are used in a variety of environments: at home, in the workplace, and in the community. Similarly, functional use of money, another academic skill, is required for using stores and restaurants in the community, riding a city bus, using a pay phone, and participating in leisure activities such as bowling or going to a movie. Other functional academic skills may include different types of reading or word recognition and use of math or number skills that are necessary to engage in a variety of daily activities.

GENERALIZED ACADEMIC SKILLS

Because the ultimate goal of educational programs for moderately and profoundly handicapped students is preparation for post-school (adult) life in a heterogeneous community setting (Brown, Nietupski, & Hamre-Nietupski, 1976), teachers must constantly make crucial decisions and monitor student progress toward this goal when selecting target skills for instruction for individual students. Skill selection and the sequence developed for instruction should be based on: 1) the individual student's current skill level; 2) the student's chronological age; 3) the number of years a student has left in school; and 4) the skills required in a student's present and potential future living environments (e.g., home, community, and vocational settings).

> **Skill selection and the sequence developed for instruction should be based on: 1) the individual student's current skill level; 2) the student's chronological age; 3) the number of years a student has left in school; and 4) the skills required in a student's present and potential future living environments (e.g., home, community, and vocational settings).**

If a student is young and has many years left in public school programs, then the selection of a developmental academic skill sequence or curriculum may be appropriate. This approach to skill development involves first teaching prerequisite skills that build, through a sequence of skills over time, into more advanced skills that are usable in daily living. At the advanced levels, a developmental sequence results in the acquisition of generalized skills, skills that can be applied across untrained situations and activities. For example, reading instruction based on a developmental or longitudinal skill sequence is likely to provide students with word attack skills. These word attack skills can then be used across situations to read new, unfamiliar materials. The students will have acquired generalized reading skills that can be used across environments and for many different reasons. Similarly, math curricula that are designed to teach a sequence of skills beginning with the basic concepts and building into an understanding of numbers and their many different applications result in generalized math skills. Students who successfully progress through these math curricula develop number skills that assist them in a variety of situations, including those that were not addressed in the instructional setting.

The development of generalized academic skills (e.g., a phonetic approach to reading, the ability to use money in *any* situation requiring money use) usually requires long-term instruction even for nonhandicapped students. In fact, a person is considered functionally literate if he/she reads at least on a fourth grade level, and some experts feel that a seventh grade reading level is required for functional literacy (Snell, 1978). This implies that an average nonhandicapped student would require 4 to 7 years of reading instruction to develop generalized reading skills that are usable in everyday life. Therefore, the number of years required for a handicapped student to become functionally literate would, no doubt, exceed 4 to 7 years, and in many cases would exceed the number of years available in public instruction. In most cases, severely handicapped students would not have enough years in public school to acquire all of the skills included in a sequence designed to teach generalized academic skills. Consequently, if such a sequence is used, instruction may result in a student acquiring some but not all of the skills necessary for application in daily living.

Although skill instruction aimed at teaching generalized academic skills may be appropriate for only a small number of severely handicapped students, knowledge of the steps involved in generalized skill instruction may assist educators in modifying and designing instructional sequences. In addition, because at least a small number of severely handicapped students will progress at an adequate rate through a developmental academic skill sequence, educators must be familiar with this approach.

Generalized Reading Instruction

As was previously stated, an individual is considered functionally literate if he/she reads on a fourth to seventh grade reading level. Functional literacy refers to an individual's ability to read written material with word recognition and comprehension skills (Snell, 1978). In order to be functionally literate, a person must have a large repertoire of sight words that will enable quick recognition of common words. A sight word repertoire in combination with word analysis skills (e.g., phonetic analysis, use of contextual cues) will assist in developing generalized reading skills (i.e., the ability to read new unfamiliar material without further training).

A sight word repertoire in combination with word analysis skills (e.g., phonetic analysis, use of contextual cues) will assist in developing generalized reading skills (i.e., the ability to read new unfamiliar material without further training).

Duffy and Sherman (1977) developed a reading sequence designed to teach generalized reading skills through a phonetic approach. This curriculum consists of two major reading components: word recognition and comprehension skills. Beginning with reading prerequisites such as matching and labeling geometric figures, the curriculum builds upon each skill in the sequence until a student can successfully read and comprehend unfamiliar material. (Refer to Duffy & Sherman, 1977, for a detailed sequential listing of reading skills.) This approach has been successfully used with mildly and some moderately handicapped learners. However, its applicability to severely handicapped learners is questionable. This may be an example of a sequence that, when used with many severely handicapped learners, results in failure to progress beyond the prerequisite level. However, the Duffy and Sherman sequence is comprehensive, clear, and adaptable for assessment and instructional purposes, and may be appropriate for some moderately handicapped learners (Snell, 1978).

The Distar Reading Program (Englemann & Bruner, 1969) is another curriculum designed to teach a phonetic approach to generalized reading skills. The Distar skill sequence begins with teaching letter sounds and progresses to skills involved in phonetically sounding out words. Distar is recommended for students with mental ages of 4 and above (Englemann, 1967). Instruction is fast paced and conducted with small groups of students. Although this program has been demonstrated to be successful with mildly handicapped and culturally deprived students, its applicability to severely handicapped students is yet to be verified. The slow progression and thorough analysis of skills leading to a level of functional literacy in the Distar sequence result in very slow progress of a severely handicapped learner toward usable skills. In fact it is questionable whether a severely handicapped student would make adequate progress to warrant use of this approach to reading instruction. Many moderately handicapped learners, on the other hand, may be able to progress through the Distar sequence to a generalized reading level.

Many other reading curricula have been developed to teach generalized reading skills. The Sullivan Programmed Reading Series (Buchanan, 1968) teaches a phonetic approach to reading through programmed self-instruction. Students are required to read and respond to items in a workbook that build into word attack skills that can be applied across situations and reading material. Although instruction in the Sullivan Series is individualized and self-paced, the material lacks immediate functionality; that is, the words read initially (e.g., man, pan, ant) are not selected based on their functional value for a student in his/her natural environment.

The Peabody Rebus Reading Program (Woodcock, Davies, & Clark, 1969) is also a programmed sequence that has been successfully used with mildly handicapped and culturally deprived young school-aged students. However, the Rebus program incorporates symbols or pictures to represent words in the early stages of the program. A gradual transition from pictures/symbols (rebuses) to the written words is made as the program progresses to higher level reading skills. The use of pictures/symbols enables students to read complete thoughts or sentences in the early stages of instruction. However, many of the symbols are abstract and require interpretation in much the same way that a written word requires interpretation (e.g., ⊂⊃ = with). Therefore, the use of the rebus symbols as a preliminary step to introducing the written words may present an unnecessary or complicating step for the more severely handicapped learner. An educator must carefully evaluate the Rebus sequence and determine its utility with individual learners.

The only commercially available reading program that was developed for mildly and moderately retarded learners is the Edmark Reading Program (1972). Unlike the previously mentioned programs, the Edmark program is based on a "whole word" approach to reading. The skills are taught in a sequence beginning with easy visual discriminations (e.g., matching pictures of familiar objects) and progresses to more difficult discriminations (e.g., matching written words) and finally to reading words, phrases, and sentences. The format for instruction is very structured and is based on the principles of learning. At the completion of the program a student has a 150-word reading vocabulary, which consists of what the authors consider high utility words. However, the words taught are not necessarily those that would be used by the learner in daily living (e.g., one of the first words taught is "horse"). The intent of the program is to teach a student reading skills that can be used across situations—generalized skills. However, generalization may be questionable with severely handicapped learners. Therefore, the selection of truly functional words may be more beneficial if taught using the Edmark format.

A number of isolated studies have been conducted to evaluate specific skill sequencing and instructional procedures designed to teach generalizable skills (e.g., Entrikin, York, & Brown, 1975; Richardson, Oestereicher, Bialer, & Winsberg, 1975). Entrikin et al. (1975) developed an instructional sequence designed to teach moderately handicapped students generalizable word recognition strategies. The program objectives included teaching students to: 1) use pictures as cues to read unknown words; 2) use initial consonant sounds as cues to read unknown words; and 3) use context cues to read unknown words. The sequence of skills was ordered from easy to hard, and completion of this sequence resulted in a student being able to use pictures, initial consonants, and context to determine an unknown word in a sentence. Although this sequence was successfully used with three moderately handicapped students, its use may be limited due to the skills identified by the authors as being prerequisites to program implementation. Skills considered prerequisite to entry into this program included: 1) rudimentary speech; 2) imitation of consonant sounds; 3) a 50-word sight vocabulary; 4) left to right eye movement when reading; 5) a reliable and valid verbal yes-no response; and 6) a basic understanding of logical and absurd relationships. Training of these prerequisites is likely to be necessary for severely handicapped learners prior to beginning instruction on the skills outlined in the Entrikin et al. sequence. Therefore, the time needed for completion of this program may be more than the time available in school for severely handicapped students. This program, however, provides a detailed step-by-step approach to the development of a generalized strategy for reading new words, and its usefulness with moderately handicapped learners has been demonstrated.

The Direct Approach to Decoding (Richardson et al., 1975) was designed to teach handicapped students a phonetic approach to word recognition. This sequence of skills included teaching: 1) letter sounds; 2) sound blending; 3) phonetic analysis of written words; and 4) word reading. Although this approach has been demonstrated to be successful with handicapped students, it is likely that severely handicapped learners will have the same difficulty progressing through this sequence as they do through other developmental sequences; that is, progress may be so slow that the skills acquired during school years may be minimal and, as a result, nonfunctional.

Generalized Math Instruction

The development of generalized math skills involves instruction through a developmental sequence of skills that is similar to the developmental sequences leading to generalized reading. Generalized math skills include competencies in: 1) rote counting; 2) one-to-one correspondence and identifying number values; 3) numeral recognition; 4) seriation and ordinal positions; 5) identifying more and less; and 6) addition and subtraction. These competencies allow a learner to respond to daily living tasks, including untrained tasks, with adequate skills. Math skills are required in numerous daily living activities. Food preparation, telephone use, time telling, grocery shopping, and money management all require the use of math skills to varying degrees.

Resnick, Wang, and Kaplan (1973) developed a developmental (hierarchically sequenced) math curriculum designed to teach generalized math skills. The curriculum provides a hierarchically ordered list of objectives within a number of math skill areas. This curriculum was not designed specifically for handicapped students. However, the sequence seems to be appropriate for any students for whom generalized skills are targeted. Table 9.1 provides a listing of these objectives by unit. Figure 9.1 presents a flow chart of the units included in the Resnick et al. sequence.

As is suggested by this flow chart, some math units are prerequisite to others (e.g., Unit 1 is prerequisite to Unit 2 and Unit 3 is to Unit 4) and some are parallel (e.g., Unit 6 is parallel to Unit 8). Therefore, prerequisite units must be taught first whereas parallel units can be taught concurrently. For example, because Units 2 and 3 are parallel, rote counting and one-to-one correspondence to 10 can be taught at the same time that numeral recognition and labeling are taught.

Traditionally, the skills included in the Resnick et al. sequence are taught in a classroom setting, in most cases through the use of paper and pencil worksheets or nonfunctional materials. For example, the counting objectives (listed in Units 1 and 2) might be taught using poker chips, pegs, beads, or blocks, and the set comparisons might be taught via worksheets that present sets of objects (e.g., balls, toys, geometric shapes) for comparison. Implicit in this approach is the assumption that the skills taught using artificial materials in artificial tasks will generalize to daily living activities requiring the same skills. Because severely handicapped students are not likely to generalize (Brown et al., 1976), this approach presents serious problems. Teachers should, instead, teach the objectives in a developmental sequence being very careful to make each objective immediately functional to the student. For example, when teaching the objective requiring a student to count a subset of objects from a larger set when given a stated numeral (Units 1 and 2, Objective E), the teacher might use silverware in the context of table setting (e.g., "Count out five spoons for table setting"). This approach will result in usable skills regardless of how far a student progresses in the math sequence. In the event that an objective in the curriculum cannot be made functional for a particular student, the teacher should reconsider the necessity for teaching that skill.

> **Teachers should teach the objectives in a developmental math sequence being very careful to make each objective immediately functional to the student.**

Within the math skill area, money management skills are frequently cited as important for successful community placement (e.g., Schalock & Harper, 1978). Therefore, teachers must consider instruction in money use for each student. As for general math and reading skills, money use has traditionally been taught through the use of a developmentally sequenced curriculum with the purpose of training generalized money skills. These

Table 9.1. A hierarchically sequenced math curriculum: Skills and subskills[a]

Units 1 and 2: Counting and one-to-one correspondence[b]

A. The child can recite the numerals in order.
B. Given a set of movable objects, the child can count the objects, moving them out of the set as he/she counts.
C. Given a fixed ordered set of objects, the child can count the objects.
D. Given a fixed unordered set of objects, the child can count the objects.
E. Given a numeral stated and a set of objects, the child can count out a subset of stated size.
F. Given a numeral stated and several sets of fixed objects, the child can select a set of size indicated by numeral.
G. Given two the child can pair objects and state whether the sets are equivalent.
H. Given two unequal sets of objects, the child can pair objects and state which set has more.
I. Given two unequal sets of objects, the child can pair objects and state which has less.

Units 3 and 4: Numerals[c]

A. Given two sets of numerals, the child can match the numerals.
B. Given a numeral stated and a set of printed numerals, the child can select the stated numeral.
C. Given a numeral (written), the child can read the numeral.
D. Given several sets of objects and several numerals, the child can match numerals with appropriate sets.
E. Given two numerals (written), the child can state which shows more (or less).
F. Given a set of numerals, the child can place them in order.
G. Given numerals stated, the child can write the numeral.

Unit 5: Comparison of sets

A. Given two sets of objects, the child can count sets and state which has more objects or that sets have same number.
B. Given two sets of objects, the child can count sets and state which has less objects.
C. Given a set of objects and a numeral, the child can state which shows more or less.
D. Given a numeral and several sets of objects, the child can select numerals which show more (less) than the set of objects.
E. Given two rows of objects (not paired), the child can state which row has more regardless of arrangement.
F. Given three sets of objects, the child can count sets and state which has most (least).

Unit 6: Seriation and ordinal position

A. Given three objects of different sizes, the child can select the largest (smallest).
B. Given objects of graduated sizes, the child can seriate according to size.
C. Given several sets of objects, the child can seriate the sets according to size.
D. Given ordered sets of objects, the child can name the ordinal position of the objects.

Unit 7: Addition and subtraction (sums to 10)

A. Given two numbers stated, set of objects, and directions to add, the child can add the numbers by counting out two subsets then combining and stating combined number as sum.
B. Given two numbers stated, set of objects, and directions to subtract, the child can count out smaller subset from larger subset and state remainder.
C. Given two numbers stated, number line, and directions to add, the child can use the number line to determine sum.
D. Given two numbers stated, number line, and directions to subtract, the child can use number line to subtract.
E. Given addition and subtraction word problems, the child can solve the problems.
F. Given written addition and subtraction problems in form: x or y; the child can complete the problems.
G. Given addition and subtraction problems in form:

$$x + \frac{+y}{y} = \Box \text{ or } \frac{-y}{x} - y = \Box;$$

the child can complete the equations.

Unit 8: Addition and subtraction equations

A. Given equation of form $z = \Box + \triangle$, the child can show several ways of completing the equation.
B. Given equation of form $x + y = \underline{\quad} + \underline{\quad}$, the child can complete the equation in several ways.
C. Given equations of forms $x + y = z + \underline{\quad} + z$, the child can complete the equations.
D. Given equations of forms $x + \underline{\quad} = y$ and $\underline{\quad} + x = y$, the child can complete the equations.
E. Given complete addition equation (e.g, $x + 7 = z$), the child can write equations using numerals and minus sign (e.g., $z - x = y$) and demonstrate relationship.
F. Given counting blocks and/or number line, the child can make up completed equations of various forms.

[a]Reprinted with permission. Resnick, L.B., Wang, M.C., and Kaplan, J. *Journal of Applied Behavior Analysis*, 1973, 6, 679–710.

[b]Unit 1 involves sets of up to five objects. Unit 2 involves sets of up to 10 objects.

[c]Unit 3 involves numerals and sets of up to five objects. Unit 4 involves numerals and sets of up to 10 objects.

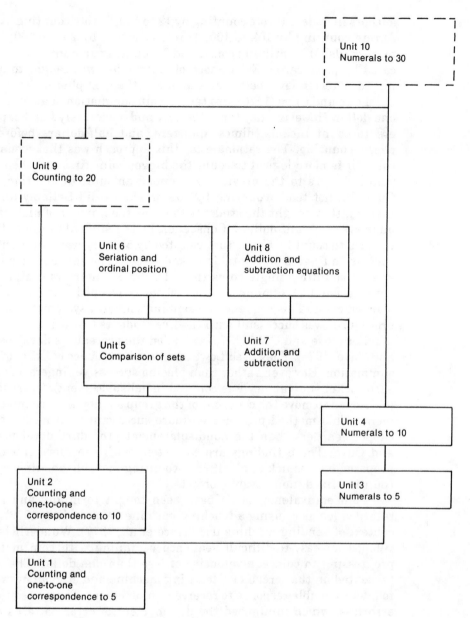

Figure 9.1. Hierarchical sequence of introductory mathematics. (Reprinted by permission. Resnick, L.B., Wang, M.C., & Kaplan, J. Task analysis in curriculum design: A hierarchically sequenced introductory mathematics curriculum. Journal of Applied Behavior Analysis, *1973, 6, 697–710.)*

available curricula, however, have not been validated with moderately or severely handicapped learners.

There are a number of instructional studies that have been conducted to evaluate skill sequencing and instructional procedures for teaching money skills to moderately and severely handicapped learners (e.g., Bellamy & Buttars, 1975; Borakove & Cuvo, 1976; Certo & Swetlik, 1980; Cuvo, Veitch, Trace, & Konke, 1978; Lowe & Cuvo, 1976; Trace, Cuvo, & Criswell, 1977; Wunderlich, 1972).

Bellamy and Buttars (1975) taught five mildly and moderately handicapped students coin summation. The sequence of skills developed by these authors included: 1) rote counting by 1's to 100; 2) rote counting by 5's to 100; 3) rote counting by 10's to 100; 4) rote counting by 25's to 100; 5) labeling price cards; 6) identifying coins; and 7) counting amounts of money as indicated by price cards. Each phase of instruction was taught to a predetermined criterion level before proceeding to the next phase.

Lowe and Cuvo (1976) also taught coin summation of amounts less than one dollar. However, they taught mildly and moderately handicapped learners to count nickels, dimes, quarters, and half-dollars before teaching penny counting. The rationale for this approach was that when summing coins, it is more logical to count the bigger coins first and then to add the pennies by 1's to the previously summed amount. In addition, Lowe and Cuvo did not teach counting by 10's or 25's as did Bellamy and Buttars. Instead, they taught the students to count the number of nickels in dimes, quarters, and half-dollars. Consequently, the students were only required to learn to count by 5's. As they counted by 5's, they were instructed to place successive fingers on the table to keep track. The sequence for instruction was: 1) counting single coins (nickels, dimes, quarters, half-dollars, and pennies); and 2) summing values of newly learned coins with previously learned coins. This sequence in combination with systematic instructional procedures was successful with the five students trained.

Borakove and Cuvo (1976) extended the procedures developed by Lowe and Cuvo (1976). They used Lowe and Cuvo's sequence of skills to teach coin summation. However, rather than placing successive fingers on the table as each nickel equivalency was counted (nondisplacement), the students were instructed to move the coins out of the group as they were counted (displacement). This method proved even more successful with moderately handicapped learners than the nondisplacement procedure developed by Lowe and Cuvo. These findings are consistent with the hierarchical sequence proposed by Resnick et al. (1973)—counting movable objects is easier than counting fixed (nonmovable) objects.

Coin equivalency skills have been taught to mildly and moderately retarded learners using a teaching machine (Wunderlich, 1972) and in the context of vending machine use (Trace et al., 1977). Wunderlich (1972) developed an easy-to-difficult sequence beginning with coin matching and progressing to coin equivalencies of less than one dollar. The tasks were presented on the screen of a teaching machine and students were required to make a double response to receive reinforcement. The procedure was near errorless, which minimized the development of error patterns or frustration. However, the cost of obtaining teaching machines and the abstract nature of this task may be prohibitive for use with severely handicapped students. If these procedures are used, the educator must be very careful to ensure that students generalize their skills to the natural environment where the skills are required.

Trace et al. (1977), however, taught coin equivalency in the context of a functional task, vending machine use. The skills considered prerequisite to entry into this program included: 1) counting to 100 by 5's and 10's; 2) naming coins and stating coin values; and 3) summing coin combinations. The skills taught in the program included selecting coins beginning with nickels alone and progressing to larger coins to equal different prices. Three responses were required: 1) price naming; 2) selecting and counting equivalent combinations of coins; and 3) depositing coins in a vending machine. An adapted vending machine was used in which only correct coin combinations would operate the machine. Therefore, if a student inserted an incorrect combination, the machine returned the money, a very natural consequence.

Finally, Cuvo, Veitch, Trace, and Konke (1978) taught change making skills to three moderately retarded adolescents. Coin summation, reading prices, and coin equivalency skills were considered prerequisite to program entry. Four response classes were taught: 1) 1¢ to 4¢; 2) 5¢ to 9¢; 3) 10¢ to 45¢ (using even multiples of 5); and 4) 11¢ to 49¢ (not using multiples of 5). Each response required three steps including price reading, coin summation, and change computation. Change making was taught in the context of making a purchase with coins. Therefore, the investigators attempted to teach the skills in the context of a functional task.

These studies conducted with handicapped students along with the literature and curricula available for nonhandicapped students provided valuable information for establishing a generalized money skill sequence. Figure 9.2 presents a hierarchically sequenced money skill curriculum for teaching generalized money skills. As in the Resnick et al. (1973) math sequence, the skills in the money sequence have been established as either sequentially ordered or parallel. Three money skill areas were identified (counting, coins/bills, and numerals) for which skills are sequentially listed.

If a generalized money skill sequence is used to teach moderately and severely handicapped learners, educators should teach each skill within the context of functional tasks rather than teaching the skills in isolated instructional settings with artificial materials or in artificial tasks. If taught in the context of daily living activities, the students will obtain skills at each step in the sequence that are immediately usable regardless of whether generalization to untrained tasks occurs.

> **If a generalized money skill sequence is used to teach moderately and severely handicapped learners, educators should teach each skill within the context of functional tasks rather than teaching the skills in isolated instructional settings with artificial materials or in artificial tasks.**

FUNCTIONAL ACADEMIC TASKS

An alternative to teaching generalized academic skills is teaching academics only as they apply to specific daily living tasks. For example, rather than teaching a phonetic approach to reading, a teacher may teach the reader words necessary for completion of a simple recipe or for recognizing the bus route a student must take to get from home to work. Similarly, an alternative to teaching generalized money use would be to teach a student to select the appropriate change for riding a bus, using a pay phone, or using a vending machine. In selecting functional academic tasks, the emphasis is on survival in community life (Snell, 1978). Therefore, teachers should be

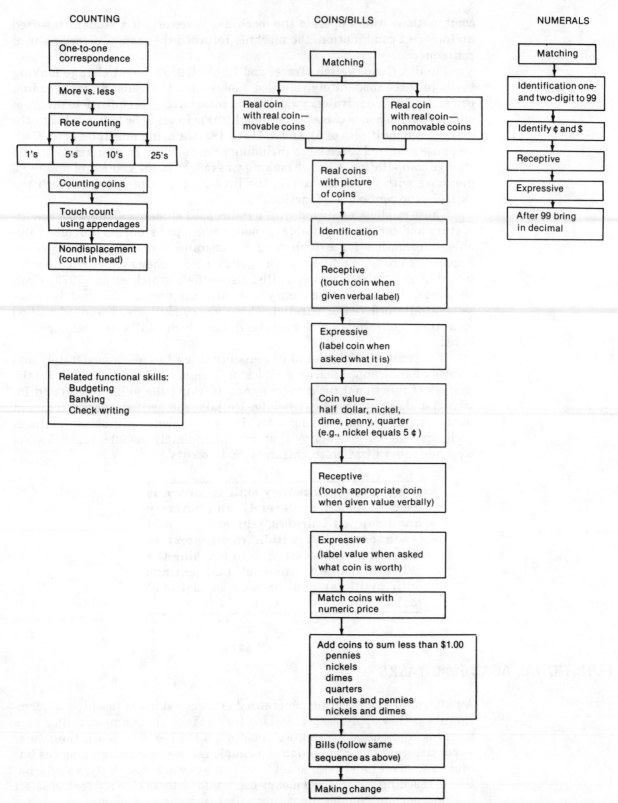

COUNTING

One-to-one correspondence
↓
More vs. less
↓
Rote counting
↓
1's | 5's | 10's | 25's
↓
Counting coins
↓
Touch count using appendages
↓
Nondisplacement (count in head)

Related functional skills:
Budgeting
Banking
Check writing

COINS/BILLS

Matching
↓
Real coin with real coin—movable coins | Real coin with real coin—nonmovable coins
↓
Real coins with picture of coins
↓
Identification
↓
Receptive (touch coin when given verbal label)
↓
Expressive (label coin when asked what it is)
↓
Coin value—half dollar, nickel, dime, penny, quarter (e.g., nickel equals 5 ¢)
↓
Receptive (touch appropriate coin when given value verbally)
↓
Expressive (label value when asked what coin is worth)
↓
Match coins with numeric price
↓
Add coins to sum less than $1.00
  pennies
  nickels
  dimes
  quarters
  nickels and pennies
  nickels and dimes
↓
Bills (follow same sequence as above)
↓
Making change

NUMERALS

Matching
↓
Identification one- and two-digit to 99
↓
Identify ¢ and $
↓
Receptive
↓
Expressive
↓
After 99 bring in decimal

Figure 9.2. Functional skill sequence for generalized use of money. (Unpublished sequence developed by A. Renzaglia and D. Browder, University of Virginia, 1980).

very familiar with the needs of each student in his/her natural environment. This approach should lead to the development of a curriculum that is designed for a specific student. As a result different functional academic tasks may be targeted for each student.

In selecting functional academic tasks, the emphasis is on survival in community life.

To generate functional academic tasks, the first step involves identifying activities in which a student would be expected to engage or activities that would increase a student's independence in community living. The next step consists of identifying the skills (academic as well as nonacademic) involved in completing those activities. The functional academic skills should be listed along with the nonacademic skills involved in the task. Table 9.2 represents a simple task analysis for use of a pay phone. As is indicated, steps 3, 4, 5, and 9 require some academic skills. This analysis does not specify the level of the skill required. Figure 9.3 presents a flow chart of the skills involved in public bus riding. This skill sequence includes functional academic skills such as money use, time telling, and reading as they relate to bus riding. In addition, this sequence presents an easy-to-difficult analysis of the academic skills within the activity. For example, time telling as represented in Figure 9.3 is broken down into sequential skills from matching the clock time to numerals to reading time by numerals to the minute.

Lichtman (1972) developed a series of simple analyses of specific functional academic tasks. Each analysis consists of a flow chart of skills that indicates a sequence for training. Figure 9.4 is a sample analysis developed by Lichtman of the skills required to use a food ad. As is indicated by this flow chart the skills listed at the bottom of the sequence are easier and prerequisite to the skills they flow into at the top of the chart.

Table 9.2.   Sample task analysis for use of a pay phone

1.   Enter phone booth
2.   Locate phone book
3.   Find appropriate number in phone book[a]
4.   Write the number or hold place in phone book[a]
5.   Select appropriate coins for the phone[a]
6.   Pick up the receiver
7.   Listen for the dial tone
8.   Insert the proper coins (quickly)
9.   Dial the correct phone number (this may be broken down into subskills)[a]
10.   Wait for the phone to ring and for someone to answer
11.   Greet the person who answers with "Hello" or "Hi"
12.   Request the target person by saying, "May I speak to (*Name*)?"
13.   Identify oneself with "This is (*Own Name*)"
14.   Give appropriate message or obtain pertinent information
15.   Respond appropriately to the target person's response by giving a proper closing routine
16.   Hang up the receiver
17.   Respond correctly when asked, "What did (*Name of Target Person*) say?

[a]Steps that require some prerequisite *academic* skills.

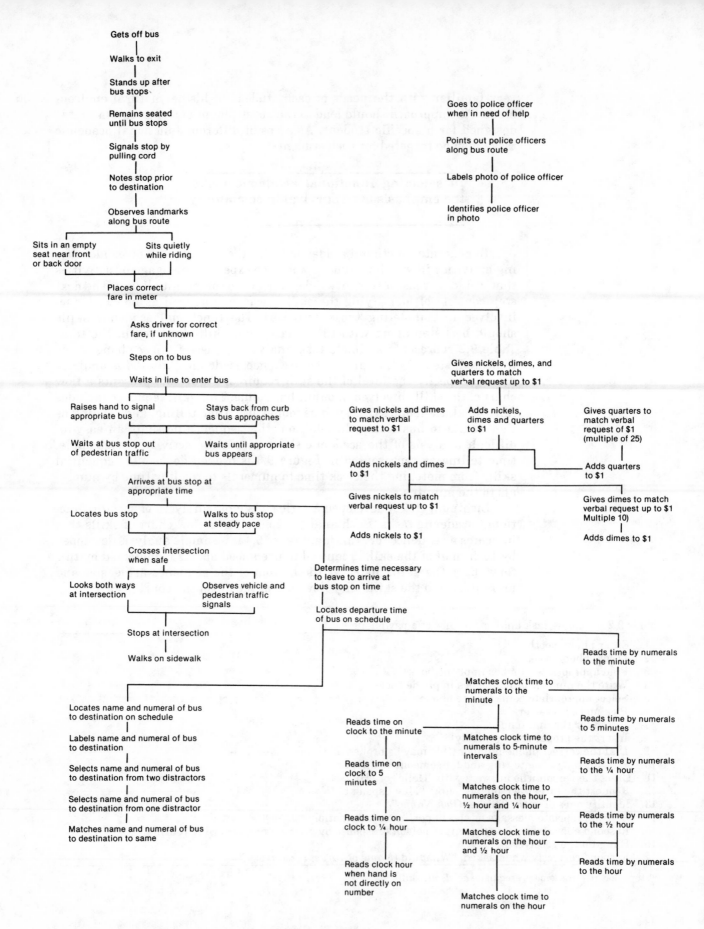

Figure 9.3. Public bus riding skills. (Unpublished sequence, J. Turner, University of Virginia, 1980.)

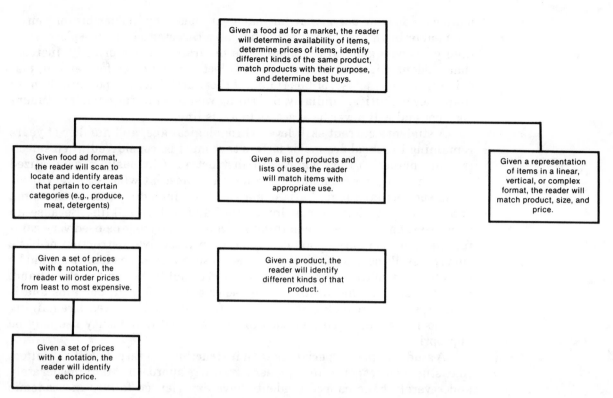

Figure 9.4. Analysis of the skills involved in using a food ad. (Reprinted with permission. Lichtman, M. Reading/everyday activities in life. New York: CAL Press, 1972.)

When teaching functional academic tasks, a teacher must determine the terminal behavior and how it will be measured prior to instruction (Snell, 1983). Because the purpose of selecting functional academic tasks is to teach immediately usable skills that directly relate to a student's daily living, measurement of the terminal behavior should include an assessment of the skills in the natural environment. For example, if selecting the appropriate coins for bus riding is the target academic skill for a particular student, that skill should not be considered required until the student has demonstrated mastery in the context of actually using the bus in the community. In addition, although it may occur, generalization to untrained academic tasks should not be expected to occur if a functional task approach is selected for instruction.

The decision to teach academics using a generalized versus a functional task approach is based on a number of variables. These variables can be addressed by answering the following questions:

1. What are the student's current and future needs?
2. What is the student's chronological age?
3. What is the student's current skill level?
4. What past experiences has the student had with instruction of the target skills?
5. How many years does the student have left in school?

Consideration of a student's current and future needs (an ecological assessment) assists a teacher in identifying those skills that are necessary for a particular student. For example, if a student will never be allowed to manage money or use money for major purchases by his/her present environment or by the group home that has been targeted as a future placement, then perhaps a generalized money use program is not a priority. Instead, that student might be taught how to select specific coins for vending machine or pay phone use, or bus riding, if those activities are potentially high frequency activities. Similarly, bus riding would not be targeted if a student does not and will never have access to a bus line.

A student's current skill level, chronological age, and number of years remaining in school are major factors that must be considered when selecting an approach to academic skill instruction. Obviously, a generalized approach would not be appropriate for an adolescent who lacks very basic skills such as language; basic domestic skills including eating, dressing, and toileting; or basic social interaction and mobility skills. Because an adolescent has few years remaining in school, time must be used very carefully, and an emphasis should be placed on intensive instruction of basic survival skills across life skill domains. In such a case, academics should be targeted only in the context of priority functional tasks. On the other hand, for a student who has acquired the basics across life skill domains and is young (perhaps preadolescent) with a sufficient number of years remaining in school, a generalized approach to reading, math, or money use may be appropriate.

A student's past experiences with instruction of a target skill also affect that student's response to a present training approach. Many moderately and severely handicapped students have experienced failure in academic skill instruction in their early school years. This may have resulted in the development of a failure set, which affects future learning of the same skills (Gold & Scott, 1971). When a failure set occurs, a student's response to a task is based on an expectation of failure and results in frustration and lack of attention to the salient features of the task. Therefore, an approach to skill instruction that does not resemble the approach used in the student's past experiences is likely to produce greater learning. Thus, if a generalized approach was used in the past and resulted in failure or little progress, perhaps a task-specific approach would prove more successful.

DEVELOPING TASK ANALYSES AND SKILL SEQUENCES

Prior to assessing a student's skill level and to beginning instruction, the target behavior must be analyzed and broken down into component skills. A skill sequence involves listing skills that are either developmentally sequential or parallel. Generally, a skill sequence can be presented in a flow chart format (e.g., the math sequence presented in Figure 9.1, the money sequence in Figure 9.2, and the analysis of use of a food ad in Figure 9.4). Each skill in a sequence can usually be task analyzed (broken down into component steps); in many instances task analyses represent a chain of motor responses. Table 9.2 presents a task analysis of pay phone use.

Task analyses or skill sequences will differ depending on how the task is conceptualized (Snell, 1978). For example, a skill sequence developed to teach generalized reading skills will differ from a task analysis designed to teach a protective reading vocabulary. Similarly, the generalized money skill sequence presented in Figure 9.2 differs from the analysis of money use for riding a public bus as presented in Figure 9.3. Regardless of how the skill is conceptualized, an analysis should produce a sequential listing of skills that indicate the behaviors required for performing the target objective.

Sidman and Cresson (1973) identified the skills they considered prerequisite to reading and comprehending single words. They conceptualized reading as a transfer from auditory-visual stimulus equivalence to purely visual equivalence. As a result of their conceptualization, an analysis of the skills considered necessary for reading includes identifying and associating visual and auditory stimuli. However, a whole word approach is advocated for severely handicapped learners rather than an approach that involves letter-sound association. Table 9.3 presents Sidman and Cresson's analysis of reading skills. This sequence can be used both to test and teach a reading vocabulary.

O'Brien (Note 5) developed a sequence of skills for telling time to the nearest quarter hour (refer to Table 9.4). The skills are presented in an easy-to-difficult sequence beginning with numeral matching. This analysis differs greatly from an analysis of time telling to the minute. O'Brien's sequence does not require counting skills, where a traditional time telling program would require counting by 1's and 5's to 60.

Even though target skills can be conceptualized differently and consequently analyzed differently, educators must be very careful to ensure that the skills being taught are functional for a student. A good skill sequence should be developed so that a student can immediately use each skill taught in the sequence; that is, each skill regardless of where it falls in the sequence of skills should be functional to the student. In some cases, this may be very difficult. Therefore, special materials may have to be used to facilitate functional use. For example, prosthetic aids (e.g., pictures for matching, coin cards to indicate proper coin combinations) may be used initially to assist a student in independence at early stages of instruction. However, as instruction progresses, the need for prosthetic aids should disappear.

Table 9.3. An analysis of reading skills based on a whole word approach[a]

Sample Stimulus (visual or auditory)	Response (name or match)	Task
Visual	Visual (match)	1. Identity picture matching: selecting a picture choice to match a sample picture
Visual	Visual (match)	2. Identity word matching: selecting a printed word choice to match a sample printed word
Auditory	Visual (match)	3. Auditory comprehension: selecting a picture choice to match a sample spoken word
Visual	Vocal (name)	4. Picture naming: naming a sample picture
Auditory	Visual (match)	5. Auditory receptive reading: selecting a printed word choice to match a sample spoken word
Visual	Visual (match)	6. Reading comprehension: selecting a printed word choice to match a sample picture
Visual	Visual (match)	7. Reading comprehension: selecting a picture choice to match a sample printed word
Visual	Vocal (name)	8. Oral reading: naming a sample printed word

[a]Reprinted with permission. Sidman, M., & Cresson, O., Jr. Reading and cross modal transfer of stimulus equivalences in severe retardation. *American Journal of Mental Deficiency,* 1973, 77, 515–523.

Table 9.4. Sequence of skills for telling time[a]

I. Reading the hour hand

Step 1: Match numeral to clock face numeral (numerals on the clock)

[a]Phase 1: 1
2: 1, 8
3: 1, 8, 5
4: 1, 8, 5, 4
5: 1, 8, 5, 4, 10
6: 1, 8, 5, 4, 10, 9
7: 1, 8, 5, 4, 10, 9, 2
8: 1, 8, 5, 4, 10, 9, 2, 6
9: 1, 8, 5, 4, 10, 9, 2, 6, 11
10: 1, 8, 5, 4, 10, 9, 2, 6, 11, 7
11: 1, 8, 5, 4, 10, 9, 2, 6, 11, 7, 3
12: 1, 8, 5, 4, 10, 9, 2, 6, 11, 7, 3, 12
13: 1, 8, 5, 4, 10, 9, 2, 6, 11, 7, 3, 12

[a]Numerals in each phase are trained to criterion level before proceeding to the subsequent phase.

Step 2: "Point to number ___ on the clock face." Shown the numeral, point to its match on the clock. In 13 phases (see above), numeral is held farther and farther from the clock.

Step 3: "Point to number ___ on the clock face." (Not shown the numeral.)

Step 4: Imitation of number name. "This is number ___. What number is this? Say ___." (Point to number on clock face.)

Step 5: Number naming. "What number is this?" (Point to number on clock face.)

Step 6: Reading the hour hand. "What number does the hour hand point to?"

II. Reading the minute hand

Step 7: Discrimination of hour and minute hand. "Point to the hour hand." "Point to the minute hand."

Step 8: Read minute hand—imitation. "What does the minute hand say? Say 'o'clock." "o'clock" "30" "15" "45"

Step 9: Read the minute hand (no verbal prompt).

III. Reading the nearest quarter-hour setting

Step 10: Read hour hand when not exactly on a number.
Phase 1: Move hour hand clockwise.
2: Only 2 numbers on clock. Hour hand between them. "Which number did the hour hand point to last?"
3: All numbers showing.
4: Hour hand between numbers and minute hand on 9.
5: Hour hand between numbers and minute hand on 3.
6: Hour hand between numbers and minute hand on 6.
7: Hour hand between or on number(s) and minute hand on 12, 9, 3, or 6. SD: "What number does the hour hand point to?" "What number does the minute hand read?" "What time is it? Say ___."

Step 11: Read time to the quarter hour. "What time is it?"

Step 12: Read time between quarter hours as, "It's about ___." SD: "What time is it? Say, 'about ___.'"

Step 13: Read time between quarter hours. No prompt. "What time is it?"
(distance from nearest quarter hour)
Phase 1: 1 minute
2: 1, 3
3: 1, 3, 5
4: 1, 3, 5, 7
5: 0, 1, 3, 5, 7

[a]Adapted from O'Brien F. Instruction in reading a clock for institutionalized retarded. Unpublished manuscript. Anna State Hospital and Southern Illinois, 1974.

> **A good skill sequence should be developed so that a student can immediately use each skill taught in the sequence.**

Another important consideration for developing skill sequences is one of generalization. If a generalized approach to academics is selected for instruction, a teacher should build into the skill sequence a method for assessing generalized use of the target skills. Similarly, if a functional task approach is selected, a method for evaluating adequate application of the target skills in the natural environment should be included in the skill sequence.

ASSESSMENT OF STUDENT SKILL LEVELS

As the development of a skill sequence is dependent on how the target behavior is conceptualized, skill assessment also depends on conceptualization. Most commercially available curricula designed to teach functional skills include a method for assessing student skills and a method for diagnosing skill deficits. The assessment is usually based on the established generalized sequence. For example, Duffy and Sherman (1977) have developed tests for each objective in their detailed skill sequence. Similarly, Wang (1973) has developed a diagnostic test based on the Resnick et al. (1973) math sequence. Although these tests are criterion referenced, they are not designed to test severely handicapped students. Additionally, the Wang (1973) assessment instrument was designed for young children and involves the use of nonfunctional materials. However, a teacher who chooses to test and teach based on these sequences can modify testing procedures to incorporate the use of functional (real) materials in natural settings.

Assessment of skills taught using a functional task approach usually involves the use of a task analysis of the target skills. For example, the task analysis of pay phone use presented in Table 9.2 can be used to assess student skills. When given instructions to use the pay phone (or given an appropriate situation for pay phone use) the student would be observed by a teacher. While observing, the teacher would record each step completed correctly and those steps performed incorrectly. The bus riding sequence (Figure 9.3) could be used in a similar fashion. However, those academic steps performed incorrectly might be analyzed further by presenting easier levels of the skills (as indicated in the flow chart in Figure 9.3) to the student for evaluation.

Sidman and Cresson's (1973) sequence (Table 9.3) presents both testing and teaching target objectives. Once a functional list of reading words has been selected, a teacher can assess student skills by presenting the materials to the student as indicated by each of the eight tasks in the sequence. This assessment, as the others previously mentioned, should indicate a student's strengths and weaknesses and where to begin instruction. However, to obtain a true picture of student skills, assessment should be conducted across trials and across days until a stable measure has been obtained. This will account for variability in a student's performance due to factors a teacher is unable to control (e.g., student's mood, bad or good days, home crises).

SELECTING A SETTING AND MATERIALS
FOR INSTRUCTION

There is little doubt that instruction in the natural environment using real materials results in the acquisition of skills that are most likely to be used at appropriate times and in appropriate places and are likely to maintain over time (Kazdin, 1980; Stokes & Baer, 1977). However, many logistical problems may arise in teaching academics when attempting to use real materials in natural settings (Langone, 1981). Access to the community may be limited due to transportation problems, and the expense involved in teaching academics (especially money use) in the natural environments (e.g., restaurants, stores) may be prohibitive. In addition, the number of teaching trials may be limited if instruction is provided only when the skill naturally occurs. Therefore, simulated training trials or massed trials in isolation may be used to augment training in the natural environment.

Prior to or in combination with instruction in the community, a teacher may simulate the natural environment in the classroom. For example, menu reading, selecting products in a grocery store, or using money to purchase groceries, clothing, items from a vending machine, or meals in a restaurant can be simulated in a classroom setting. However, if a teacher chooses to simulate, an attempt should be made to create an environment in the classroom that resembles as closely as possible the natural setting. Furthermore, a teacher should never consider a skill acquired until mastery of that skill has been demonstrated in the natural environment. Because functional academic skills are used across life skill domains, they can frequently be taught in the context of other life skills. For example, money is the natural reinforcer for work. Therefore, students participating in vocational training should receive money from the beginning as a reward. The money earned can be used to teach money value, purchasing skills, or budgeting and banking skills as appropriate for the individual student. Similarly, phone use can be taught for the purpose of initiating leisure time activites with friends (e.g., Nietupski & Williams, 1974). By teaching phone skills in this context, the reinforcers are built in (naturally occurring).

A teacher should never consider a skill acquired until mastery of that skill has been demonstrated in the natural environment.

Developing Instructional Programs

Once a task analysis has been developed and the setting and materials have been selected for instruction, an instructional program must be developed. Specifically, prompting and reinforcement strategies must be selected and described with enough detail to promote consistency within and between trainers.

Prompting

Two general types of prompting procedures are available to teachers. These are *instructional prompts*, which refer to what a teacher should do to promote correct responding, and *stimulus prompts,* which involve modifying the task materials to assist correct responding.

Instructional Prompts Instructional prompts involve verbal assists, gestural prompts, teacher models, and physical assists that facilitate task completion while minimizing errors. These prompts can be used in a least-to-most intbecive hierarchy (e.g., verbal, model, then physical assists) or a most-to-least intrusive hierarchy (e.g., physical, model, then verbal), or each prompt can be used independently. For a more in-depth discussion of a least intrusive prompt system, refer to Chapters 3 and 8. Table 9.5 presents a sample instructional program using a least-to-most intrusive prompting procedure for teaching coin selection for using a drink machine.

An alternative to a hierarchy of prompts is the use of one functional prompt to assist correct performance. For example, if a student responds well to gestural prompts, perhaps the teacher might choose to *point* to the correct selection of coins when the student needs assistance. However, if a single prompt is selected, a method for fading that prompt should be incorporated into the program. Time delay (Snell & Gast, 1981) is a potentially effective method of fading a prompt. Time delay consists of gradually increasing the amount of time between the instructional cues for the task and the delivery of the prompt. By increasing the time (delaying the prompt) the teacher expects the student to begin anticipating a correct response before the prompt is delivered. For an in-depth discussion of time delay, see Snell and Gast (1981).

The decision to select one instructional prompting procedure over another should be based on the skills of the student, the difficulty of the task, and the type of task being trained. Students who are severely motorically impaired may not perform well when taught with a least intrusive prompting system, especially if the system incorporates a verbal or model prompt. In many cases, severely motorically impaired students understand the instructional cue but do not have enough control over their motor movements to perform a step. Therefore, verbal or model prompts would not assist and in many cases would serve as stimuli for frustration. It should not be assumed, however, that this is true for all motorically impaired students. Each student should be approached as an individual, and prompting procedures should be selected based on the performance of the individual.

Task difficulty may suggest the use of one prompting procedure over others. Cuvo and his colleagues used a most-to-least intrusive prompting procedure to instruct difficult steps (e.g., Cuvo, Jacobi, & Sipko, 1981; Cuvo, Leaf, & Borakove, 1978). The rationale presented for this approach was that the most-to-least intrusive prompting procedure provides more assistance in the early stages of learning and decreases assistance as the student's skills increase, thus minimizing errors. At this time, however, little evidence is available supporting the use of one instructional prompting procedure over others.

Stimulus Prompts Modifications of task materials including color coding, picture prompts, directional cues, and textural prompts have been used to facilitate correct performance. If stimulus prompts are used, the teacher should select a stimulus that is functional to the student. For exam-

Table 9.5. Sample program format: Teaching coin selection skills for using a drink machine

Time of Program: Morning and afternoon break

Student(s): Sally, Joe, Sam, and Sara

1. *Specific Program Objective:*
   When given own coin purse with at least one quarter, one dime, one nickel, and one penny, and told, "(Name), get drink money," he/she will get the quarter and nickel on four out of five probes on three consecutive days.

   Rationale: Discriminating coins for the drink machine is a functional skill that will provide more independence in the vocational and community settings.

2. *Student Characteristics that:* 1) assist: Can identify coins (quarter, dime, nickel, and penny); can open/close change purse; follows verbal, model, and physical prompts.
   2) hinder:

3. *Behavior Change Procedures:*
   Baseline/probe: Give student his/her own change purse with at least one quarter, one dime, one nickel, and one penny in it and say, "(Name), get out your drink money." Wait 3 seconds for response; score (+) for correct response and (−) for incorrect, inappropriate, or no response. Probe five trials each day during baseline and first five trials during training. Do not reinforce or prompt. Reinforcement may be given for behavior not related to correct performance of task (e.g., "Good sitting, *Name*").

   Training: Conditions and setting are the same as for probes. Train using a system of least prompts. Give the instructional cue, "(Name), get out your drink money." Wait 3 seconds for a response. If correct, reinforce and record (+). If the student responds incorrectly or does not respond, provide a verbal prompt (e.g., "Get out a quarter and a nickel"). If the student responds correctly, reinforce and record (V). If an incorrect or no response is made, model the response while giving a verbal prompt (e.g., "Get out a quarter and a nickel like this. Now you do it"). If a correct response follows the model, reinforce and record (M). If an incorrect or no response is made in 3 seconds, physically prompt the student through the task while verbally prompting. Reinforce and record (P). Conduct ten training trials using these procedures.

4. *Reinforcers:*
   Praise and a chip given for each correct or prompted response. Fifteen chips are exchanged for keeping the quarter and nickel and the opportunity to buy a drink with the money. When the student gets three consecutive correct responses with one prompt, do not reward performance requireing a more intrusive prompt.

5. *Data Collection Method:*
   Baseline probe: Record (+) for correct response and (−) for incorrect, inappropriate, or no responses.

   Training: Record level of prompt required for correct response: (+) no prompt, (V) verbal, (M) verbal plus model, or (P) verbal plus physical. Underline three consecutive correct responses at a certain prompt level to indicate no more reinforcement at a more intrusive prompt level.

6. *Criterion To Be Met for Success:*
   Four out of five correct probe trials on three consecutive days.

7. *Maintenance and Generalization Procedures:*
   Fade praise and chips by using the coin discrimination task as part of the reward procedure for another task (i.e., vocational task) that is being rewarded with praise and chips. Generalize using other trainers and different work areas. Train other coin combinations for drink machine after criterion is met for quarter and nickel.

---

ple, if a picture prompt is used, the student should be able to respond correctly to the picture prior to using it as a prompt. Stimulus prompts are frequently used to mark the temperature required for operating stove dials, to mark the dial settings on a washing machine, or to assist a student in recognizing his/her name through color coding of the letters in the student's name.

If stimulus prompts are used, the teacher should select a stimulus that is functional to the student.

Miller and Miller (1968) used stimulus prompts that accentuated the meaning of sight words being trained. For example, the word "look" was presented as "look" to accentuate its meaning and to facilitate correct labeling. Unfortunately, not all words can be modified to accentuate their meanings.

Dorry and Zeaman (1973, 1975) and Dorry (1976) investigated the use of pictures to facilitate the acquisition of a sight word vocabulary. They found that the use of pictures did facilitate sight word acquisition, and through the use of a picture fading technique severely handicapped students eventually learned to read the words without assistance. Dorry and Zeaman found that a picture fading technique was more effective than other types of fading techniques for sight word acquisition. Their conclusion was that by fading the picture gradually while the written word remained at full intensity, the learner's attention was gradually shifted from the picture to the word. In addition, this procedure was errorless, avoiding the development of a failure set. Figure 9.5 demonstrates the picture fading technique with the word "Coke." As with Miller and Miller's (1968) technique, the picture fading technique can only be used for words that can be pictorially represented. Stimulus and instructional prompts can be used individually or in combination. In most instances when stimulus materials have been modified, instructional prompts are used to facilitate correct performance in response to the modified task. However, once responding has met a criterion level with prompts, the prompts should be faded so that the student eventually responds to the natural cues of the task.

Reinforcement

The type and schedule of reinforcement should be delineated prior to task instruction and should resemble the natural reinforcers and schedules when possible. Types of reinforcement, of course, depend on the student and what has been identified as reinforcing to him/her. However, whenever possible the natural reinforcers for the target behavior should be used. For example, instruction in money use should be rewarded by allowing a student to earn and spend money. Similarly, telephone use can be rewarded by allowing a student to call a friend, and menu reading can be rewarded by taking a student to a restaurant to order and eat a meal. If the natural reinforcers are used from the beginning of instruction, fading of the reinforcement is unnecessary.

USE OF PROSTHETIC AIDS

In many instances a teacher may be faced with a student who has very little time left in school and/or a student with extreme skill deficits for whom a generalized or a functional task approach with an objective of total independence in task performance is unlikely to result in success. Therefore, the teacher should consider the use of prosthetic devices to assist student performance, or perhaps an alternative method of task performance should be considered.

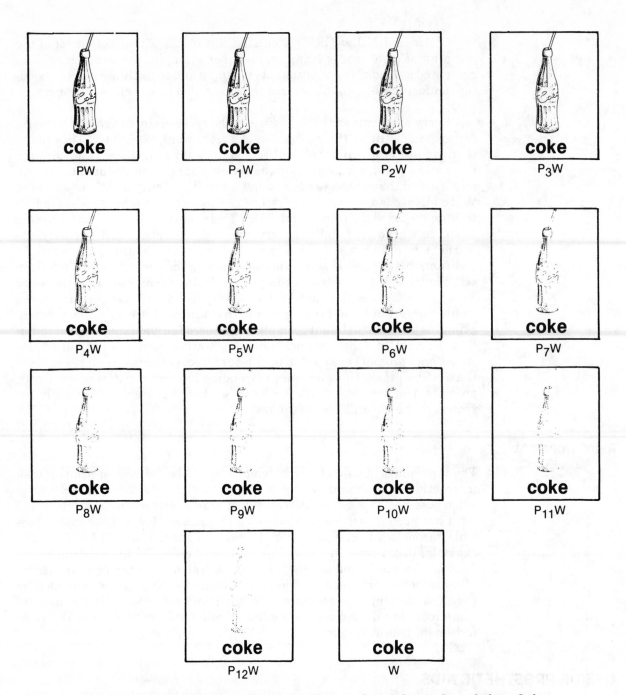

Figure 9.5. Picture fading technique used to teach a sight word vocabulary. Subscripts 1 through 12 indicate the degrees of the fading sequence. (Reprinted with permission. Renzaglia, A.M., The effect of the number of faded steps in a fade-picture-out instructional procedure on the reading acquisition, retention and transfer of moderately and severely retarded individuals. 1978. Unpublished doctoral dissertation. Madison: University of Wisconsin–Madison.)

> **The teacher should determine whether there is enough time to teach total independence or if prosthetic aids or an alternative approach would meet the student's needs with greater efficiency.**

Prosthetic Devices

Prosthetic devices are extra task materials that assist a student in correct performance. In essence they are a type of stimulus prompt, but in many cases the extra stimulus will never be faded or removed. For example, if a student is being trained bus riding skills and as a part of the sequence he/she is required to identify the appropriate bus by number but this skill has been identified as too difficult, perhaps the teacher could provide the student with a wallet-sized card with the bus number printed on it. The student would then be required merely to match the bus number with the number on the card. This card is an example of a prosthetic device. Another example of a prosthetic device is the use of a small pocket timer in a vocational setting in the event that a student cannot tell time. The timer could be set for the time allowed for breaks or for lunch, thus assisting the student in returning to work on time. Similarly, for nonverbal students who are required to know their names and addresses for a targeted vocational placement, an identification card could be issued with the student's name and address printed on it. Therefore, when the student is required to respond to requests for name and address, he/she can provide the identification card.

Figure 9.6 represents three prosthetic aids that can be used for activities requiring money use (i.e., bus riding, bowling shoe rental, and bowling. These cards can be made wallet-sized so that a student is able to carry them with little difficulty. Use of these cards simply involves matching coins to the values on the cards and using those matched coins to purchase the activity. Similar coin cards can be designed for many activities for which prices remain relatively constant.

Nietupski, Certo, Pumpion, and Belmore (1976) designed a prosthetic aid for grocery shopping. The aid was a three-ring binder that fit in the seat of a shopping cart and contained pictures of the items to be purchased and the money required rounded up to the nearest dollar. With the use of this device, basic match-to-sample skills were all that were required. Therefore, students could successfully grocery shop without assistance even though they do not have the money or reading skills that might be expected.

If the decision is made to teach a student to use a prosthetic device rather than to teach total task independence, the device should be carefully designed to permit ease of use. The discrimination involved in use of the device and the intrusiveness of the device should be minimized.

Alternative Approaches

With the increase in high technology, equipment has become available to the general public that lessens the demands on people in academic task performance. For example, calculators have become readily available and digital clocks have become prevalent.

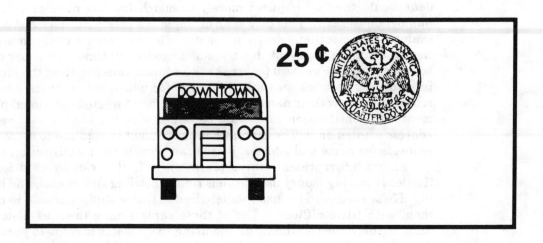

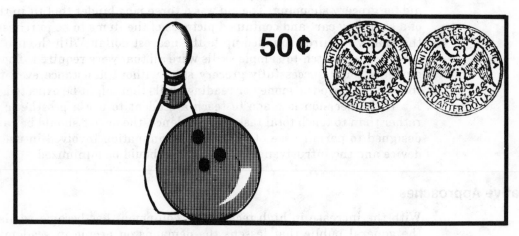

Figure 9.6. *Sample prosthetic aids for selecting the appropriate coins for bus riding and bowling.*

A number of educators have investigated the use of calculators by severely handicapped learners to perform simple math skills and to make purchases in community stores (Smeets & Kleinloog, 1980; Wheeler et al., 1980). Although these investigators were successful in training severely handicapped learners to use calculators, teachers must be cautious in this approach. If a severely handicapped student does not have the math skills to calculate costs without a calculator, that student will not have the skills to detect an error made when using the calculator. Therefore, the potential for problems exists.

Digital clocks provide an alternative to conventional clocks for time telling. It seems obvious that digital clocks are easier to read than conventional clocks, and for many students this is true. However, digital clocks do lack the time perspective provided by conventional clocks. That is, for students who do not have number seriation skills, the digital clock does not indicate time in relationship to other times. Therefore, a student would be unable to judge the amount of time remaining before a scheduled time or, even more of a problem, a student would be unable to determine that the target time had passed.

In the event that alternative approaches to task performance exist, a teacher should certainly consider their use. There is little doubt that with the growing influence of high technology on community life, new and more efficient methods for approaching functional academic tasks will continue to be developed. However, teachers must critically evaluate these new approaches for potential problems in use with severely handicapped students.

SUMMARY

Functional academic skills have traditionally been a major emphasis of educational programs for all students including moderately and severely handicapped students. However, traditional approaches have frequently resulted in severely handicapped students failing to progress in an academic curriculum beyond prerequisite skill levels. Therefore, students have graduated from public school programs lacking skills that are functional (usable) in daily community living.

To avoid these problems, teachers must define the need for academics based on the needs of individual students in their present and potential community living setting. Once these needs are established, a teacher must decide on either a generalized or a functional task approach for instructions. However, regardless of the approach selected, the ultimate objective for each student must be performance of the target skills in the natural settings. More research is needed to assist teachers in facilitating skill generalization to natural settings. In addition, continued evaluations of the use of prosthetic aids and alternative approaches to skill performance will assist educators in providing efficient and effective academic programs for their students.

10

ADVOCACY AND COMMUNITY INTEGRATION

LEARNING GOALS

1. *Define advocacy; identify at least six forms of advocacy.*
2. *Describe the importance of advocacy in education and community integration.*
3. *Describe three target settings where citizen advocacy can occur for moderately and severely handicapped individuals.*
4. *Identify and discuss four major guidelines in establishing a community integration program.*
5. *Highlight five advocacy strategies which might be used to facilitate work adjustment into competitive employment.*

Throughout much of this book there has been an emphasis on developing *competence* in moderately and severely handicapped individuals. We have stressed the value of functional curriculum and the application of systematic training procedures. These are important aspects of program planning and implementation and should not be minimized.

It has become increasingly evident to us that if moderately and severely handicapped people are to be placed into minimally restrictive vocational and community living environments, then training in and of itself will not be sufficient for most individuals. There will be a need to relate to and depend on, at some point, other citizens in the community. In most cases these citizens will be nonhandicapped and/or more competent in community living. We cannot hope to have professional staff at the side of handicapped students and/or clients at all times. Parents of handicapped individuals realized this long before many special educators ever thought of community integration.

Thus, it is necessary to rely on nonhandicapped citizens in a given community for support. These citizens must support programs either indirectly with tax dollars and votes for special education programs or directly through volunteer work in Special Olympics, assistance as co-workers in job environments, or helping families cope with stressful situations. For special education professionals to pretend that nonhandicapped individuals are *not* a major part of helping moderately and severely handicapped individuals attain independence is a dangerously naive assumption. In this, our final chapter, we relate how *advocacy* can play an important complementary role to training programs that take place in community settings and describe how to establish a community integration program.

ADVOCACY: ITS CRUCIAL ROLE IN COMMUNITY INTEGRATION

Defining Advocacy

Simply put, advocacy involves speaking for or acting on behalf of a handicapped individual. Advocacy cannot be a passive process. It must be *planned* and not left to chance. Biklen (1979) says advocacy is best defined:

> . . . *as an independent movement of consumers (e.g., parents, people with disabilities, children) and their allies to monitor and change human service agencies.* (p. 310)

As we will see later in the chapter, advocacy can take different forms and roles. The form of advocacy undertaken should fit the needs of the client and the population. Traditionally, advocacy has not regularly interfaced with instructional practices exhibited by teachers and other service providers. Frequently, instructional service delivery is somewhat independent of active efforts at advocacy. In this book we suggest that training and advocacy must go hand-in-hand.

Biklen (1979), a noted expert in the study of advocacy, has observed principles by which advocates attempt to promote quality human services. These include:

> *Advocates attempt to identify those conditions which make a person dependent . . . the advocate helps the person to achieve human services as a right.*
> *Advocates try to understand the person's feelings, experiences, and needs through his own words and accounts.*
> *Advocates do not express pity but rather anger about the conditions and attitudes in this society that dehumanize those who have disabilities.*
> *Advocates must sometimes be willing to accept the disdain and criticism of those agencies and people whom they question.* (p. 310)

There are many types of advocates. One can be a paid lobbyist in Washington, D.C., who advocates all the time with legislators on behalf of the handicapped. On the other hand, one might only be a concerned citizen and/or neighbor who is anxious to help handicapped people be assimilated into the community. Both types of advocates are important but for different reasons.

Why Do We Need Advocacy?

Advocacy must become far more pervasive than the paid lobbyist or an executive director of the state association. If our ultimate programmatic goal is to help moderately and severely handicapped individuals improve the quality of their life and facilitate adjustment in the community, then training is only one aspect of this process and *citizen advocacy* is imperative. If, on the other hand, segregated residential living and social isolation is expected (i.e., long-term institutionalization), then naturally advocacy will have a diminished role.

We need active efforts at advocacy for several reasons. First, there are not enough special education professionals to accommodate all of the handicapped persons into the community; we need *help* from concerned citizens. Second, it is important that false myths and perceptions of moderately and severely handicapped individuals be erased. Improved knowledge and information comes about best through periodic contact. Advocates can facilitate this contact. Third, much more money and financial support are necessary to improve programs and even to retain the present level. Nonhandicapped citizens carry much more impact with legislators who appropriate dollars for programs. Finally, and perhaps most importantly, the moderately and severely handicapped people we work with need to know and feel that nonhandicapped citizens and neighbors *care* about them and accept them. These feelings cannot possibly emerge in secluded or isolated residential settings.

> **If our ultimate programmatic goal is to help moderately and severely handicapped individuals improve the quality of their life and facilitate adjustment in the community, then training is only one aspect of this process and citizen advocacy is imperative.**

Therefore, the question then becomes: How do we implement efforts at advocacy? What methods are available? In the section below several suggestions are given.

Forms of Advocacy

There are a variety of advocacy methods that have merit. Biklen (1979) has done an excellent job of listing and describing techniques. Most readers are probably familiar with most of these ideas:

1. Demonstrations (i.e., sit-ins, marches)
2. Demands
3. Letter writing
4. Newsletters and other communications
5. Lobbying
6. Boycotts
7. Court action and legal advocacy
8. Negotiation
9. Model program demonstration

Another advocacy method is *pairing* a citizen advocate with a protege. This approach to advocacy is an excellent form of direct line communication about the handicapped person to the citizen. Other writers stress the importance of carefully matching the characteristics of both citizens and proteges. For example:

> *Wolfensberger (1972) argues that whether the advocate is to serve primarily an instrumental or an expressive she depends on the client's needs, degree of independence, and type of residence; while reinforcing the notion that the protege's needs and characteristics are important in matching.* (Danker-Brown et al., 1979, p. 137)

We believe that increased contact and the subsequent communication of accurate information between professionals and nonhandicapped citizens overcomes many of the misperceptions and anxieties that are held in the community. Consider how a neighbor might feel if a mentally retarded adult walked by her house every day with his head rocking sideways and singing to himself. This behavior looks peculiar. If the neighbor, however, is aware that the individual is partially visually impaired and that a program is being developed to reduce these rocking "blindisms," then more tolerance might be exhibited. Furthermore, it should be pointed out to the neighbor that no harm has been or will be done. Hence, communication by professionals to lay people in the community is a very important and overlooked method of advocacy.

Peer tutoring is another form of advocacy that has only been used in a limited fashion between moderately or severely handicapped and nonhandicapped children. Interaction and assistance on the part of normal children with severely handicapped peers is an excellent means of educating other children who are not involved. The peer tutor serves as a model to others; gifted children and school leaders, because of their high credibility to begin with, are good targets for becoming advocates.

One of the best forms of advocacy can be displayed by the client. Competence and acceptable social behavior and appearance are crucial elements for community integration. A handicapped individual who adjusts to the location of the community (i.e., rural, inner-city, suburban) and its social standards will serve as the best advocate in the long run. Exhibition of appropriate behavior is ultimately more acceptable than a nonhandicapped person who is always present.

For some severely physically handicapped people, however, there may be a need for a constant caregiver who also functions as an advocate. In these situations it is best for the caregiver to allow the handicapped person as much individuality as possible.

Target Settings for Advocacy

In order to understand the wide range of places in which advocacy may occur this section highlights representative settings. This section is aimed at professionals looking for ways to improve community integration of their students or clients.

Church For those severely handicapped children who cannot talk, the fellowship of Sunday school classes can be most beneficial when in the presence of nonhandicapped peers. An advocate might: 1) communicate with the other children and teacher about the severely handicapped child's characteristics; 2) stay with all the children for a reasonable period of time to help with the adjustment; and 3) help solicit a child in the group who will serve as a "special friend."

Work at the Local Factory In the case of a motorically impaired individual (labeled as cerebral palsied and with difficult-to-understand verbalizations) who has become recently employed in a factory, advocacy might be helpful. A counselor or friend might accompany the individual to work initially, help assess the composition of co-workers in the environment, and possibly solicit support from a cooperative floor supervisor or line leader. Once the individual becomes accustomed to the routine, the advocate can maintain a less active role.

> **A counselor or friend might accompany the individual to work initially, help assess the composition of co-workers in the environment, and possibly solicit support from a cooperative floor supervisor or line leader.**

Participation in an After-School Cooking Class Similar to integration into Sunday school classes, secondary students who wish to participate in an afternoon cooking class with nonhandicapped peers should be encouraged to do so. An advocate might help arrange transportation and initially review the appropriateness of the class for the student. Upon placement into the class, the advocate would then attend the class for a period of time to help the handicapped student feel more comfortable and to maximize whatever skills he/she has.

Sibling Advocacy in the Neighborhood Brothers and sisters of handicapped children have acted on behalf of their siblings for a long time. This is one excellent form of advocacy provided it does not become either burdensome or confrontational. A brother or sister may serve as a superb model for the handicapped child. Active siblings can promote acceptance for their handicapped brother or sister in the neighborhood.

Table 10.1 presents a small sample of several of the community experiences that have been observed by the authors and their colleagues with moderately and severely handicapped youths over the past 2 years. Advocacy has played a major role in helping moderately and severely handicapped people "make it" in community settings. The target goals in the fourth column of the table are suggestions for educational objectives that teachers can work toward, depending of course on their student's individual needs.

A CASE STUDY ANALYSIS OF ADVOCACY IN A COMPETITIVE WORK SETTING

Although the guidelines and examples provided so far are illustrative of community-based advocacy, it is helpful to describe and relate the actual process of *how* to advocate for a severely handicapped person in a predominantly nonhandicapped environment. One setting in which there is an increasing amount of success in using this approach is job placement in competitive employment (nonsheltered) situations (Wehman, 1981). Below are described several specific advocacy strategies that may be utilized in job placement and retention programs for severely handicapped persons. A basic assumption is made that a teacher, counselor, or other paraprofessional is initially available at the work environment on a frequent basis and follows many of the job placement and follow-up guidelines described in the previous chapter on competitive employment.

Informing Co-Workers of Client's Behavioral Characteristics

In order to heighten co-workers' sensitivity and awareness of the client's unique characteristics it is usually a good practice to discuss with workers, individually, the incoming client. For example, if Robert is beginning work for the first time competitively in a laundry room, yet cannot hear and is severely mentally retarded, it is helpful to alert co-workers to these disabilities. By pointing out the positive features of Robert's abilities and his strengths (i.e., strong work attitude and parental support), co-workers are able to view Robert with a more balanced perspective.

Similarly, it is generally wise to discuss some of the realistic expectations for and potential of a disabled client with a certain job. There is a wide variability between what nonhandicapped co-workers perceive as a disabled employee's work capacity. This is especially true in jobs where there are many uneducated or predominantly illiterate nonhandicapped persons employed. If co-workers are made aware of the client's personality and learning characteristics, it usually facilitates the early days of the placement and makes it easier for the staff to fade assistance.

> **There is a wide variability between what nonhandicapped co-workers perceive as a disabled employee's work capacity.**

Maintaining Regular On-Site Contact

Perhaps the most critical element in successful on-the-job training programs with severely disabled workers is the sustained presence (i.e., training and/or advocacy of a job counselor or teacher). Bearing in mind that most moderately or severely retarded trainees have little experience at independent functioning in *natural work environments* or *community environments*, it is apparent that the initial entry to these settings will be difficult without assistance.

The presence of staff, initially, is necessary for the following reasons:

1. To help train the client in specific job functions
2. To help train the client in appropriate social behaviors
3. To help the client and co-workers communicate, or at least get adjusted to each other's communication system
4. To demonstrate to parents the commitment to helping the client adjust
5. To observe and record the client's progress

Although this approach may be criticized as being too costly or resulting in a difficult fading of staff, it is the most realistic for many severely retarded persons, especially those who never received training in natural environments. Furthermore, it is possibly the most effective form of advocacy because it is ongoing and sensitive to changes in the attitudes of workers and supervisors.

Helping Client Complete Job

As an extension of the previous advocacy strategy, helping a client complete a job may also be utilized as an advocacy strategy. This should not necessarily be construed as performing all of the job for the worker. However, in some cases it may be quite appropriate to provide physical assistance when a worker is having difficulty learning a particular aspect of the job.

Reinforcement of Nonhandicapped Co-Workers

Looking for opportunities to praise, compliment, or *thank* nonhandicapped co-workers for their support and assistance in helping a client adjust is another advocacy strategy. Providing recognition to an employee through a written letter with a copy to the personnel director can be an even more effective means of displaying gratitude to co-workers.

Table 10.1 Community Integration Summary Sheet (community generalization training during school hours)

Student	Age	Behavioral characteristics	Community setting	Primary target behavior for change	Secondary target behavior for change	Program status	Parent acceptance	Student response to experience
Bruce	14	Severe retardation/ nonambulatory/ wheelchair/nonverbal/good receptive language skills	Fast-food restaurant (McDonald's)	Ordering food with communication cards	Transferring from wheelchair to car	Ongoing (weekly)	High	Shows great enjoyment
Connie	19	SPH/nonambulatory/ wheelchair (quad.)/ some limited verbalizations	Fast-food restaurant (McDonald's)	Ordering food verbally	Transferring from wheelchair to car	Ongoing	Moderate	Improved attendance to school
Roger	18	SPH/ambulatory/exhibits echolalic speech only/continual stereotypical behavior	Fast-food restaurant (McDonald's)	Ordering food verbally	Reduction of stereotypical behavior	Ongoing	High	Improved behavior while in community
Jean	14	SPH/exhibits hyperactive, stereotypical and aggressive behavior/visually impaired/nonverbal	Fast-food restaurant (McDonald's)	Ordering food with communication cards	Increasing appropriate social behavior	Ongoing	High, but "worried"	Appropriate behavior
Alan	14	SPH/nonambulatory/wheelchair/ nonverbal	Pinball (7-11 store)	Ordering soda with communication cards	Independent transfer from car	Ongoing	High	Shows great enjoyment
Bill	19	SPH/nonambulatory (quad.)/some verbal behavior	Pinball (7-11 store)	Ordering soda at counter	Transfer from car (assisted)	Ongoing	Moderate	Improved attendance to school

Name	Age	Characteristics	Setting	Objective	Objective	Status	Progress	Comments
Greg	18	SPH/ambulatory/only echolalic speech/continual stereotypical behavior	Pinball	Getting out of car independently	Reduction of stereotypical behavior	Ongoing	High	Improved behavior while in community
Ed	20	Moderate retardation/ambulatory/severe speech impairment/receptivity good/understands most simple conversation/no academic skills	Grocery store	Will shop using a short list, words, and/or pictures	Will recognize change, $1.00 and $5.00 bill, and wait for change when making purchase	Ongoing (weekly)	Data being compiled	
Leo	18	Moderate retardation/ambulatory/speech impaired/moderately visually impaired/expressive language limited	Grocery store	Will shop using a short list, words, and/or pictures	Will recognize change, $1.00 and $5.00 bill, and wait for change when making purchase	Ongoing (weekly)	Data being compiled	
Ruth	20	Moderate retardation/ambulatory/good expressive and receptive language/no academic skills	Grocery store	Will shop using a short list, words, and/or pictures	Will recognize change, $1.00 and $5.00 bill, and wait for change when making purchase	Ongoing (weekly)	Data being compiled	
Wayne	17	SPH/ambulatory but no endurance and lacks stability/nonverbal/very limited receptive language/one-step commands	Fast-food restaurant (Hardee's)	Following one-step commands	Increase distance of independent walking on community terrain	Began 2/3/81; ongoing	High	Follows commands and moves much more quickly in restaurant environment

It is critical that a positive co-worker attitude toward handicapped employees *not* be taken for granted. It cannot be assumed that this attitude is normal and therefore should go unreinforced. Without embarrassing co-workers, subtle reinforcement can serve to strengthen relationships between handicapped and nonhandicapped employees.

Providing recognition to an employee through a written letter with a copy to the personnel director can be an even more effective means of displaying gratitude to co-workers.

Providing Parental Support in Problem Situations

Parental assistance and support plus regular communication eventually may lead to conversion of the most recalcitrant parents or family members. Placement of a client for the first time competitively will result in the following type of questions:

1. "What happens to John's SSI payment?"
2. "How does John get to work?"
3. "Will John get too tired? He's never worked 40 hours a week."
4. "Will John be alright? Will his co-workers take advantage of him?"
5. "John doesn't need to work. We give him all the money he needs."

In order to respond intelligently and persuasively to these points, reasonable answers must be carefully thought out. It may be that parents who are extremely concerned might come to the job placement from time to time to see John work. In another problem situation a representative from the Disability Determination Office might visit the parents and explicitly describe SSI rules and provisions.

Once parents trust staff, then they may become very strong advocates of a job placement program. Such parents can help influence other reluctant parents as well. However, before reaching this level of trust, the *informational advocacy* described above is necessary. Parents may respond negatively only because they are frustrated and do not know where to get satisfactory answers.

Reinforcing Employers

As noted earlier, co-worker reinforcement is necessary. Equally important is recognition for employers who are willing to hire severely disabled employees. There are a number of ways to draw attention to the floor supervisor or department director who supports disabled employees. These include:

1. Employer plaques or commendations that leave a permanent reminder in the employer's office
2. Reports to the television or newspaper media describing the employer's efforts

3. Newsletters for other employers that describe the affirmative action efforts of your employer
4. Letters to the employer's supervisor expressing thanks for assistance and support
5. Written or verbal thanks and compliments directly given to the supervisor

Although these techniques are surely not extensive, it is once again a question of not leaving the willing employer unattended or taken for granted. Employers can and do vacillate; that is, they change their minds about hiring handicapped persons frequently at times without apparent reasons. Also, they are under covert pressure from other subordinates not to hire severely disabled people to do an equivalent job. Meeting these pressures successfully and maintaining an affirmative action for severely disabled workers must be reinforced.

COMMUNITY INTEGRATION

As has been noted throughout this text, special education literature has been marked increasingly with references to educational integration and community integration. Although not always clearly defined, it is generally accepted that educational integration refers to placement of handicapped students in regular classes or in special classes situated in regular schools (Stainback, Stainback, & Jaben, 1981). Community integration (Novak & Heal, 1980), on the other hand, is taken to mean placement of handicapped individuals into community residences, facilities, and activities that are in proximity to nonhandicapped citizens.

For moderately and severely handicapped children both educational and community integration are vital for their full development. Advocacy can play a major role in facilitating both types of integration. It is imperative that students have the opportunity to interact with nonhandicapped individuals of their own age and that these peers learn how to interact and relate to the severely handicapped students. Educational integration is best accomplished through careful placement of severely handicapped classes through different parts of the regular school building. Placement should be made in chronologically age-appropriate schools (i.e., secondary students should go to regular high schools). Community integration should take place for severely handicapped children and youth *during* school hours and *after* school hours. Instructional activities that are to take place in the community must be carefully orchestrated by teachers, parents, and administrators (Wehman & Hill, 1980).

It is imperative that students have the opportunity to interact with nonhandicapped individuals of their own age and that these peers learn how to interact and relate to the severely handicapped students.

It is the purpose of this section to describe how to develop, implement, and evaluate a community integration program for severely handicapped children and youths. The focus is on providing practical guidelines for establishing a community integration program that is consistent with the child's needs and family's ability to follow through on the program. The process of advocacy is a constant thread that runs through the flow chart sequence of programmatic activities presented.

Criteria for Selecting Target Objectives for Community Integration

The best vehicle for programmatically administering a community integration program is the IEP. As the educational blueprint for the child's service needs and programmatic goals, it is this tool that should be used to identify community integration objectives. Objectives should reflect parental needs and abilities to assist in maintaining the program, the child's functioning level and interests, and a coordination with other objectives on the IEP. Before a community integration program can be implemented, specific instructional objectives must be identified. This avoids the pitfall of activities that are perhaps isolated in nature and that would not be retained over the long run. We have listed these specific criteria points below as a guideline for determining target goals:

What activities and resources are available near the student's home?

What leisure time and domestic (shopping) patterns does the student's family follow regularly, and how does the student participate in these activities?

What social interaction strengths or deficits does the student have that require remediation in the community?

What motor and/or self-care strengths or deficits does the student have that require remediation in the community?

What communication strengths or deficits does the student have that require remediation in the community?

What community integration activities do parents rate as a high priority (e.g., use of leisure time during shopping?)

Based on a ranking of possible community integration activities, what targets are of the highest priority?

It must be noted that the functional utility of the other IEP objectives will be enhanced if they are practiced in natural community settings. For example, the student who practices use of picture communication cards in the classroom day in and day out should have the opportunity to use these cards under teacher supervision in a community integration setting such as a fast-food restaurant. In Table 10.2 are four sample instructional objectives (annual and short-term) for community integration.

Activities Involved in Identifying and Securing Community Integration Placements

Figure 10.1 shows a flow chart of activities for initiating a community integration placement for an individual student. Examples of environments in which a community integration placement can be made are:

1. Any community store/restaurant/agency that the family may utilize for errands

| Table 10.2. Community integration area (annual goals and short-term objectives) ||
Annual Goals	Short-Term Objectives
1. John will develop skills (at least four measurable skills) to participate more fully in less restrictive community environments with friends/family.	Following a companion at all times, John will operate grocery cart to 90% criterion over three consecutive trials in community.
2. Sandra will exhibit appropriate social behavior in at least three community environments.	Sandra will comply with three directional commands (e.g., "Let's sit over here"), within 10 seconds (and will run away from the trainer zero times) over three consecutive trials at the community recreation center.
3. Steve will exhibit social interaction skills with nonhandicapped persons in three different community settings.	Steve will greet at least five fellow scouts through waving, smiling, or picture cards during the first 10 minutes of the meeting over three consecutive meetings.
4. Angela will generalize functional use of picture card communication to three different community environments.	Angela will order refreshments at bowling alley snack bar without assistance from trainer over three consecutive trials.

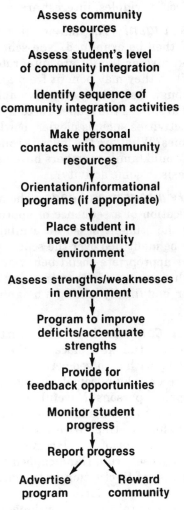

Assess community
resources
↓
Assess student's level
of community integration
↓
Identify sequence of
community integration activities
↓
Make personal
contacts with community
resources
↓
Orientation/informational
programs (if appropriate)
↓
Place student in
new community
environment
↓
Assess strengths/weaknesses
in environment
↓
Program to improve
deficits/accentuate
strengths
↓
Provide for
feedback opportunities
↓
Monitor student
progress
↓
Report progress
↙   ↘
Advertise   Reward
program   community

Figure 10.1. Flow chart of activities for initiating a community integration placement.

2. Any club, group, troop, etc. that nonhandicapped peers may join (e.g., 4-H, scouts, church groups)
3. Any school activity or community recreational facility used by nonhandicapped age peers (e.g., pep rallies, pinball arcade, classes at community recreation center, boy's club, community pool)

The activities described in Figure 10.1 may seem overwhelming for a single classroom teacher in addition to other duties. It may be useful therefore, for teachers of similar age groups to work together, enlisting the administrator's help as much as possible for contacts and suggestions. Each of these activities is briefly described below.

Assess Community Resources The development of a community integration program should begin by assessing the currently available community resources rather than identifying ideal community services for the handicapped. This approach emphasizes integration in activities which already exist and are readily accessible for handicapped students and their families. Available activities could be classified according to appropriate age levels, cost variables, interest areas, neighborhoods, and so forth.

Assess Student The individual student's level of community integration should then be examined. Non-school activities indicate how well the student and his/her family are integrated in their community as well as what activities they may benefit from and enjoy. This step could be accomplished through a simple survey. Examples of items that could be included in a survey are: Does the student accompany parents on errands, to church, to leisure activities such as movies, bowling, etc., to appointments, to visit friends' homes? What are the favorite community leisure activities of family members? Would family members have the time to transport the student on a weekly basis to some activity?

Identify Integration Needs The above information leads directly to the identification of a sequence of appropriate community integration activities for the student based on availability, need, and interest. The sequence can be identified over the school year, beginning, for example, with training for appropriate social behavior and skill development in a laundromat with a parent, and then training for appropriate behavior in church by mid-year, and finally joining a neighborhood scout troop during the last quarter.

Contact Communities The fourth activity that must be accomplished before a student is placed in the new community environment is an initial meeting with involved persons. Even if the selected environment is a grocery store or a laundromat, discussing the philosophy of the program with appropriate persons is useful. With clubs or scout troops this meeting is essential. The need for additional orientation programs can also be determined from this meeting. With a club-type activity, if possible, try to observe the activity prior to placement of the student. Many community activities are loosely run. Handicapped students and families may be disappointed because of fluctuation in the size of the group, age range of members, schedule, and so forth. Try also to identify essential prerequisite skills, environmental barriers, or dangers.

Orientation Programs   Some community groups or activities may require a structured orientation program. Visual materials such as a slide show of handicapped and nonhandicapped youths together are useful. It is necessary to not take for granted the knowledge base relevant to severely handicapped individuals that citizens in the community possess.

Placement   Finally, the student is placed in the new community environment. Prior planning should be accomplished to ensure that the student disrupts the environment as little as possible (i.e., he should arrive and leave on time, wear appropriate clothing, etc.). The student initially should be accompanied by a staff person who may function as a trainer/advocate. This individual assists in introductions, interactions, and participation to the maximum extent possible.

Assess Student and Provide Intervention   The trainer/advocate also assesses the student's strengths and deficits in the new setting. As the integration activities continue, the trainer also develops programs and objectives to improve these deficits and accentuate the handicapped student's strengths. Intervention strategies are more fully discussed below.

Feedback Opportunities   In order to maintain the interest and commitment of others, related persons should have an opportunity to provide feedback and suggestions. A simple feedback survey can be sent out each month to parents, other teachers, administrators, and nonhandicapped participants in the activities. This might be done in conjunction with personal contacts and phone conversations.

Monitor and Report Progress   A method to monitor student progress should be accomplished in order to provide accountability and to ensure progress on individual objectives such as picture card use and general social acceptance in the setting. Progress reports should also be sent to related staff persons and/or family members periodically to keep them informed and interested.

Advertise Programs   The program itself may be unique and innovative; therefore, the next step is to advertise the efforts being accomplished. Invite community VIP's, parents, and the media to observe. These activities will help to continue such efforts even in the face of reduced funding.

Provide Reinforcement   Finally, the community can also be rewarded for its help, participation, and interest by simple social praise, giving extra snapshots of the activities or a certificate of thanks to involved persons.

STRATEGIES FOR INTERVENTION IN COMMUNITY SETTING

Systematic instructional strategies used within a good classroom program can and should also be used in community settings. Community training should not be viewed simply as a post-test environment for classroom training, but rather as an arena for continued training. Techniques such as chaining, fading, prompt hierarchies, simple/complex reinforcement schedules, role playing, behavior rehearsal, feedback, and practice are all viable strategies in full view of the nonhandicapped community as well. There are, however, several important considerations that should be emphasized.

First, because the ultimate goal of all instruction is to enable the student to respond to natural environmental cues, community trainers must identify and utilize these cues/prompts throughout the program. After identification of natural cues at work within an environment, techniques such as establishing a specific waiting period prior to teacher prompting, systematic use of pairing and redundant cueing, and reinforcement for self-initiated behaviors are essential in establishing natural control. Fortunately, the menu of reinforcers is usually far more varied and powerful in the natural settings.

Another important consideration regarding instruction in community environments is that the instructional techniques utilized actually serve as models of treatment and a form of advocacy for the handicapped student. Nonhandicapped citizens will probably view the trainer as an expert and will model his/her approach. Thus, it is important to present age-appropriate techniques, emphasizing understanding and respect for the student as a fellow human. Preparation through heavy emphasis on simulated practice and role playing prior to entering the community environment will help students be viewed in a more credible light. In addition, the trainer *should* talk to nonhandicapped persons to describe the program philosophy and emphasize the student's strengths.

EVALUATION OF THE EFFECTIVENESS OF COMMUNITY PLACEMENT

It is not sufficient to identify appropriate instructional targets, locate viable placements, and implement intervention strategies. The effectiveness of the program, regardless of duration, must be evaluated. An assessment of the program must be made in order to determine whether staff were correct in their judgment to place the individual. More importantly, an evaluation will yield information relevant to the success of the placement. There are several specific dimensions that can be assessed.

First, the instructional objective that has been targeted can be monitored for completion. For example, if it was decided initially that Ron will be taught to independently order a soda at the local ice cream shop, then a postinstructional evaluation should indicate whether he can now perform this skill and, if not, where he is deficient. This evaluation is completed by direct observation and recording.

The second form of evaluation should be a coding of the acceptance that the teacher feels of the activity. The teacher's attitude and belief in the value of the program will influence other such programs taking place.

A third source of feedback must come anecdotally and formally from the nonhandicapped consumers or participants at the setting. The social acceptance of the severely handicapped student by nonhandicapped individuals is perhaps the most important feature of the experience.

Another evaluative aspect of the program must be the expressions of pleasure and, if possible, verbal statements by the child indicating preference for the activity. A community integration experience that is devoid of this behavior defeats the purpose of facilitating these types of integration activities.

Finally, the parent and family reactions are crucial to assess. If there is little interest or it does not actually help the family in some way, then it is not unlikely that follow-through and subsequent opportunity to engage in the activity will be limited. Parents must be continually monitored and invited to participate in the early stages of any community integration activities, especially those that occur after hours.

The sum total of the evaluation data will help staff make decisions about the selection of future community placements. Furthermore, these data will help document the importance of expanding school instructional activities beyond the classroom on a regular basis. Such data also will be helpful in demonstrations of competence by the child to parents and other agencies such as Parks and Recreation and Vocational Rehabilitation.

SUMMARY

In this chapter we have defined advocacy and explained its importance in the context of instruction. Numerous types of advocacy were described as well as several target settings in which advocacy might take place on behalf of a moderately or severely handicapped person. These descriptions of advocacy were then followed by an outline of how to develop and implement a community integration training program using advocacy as a major aspect of the program. Finally, specific advocacy examples were presented in the context of a competitive employment job placement.

REFERENCES

Alberti. *Assertiveness*. San Luis Obispo: Impact Publishers. 1977.

Alberto, P., & Schofield, P. An instructional pattern for the severely handicapped. *Teaching Exceptional Children,* 1979 *12*(1).

Amary, I. *Creative recreation for the mentally retarded*. Springfield, Illinois: Charles C Thomas, 1975.

American Association on Mental Deficiency. *Manual on terminology and classification in mental retardation*. Washington: American Association on Mental Deficiency, 1977.

American Psychological Association. *Diagnostic and statistical manual on mental disorders*. Washington: American Psychological Association, 1968.

ANSI A117.1. Making buildings and facilities accessible to and usable by handicapped. New York: American National Standards Institute, Inc., 1961.

Baker, B., Seltzer, G. B., & Seltzer, M. *As close as possible*. Boston: Little, Brown, & Co., 1977.

Bandura, A. *Principles of behavior modification*. New York: Holt, Reinhart, & Winston, 1969.

Barnes, K. Pre-school play norms: A replication. *Developmental Psychology,* 1971, *5*, 99–103.

Bates, P. The effectiveness of interpersonal skills training on the social skill acquisition of moderately and mildly retarded adults. *Journal of Applied Behavior Analysis,* 1980, *13*, 237–248.

Bates, P., & Harvey, J. Social skills and the mentally retarded: An empirical analysis of the research. In O. C. Karan (Ed.), *Habilitation practices with the severely developmentally disabled,* Madison, Wisconsin: R & T Center, 1979.

Bates, P., & Renzaglia, A. Community-based recreation programs. In P. Wehman (Ed.), *Recreation Programming for Developmentally Disabled Persons.* Baltimore: University Park Press, 1978.

Bates, P., Renzaglia, A., & Clees, T. Improving the work performance of severely/profoundly retarded adults: The use of a changing criterion procedural design. *Education and Training of the Mentally Retarded,* 1980, *15,* 98–104.

Bates, P., Renzaglia, A., Robertson, J., Brereton, D., & Clees, T. Woodworking skill acquisition: A multiple baseline demonstration of program effectiveness. *Vocational Evaluation and Work Adjustment Bulletin, 13,* 133–137.

Bauman, K., & Iwata, B. Maintenance of independent housekeeping skills using scheduling plus self-recording procedures. *Behavior Therapy,* 1977, *8,* 554–560.

Becker, W. C., & Engelmann, S. Systems for basic instruction: Theory and applications. In A. Catania & T. Brigham (Eds.), *Handbook of applied behavior analysis: Social and instructional processes.* New York: Irvington Publishers, 1978.

Bellamy, T., & Buttars, E. L. Teaching trainable level retarded students to count money: Toward personal independence through academic instruction. *Education and Training of the Mentally Retarded,* 1975, *10*(1), 18–25.

Bellamy, G. T., Horner, R., & Inman, D. *Vocational training of severely retarded adults*. Baltimore: University Park Press, 1979.

Bellamy, G., Inman, D., & Yeates, J. Workshop supervision: Evaluation of a procedure for the production management with the severely retarded. *Mental Retardation,* 1978, *16,* 317–319.

Bellamy, G., Peterson, L., & Close, D., Habilitation of the severely and profoundly retarded: Illustrations of competence. *Education and Training of the Mentally Retarded,* 1976, *10,* 174–186.

Belmore, K., & Brown, L. Job skill inventory strategy for use in a public school vocational training program for severely handicapped potential workers. In N. Haring & D. Bricker (Eds.), *Teaching the severely handicapped,* Vol. III, Columbus, Ohio: Special Press, 1978.

Benoit, E. P. The play problem of retarded children: A frank discussion with parents. *American Journal of Mental Deficiency,* 1955, *60,* 41–45.

Bernhardt, A. J., Hersen, M., & Barlow, D. H. Measurement and modification of spasmodic torticollis: An experimental analysis. *Behavior Therapy,* 1972, *3,* 294–297.

Biklen, D. *Community imperative: A refutation of all arguments in support of deinstitutionalizing anybody because of mental retardation*. Syracuse: Human Policy Press, 1979.

Blackhurst, E. A. Sociodrama for the adolescent mentally retarded. *Training School Bulletin*, 1966, *63*, 136–142.

Blackman, L., & Siperstein, G. *Employment of the mentally retarded in a competitive industrial setting: Final report.* Albertson, Long Island: Hiram Resources Center, 1967.

Blatt, B., Bogdan, R., Biklen, D., & Taylor, S. From institution to community: A conversion model. In E. Sontag, J. Smith, & N. Certo (Eds.), *Educational programming for the severely and profoundly handicapped.* Reston, Virginia: The Council for Exceptional Children, 1977.

Board of Trustees of The California State University and Colleges. *Way to go.* Baltimore: University Park Press, 1978.

Borakove, L. S., & Cuvo, A. J. Facilitative effects of coin displacement on teaching coin summation to mentally retarded adolescents. *American Journal of Mental Deficiency,* 1976, *81*, 350–356.

Bowe, F. Transportation: A key to independent living. *Archives of Physical Medical Rehabilitation,* 1979, *60*, 473–486.

Boyan, C. A flexible approach to career development: Balancing vocational training and training for independent living. *Education and Training of the Mentally Retarded,* 1978, *13*, 209–213.

Bradley, V. J. *Deinstitutionalization of developmentally disabled persons: A conceptual analysis and guide.* Baltimore, University Park Press, 1978.

Bradtke, L., Kirkpatrick, W. Q., & Rosenblatt, K. P. Intensive play—A technique for building affective behaviors in profoundly mentally retarded young children. *Education and Training of the Mentally Retarded,* 1972, *7,* 8–13.

Brody, G. H., & Stoneman, Z. Social competencies in the developmentally disabled. *Mental Retardation,* 1977, *15*(4), 41–43.

Brolin, D. E. *Vocational preparation for persons with handicaps.* Columbus, Ohio: Charles E. Merril, 1982.

Brown, L. Instructional programs for the trainable level retarded. In L. Mann and D. Sabatin (Eds.), *First annual review of special education.* New York: Grune & Stratton, 1973.

Brown, L., Bellamy, G. T., & Sontag, E. *The development and implementation of a public school prevocational training program for trainable retarded and severely emotionally disturbed children.* Madison, Wisconsin: Madison

Public School, 1971.

Brown, L., Branston, M., Hamre-Nietupski, S., Johnson, I., Wilcox, B., & Gruenewald, L. A rationale for comprehensive longitudinal interactions between severely handicapped students and nonhandicapped students and other citizens. *AAESPH Review,* 1979.

Brown, L., Branston, M., Hamre-Nietupski, S., Pumpian, I., Certo, N., & Gruenewald, L. A strategy for developing chronological age-appropriate and functional curricular content for severely handicapped adolescents and young adults. *Journal of Special Education,* 1979, *13,* 81–90.

Brown, L., Branston-McClean, M., Baumgart, D., Vincent, L., Falvey, M., & Schroeder, J. Utilizing the characteristics of a variety of current and subsequent least restrictive environments as factors in the development of curricula content for severely handicapped students. *AAESPH Review,* 1979.

Brown, L., Branston-McClean, M. B., Baumgart, D., Vincent, L., Falvey, M., & Schroeder, J. Using the characteristics of current and subsequent least restrictive environment in the development of curricular content for severely handicapped students. *AAESPH Review,* 1979, *4*(4), 407–424.

Brown, L., Falvey, M., Baumgart, D., Pumpian, D., Schroeder, J., & Gruenwald, L. (Eds.). *Strategies for teaching chronological age appropriate functional skills to adolescent and young adult severely handicapped students.* Madison, Wisconsin: Madison Metropolitan Schools, 1979.

Brown, L., Nietupski, J., & Hamre-Nietupski, S. Criterion of ultimate functioning. In M. Thomas (Ed.), *Hey don't forget about me!* Reston, Virginia: Council for Exceptional Children, 1976.

Brown, L., & Pearce, E. Increasing the production rates of trainable retarded students in a public school simulated workshop. *Education and Training of the Mentally Retarded,* 1970, *5,* 15–22.

Bryan, T. H., & Bryan, J. H. The social-emotional side of learning disabilities. *Behavior Disorders,* 1977, *2,* 141–145.

Buchanan, C. D. *Teacher's guide to programmed reading* (Book 1, Series 1, revised ed., Sullivan Associates Program). St Louis: Webster Division, McGraw-Hill, 1968.

Burton, T., & Hirshoren, A. The education of severely and profoundly handicapped children: Are we sacrificing the child to the concept? *Exceptional Children,* 1979, *45,* 598–602.

Carney, I. H., Menchetti, B. M., & Orelove, F. P. Community transportation: Teaching moderately handicapped adults to ride the Champaign-Urbana mass transit system. In B. Wilcox, F. Kohl, & T. Vogelsberg (Eds.), *The severely and profoundly handicapped child.* Springfield, Illinois: State Board of Education, 1977.

Certo, N., Brown, L., Belmore, K., & Crowner, T. A review of secondary level educational service delivery models for severely handicapped students in the Madison Public Schools. In *Educational programming for the severely and profoundly handicapped.* Reston, Virginia: Council for Exceptional Children, 1977.

Certo, N., Schwartz, R., & Brown, L. Community transportation: Teaching severely handicapped students to ride a public bus system. In L. Brown, T. Crowner, W. Williams, & R. York (Eds.), *Madison's alternative for zero exclusion: A book of readings,* Vol. V. Madison, Wisconsin: Madison Public Schools, 1975.

Certo, N., & Swetlik, B. Making purchases: A functional money use program for severely handicapped students. In L. Brown, N. Certo, K. Belmore, & T. Crowner (Eds.), *Madison's alternative for zero exculsion: Papers and programs related to a public school services for secondary age severely handicapped students* (Vol. IX, Part 1). Madison, Wisconsin: Madison Public Schools, 1980.

Chiang, S. J., Iwata, B. A., & Dorsey, M. F. Elimination of disruptive bus riding behavior via token reinforcement on a "distance-based" schedule. *Education and Treatment of Children,* 1979, *2,* 101–109.

City of White Plains v.˙*Ferraioli,* 34 N.Y. 2d 300, 357 N.Y.S. 2d 449, 313 N. E. 2d 756 (N.Y. Ct. of App., 1974).

Clarke, J., Greenwood, L., Abramowitz, & Bellamy, G. Summer jobs for vocational preparation of moderately and severely retarded adolescents. *Journal of the Association of the Severely Handicapped,* 1980, *5,* 24–37.

Cohen, J. S. Employer attitudes toward hiring mentally retarded individuals. *American Journal of Mental Deficiency,* 1976, *67,* 705–713.

Cohen, M., & Close, D. Retarded adults' discrete work performance in a shel-

tered workshop as a function of overall productivity and motivation. *American Journal of Mental Deficiency,* 1976, *80,* 733–743.

Coon, M. E., Vogelsberg, R. T., & Williams, W. Effects of classroom public transportation instruction on generalization to the natural environment. *Journal of the Association for the Severely Handicapped,* 1981, *6,* 46–53.

Cortazzo, S., & Sansone, R. Travel training. *Teaching Exceptional Children,* 1976, *43,* 78–84.

Crnic, K., & Pym, H. Training mentally retarded adults in independent living skills. *Mental Retardation,* 1979, *17*(1), 13–16.

Cronin, K., & Cuvo, A. Teaching mending skills to mentally retarded adolescents. *Journal of Applied Behavior Analysis,* 1979, *12,* 401–406.

Crosson, J. A technique for programming sheltered workshop environments for training severely retarded workers. *American Journal of Mental Deficiency,* 1969, *73,* 814–818.

Cullinhan, D., Kauffman, J. M., & LaFleur, N. K. Modeling: Research with implications for special education. *Journal of Special Education,* 1975, *9*(2), 213–221.

Cuvo, A. Validating task analysis of community living skills. *Vocational Evaluation and Work Adjustment Bulletin,* 1978, *11,* 13–21.

Cuvo, A., & Davis, P. Home living for developmentally disabled persons: Instructional design and evaluation. *Exceptional Education Quarterly,* 1981, *2,* 87–98.

Cuvo, A. J., Jacobi, E., & Sipko, R. Teaching laundry skills to mentally retarded students. *Education and Training of the Mentally Retarded,* 1981, *16*(1), 54–64.

Cuvo, A., Jacobi, E., & Sipko, R. Teaching laundry skills to mentally retarded students. *Mental Retardation,* in press.

Cuvo, A. J., Leaf, R., & Borakove, L. Teaching janitorial skills to the mentally retarded: Acquisition, generalization and maintenance. *Journal of Applied Behavior Analysis,* 1978, *11,* 345–355.

Cuvo, A. J., Veitch, V. D., Trace, M. W., & Konke, J. L. Teaching change computation to the mentally retarded. *Behavior Modification,* 1978, 531–548.

DeJung, J. E., Holen, M. C., & Edmondson, B. Test of social influence for retarded adolescents: Measuring social cue perception. *Psychological Reports,*

1973, *32*, 603–618.

DeRoo, W., & Haralson, H. Increasing workshop production through self-visualization on videotape. *Mental Retardation,* 1971, *9,* 22–25.

DeVore, S. *The profoundly retarded.* Springfield, Illinois: Charles C Thomas, 1979.

Dorry, G. W. Attentional model for the effectiveness of fading in training reading vocabulary with retarded persons. *American Journal of Mental Deficiency,* 1976, *81,* 271–279.

Dorry, G. W., & Zeaman, D. The use of a fading technique in paired-associate teaching of a reading vocabulary with retardates. *Mental Retardation,* 1973, *11*(6), 3–6.

Dorry, G. W., & Zeaman, D. Teaching a simple reading vocabulary to retarded children: Effectiveness of fading and nonfading procedures. *American Journal of Mental Deficiency,* 1975, *79,* 711–716.

Duffy, G. G., & Sherman, G. B. *Systematic reading instruction* (2nd ed.) New York: Harper & Row, 1977.

Eagle, F. Prognosis and outcome of community placement of institutionalized retardates. *American Journal of Mental Deficiency,* 1976, *72,*(2), 232–243.

Edmark reading program: Teacher's guide. Seattle: Edmark Associates, 1972.

Edmondson, B., Leland, H., & Leach, E. Increasing social cue interpretations by retarded adolescents through training. *American Journal of Mental Deficiency,* 1967, *71,* 1017–1024.

Edwards, J. *Social/sexual training for the severely handicapped.* Paper presented at the seventh annual conference of The Association for the Severely Handicapped, Los Angeles, October 30 to November 1, 1980.

Eisler, R. M., & Hersen, M. Behavioral techniques in family oriented crisis intervention. *Archives of General Psychiatry,* 1973, *28,* 111.

Emmel, N. Litigation concerning community integration. In A. R. Novak & L. W. Heal (Eds.), *Integration of developmentally disabled individuals into the community.* Baltimore: Paul H. Brookes, 1980.

Englemann, S. Classroom techniques: Teaching reading to children with low mental age. *Education and Training of the Mentally Retarded,* 1967, *2,* 193–201.

Englemann, S., & Brunner, E. C. *Distar reading: An instructional system.* Chicago: Science Research Associations, 1969.

Entrikin, D., York, R., & Brown, L. Teaching trainable level multiply handicapped students to use picture cues, contact cues, and initial sounds to determine the labels of unknown words. In L. Brown, T. Crowner, W. Williams, & R. York (Eds.), *Madison's alternative for zero exclusion: A book of readings* (Vol. 5). Madison, Wisconsin: Madison Public Schools, 1975.

Favell, F. Reduction of stereotypes by reinforcement of toy play. *Mental Retardation,* 1973, *1*(4), 24–27.

Favell, F., & Cannon, P. R. Evaluation of entertainment materials for severely retarded persons. *American Journal of Mental Deficiency,* 1977, *81*(4), 357–361.

Ferleger, D., & Boyd, P. A. Anti-institutionalization: The promise of the Pennhurst case. In R. J. Flynn & K. E. Nitsch (Eds.), *Normalization, social integration, and community services.* Baltimore: University Park Press, 1980.

Flexer, R. W., & Martin, A. S. Sheltered workshops and vocational training settings. In M. Snell (Ed.), *Systematic instruction of the moderately and severely handicapped.* Columbus, Ohio: Charles E. Merrill, 1978.

Foster, R. *Camelot behavior checklist.* Lawrence, Kansas: Behavioral Systems, 1974.

Gallup Organization Report for the President's Committee on Mental Retardation. Public attitudes regarding mental retardation. In R. Nathan (Ed.), *Mental retardation: Century of decision* (No. 040-000-00343-6). Washington, D.C.: U. S. Government Printing Office, 1976.

Gambrill, E., & Richey, C. An assertive inventory for use in assessment and research. *Behavior Therapy,* 1975, 550–561.

Gesell, A. *The first five years of life.* New York: Harper Bros., 1940.

Gibson, F. W., Lawrence, P. S., & Nelson, R. O. Comparison of three training procedures for teaching social responses to developmentally disabled adults. *American Journal of Mental Deficiency,* 1976, *82*(4), 379–387.

Gold, M. Stimulus factors in skill training of the retarded on a complex assembly task: Acquisition, transfer, and retention. *American Journal of Mental Deficiency,* 1972, *76,* 517–526.

Gold, M. Factors affecting production by the retarded: Base rates. *Mental Retar-*

dation, 1973, *11,* 9–11. (a)

Gold, M. Research on the vocational habilitation of the retarded: The present, the future. In N. Ellis (Ed.), *International review of research in mental retardation,* Vol. 6. New York: Academic Press, 1973. (b)

Gold, M. W. Task analysis of a complex assembly task by the retarded blind. *Exceptional Children,* 1976, *43,* 78–84.

Gold, M., & Barclay, C. The learning of difficult visual discriminations by the moderately and severely retarded. *Mental Retardation,* 1973, *11,* 9–11.

Gold, M., & Pomerantz, D. Issues in prevocational training. In M. Snell (Ed.), *Systematic instruction of the moderately and severely handicapped.* Columbus, Ohio: Charles E. Merrill, 1978.

Gold, M. W., & Scott, K. G. Discrimination learning. In W. B. Stevens (Ed.), *Training the developmentally young.* New York: John Day, 1971.

Goldfried, M. R., & D'Zurilla, T. J. A behavioral analytic model for assessing competence. In C. D. Spielberger (Ed.), *Current topics in clinical and community psychology* (Vol. 1). New York: Academic Press, 1969.

Goldstein, H. Social and occupational adjustment. In H. Stevens & R. Heber (Eds.), *Mental retardation: A review of research.* Chicago: University of Chicago, 1964.

Goldstein, H. Construction of a social learning curriculum. *Focus on Exceptional Children,* 1969, *1,* 1–10.

Gordon, S., O'Connor, N., & Tizard, J. Some effects of incentive on the performance of imbeciles on a repetitive task. *American Journal of Mental Deficiency,* 1955, *60,* 371–377.

Granger, C., & Wehman, P. Sensory stimulation. In P. Wehman (Ed.), *Recreation programming for the developmentally in disabled persons.* Baltimore: University Park Press, 1979.

Greene, B. F., Bailey, J. S., & Barber, F. An analysis and reduction of disruptive behavior on school buses. *Journal of Applied Behavior Analysis,* 1981, *14,* 177–192.

Greenleigh Associates. *The role of the sheltered workshop in the rehabilitation of the severely handicapped.* Report to the U. S. Department of Health, Education and Welfare. Washington, D.C.: Rehabilitation Services Administration, 1975.

Gruber, B., Reeser, R., & Reid, O. H. Providing a less restrictive environment for profoundly retarded persons

by teaching independent walking skills. *Journal of Applied Behavior Analysis,* 1979, *12,* 285–297.

Halderman v. *Pennhurst State School,* 446 F. Supp. 1295 (E.D.Pa., 1978) aa'd, 612 F. 2d 84 (3rd Cir., 1979).

Hall, G., Sheldon-Wildgen, J., & Sherman, J. Teaching job interview skills to retarded clients. *Journal of Applied Behavior Analysis,* 1980, *13,* 433–442.

Hallahan, D. P., & Kauffman, J. M. *Exceptional children: Introduction to special education.* Englewood Cliffs, New Jersey: Prentice-Hall, 1978.

Hamre-Nietupski, S., & Williams, W. Implementation of selected sex education and social skills to severely handicapped students. *Education and Training of the Mentally Retarded,* 1977, *12* (4).

Hansen, C. History of vocational habilitation of the handicapped. In C. L. Hansen (Ed.), *Expanding opportunities: Vocational education for the handicapped.* Seattle, Washington: PSAS, University of Washington, 1980.

Heal, L. W., Novak, A. R., Sigelman, C. K., & Switzky, H. N. Characteristics of community residential facilites. In A. R. Novak & L. W. Heal (Eds.), *Integration of developmentally disabled individuals into the community.* Baltimore: Paul H. Brookes, 1980.

Heal, L. W., Sigelman, C. K., & Switzky, H. N. Research on community residential alternatives for the mentally retarded. In N. Ellis (Ed.), *International review of research in mental retardation* (Vol. 9). New York: Academic Press, 1978.

Heimstra, N. W., Nichols, M. A., & Martin, G. An experimental methodology for analysis of child pedestrian behavior. *Pediatrics,* 1969, *44,* 832–838.

Heimstra, N. W., & Struckman, D. L. Relationship between children's perception of hazard scores and accidents. Unpublished report, Human Factors Laboratory, University of South Dakota, Vermillion, 1973.

Hersen, M., & Bellack, A. S. A multiple baseline analysis of social skills training in chronic schizophrenics. *Journal of Applied Behavior Anlaysis,* 1976, *9,* 239–245.

Hersen, M., & Bellack, A. S. Assessment of social skills. In A. R. Ciminero, K. S. Calhann, & H. E. Adams (Eds.), *Handbook for behavioral assessment.* New York: John Wiley, 1977.

Hersen, M., Eisler, R. M., & Miller, P. M. An experimental analysis of generalization in assertive training. *Behavior Research and Therapy*, 1973, *11*, 443–451.

Hill, J. W. Use of an automated recreation device to facilitate independent leisure and motor behavior in a profoundly retarded male. *Journal of the Association for the Severely Handicapped*, in press.

Hill, M., & Wehman, P. Employer and co-worker perceptions of moderately and severely retarded workers. Invited article in the *Journal of Contemporary Business*, February, 1980.

Hill, J., Wehman, P., & Horst, G. Toward generalization of appropriate leisure and social behavior in severely handicapped youth: Pinball machine use. *Journal of the Association for the Severely Handicapped*, 1982, *6*(4), 38–44.

Hill, J., Wehman, P., & Pentecost, J. H. Developing job interview skills in severely developmentally disabled clients. *Vocational training and placement of severely disabled persons: Project Employability* (Vol. I). Richmond, Virginia: School of Education, Virginia Commonwealth University, 1979.

Hopper, C., & Wambold, C. Improving the independent play of severely mentally retarded children. *Education and Training of the Mentally Retarded*, 1977, *13*(1), 42–46.

Hopperton, R. *Zoning for community homes: A handbook for municipal officials.* Columbus, Ohio: The Law Reform Project, Ohio State University, December, 1975.

Horner, R., & Bellamy, G. T. Structured employment. In G. T. Bellamy, G. O'Connor, & O. C. Karan (Eds.), *Vocational rehabilitation of the severely handicapped.* Baltimore: University Park Press, 1977.

Horner, R., & Bellamy, G. Long-term structured employment: Productivity and productive capacity. In G. Bellamy, G. O'Connor, & O. Karan (Eds.), *Vocational habilitation for developmentally disabled persons: Contemporary service strategies.* Baltimore: University Park Press, 1978.

Horner, R., Lahren, B., Schwartz, T., O'Neill, C., & Hunter, J. Dealing with the low production rates of severely retarded workers. *AAESPH Review*, 1979, *4*, 202–212.

Horner, R. H., Sprague, J., & Wilcox, B. General case programmiong for community activities. In B. Wilcox & G. T. Bellamy (Eds.), *Design of high school programs for severely handicapped students.* Baltimore: Paul H. Brookes, 1982.

Huddle, D. Work performance of trainable adults as influenced by competition, cooperation, and monetary reward. *American Journal of Mental Deficiency*, 1979, *74*, 43–49.

Irvin, L., & Bellamy, G. Manipulation of stimulus features in vocational skill training of the severely retarded: Relative efficacy. *American Journal of Mental Deficiency*, 1977, *81*, 486–491.

Jackson, G. The use of visual orientation feedback to facilitate attention and task performance. *Mental Retardation*, 1979, *17*, 281–284.

Jens, K., & Shores, R. Behavioral graphs as reinforcers for work behavior of mentally retarded adolescents. *Education and Training of the Mentally Retarded*, 1969, *4*, 21–26.

Jennings, R. D., Burke, M. A., & Onstine, B. W. Behavioral observations and the pedestrian accident. *Journal of Safety Research*, 1977, *1*, 26–33.

Johnson, B., & Cuvo, A. Teaching cooking skills to mentally retarded persons. *Behavior Modification*, in press.

Johnson, F., Ford, A., Pumpian, I., Stengart, J., & Wheeler, J. *A longitudinal listing of chronological age-appropriate and functional activities for school-aged moderately and severely handicapped students.* Madison, Wisconsin: Madison Metropolitan Schools, 1980.

Johnson, J. L., & Mithaug, D. E. A replication of sheltered workshop entry requirements. *AAESPH Review*, 1978, *3*, 116–122.

Johnson, M., & Bailey, F. The modification of leisure behavior in a half-way house for retarded women. *Journal of Applied Behavior Analysis*, 1977, *10*(1), 273–282.

Justen, J. Who are the severely handicapped? A problem in definition. *AAESPH Review*, 1976, *1*, 1–12.

Kale, R. J., Kaye, J. H., Whelan, P. A., & Hopkins, B. L. The effects of reinforcement on the modification, maintenance and generalization of social responses of mental patients. *Journal of Applied Behavior Analysis*, 1968, *1*, 307–314.

Kallman, W. M., Hersen, M. J., O'Toole, D. H. The use of social reinforcement in a case of conversion reaction. *Behavior Therapy*, 1975, *6*, 411–413.

Kastner, L. S., Reppucci, N. D., & Pezzoli, J. J. Assessing community attitudes toward mentally retarded persons. *American Journal of Mental Deficiency*, 1979,

84, 137–144.

Kazdin, A. Toward a client administered token reinforcement program. *Education and Training of the Mentally Retarded,* 1973, *8,* 4–11.

Kazdin, A. E. *Behavior modification in applied settings.* Homewood, Illinois: Dorsey Press, 1975.

Kazdin, A. E. Assessing the clinical or applied importance of behavior change through social validation. *Behavior Modification,* 1977, *1,* (4), 427–451.

Kazdin, A. *Behavior modification in applied settings* (revised ed.). Homewood, Illinois: Dorsey Press, 1980.

Kazdin, A., & Polster, 1973.

Kelly, J. A., & Drabman, R. S. The modification of socially detrimental behavior. *Journal of Behavior Therapy and Experimental Psychiatry,* 1977, *8,* 101–104.

Kelly, J. A., Furman, W. F., Phillips, J., Hathorn, S., & Wilson, T. Teaching conversational skills to retarded adolescents. *Child Behavior Therapy,* 1979, *1,* 85–97.

Kelly, J. A., Laughlin, C., Claireborne, M., & Patterson, J. A group procedure for teaching job interview skills to formerly hospitalized psychiatric patients. *Behavior Therapy,* 1979, *10,* 299–310.

Knapczyk, D. Task analytic assessment of severe learning programs. *Education and Training of the Mentally Retarded,* 1975, *10,* 24–27.

Knight, A. S. Attitudinal, social, and legal barriers to integration. In P. Roos, B. M. McCann, & M. R. Addison (Eds.), *Shaping the future: Community-based residential services and facilities for mentally retarded people.* Baltimore: University Park Press, 1980.

Kubat, A. Unique experiment in independent travel. *Journal of Rehabilitation,* 1973, *2,* 36–39.

Lake v. *Cameron,* 364 F 2d 657 (D.C. Cir., 1966).

Lambert, N., Windmiller, M., Cole, L., & Figueroa, R. *AAMD adaptive behavior scale: Public school version* (1974 revision). Washington, D.C.: American Association on Mental Deficiency, 1975.

Langone, J. Curriculum for the mentally retarded . . . or "what do I do when the ditto machine dies!" *Education and Training of the Mentally Retarded,* 1981, *16*(2), 150–161.

Laski, F. The right to live in the community: The legal foundation. In P. Roos, R. M. McCann, & M. R. Addison (Eds.),

Shaping the future: Community-based residential services and facilities for mentally retarded people. Baltimore: University Park Press, 1980.

Laus, M. D. Orientation and mobility instruction for the sighted mentally retarded. *Education and Training of the Mentally Retarded,* 1974, *9,* 70–73.

Lensink, B. R. Establishing programs and services in an accountable system. In P. Roos, B. M. McCann, & M. R. Addison (Eds.), *Shaping the future: Community-based residential services and facilities for mentally retarded people.* Baltimore: University Park Press, 1980.

Lessard v. *Schmidt,* C.A. No. 71-C-602 (E.D.Wi. D.C., 1972).

Levy, S., Pomerantz, D., & Gold, M. Work skill development. In N. Haring and L. J. Brown (Eds.), *Teaching the severely handicapped* (Vol. 1). New York: Grune & Stratton, 1976.

Lichtman, M. *Reading/everyday activities in life: Examiner's manual.* New York: CAL Press, 1972.

Lippman, L. The public. In R. Kugel, & A. Shearer (Eds.), *Changing patterns in residential services for the mentally retarded* (revised ed.). (DHEW No. (OHD) 76-21015). Washington, D.C.: President's Committee on Mental Retardation, 1976.

Lowe, M. K., & Cuvo, A. J. Teaching coin summation to the mentally retarded. *Journal of Applied Behavior Analysis,* 1976, *9,* 483–489.

Lynch, K. Toward a skill-oriented prevocational program for trainable and severely mentally impaired students. In G. T. Bellamy, G. O'Connor, & O. Karan (Eds.), *Vocational rehabilitation of severely handicapped persons: Contemporary service strategies.* Baltimore: University Park Press, 1979

Marchant, J., & Wehman, P. Teaching table games to severely handicapped students. *Mental Retardation,* 1979, *17,* 150–152.

Marholin, D., O'Toole, K. M., Touchette, P. E., Berger, P. L., & Doyle, D. A. "I'll have a Big Mac, large fries, large Coke and apple pie" or teaching adaptive community skills. *Behavior Therapy,* 1979, *40,* 236–248.

Martin, A., & Morris, J. L. Training a work ethic in severely mentally retarded workers: Providing a context for the maintenance of skill performance. *Mental Retardation,* 1980, *18,* 67–71.

Martin, G., Palotta-Cornick, A., Johnstone, G., & Goyos, A. A supervisory strategy to improve work performance for lower functioning retarded clients in a sheltered workshop. *Journal of Applied Behavior Analysis*, 1980, *13*, 183–190.

Martin, J., Rusch, F., James, V., Decker, P., & Trytol, K. The use of picture cues in the preparation of complex meals. *Applied Research in Mental Retardation*, 1982, *3*, 105–119.

Matson, J. Preventing home accidents: A training program for the retarded. *Behavior Modification*, 1980, *4*(3), 397–410. (a)

Matson, J. L. A controlled group study of pedestrian-skill training for the mentally retarded. *Behavior Research and Therapy*, 1980, *18*, 99–106. (b)

Matson, J., & Andrasik, F. Training leisure time and social interaction skills to mentally retarded adults. *American Journal of Mental Deficiency*, 1982, *86*, 533–542.

McFall, R. M., & Twentyman, C. T. Four experiments on the relative contributios of rehearsal, modeling and couching to assertion training. *Journal of Abnormal Psychology*, 1973, *81*, 31–34.

McGaughey, R. From problem to solution: The new focus in fighting environmental barriers for the handicapped. *Rehabilitation Literature*, 1976, *37*(1), 10–13.

Mental Health Law Project. *Combatting exclusionary zoning: The right of handicapped people to live in the community.* Washington, D.C.: Mental Health Law Project, 1978.

Meichenbaum, D. *Cognitive behavior modification: The integrative approach.* New York: Plenum, 1977.

Mickenberg, N. H. A decade of deinstitutionalization: Emerging legal theories and strategies. *Amicus*, 1980, *5*(3), 54–63.

Miller, A., & Miller, E. Symbol accentuation: The perceptual transfer of meaning from spoken to printed words. *Journal of Mental Deficiency*, 1968, *73*, 200–208.

Minkin, N., Brauckman, L. J., Minkin, B. L., Timbers, G. D., Timbers, B. J., Fixsen, P. J., Phillips, E. L., & Wolf, M. M. The social validation and training of conversational skills. *Journal of Applied Behavior Analysis*, 1976, *9*, 127–139.

Mithaug, P., Hagmeier, L., & Haring, N. The relationship between training activities and job placement in vocational education of the severely and profoundly handicapped. *AAESPH Review*, 1977, *2*,(2), 25–46.

Mithaug, D., Mar, D., & Stewart, J. *Prevocational assessment and curriculum guide.* Seattle: Exceptional Education, 1978.

Mithaug, D., Mar, D., Stewart, J., & McCalmon, D. Assessing prevocational competencies of profoundly, severely, and moderately retarded persons. *Journal of the Association for the Severely Handicapped*, 1980, *5*, 270–284.

Moon, S., & Renzaglia, A. Physical fitness with the mentally retarded: A critical review. *Journal of Special Education*, 1982.

Morales v. *Turman*, 383 F. Supp. 53, 125 (E.D. Tex., 1974), rev'd 535F. 2d 964 (5th Cir., 1976), reinstated 430 U.S. 322 (1977).

Morris, R., & Dolker, M. Developing cooperative play in socially withdrawn retarded children. *Mental Retardation*, 1974, *12*(6), 24–27.

National Association of Superintendents of Public Residential Facilities for the Mentally Retarded. *Residential programming: Position statements.* Washington, D.C.: President's Committee on Mental Retardation, 1974.

Neef, N. A., Iwata, B. A., & Page, T. J. Public transportation training: In vivo versus classroom instruction. *Journal of Applied Behavior Analysis*, 1978, *11*, 331–344.

Nelson, R., Gibson, F., Jr., & Cutting, D. S. Video-taped modeling: The development of 3 appropriate social responses in a mildly retarded child. *Mental Retardation*, 1873, *11*(6), 24–27.

Neufeld, G. R. Deinstitutionalization procedures. *AAESPH Review*, 1977, *2*, 15–23.

Newcomer, B., & Morrison, T. Play therapy with institutionalized mentally retarded children. *American Journal of Mental Deficiency*, 1974, *18*, 727–733.

New York Association for Retarded Children v. *Carey.* 1975.

New York Association for Retarded Children v. *Rockefeller.* E.D.N.Y., 357 F. Supp. 752, 762–763., 1973.

Nietupski, R., Certo, N., Pumpian, I., & Belmore, K. Supermarket shopping: Teaching severely handicapped students to generate a shopping list and make purchases functionally linked with meal preparation. In L. Brown, N. Certo, K. Belmore, & T. Crowner (Eds.), *Madison's alternative for zero exclusion: Papers and programs related to public school services for secondary age severely handicapped students* (Vol. VI, Part 1). Madison, Wisconsin: Madison Public Schools, 1976.

Nietupski, J., & Williams. Teaching severely handicapped students to use the telephone to initiate selected recreational activities and to respond appropriately to telephone requests to engage in selected recreation activities. In L. Brown et al. (Eds.), *A collection of papers and programs related to public school services for severely handicapped students* (Vol. 4). Madison, Wisconsin: Madison Public Schools System, 1974.

Nihira, L., & Nihira, K. Normalized behavior in community placement. *Mental Retardation*, 1975, 13(2), 9–13.

Nirje, B. The normalization principle and its management implications. In R. Kugel & W. Wolfensberger (Eds.), *Changing patterns of residential services for the mentally retarded.* Washington, D.C.: President's Committee on Mental Retardation, 1969.

Nirje, B. Tenets of normalization. In Canadian Association for the Mentally Retarded, *Orientation manual on mental retardation.* Toronto: National Institute on Mental Retardation, 1977.

Novak, A., & Heal, L. (Eds.). *Integration of developmentally disabled individuals into the community.* Baltimore: Paul H. Brookes, 1980.

Nutter, D., & Reid, D. Teaching retarded women a clothing selection skill using community norms. *Journal of Applied Behavior Analysis,* 1978, 11, 475–487.

Olshansky, S. Job placement: Another discovery. *Rehabilitation Literature* 1977, 38, 116–119.

Page, T. J., Iwata, B. A., & Neef, N. A. Teaching pedestrian skills to retarded persons: Generalization from the classroom to the natural environment. *Journal of Applied Behavior Analysis,* 1976, 9(4), 433–444.

Paloutzian, R. F., Hasazi, J., Streifel, J., & Edgar, C. Promotion of positive social interaction in severely retarded young children. *American Journal of Mental Deficiency,* 1971, 75, 519–524.

Parten, M. B. Social play among preschool children. *Journal of Abnormal Psychology,* 1932, 28, 136–147.

Perske, R. The dignity of risk. In W. Wolfensberger (Ed.), *The principle of normalization in human services.* Toronto, National Institute on Mental Retardation, 1972.

Perske, R. P. *New life in the neighborhood: How persons with retardation or other disabilities can help a good community better.* Nashville, Tennessee: Parthenon, 1980.

Peterson, N., & Haralick, J. G. Integration of handicapped and nonhandicapped pre-schoolers: An analysis of play behavior and social interaction. *Education and Training of the Mentally Retarded,* 1977, 12(3), 235–245.

Piaget, J. *Play, dreams and imitation in childhood.* New York: W. W. Norton, 1962.

Pieper, B., & Cappuccilli, J. Beyond the family and the institution: The sanctity of liberty. In T. Apolloni, J. Cappuccilli, & T. P. Cooke (Eds.), *Achievements in residential services for persons with disabilities: Toward excellence.* Baltimore: University Park Press, 1980.

Premack, D. Reinforcement theory. In D. Levin (Ed.), *Nebraska symposium on motivation,* 1965.

Quilitch, H. R., & Risley, T. The effect of play materials on social play. *Journal of Applied Behavior Analysis,* 1973, 6, 575–578. Lincoln, Nebraska: University of Nebraska Press, 1965, 123–180.

Reading, B. J. Pedestrian protection through behavior modification. *Traffic Engineering,* 1973, 43, 14–23.

Redd, W. H. Generalization of adults stumulus control of children's behavior.

Reid, D., Willis, B., Forman, P., & Brown, K. Increasing leisure activity of physically disabled retarded persons through modifying resource availability. *AAESPH Review,* 1978, 3(2), 78–93.

Resnick, L., Wang, M., & Kaplan, J. Task analysis in curriculum design: A hierarchically sequenced introductory mathematics curriculum. *Journal of Applied Behavior Analysis,* 1973, 6, 679–710.

Revell, W. G., Kriloff, L. J., & Sarkees, M. D. Vocational evaluation. In P. Wehman and P. J. McLaughlin (Eds.), *Vocational curriculum for developmentally disabled persons.* Baltimore: University Park Press, 1980.

Renzaglia, A., & Bates, P. Socially appropriate behavior. In M. Snell (Ed.), *Systematic instruction of the moderately and severely handicapped* (2nd ed.). Columbus, Ohio: Charles E. Merrill, 1983.

Renzaglia, A., Wehman, P., Schutz, R., & Karan, O. Use of cue redundancy and positive reinforcement to accelerate production in two profoundly retarded workers. *British Journal of Social and Clinical Psychology,* 1978, *17,* 183–187.

Reynolds, R. Normalization. In P. Wehman, & S. Schleien (Eds.), *Leisure programs for handicapped persons.* Baltimore: University Park Press, 1981.

Rich, A. R., & Schroeder, H. E. Research issues in assertiveness training. *Psychological Bulletin,* 1976, *83*(6), 1081–1096.

Richardson, E., Oestereicher, M., Bialer, I., & Winsberg, G. Teaching beginning reading skills to retarded children in community classrooms: A programmatic case study. *Mental Retardation,* 1975, *13*(1), 11–15.

Risley, R., & Cuvo, A. Training mentally retarded adults to make emergency telephone calls. *Behavior Modification,* 1980, *4,* 513–525.

Robinson-Wilson, M. A. Picture recipe cards as an approach to teaching severely and profoundly retarded adults to cook. Education and Training of the Mentally Retarded, 1977, 12, 69–73.

Rothbart, M. Perceiving social injustice: Observations on the relationship between liberal attitudes and proximity to social problems. *Journal of Applied Social Psychology,* 1973, *3,* 291–302.

Rusch, F. Toward the validation of social/vocational survival skills. *Mental Retardation,* 1979, *17,* 143–145.

Rusch, F., & Mithaug, D. *Vocational training for mentally retarded adults: A behavior analytic approach.* Champaign, Illinois: Research Press, 1980.

Rusch, F., & Schutz, R. Vocational and social work behavior research: An evaluative review. In J. L. Matson & J. R. McCartney (Eds.), *Handbook of behavior modification with the mentally retarded.* New York: Plenum Press, in press.

Rychtarick, R. G., & Bornstein, P. H. Training conversational skills in mentally retarded adults. *Mental Retardation,* 1979, *17*(6), 289–293.

Saenger, G. The adjustment of severely retarded adults in the community. In H. B. Robinson & N. M. Robinson (Eds.), *The mentally retarded child.* New York: McGraw-Hill, 1965.

Sailor, W., & Mix, B. *The TARC assessment system.* Lawrence, Kansas: H & H Enterprises, 1975.

Salter, A. *Conditioned reflex therapy.* New York: Capricorn, 1949.

Salvatore, S. The ability of elementary and secondary school children to sense oncoming car velocity. *Journal of Safety Research,* 1974, *6*(3), 118–125.

Schalock, R. *Independent living screening test.* Mid-Nebraska Mental Retardation Services, 1975.

Schalock, R., & Harper, R. Placement from community-based mental retardation programs: How well do clients do? *American Journal of Mental Deficiency,* 1978, *83,* 240–247.

Scheerenberger, R. C. A model for deinstitutionalization. *Mental Retardation,* 1974, *12*(6), 3–7.

Scheerenberger, R. C. Public residential services for the mentally retarded. In N. R. Ellis (Ed.), *International review of research in mental retardation* (Vol. 9). New York: Academic Press, 1978.

Scheerenberger, R. C. The impact of court actions on recent trends in service delivery. In P. Roos, B. M. McCann, & M. R. Addison (Eds.), *Shaping the future: Community-based residential services and facilities for mentally retarded people.* Baltimore: University Park Press, 1980.

Schleien, S., Kiernan, J., Ash, T., & Wehman, P. Developing cooking skills in a profoundly retarded woman. *Journal of the Association for the Severely Handicapped,* 1981.

Schleien, S., Kiernan, J., & Wehman, P. Evaluation of an age-apppropriate leisure skills program for mentally retarded adults. *Education and Training of the Mentally Retarded,* 1981, February, 13–19.

Schleien, S., Wehman, P., & Kiernan, J. Teaching leisure skills to severely handicapped individuals: An age-appropriate darts game. *Journal of Applied Behavior Analysis,* 1982.

Schroeder, S. Parametric effects of reinforcement frequency, amount of reinforcement, and required response force on sheltered workshop behavior. *Journal of Applied Behavior Analysis,* 1972, *5,* 431–441.

Screven, C., Straka, J., & Lafond, R. Applied behavioral technology in a vocational rehabilitation setting. In W. Gardner (Ed.), *Behavior modification in mental retardation.* Chicago: Aldine Publishing Company, 1971.

Segal, S. P., Baumohl, J., & Moyles, E. W. Neighborhood types and community reaction to the mentally ill: A paradox of intensity. *Journal of Health and Social Behavior,* 1980, *21,* 345–359.

Serber, M. Teaching the non-verbal components of assertive training. *Journal of Behavior Therapy and Experimental Psychology,* 1972, *3,* 179–183.

Shelton v. Tucker, 364 U.S. 479, 488, 1960.

Sidman, M., & Cresson, O., Jr. Reading and cross modal transfer of stimulus equivalences in severe retardation. *American Journal of Mental Deficiency,* 1973, *77,* 515–523.

Sigelman, C. K. A Machiavelli for planners: Community attitudes and selection of a group home site. *Mental Retardation,* 1976, *14*(1), 26–29.

Skills to Achieve Independent Living (SAIL), Dallas, Texas: Melton Peninsula, Inc., 1979.

Smeets, P. M., & Kleinloog, D. Teaching retarded women to use an experimental pocket calculator for making financial transactions. *Behavior Research of Severely Developmental Disabilities,* 1980, *1,* 1–20.

Smith, R. *Methods of clinical teaching.* New York: McGraw-Hill, 1975.

Snell, M. (Ed.), *Systematic instruction for the moderately and severely handicapped.* (2nd ed.) Columbus, Ohio: Charles E. Merrill, 1983.

Snell, M. Daily living skills: Instruction of moderately and severely retarded adolescents and adults. In J. Kauffman, & D. Hallahan (Eds.), *Handbook of special education.* Englewood Cliffs, New Jersey: Prentice-Hall, 1981.

Snell, M. E. Functional Reading. In M. E. Snell (Ed.), *Systematic instruction of the moderately and severely handicapped* (revised ed.). Columbus, Ohio: Charles E. Merrill, 1983.

Snell, M. Teaching bedmaking to severely retarded adults through time delay. *Analysis and Intervention in Developmental Disabilities,* in press.

Snell, M. E., & Gast, D. L. Applying time delay procedure to the instruction of the severely handicapped. *Journal of the Association for the Severely Handicapped,* 1981, *6,* 3–14.

Snyder, J. E., Apolloni, T., & Cooke, T. Integrated settings at the early childhood level: The role of non-retarded peers. *Exceptional Children,* 1977, *43*(5), 262–269.

Sowers, J., Rusch, F. R., & Hudson, C. Training a severely retarded young adult to ride the city bus to and from work. *AAESPH Review,* 1979, *4,* 15–22.

Spears, D. L., Rusch, F. R., York, R., & Lilly, M. S. Training independent arrival behaviors to a severely mentally retarded child. *Journal of the Association for the Severely Handicapped,* 1981, *6,* 40–45.

Spellman, C., DeBriere, T., Jarboe, D.,

Campbell, S., & Harris, C. Pictorial instruction: Training daily living skills. In M. Snell (Ed.), *Systematic instruction of the moderately and severely handicapped.* Columbus, Ohio: Charles E. Merrill, 1978.

Spooner, F., & Hendrickson, B. Acquisition of complex assembly skills through the use of systematic training procedures: Involving profoundly retarded adults. *AAESPH Review,* 1976, *1,* 14–25.

Stainback, S., & Stainback, W. Influencing the attitudes of regular class teachers about the education of severely retarded students. *Education and Training of the Mentally Retarded,* 1982, *17*(2), 88–92. (a)

Stainback, W., & Stainback, S. Nonhandicapped students perceptions of severely handicapped students. *Education and Training of the Mentally Retarded,* 1982, *17*(3), 177–182. (b)

Stainback, W., Stainback, S., & Jaben, T. Providing opportunities for interaction between severely handicapped students. *Teaching Exceptional Children,* 1981, 13, 72–75.

Stainback, W., Stainback, S., Raschke, D., & Anderson, P. Three methods for encouraging interactions between severely retarded and nonhandicapped students. *Education and Training of the Mentally Retarded,* 1981, *16*(3), 188–193.

Stanfield, J. S. Graduation: What happens to the retarded child when he grows up? *Exceptional Children,* 1973, *39,* 548–552.

Stein, J. Physical education, recreation, and sports for special populations. *Education and Training of the Mentally Retarded,* 1977, *12,* 4–13.

Sternant, J., Messina, P., Nietupski, J., Lyon, S., & Brown, L. Occupational and physical therapy services for severely handicapped students. In E. Sontag (Ed.), *Educational programming for the severely and profoundly handicapped.* Reston, Virginia: Council on Exceptional Children, 1977.

Stickney, P. Strategies for gaining community acceptance of residential alternatives. In P. Stickney (Ed.), *Gaining community acceptance: A handbook for community residence planners.* White Plains, New York: Westchester Community Service Council, 1976.

Stokes, T., & Baer, D. An implicit technology of generalization. *Journal of Applied Behavior Analysis,* 1977, *10,* 341–367.

Stokes, T. F., Baer, D. M., & Jackson, R. L. Programming the generalization of a greeting response in four retarded children. *Journal of Applied Behavior Analysis,* 1974, *7,* 599–610.

Strain, P. Increasing social play of severely retarded pre-schoolers. *Mental Retardation,* 1975, *13*(6), 7–9.

Strain, P. S., & Carr, T. H. The observational study of social reciprocity. *Mental Retardation,* 1975, *13*(4), 18–19.

Strain, P., Cooke, T., & Appolloni, T. *Teaching exceptional children: Assessment and modification of social behavior.* New York: Academic Press, 1976.

Strain, P. S., & Shores, R. E. Social reciprocity: A review of research and educational implications. *Exceptional Children,* 1977, *43*(8).

Suchman, E. A. *Behavioral approaches to accident research.* New York: Association for the Aid fo Crippled Children, 1961.

Sulzar-Azaroff, B., & Mayer, L. *Applying behavior modification techniques for children and youth.* New York: Houghton-Mifflin, 1977.

Thompson, M. M. *Housing for the handicapped and disabled: A guide for local action.* Washington, D.C.: The National Association of Housing and Redevelopment Officials, 1977.

Thorensen, C., & Mahoney, M. *Behavioral self-control.* New York: Holt, Rinehart, Winston, 1974.

Thrasher, L. M. Right to treatment litigation: Constitutional theory, relief, and preparation. In P. Roos, B. M. McCann, & M. R. Addison (Eds.), *Shaping the future: Community-based residential services and facilities for mentally retarded people.* Baltimore: University Park Press, 1980.

Tobias, J., & Cortazzo, A. D. Training severely retarded adults for greater independence in community living. *Training School Bulletin,* 1963, *60,* 23–37.

Tobias, J., & Gorelick, J. Teaching trainables to travel. *The Digest of the Mentally Retarded,* 1968, *9,* 175–181.

Touchette, P. Transfer of stimulus control: measuring the amount of transfer. *Journal of the Experimental Analysis of Behavior,* 1971, *15,* 347–354.

Trace, M. W., Cuvo, A. J., & Criswell, J. L. Teaching coin equivalence to the mentally retarded. *Journal of Applied Behavior Analysis,* 1977, *10,* 85–92.

Trower, P., Yardley, K., Bryant, B., & Shaw, P. Treatment of social failure. *Behavior Modification,* 1975, *6*(2), 220–229.

Turnbull, A., Strickland, B., & Brantley, J. *Designing and implementing individualized educational programs.* Columbus, Ohio: Charles E. Merrill, 1978.

Turner, S. M., Hersen, M., & Bellack, A. S. Social skills training to teach prosocial behaviors in an organically impaired and retarded patient. *Journal of Behavior Therapy and Experimental Psychiatry,* 1978, *9,* 253–258.

U. S. Department of Labor. *Sheltered workshop study, workshop survey* (Vol. 1) Washington, D.C.: U. S. Department of Labor, 1977.

van den Pol, R., Iwata, B. A., Ivancic, M. T., Page, T. J., Neef, N. A., & Whitley, F. P. Teaching the handicapped to eat in public places: Acquisition, generalization and maintenance of restaurant skills, 1981.

Van Houten, R. Social validation: The evaluation of standards of competency for target behaviors. *Journal of Applied Behavior Analysis,* 1979, *12*(4), 581–592.

Venn, J., DuBose, R., & Merbler, J. Parent and teacher expectations for the adult lives of their severely and profoundly handicapped children. *AAESPH Review,* 1977, *2*(4), 232–238.

Villiage of Belle Terre v. *Borass,* 416 U.S. 1, 94, S. Ct. 1536, 39 L.Ed. 2d 797 (1974).

Voeltz, L. Children's attutudes about handicapped children. *American Journal of Mental Deficiency,* 1980, *84*(5), 455–464.

Voeltz, L. Effects of structured interactions with severely handicapped peers on children's attutudes. *American Journal of Mental Deficiency,* 1982.

Voeltz, L., Biel-Wuerch, B., & Wilcox, B. Leisure and recreation: preparation for independence, integration, and self-fulfillment. In B. Wilcox, & G. T. Bellamy (Eds.), *Design of high school programs for severely handicapped students.* Baltimore: University Park Press, 1982.

Vogelsberg, R. T., & Rusch, F. R. Training severely handicapped students to cross partially controlled intersections. *AAESPH Review,* 1979, *4*(3), 264–273.

Vogelsberg, R. T. & Rusch, F. R. Community mobility training, In F. Fusch & D. Mithaug (Eds.), *Vocational training for mentally retarded adults.* Champaign, Illinois: Research Press, 1980. (a)

Vogelsberg, R., & Rusch, F. Training severely handicapped students to cross partially controlled intersections. *AAESPH Review*, 1980. (b)

Vogelsberg, R., Anderson, J., Berger, P. Haselden, T., Mitwell, S., Schmidt, C., Skowron, A., Ulett, D., & Wilcox, B. Programming for apartment living: A description and rationale of an independent living skills inventory. *Journal of the Association for the Severely Handicapped*, 1980, *5*(1), 38–54.

Walls, R., Zane, T., & Thuedt, J. Trainers' personal methods compared to two structured training strategies. *American Journal of Mental Deficiency*, 1980, *4*, 495–507.

Wang, M. C. Diagnostic tests for the quantification curriculum. Units 1–8. Pittsburgh: University of Pittsburgh, 1973.

Wehman, P. Behavioral self control with the mentally retarded. *Journal of Applied Rehabilitation Counseling*, 1975, *6*, 27–34.

Wehman, P. Vocational training of the severely retarded: Expectations and potential. *Rehabilitation Literature*, 1976, *37*(8), 233–256.

Wehman, P. Applications of behavior modification techniques to play problems of the severely and profoundly retarded. *Therapeutic Recreation Journal*, 1977, *11*(1), 17–23. (a)

Wehman, P. *Helping the mentally retarded acquire play skills: A behavioral approach*. Springfield, Illinois: Charles C Thomas, 1977. (b)

Wehman, P. Research on leisure time and the severely developmentally disabled. *Rehabilitation Literature*, 1977, *38*(4), 98–105. (c)

Wehman, P. Effects of different environmental conditions on leisure time activity of the severely and profoundly handicapped. *Journal of Special Education*, 1978, *11*(2), 183–193; 217–231. (a)

Wehman, P. Leisure skill programming for severely and profoundly handicapped students; state of the art. *British Journal of Social and Clinical Psychology*, 1978, *17*. (b)

Wehman, P. *Curriculum design for severely and profoundly handicapped students*. New York: Human Sciences Press, 1979. (a)

Wehman, P. Instructional strategies for improving toy play skills of severely and profoundly handicapped children. *AAESPH Review*, 1979, *4*(2). (b)

Wehman, P. Teaching recreational skills to severely and profoundly handicapped persons. In E. Edgar, & R. York (Eds.), *Teaching the severely handicapped* (Vol. IV). Seattle: AAESPH, 1979. (c)

Wehman, P. Toy Play. In P. Wehman (Ed.), *Recreation programming for developmentally disabled persons*. Baltimore: University Park Press, 1979, 37–64; 200–207. (d)

Wehman, P. *Competitive employment: New horizons for the severely disabled*. Baltimore: Paul H. Brookes, 1981.

Wehman, P., & Hill, J. (Eds.). *Vocational training and placement of severely disabled persons: Project employability* (Vol. I). Richmond, Virginia: School of Education, Virginia Commonwealth University, 1979. (a)

Wehman, P., & Hill, J. *Vocational training and placement of severely disabled individuals* (Vol. II). Richmond, Virginia: School of Education, Virginia Commonwealth University, 1979. (ERIC Document Reproduction Service No. ED 176 110). (b)

Wehman, P., & Hill, J. *Instructional programming for severely handicapped youth: A community integration approach*. Richmond, Virginia: School of Education, Virginia Commonwealth University, 1980.

Wehman, P., & Hill, M. *Vocational training and placement of severely disabled persons: Project employability* (Vol. III). Richmond, Virginia: School of Education, Virginia Commonwealth University, 1982.

Wehman, P., Hill, J., & Koehler, F. Helping severelyhandicapped persons enter competitive employment. *Journal of the Association for the Severely Handicapped*, 1979, *4*, 274-290.

Wehman, P., Hill, J., and Koehler, F. Placement of developmentally disabled individuals into competitive employment: Three case studies. *Education and Training of the Mentally Retarded*, 1979, *14*(2).

Wehman, P., & Marchant, J. Developing gross motor recreational skills in children with severe behavioral handicaps. *Therapeutic Recreation Journal*, 1977, *11*(1), 17–23.

Wehman, P., & Marchant, J. Improving free play skills of severely retarded children. *The American Journal of Occupational Therapy*, 1978, *32*(2), 100–104.

Wehman, P., & McLaughlin, P. (Eds.). *Vocational curriculum for developmentally disabled persons*. Baltimore: University Park Press, 1980.

Wehman, P., & McLaughlin, P. *Program development in special education.* New York: McGraw-Hill, 1981.

Wehman, P., Renzaglia, A., Berry, G., Schutz, R., and Karan, O. C. Developing a leisure skill repertoire in severely and profoundly handicapped adolescents and adults. *AAESPH Review,* 1978, *3*(3), 162–172.

Wehman, P., Renzaglia, A., Schutz, R., Gray, J., James, S., & Karan, O. Training leisure time skills in the severely and profoundly handicapped: Three recreation programs. In O. C. Karan et al. (Eds.), *Habilitation practices with the severely developmentally disabled* (Vol. 1). Madison, Wisconsin: R & T Center, 1976.

Wehman, P., Renzaglia, A., & Schutz, R. Behavioral training strategies in sheltered workshops for the severely developmentally disabled. *AAESPH Review,* 1977, *2*, 24–31.

Wehman, P., & Schleien, S. Assessment and selection of leisure skills for severely and profoundly handicapped persons. *Education and Training of the Mentally Retarded,* 1980, *14*(3), 50–58. (a)

Wehman, P., & Schleien, S. Leisure skills programming for severely handicapped children. In G. Cartlege & S. Cartwright (Eds.), *Teaching social skills to exceptional children.* New York: Pergamon Press, 1980. (b)

Wehman, P., & Schleien, S. *Leisure for handicapped persons: Adaptations, techniques, and curriculum.* Baltimore: University Park Press, 1981.

Wehman, P., & Schleien, S., & Kiernan, J. Age-appropriate recreation programs for severely handicapped individuals. *Journal of the Association for the Severely Handicapped,* 1980, *5*(4), 395–407.

Wehman, P., Schutz, R., Renzaglia, A., & Karan, O. The use of positive practice training in work adjustment with two profoundly retarded adolescents. *Vocational Evaluation and Work Adjustment Bulletin,* 1977, *14*, 14–22.

Wehman, P., Schutz, R., Bates, P., Renzaglia, A., & Karan, O. Self-management programs with mentally retarded workers: Implications for developing independent vocational behavior. *British Journal of Social and Clinical Psychology,* 1978, *17*, 57–64.

Wheeler, J., Ford, A., Nietupski, J., Loomis, R., & Brown, L. Teaching moderately and severely handicapped adolescents to shop in supermarkets using pocket calculators. *Education and Training of the Mentally Retarded.* 1980, *15*(2), 105–117.

Whitehead, C. Sheltered workshops in the decade ahead: Work and wages or welfare. In G. T. Bellamy, G. O'Connor, & O. C. Karan (Eds.), *Vocational rehabilitation of severely handicapped persons.* Baltimore: University Park Press, 1979.

Whitman, T. L., Mercurio, J. R., & Caponigri, V. Development of social responses in two severely retarded children. *Journal of Applied Behavior Analysis,* 1970, *3*, 133–138.

Wilcox, B., & Bellamy, G. T. *Designing high school programs for severely handicapped students.* Baltimore: Paul H. Brookes, 1982.

Williams, L., Martin, G. L., McDonald, S., Hardy, L., & Lambert, S. L. Effects of back scratch contingency on reinforcement for table serving on social interaction with severely retarded girls. *Behavior Therapy,* 1975, *6*(2), 220–229.

Williams, W., Hamre-Nietupski, S., Pumpian, I., McDaniel-Marx, J., & Wheeler, J. Teaching social skills. In M. Snell (Ed.), *Systematic instruction for the moderately and severely handicapped.* Columbus, Ohio: Charles E. Merrill, 1978.

Wolf, M. M. Social validity: The case for subjective measurement or how applied behavior analysis is finding its heart. *Journal of Applied Behavior Analysis,* 1978, *11*, 203–214.

Wolfensberger, W. *Principles of normalization.* Toronto: National Institute of Mental Retardation, 1972.

Wolfensberger, W. The definition of normalization: Update, problems, disagreements, and misunderstandings. In R. J. Flynn and K. E. Nitsch (Eds.), *Normalization, social integration, and community services.* Baltimore: University Park Press, 1980.

Wolpe, J. *Psychotherapy by reciprocal inhibition.* Stanford, California: Stanford University Press, 1958.

Wolpe, J., & Lazarus, A. A. *Behavior therapy techniques.* New York: Pergamon Press, 1966.

Woodcock, R. W., Davies, C. O., & Clark, C. R. *The Peabody rebsus reading program supplementary lessons kit: Manual of lessons.* Circle Pines, Minneapolis: American Guidance Service, 1969.

Wunderlich, R. Programmed instruction: Teaching coinage to retarded children. *Mental Retardation,* 1972, *10*(5), 21–23.

Wyatt v. *Stickney,* 344 F. Supp. 343, 344, F. Supp. 387 (M.D.Ala., 1972), aff'd sub. nom. *Wyatt* v. *Aderholt,* 503 F. 2d 1305 (5th Cir., 1974).

Yeaton, W. H., & Bailey, J. S. Teaching pedestrian safety skills to young children: An analysis and one-year follow-up. *Journal of Applied Behavior Analysis,* 1978, *11,* 315–330.

York, R., Williams, W., & Brown, P. Teacher modeling and student imitations: An instructional procedure and teacher competency. *AAESPH Review,* 1976, *1*(8), 11–15.

Zider, S., & Gold, M. W. Behind the wheel training for individuals labeled moderately mentally retarded. *Exceptional Children,* 1981, *47,* 632–639.

Zimmerman, J., Overpeck, C., Eisenberg, H., & Garlick, B. Operant conditioning in a sheltered workshop. *Rehabilitation Literature,* 1969, *30,* 323–334.

Zohn, C., & Bornstein, P. Self monitoring of work performance with mentally retarded adults: Effect upon work productivity, work quality, and on-task behavior. *Mental Retardation,* 1980, *18,* 19–25.

NOTES

1. Johnson, J. *Description of the Living Environment Needs Inventory (LENI).* Unpublished manuscript. Project PRIDE, Parsons Research Center, Parsons State Hospital and Training Center, Parson, Kansas.
2. Friend, D., Campbell, S., & Johnson, J. *Meal preparation.* Unpublished manuscript. Project MESH, Bureau of Child Research, University of Kansas, Kansas University Affiliated Programs at Parsons.
3. Campbell, S., & Johnson, J. *Domestic skills programs.* Unpublished manuscript. Project MESH, Bureau of Child Research, University of Kansas, Kansas University Affiliated Programs at Parsons.
4. Johnson, J. *Picture reading program.* Unpublished manuscript. Project MESH, Bureau of Child Research, University of Kansas, Kansas University Affiliated Programs at Parsons.
5. O'Brien, J. G. *Death by ounces.* A Voice in Society Series Presentation of the Travelers Insurance Company, Hartford, Connecticut, 1972.
6. Renzaglia, A. *Community-based workshops: Entrance criteria for the severely developmentally disabled.* Unpublished masters thesis. University of Wisconsin, Madison, 1976.